SRICHANDRAJI MAHARAJ

GREAT SAINTS OF INDIA SERIES

SRICHANDRAJI MAHARAJ

By
O.P. Ralhan

ANMOL PUBLICATIONS PVT. LTD.
NEW DELHI - 110 002 (INDIA)

ANMOL PUBLICATIONS PVT. LTD.

4374/4B, Ansari Road, Daryaganj
New Delhi - 110 002
Ph.: 23261597, 23278000
Visit us at: www.anmolpublications.com

First Published, 2004

ISBN 81-261-1828-8

PRINTED IN INDIA

Published by J.L. Kumar for Anmol Publications Pvt. Ltd., New Delhi - 110 002 and Printed at Mehra Offset Press, Delhi.

Contents

Preface

Once Guru Nanak had collected three bundles of grass for his cows and buffaloes and he desired to have them taken home. The grass was wet and muddy. Since no one was willing for the task, the Guru asked his sons Sri Chand and Lakshmi Chand to carry the bundles. They too evaded the duty, saying that labourers could do the job, quoted Shrimati Mridula Oberoi in her book, *'Life and Times—The Sikh Gurus'* (Madhuban Educational Books; a division of Vikas Publishing House Private Ltd.) Lehna, who had just arrived there, bowed before the Guru and said most humbly, "Consider me as your labourer and give me this job to do".

She further added, on another occasion, Guru Nanak sent for his sons at the dead of night and asked them to wash his soiled clothes. His sons protested in a chorus, "There is no water around. Even if we manage to wash your clothes, how are they ever going to dry at this unearthly hour?"

The Guru made the same request to Lehnaji. He at once set about doing the assigned task with all sincerity. Early next morning he presented his master with clean, washed and dried clothes.

One winter night it poured so heavily that a part of the wall of the Guru's house collapsed. Around midnight he asked his sons to repair it. They said, "It is dark and bitterly cold. Besides, it is not our job to build or repair walls. Tomorrow morning we shall summon masons and labourers to do the work."

The Guru said to his sons, "Since it is the Guru's work, it must only be done by his Sikhs; and it must be done immediately without any further delay."

Lehnaji, who happened to be standing next to the Guru offered his services. He started building the wall. When he was nearly half way through, the Guru said that the wall was not straight. He asked him to demolish the half built wall and build it again. Lehnaji obeyed his master and started rebuilding the wall with utmost care. But the Guru was still not satisfied. He had to pull it down once more. This carried on several times.

The Guru's own sons tried to discourage Lehnaji against this task assigned to him. They said, "You can never please him. Give up the work."

But Lehnaji said, "A servant must do his master's work. It is for the master to decide what work he should assign to his servant."

Dr. Gopal Singh in his book A History of the Sikh People has written that the ascetic son of Guru Nanak, Sri Chand, though disinherited by the father, was still alive and preaching his gospel of renunciation as an Udasi though he was mature and disinterested enough not to come actively in the way of the third Guru. But it was really hard for the common run of the Sikhs "to choose between Guru Nanak's son and the nominee of his nominee". Gurudas and the bards Satta and Balwand hinted that both of the Guru's sons were disobedient.

Some scholars have said that like Datu (Son of Guru Angad), Sri Chand, the eldest son of Guru Nanak, also lay his claim to the Guru Gaddi on the plea that Guru Angad had got no right to appoint his successor and Guruship must revert to him automatically since it belonged to his father, who passed it on to Guru Angad without conferring on him the powers to pass it on to others. Sri Chand, partly because of his own piety and partly because of the general tendency on the part of the people to put a premium on celibacy and asceticism was attracting people towards him. According to Gokal Chand Narang, "the tide was turning in his favour and it required all the power and statesmanship of Amar Das to save the infant church from an early death". Happily for Sikhism, the old Guru rose to the occasion. The Guru appealed to the people by pointing out the example set by Guru Nanak himself to learn, "how one could live in the world and still not be of the world". According to Macauliffe circular letters were sent to the people enjoining upon them that asceticism was foreign to the creed of Guru Nanak.

Though I have spent my entire life in various libraries but I did not happen to go through any authenticated biography of Baba Srichandji. I was ignorant about this great Udasin saint who devoted his entire life to save the Hindu religion from muslim rulers. Pandit Madan Mohan Malviya had once said that Hindu community is grateful to Guru Tegh Bahadur who while sacrificing his life safeguard the Hindu community. It will not be out of place to mention here that Hindus will remain always grateful not only to Guru Tegh Bahadurji Maharaj but also Guru Arjun Dev Ji, Guru Gobind Singh, Bhai Mati Das, Bhai Sati Das, Bhai Dayal and so many other stalwarts of that period who laid down their lives.

It is very strange and pains me to point it out that the Yogi who was the incarnation of Lord Shiva and devoted his entire life to safeguard the interests of Hindu community like Tulsidas Ji, Kabir Sahib and other Hindu saints who had to face tortuous attitude of Lodhis, Mughals and other Muslim rulers during their life time ignored and never brought to light His contribution to reform anti-Hindu elements and save the Hindus from conversion. The Indian scholars and historian in particulars have done a grave injustice to Baba Sri Chand Ji who in his 150 years long life not only in India but also in so many foreign countries propagated the Vedic religion and whose life is full of miracles. Baba Sri Chand Ji Maharaj's contribution to help save Hindu religions should have been recorded in the annals of Indian History in Golden words.

The grave injustice towards this great saint by the scholar community has compelled and inspired me to undertake this project within my meagre source of income as no body has so far dared to undertake the project of Bhagwan Sri Chand's biography. It is most disgusting that in the presence of numerous universities and thousands of Udasin Akharas and Research Centres in India, no such institution has assigned this project to any scholar. But to talk of any financial assistance from any Udasin Akharas no body bothers even to reply my requests to help support and to complete this project. Unfortunately near about all the Dhunas/Akharas/Ashram/Maths and Dharamsalas established by Baba Sri Chand Ji and his great followers have been converted as personal properties and no body bothers to remember the motive of the establishments and have completely forgotten the constitution written by Shri Nirwan Priyatam Dasji Maharaj to manage the institutions set up by this Sect.

This book would not have seen the light of the day if Master Gyandra Ji an ardent follower and disciple of Baba Nirbandhan Dev (Udasin Ashram, Okhla, Delhi) have not come in my life. Gyandra Ji is the luckiest person on earth to whom Baba Nirbandhan Dev Ji Maharaj assigned the job of Hindi translation of Mukhwak of Baba Sri Chand—(written by Baba Sri Chand Ji Maharaj is in the possession of Gyandra Ji who is the present Mahant of this Ashram). It will not be out of place to mention here when he was busy in translating these sacred manuscripts written by Baba Sri Chand Ji— miraclously he died in Irwin Hospital and after cremation he was found alive and still alive and looking after this Ashram as desired by his Guru (Please see detail report under the sub title "Udasin Bhagats" and this biography of a great son of mother India according to Mahant Baba Anantanand Ji Maharaj Mahant of Sangalwala Akhara, Amritsar). The life of Bhagwan Sri Chandra the Udasin Acharya, has so many lessons for our spiritual upliftment—such as equanimity impartiality, love, affection, valour, self service, patriotism, faithfulness, self denied, simplicity, morality, virtuousness, forbearance (tolerance), contentment, restraint, etc. could not have been completed if Mahant Swami Raghwanand Ji Maharaj "Udasin" President Shri Guru Ramrai Udasin Ashram, Aram Bagh, Panchkuian Road, New Delhi-110055 and Mahamandleshwar Doctor Sant Devi Samvidanand Udasin could not have helped me liberally. They have been so kind and nice towards me that they put entire collection of books on Baba Sri Chand in their Ashram Library— Sarvanand Library on my disposal. I am really very grateful of both these great souls and thankful of Kumari Mamta Ji. She also helped me a lot in this venture.

I am also grateful of Mahant Anantanand ji Maharaj who permitted me to take notes liberally from his books. I am also indebted to Shri Jeevan Prakash Jeevan and Dr. Gyanendra Singh Ji whose books proved guidelines for this project.

Dear reader I am not a good translator if you come across any such mistake in my translation/grammatical or any other in this book because I have attempted to translate the material from various Urdu, Hindi and Punjabi books. All mistakes are mine. Hoping you would be kind enough to forgive me and try to follow the spirit and great ideals set up by Bhagwan Shri Sri Chandra Ji Maharaj—who was the Saviour of Sanatan Dharma in India in the real sense.

I am also thankful to my publisher.

O.P. Ralhan

52-B, Pocket A-3 DDA Flats,
(Everest Apartments)
Kalkaji Extension, New Delhi-19

1

The Political Conditions (1494-1643 A.D.)

When Guru Nanak was born in 1469 A.D. Bahlol Lodi (1451-1489) was ruling Northern India. His successor was Sikandar Lodi who ruled from 1489 to 1517 A.D. He was succeeded by Ibrahim Lodi (1517-1526 A.D.). Guru Nanak saw the laying of foundation of the Mughal Empire by Babar, who was succeeded by his son Humayun, during the life time of the Guru.

From the tenth century onwards, successive hordes of Muslim invaders had poured in from central Asia. As the highway to Delhi lay through the Punjab the great sufferings had been caused to the people of this province. The Afghans and Turks established their rule and various Muslim dynasties ruled Northern India. Foreign rulers and their foreign functionaries ruled through their military strength. The exploited people are fleeced them. They committed untold atrocities, imposed *Jazia* (a personal tax on all non-Muslims) and otherwise taxed them heavily. All avenues of higher service were closed to the Hindus, who could not get employment except to the lower posts. Hindu temples were razed to the ground and a large number of Muslim mosques were erected. Hindu schools were closed and every effort was made to crush Hindu culture and civilization. A great many Hindus were converted to Islam on the point of sword and the spirit of the people was crushed. There was a wide gulf created between the rulers and the ruled and between the Hindus and the Muslim population-so much so that Hindu Fakirs were subjected to all types of humiliations and were made to dress differently from the Muslim Fakirs. There are complete segregation between the Hindus and Muslims— their rites, customs and ceremonies and their way of living. The masses were greatly demoralised and emasculated. Not a single leader of note was produced by the Hindus during the past five centuries. All this time a very low status was assigned to the Hindus. They were required to put marks on their foreheads or attach other distinguishing marks to their dress. They were forbidden to eat grain of a superior quality, to wear rich apparel or to ride good horses, or in palanquins and carriages. In Dera Ghazi Khan district a Hindu could ride only a donkey. The law of blasphemy was strictly enforced and capital punishment was inflicted for any criticism of Islam. Bodhan Brahmin was executed by Sikandar Lodi (1485-1517) for saying that Hinduism was as good a religion as Islam. Conversion of Hindus was a frequent occurrence and it was done on a mass scale on occasions and in certain parts of the country.

As stated by Professor Arnold Toynbee in the sacred writings of the Sikhs, page 10 (a Unesco Publication), "their India, where Islam has impinged on Hinduism violently. On the whole, the story of the relations between these two great religions on Indian ground has been and unhappy tale of mutual misunderstanding and hostility".

Guru Nanak was 20 years old when Sikandar Lodi ascended the throne. Even as a Prince, he had been a bigoted Muslim and wanted to kill all the Hindus who had assembled at Thanesar for a bath in the sacred tank. Praising of him Abdulla, the author of Tarikh-e-Dandi, writes: "He was so zealous a Musalman that he utterly destroyed diverse places of the infidels, and left not a vestig remaining of them. He entirely ruined the shrines of Mathura, the mines of heathenism and turned their principal places of worship into caravan sarais and colleges. Their stone images were given to butchers for using as weights for weighing meat and all the Hindus were strictly prohibited from shaving their heads and beards and performing their ablutions. He thus put an end to all idolatrous rites of the infidels there, and no Hindus, if he wished to have his head or beard shaved could get a barber to do it. Every city thus conformed as he desired to the custom of Islam." The famous idols of Nagarkot and Jawalamukhi were broken to pieces, which were given to butchers.

Political conditions were much worse. As pointed out by Guru Nanak: "This age is like a dragon sword--the kings are butchers; Goodness had taken wings and flown". He further adds— "There is no one who recieveth or giveth not bribes. The king administers justice only when his palm has been greased".

Guru Nanak was also an eye-witness to the treatment meted out to the people by the Mughal invaders in 1521. He was on his way back after touring the Muslim countries. He must have had some idea of the preparations Babar had been making in Afghanistan for invading the Punjab, which he had twice in 1505 and in 1519. On both these occasions Nanak was not in Punjab. He was returning from his tour on foot not far behind the invaders who came on Irani and Iraqi horses. Before reaching his home town, he stayed at Sayyidpur (now known as Eminabad) with his favourite disciple, Lalo, about 50 miles from Lahore in Gujranwala district. When Lalo spoke of the atrocities practised by Afghan officers and soldiers, Guru Nanak replied:

As the world of the Lord descendeth upon me;

So I make it known, friend Lalo;

With evil as his best man,

Bringing a crowd of sins as his bridal procession,

Like a bridegroom Babar has hastened from Kabul,

To seize by force as his bride, O Lalo,The wealth of Hindustan.

Modesty and righteousness both have vanished,

Falsehood leading the Van, holds the field, O Lalo;

Both the Qazi and the Brahmin are out of the work;

The devil reads the marriage service.

Muslim women, who read the Quran,

In their agony will cry on God, O Lalo;

Hindu women of high caste or low caste

Will meet with the same dire fate, Men will sing hymn's in praise of Murder, O Nanak,

And instead of safforn smear themselves with blood.

Babar arrived at Sayyidpur shortly afterwards. Nanak was still there. The town was mostly inhabited by rich Hindu traders and Zamindars. They offered considerable resistance in order to save themselves from surrendering their wealth and women. The infuriated Babar, and he ordered a general massacre of the people. All the young women were reduced slavery. Others were forced to grind corn and cook food for the troops. The town was looted and then destroyed by fire. Nanak and Lalo were forced to carry heavy loads of looted property on their heads to the camp and then compelled to grind corn.

The barbarous treatment of prisoners in the camp, particularly of women, broke the tender heart of Nanak. The shock and pain were too acute for him to bear.[1]

According to Puratan Janam Sikhi's--on reaching Sayyidpur Babar ordered slaughtering of every body whosoever came his way, houses were looted and then razed to the grounds, and the surrounding countryside was devastated.

At some stage the Guru and Mardana were seized and commited to the Sayyidpur prison under the supervision of a certain Mir Khan. Both were made to do forced labour, Guru Nanak as a coolie and Mardana as a horse attendant. Mir Khan, when he came to watch the prisoners, was startled to observe that the Guru's load remained suspendid a full cubit above his head and that the horse followed Mardana without any help. This information was conveyed to Babar who declared, 'Had I known there were such faquirs here I should not have destroyed the town'. He accompanied Mir Khan to where the prisoners were working and observed that a hand-mill which had been issued to Guru Nanak turned without any assistance.

Babar then approached the Guru who uttered two verses. Hearing these the Mughal fell and kissed the feet, and offered him a favour. Guru Nanak asked for all the prisoners to be released, and Babar at once issued orders to free them and restore their property. The prisoners, however, refused to go unless Guru Nanak accompanied them.[2]

Shrimati Mridula Oberoi has recorded this incident in the following words:-

Towards the end of their travels, Guru Nanak and Bhai Mardana happened to visit Eminabad a second time. As was their practice, they went to Bhai Lalo's house and stayed with him.

Around that time Emperor Babar had defeated and imprisoned the people of Eminabad. Many of them had been killed. Their houses were looted and the poor unhappy people were made to carry their own looted property to Babar's camp.

Guru Nanank and Bhai Mardana were also taken prisoners and given a heavy load to carry. Guru Nanak's heart ached with sorrow at the misery of the people around him. He began to sing sweet, holy songs in praise of God, which brought great solace to the sufferers.

Babar's men reported this incident to him. Babar decided to visit the prison and see things for himself. When he reached the prison, he found Guru Nanak sitting peacefully with his eyes closed. He was singing in a melodious voice while all the prisoners sat with folded hands. Even though he could not follow the words, Babar too joined the crowd. He seemed to be under a magic spell.

When Guru Nanak stopped singing Babar asked him the meaning of the hymn. Guru Nanak boldly explained to him that he was singing about the Emperor's cruelty and the plight of the victims.

> Babar ruled over Khurasan and hath terrified Hindustan. The creator taketh no blame to Himself; it was death disguised as a Mughal who made war on us.
>
> When there was such slaughter and lamentation didst not Thou,
>
> O God, feel pain?
>
> Creator, Thou belongest to all....

Babar was impressed by Guru Nanak's courage and truthfulness. He said to him, "What can I do for you?" Guru Nanak at once said, "Set the prisoners free and return their property and wealth which your men have so mercilessly plundered. Babar readily agreed to his request.[3]

Humayun and Guru Angad

During Guru Angad's times (1539-1552), Humayun came to the throne of India (1530-1540). He had to fight two consecutive battles against Sher Shah Suri and was defeated in the second battle. Near Kanauj, he suffered yet another defeat and was obliged to flee from India. He made his way to Lahore. At Lahore he enquired for some priest who could perform miracles and help him regain his throne. He was informed of the greatness of the late Guru Nanak and his successor Guru Angad, and advised to seek the latter's assistance.

Humayun then proceeded to Khadur to meet the Guru. At that time the Guru was in deep meditation while his ministrels were playing and singing the Guru's hymns. The Emperor was kept standing. He was offended and, in a fit of rage, put his hand on the hilt of the sword and drew it out of the scabbard. He wanted to cut off the Guru's head with the sword.

The Guru opened his eyes and looked at Humayun.

Then he smiled and said, "when you should have used your sword against Sher Shah, you failed to do so. Now when you came amongst the men of God, instead of saluting them respectfully, you desire to draw your sword on them. You fled from the battlefield in a cowardly manner and now you are posing as a hero who wishes to attack religious men."

Humayun hung his head in shame and craved the Guru's spiritual assistance. The Guru said", I shall pray for you. You will get back your kingdom after sometime. But do not forget God even then. Be a just and kind ruler.[4]

Dr. Gopal Singh has narrated this incident as under—It is said that Babar's son, Humayun, having been defeated by Sher Shah, was fleeing India via Lahore and hearing the repute of the Guru came to call upon him at Khadur for his blessings, with a good number of presents. The Guru was absorbed in his meditation, and no one dared disturb him. The fugitive king waited so long that he was enranged and put his hand to the hilt of his sword to strike the Guru. The consternation that ensued among the devout shook the Guru out of his trance and seeing what was happening reprimanded the royal visitor saying: "It is unchivalrous for a king to flee from the battle field and vent his wrath upon men of God." Humayun begged his forgiveness. The Guru in his compassion granted him pardon and, it is said, blessed him saying that though his path may be arduous and long he would win back the throne of Hindustan. When after a time, Humayun succeeded to the throne of Delhi again, he wanted to do some favour to the Guru. By this time, Guru Angad was no more and his successor, Guru Amar Das, sent back the reply to the emperor that the only favour the Guru's house asked of him was that he be just to all people alike.[5]

In the year 1567 A.D. when Akbar visited Lahore, he made a call on Guru Amar Das (1479-1574) at Goindwal. His fame as a great spiritual leader had already reached the ears of the emperor, but when he saw the non-sectarian, though earth-aware atmosphere of the holy sanctury he was deeply impressed. On being told that the Guru would see no one, high or low, till one had partaken of the food from the common kitchen (Langar), Akbar, a man of broad sympathies and high culture, welcomed the idea and partook of the food distributed there sitting in a row with his subjects of humble origin. Before departing, Akbar wanted to endow this unique institution (where all men, irrespective of creed, caste or station, could satisfy their hunger in such large numbers) with the revenue of several villages. But the Guru refused to accept any imperial offerings saying that the Guru's kitchen must be self-supporting and depend only upon the small offerings of the devout. According to some historians, the emperor not willing to disregard the Guru's wishes in this behalf, bestowed the Jagir on the Guru's daughter, Bibi Bhani, instead which fact is, however, not substantiated by the imperial records. According to the Gazetteer of Amritsar (1883-1884), it was Guru Ram Das who first settled near the tank of Amritsar about 1547 A.D., and obtained a grant of the site with 500 bighas from Akbar in 1577, and paid to the Zamindars of Tung who owned the land a consideration of Rupees Seven Hundred Akbari.[6]

Visit of Akbar to Goindwal

Emperor Akbar's visit has been recorded by another author as follows: Another important event of the Guru's pontificate was the respect shown by Akbar for the Guru (Guru Amar Das) and his teachings. Guru Amar Das could lay claim to many of the hill chieftains among his followers who contributed thousands to the funds of the church but the greatest triumph of the church in the eyes of the people was scored when the Guru's fame brought Akbar to his doors. According to Gyan Singh, "Akbar sent a trusted official, one Bhagwan Das Khatri of Sirhind, to beseech the Guru to pray for his success". The Guru was then engaged in the constructions of a Baoli and is stated to have said that the Chittor would fall as soon as the wheel of the well would settle in position. The siege ended in Akbar's victory and he visited Goindwal. He took his meal at the temple of Bread (Langar) and met the Guru. The working and the laudable objectives of the institution of the free kitchen impressed him so much that he made an offer of eighty four villages. But the Guru declined the offer and uttered, I wish not that the langar should be run by one man. The institution owes its existence to the people, let them run it. Even then "Akbar got effected the deed of 84 villages in the name of Bibi Bhani where the city of Amritsar was raised."

How far the reason embodied in the tradition is correct it is very difficult to judge because of scanty historical material but Akbar's friendly visit was undoubted. The friendship of Akbar with the Guru operated in two ways for the benefit of church. In the first place, it increased the prestige of the Guru and made their mission more popular with the higher classes of the society. Yatha Raja Tatha Praja (यथा राजा तथा प्रजा) (As is the king, so are the subjects). The truth of this proverb is nowhere better illustrated than in India, the land of its birth. The early recruits to all new churches are the caste-aways of established organisations. The early Sikhs too were mostly those who could hardly claim high places in the Hindu society. The attention of the sovereign, however, tolerant and broad minded by nature he may be, are bound to tell in favour of the object of his attention and as Panth Prakash says that the very fact of Akbar's doing homage to the Guru brought crowds of followers to the fold of Sikhism.

The other way in which Akbar's friendship was utilized was that the Guru took advantage of it to relieve oppression of popular sufferings. Two examples of this are recorded in Panth Prakash and other books. In the first instance, Guru Amar Das and his followers were exempted from paying pilgrimage tax while they visited Haridwar. Secondly, when the Guru put the case of the peasantary before the Emperor and asked him to remit the whole land tax for the year, in view of the likely loss to the peasants because of executed sudden fall in the prices of the grains owing to the rich harvest and Emperor's marching off the Punjab, Akbar readily consented.

This timely intercession for the sake of peasants

immensely increased the popularity of the Guru and made him an idol with the peasantary of Majha and Malwa who, in course of time, provided almost all the fighting strength of Guru Gobind Singh.[7]

Guru Nanak was so impressed by Baba Lehnaji's humble services that he found a true successor in him. He addressed Baba Lehnaji, "You have become so dear to me that you seem a part of me. You are my Angad, a part of my body".

Thus his name was changed to Guru Angad and he became the second Sikh Guru in preference to Guru Nanak's own sons. Guru Nanak told his unhappy sons that Angad alone had proved himself worthy of the guruship.

He said, "Guruship is a position which depends on self-sacrifice and Angad has exhibited this virtue in the highest degree. His sincere devotion and extreme humility have won him this honour".

Guru Angad nominated Shri Amardas as his successor. He bathed him, dressed him in new clothes and seated him on the Guru's gaddi or throne. He placed five copper coins and a coconut before him. He ordered Bhai Buddha, a senior Sikh, to apply 'tilak' on his forehead. Than the Guru bowed before Shri Amardas. He said before everyone present, "Shri Amardas is Guru Amardas now. He will be the Guru after me".

Guru Amardas established his headquarters at Goindwal. His growing popularity made Guru Angad's son Shri Datu, very jealous and angry. He publically declared, "Amru (Guru Amardas) was my father's servant. He is my servant now. My father's throne is mine and I am the Guru". Saying this, Datu gave the Guru a hard kick . The Guru fell from his seat and Datu planted himself on the Guru's throne.

Despite the insult and physical hurt caused to him by Datu, the Guru said, "Please pardon me if my old hard bones hurt your tender foot". After saying so, Guru Amardas left Goindwal and went into hibernation in his home village Basarka. He refused to meet anyone or see any of his Sikhs.

None of the Sikhs acknowledged Datu as their Guru. Datu forced himself on the Guru's throne at Goindwal, but still could neither command their respect nor love. In a huff he gathered all the wealth that could lay his hands on, loaded it on a camel and set off for Khadur Sahib. On the way he was robbed. One of the robbers struck Datu on the same foot with which he had kicked Guru Amardas. His foot swelled up causing him great pain. It is said that he lived with the pain for the rest of his life.

With the help of Bhai Buddha, Guru Amardas's followers persuaded him to come out of hiding and return to Goindwal.[8]

Before his death, Guru Amardas appointed Jetha, husband of his second daughter Bibi Bhani as his successor and gave him, the name of Guru Ramdas. (1534-1581).

It was Guru Ramdas devotion, patience and humility which won him the guruship. Even Guru Nanak's elder son, Baba Sri Chand, who bore a grudge against his father for not nominating him as his successor, succumbed to his sweet humility.

Baba Sri Chand was an 'Udasi, one who has given up worldly life. He wore long hair and wandered about as a naked hermit. He refused to meet Guru Angad or Guru Amardas, but now that a long time had elapsed since his father's death, and he had partially forgotten his imaginary grievances, he decided to visit Guru Ramdas.

When he arrived in the suburbs of Goindwal, Guru Ramdas went out to receive and welcome the holy visitor. He made him an offering of a beautiful horse and five hundred rupees in cash. Sri Chand found in Guru Ramdas the very image of his father Guru Nanak. During their conversation, Sri Chand remarked that he had grown a very long beard and asked the purpose for doing so. Guru Ramdas replied in a humble voice, "O holly Sir, I have grown this long beard in order to wipe with it the feet of holy men like you". Saying this the Guru actually started wiping Baba Sri Chand's feet with his long black beard. Baba Sri Chand was overwhelmed. He drew back his feet and said, "You are in my father's place. I should show respect to you. Because of your sweetness and humility you have taken my father's place. I have none of these virtues. I now understand and appreciate my father's gestures in not nominating me as his successor".[9]

On the nomination of Guru Amar Das ((A.D. 1479 - A.D. 1574) as third Guru the sons of the second Sikh Guru Angad at the investiture of Guru Amardas — Dasu and Datu felt much upset and claimed that it was their hereditary right to assume the pontificate. On the advice of their mother, Mata Khivi, Dasu withdrew his claim, but Datu remained adamant and declared himself as the Guru. Guru Amar Das, with a view to avoiding any trouble, retired to Goindwal. Much enraged at this, Datu went to Goindwal and committed insane act of kicking him in the chest while he was giving instructions to the congregation. Guru Amardas displayed extraordinary patience and said, "Oh Honoured Sir, pardon me; my old bones must have hurt your tender feet", and left Goindwal for his native village, Basarka.

Datu, however, could not convince the Sikhs of the legitimacy of his claim and in despair, left for Khadur Sahib. In the meantime, prominent Sikhs such as Baba Buddha etc. prevailed upon Guru Amar Das to return to Goindwal and resume his work.

Like Datu, Sri Chand, the eldest son of Guru Nanak, also lay his claim to the Guru Gaddi on the plea that Guru Angad had got no right to appoint his successor and Guruship must revert to him automatically since it belonged to his father, who passed it on to Guru Angad without conferring on him the powers to pass it on to others. Sri Chand, partly because of his own piety and partly because of the general tendency on the part of the people to put a premium on celibacy and asceticism was attracting people towards him. According to Gokal Chand Narang, the "tide was turning in his favour and it required all the power and statesmanship of Amar Das to save the infant church from an early death." Happily for

Sikhism, the old Guru rose to the occasion. The Guru appealed to the people by pointing out the example set by Guru Nanak himself to learn, "how one could live in the world and still not be of the world." According to Macauliffe circular letters were sent to the people enjoining upon them that asceticism was foreign to the creed of Guru Nanak.

In this connection, the author of Mehma Prakash relates that once a man named Gangu, enquired from the Guru as to which was the correct path to salvation. The Guru told him that he should start business at Delhi, earn his livelihood through honest means and give a part of it to the needy.

In this way, the Guru achieved a remarkable success in overcoming the danger from Udasis and thier leader Sri Chand. This successor primarily due to the definite and firm stand taken by the Guru himself.

The step was, however, pregnant with far reaching consequences. The Sikhs were separated from Udasis and thus raised above asceticism were free and fit to follow the course of national progress which depends alike on spiritual attainments and material uplift.[10]

Jahangir and Guru Arjun Dev

Upto the time of Akbar, and Mughal Emperors had not greatly interfered with this peaceful movement. But the ever growing popularity and influence of Sikhism perturbed Jahangir, who had little of the mildness and tolerance of his father. As a Mohammedan, he thought it was his duty to bring the infidels to the fold of Islam. Thus the bigotary of Emperor Jahangir was stirred up. He himself writes in his autobiography:

"On the banks of the river Beas, there stands a village Goindwal, where dwells a person Arjun by name. He is known as Guru. He has taken into his folds quite a number of Hindus, as also simple Mohammedans by influence of his ways and manners. His purity and saintliness is being loudly proclaimed on all sides and worshippers from all parts of the country rally round him. They manifest complete faith in him and pay their homage to him. This movement has been going on for the past three to four generations. I have been contemplating for a long time either to end this movement or to convert the Guru to Islam".

A pretext was soon created for hauling up the Guru on charge of sedition. Chandu, the Dewan, conspired with servile informers and invented the story that the Guru had helped Khusrau, the rebellous son of the Emperor Jahangir, while he was passing through Goindwal and that the Guru had applied a 'tilak' on his forehead as a token of his blessings. The Emperor grabbed this opportunity of giving vent to his pent-up feelings and rage.

Referring to these allegations, Jahangir writes in his autobiography: "I was already fully aware of his heresies and as I was now informed of him, I ordered that the Guru be brought into my presence and I conferred all his belongings to Murtza Hussain Khan and further ordered that he should be tortured to death under the law of Yusa". Power-mad Monarchs are often blind to truth and reason. The following day the Emperor left Lahore for Kashmir, with no effort to know or seek the truth behind all these allegations against the Guru; and even before the Guru could be brought to Lahore.

Jahangir's son Khusrau, had rebelled against him. He was fleeing towards Lahore and the Emperor was closely pursuing him. On the way he mercilessly massacred all those who were reported to have helped Khusrau in any way. The Emperor's diary shows that on the 16th Zeeulhaj he was at Serai Qaziwali. On the 17th he reached Goindwal starting the same morning from Sultanpur. He knew that Guru Arjun lived at Goindwal. If the Guru had really helped Khusrau in any way, the Emperor would have surely dealt with him then and there. But there was no report against him. From there, the Emperor marched on the Jaipal, a village seven miles from Lahore and stayed there still the 28th. He heard nothing against the Guru till then.

On the 3rd of Muharram, Khusrau was arrested and 700 of his companions were impaled alive on spikes pitched outside the Lahore gates. Some of them were sewn up in wet cowhides and ass-hides. The Emperor remained at Lahore till the 8th. It was not until the 7th that he was suddenly informed that Guru Arjun had applied a tilak on Khusrau's forehead in token of his blessings. It was an utterly false charge that was brought against the Guru. Chandu, the Dewan had conspired with some fanatic Mohammedans and fabricated the whole story.

Chandu bore a grudge against the Guru. His malice was due to the Guru's refusal to accept his daughter in marriage to his son Har Gobind. Chandu had spoken contemptuously of the house of Guru Nanak and therefore the Guru refused his offer. But Jahangir, who for reasons of his own, had long since been contemplating to take some strong action against the Guru, now found a good excuse to order that he should be arrested and tortured to death.

After the Emperor left for Kashmir, the Guru was brought to Lahore. Murtza Hussain Khan handed him over to Chandu, the Dewan who devised the tortures inflicted upon the Guru. Guru Arjun was made to sit on red hot iron and burning sand was poured over his bare body. But the Guru remained calm and tranquil throughout, and his face flushed with divine glory.

When Hazrat Mian Mir, a Muslim saint, who had laid the foundation stone of the Golden Temple, heard this tale of sorrow, he rushed to see the Guru. Tears trickled down the cheeks of the aged Mian Mir when he saw the ghastly scene. He cried like a child and said: "Master! I cannot bear to see these horrors inflicted on you". But the Master comforted him and asked him to look up. When lo! the hosts of Heaven were seen hovering around the Guru and angels good awaiting his commands. But the Guru was unruffled, quite calm and tranquil and full of ineffable peace.

He completely resigned himself to the Will of God, and

submitted cheerfully to the most agonising physical torture, and said: "Sweet be Thy Will, My Lord, Thy Grace alone I beseecheth". — Mian Mir then bowed and left in silence.

At last Chandu made up his mind to kill Guru Arjun by suffocating him in a fresh cowhide, in which he was to be sewn up. The Guru asked for a bath in Ravi River. He was permitted to bathe, as Chandu revelled in the thought that the Guru's body full of blisters would undergo greater pain when it would be dipped in cold water. Crowds of people watched him, calm but deeply afflicted while the Master stood in water and had a dip and disappeared[11].

Shrimati Mridula Oberoi about the Martyrdom of Guru Arjun has recorded that for five days the Guru was tortured in various ways. The Emperor's officers poured burning sand on him, seated him in a red-hot cauldron and bathed him in boiling water. The Guru bore all these tortures without a sign of groan. Guru Arjun kept repeating the following verse during the period of his torture.

When very great troubles befall,

and no body receiveth one;

When enemies pursue, and relations flee away;

When all from whom man looked for assistance have fled,

and all succours are at an end;

If he then remembers God, no hot wind shall strike him.

Several jogis and religious men appealed for the release of the Guru. Mian Mir the Muslim saint whom even, Jahangir respected went to see his friend Guru Arjun and said to him, "May I appeal to the Emperor for your release? May I ask him to punish these people who are torturing you?" The Guru replied, "No brother. All is happening according to God's will. Men who stand for truth have to suffer often. Their sufferings gives strength to the cause of truth. Go, brother, pray for me. Pray for the success of my cause. Prey for victory to Truth."

On the fifth day, the Guru was taken to the river Ravi. With its ice cold water he bathed his feet and hands. Then he went into the river and bathed his whole body. All along, he was reciting the Japji Sahib. Before leaving his mortal coil, he declared his son Sri Hargobind as his successor.[12] This happened on 30th May 1606 A.D. at Lahore (now in Pakistan).[13]

According to Doctor Gopal Singh— The story of Chandu, a Diwan (Finance Minister) of Akbar at Delhi (Macauliffe, the Sikh Religion, III pp. 70-76) whose daughter had been refused by the Guru for his son, for he had spoken some derogatory words about his house which the Sikhs of Delhi resented, and linking up of this family feud with the subsequent martyrdom of Guru Arjun by the Sikh chroniclers seems to be a pure forgery and a fantasy.. In the first place, as we shall see, Jahangir himself admits his total responsibility in his Tuzak (memoirs) for the Guru's martyrdom. Secondly, there is no historical evidence of a Chandu having been the emperor's Diwan at Delhi or even at Lahore. Possibly, like the story of Guru Nanak's supposed blessings to Babur for sovereignty over India upto his seventh generation, this story was also given currency by clever sycophants of the emperor, or the Guru's detractors like Prithia, in order to wash the guilt off the emperor's name or the real culprits behind the scene.[14]

When on October 17, 1605 Akbar died and was succeeded by Jahangir, notorious for his lax moral life which he tried to get condoned by the ulema by dancing to their orthodox views on Islam (His first wife, daughter of Raja Bhagwan Das and mother of Khusru, took opium and died on account of his ill treatment of her, though in his Tuzak (memoir) he blames her death (1604) on Khusru's attitude towards him(!) (Vol. I, pp. 55-56 tr. by Beveridge). Akbar wanted to disinherit him in favour of Khusru for his disloyalty (and his wanton cruelty and exclusive use of opium and liquor) arrested him and put him in chains, for ten days, slapped and abused him (Nov. 1604) but later reconciliation was affected through Akbar's mother and his wives (Abul Fazals Akbar Nama, Tr. by Beveridge, III p.1244).

Reports were reaching his ears through Sheikh Ahmad Sirhindi, popularly known as Mujadid Alif Sani, an extremely bigoted and well known Sunni divine of Sirhind, of the growing influence of the Guru, particularly among the Muslims. The Sheikh therefore, might also have urged the king-emperor to counteract and destroy him. (In his letter to Sheikh Farid Bukhari, alias Murtaza Khan, Governor of Lahore, the Mujadid approves gleafully of the execution of the Guru in these words: "The execution at this time of the accused of Goindwal... with whatever motive... is an act of highest grace for the followers of Islam." (Maktubat-i-Imam Rabbani, Vol. I, part iii letter, No. 193).

Jahangir was therefore looking out for a suitable opportunity. He took the advantage of Khusrus rebellion and his meeting with Guru Arjun Dev. He writes in Tuzak-i-Jahangiri. In these days, Khusru passed through this way (That Guru Arjun received and honoured Khusru in his court was not without reason. The British Ambassador in the court of Jahangir, Sir Thomas Roe (in his Embassy, ed. by Foster, 1889, 2 Vols) has this to say of him:- "Sultan Khusru, the eldest brother of Prince Khurram (Late Shah Jahan) is both extremely beloved and honoured of all men (almost adored and very justly) for his noble parts. If he prevails in his rights, his kingdom will be a sanctuary for Christians, whom he loves and honours, favouring learning, valour, the discipline of war, and abhoring all covetousness. If the other (Khurram wins), we shall be the loser. He is a hater of all christians, proud, subtile, false and barbarously tyrannous".)

This foolish person resolved to call on him. Khusro halted for a time at this place and this man came to see him and discoursed with him on many matters and also applied with saffron to his forehead what the Hindus call *Kashakeh* (Tilak) and consider as a good omen. When I heard this account personally, I already knew about his false pretences. So I ordered that he be brought into my presence, that his property be confiscated and his sons and other possessions be made over to Murtaza Khan and he be dealt with (put to death) in accordance with the political (siyasat) and the common law of the land (yasa)".

This unassailable evidence makes three things obvious:-

1. That the Guru's "political crime" of "calling upon" Khusro and applying a saffron marks to his forehead, was an after thought on the part of Jahangir who had already made up his mind either to put the Guru to death or to bring him into the fold of Islam, not because he was a political rebel, but because innocent Muslims as much as Hindus were accepting him as their spiritual leader.

2. There is no mention in the king's memoirs of any heavy fine having been imposed upon the Guru who being unable to pay was put to death, or his son later put into prison for that reason *Dabistan*, however, mentions a fine having been imposed, though all Sikh historical records are silent about it.

3. The story of a Chandu having anything to do with this martyrdom is a concoction of the Sikh chroniclers, like the authors of *Mehma Prakash* and *Gurupratap Surya Granth*. It may be that some Hindu employees of Murtaza Khan called Chandu may have been associated with the process of extreme tortures inflicted for five consecutive days on the Guru (May 24-29, 1606 A.D.) which led to the currency of the story in order to mitigate the wrath of the people against the emperor and his regime. It is clear therefore, that Guru was tortured to death not so much for political as for religious seasons. The emperor's orders were carried out in every detail on May 30, 1606 A.D. ...[15]

Jahangir (1605-1626 A.D.) and Guru Hargobind (1595-1645 A.D.)

On seeing the prosperity of the Guru, his cousin Meharwan, the son of his paternal uncle, Prithi Chand, grew very jealous and conspiring with Chandu Lal complained to the Emperor Jahangir, that having abandoned the practice of his ancestors, the Guru had buckled on the sword, and organised a regular army, and had begun to dispose judicial cases like the King's law courts. He also represented that these facts were injurious to the interests of the state and prayed the Emperor to adopt measures to stop them. Chandu Lal reminded the Emperor of the imposition of fine of Rs.100,000 on the deceased Guru Arjun and suggested its recovery from his son. The Emperor deputed two Sardars to fetch Guru Hargobind.

On his part also the Guru was seeking an opportunity to have an interview with the Emperor, so that Chandu Lal might be chastised for his cruelty. On the arrival of the Sardars, he at once made necessary arrangements for his household and the temple at Amritsar, and started on 3rd Jeth Sambat 1673 (May 1616 A.D.) to Delhi with 100 horses. When the Guru reached Delhi the Emperor received him with due marks of honour and respect and during the interview he was very much pleased by what he saw. He granted Rs. 500 for the langar and issued orders for the necessary supply of grain and fodder for horses. At the same time he gave him permission to attend the court daily. On several occasions the Guru accompanied the Emperor to his sports. The Guru's rising in the estimation of the Emperor grieved his father's enemy, Chandu Lal, who made several unsuccessful attempts to injure him. However, on an occasion when the Emperor was attacked with high fever for three successive days, the old snake, Chandu Lal, found opportunity to bite. He bribed the royal astronomer to attempt the removal of the Guru from the royal presence. The astronomer told the Emperor that an evil star (Sarh Sati) had appeared which fore-boded evil to His Majesty for 7½ years, unless a pious faqir like the Guru, should repeat holy hymns for 40 days in some suitable place in the South. Then Chandu Lal came in and pretended to praise the Guru much and suggested that the Fort of Gwalior was the most suitable and convenient locality for the purpose. The Emperor was deceived and a message was sent to the Guru accordingly. The latter did not think it proper to enter into a discussion at the time and carried out the royal wishes at once and left for Gwalior with 5 Sikhs. When he had been there for some days, Chandu Lal sought an opportunity to explain the prosperous condition of the Guru and the advisability of levying the fine of Rs.100,000 and suggested that until the amount was paid in, the Guru should be told to remain in the Fort as a State Prisoner. His Majesty agreed and orders were issued accordingly. Some months later, the news of the fact reached Amritsar and the Guru's mother deputed Baba Buddha to procure his release on payment of the fine. About 2000 Sikhs accompanied him. They gathered round the fort and bowed before its walls in worship of the Saint undergoing persecution there. They asked for permission to pay the fine, but the Guru forbade them on pain of curse and excommunication and it was never paid in.

The Guru was ever busy in contemplation and did not care about his imprisonment, but the Sikh Nation was deeply concerned. At the time the famous Faqir, Mian Mir, happened to visit Delhi and obtained an interview with the Emperor. During the conversation the latter stated the troubled nature of his dreams, which the former attributed to the incarceration of the innocent Guru. At the same time he showed the Emperor how Chandu Lal had been cruel and hard upon the deceased Guru Arjun on account of a private grudge and how for that same reason he was bent upon doing mischief to the Guru. He added that for such acts, though the subordinates were directly responsible the Rulers were also liable to suffer. By these remarks the Emperor was much affected and ordered the immediate release and return of the Guru to Delhi. On his arrival there precious presents were sent to him, and His Majesty apologised and sought forgiveness for his past treatment of the Guru. On his way back from Kabul the Emperor fell ill and died at Bhimbar on the morning of 28th October 1627 A.D. (Samvat 1684). He was succeeded by his son Shah Jahan.[16]

Harcharan Singh Sobti has mentioned that Sixth Guru of the Sikhs Guru Hargobind was imprisoned in the fort of

Gwalior for one year. When he was released he insisted upon that his 52 fellow prisoners, who were Rajputs Rajas, should also be set free. It was agreed upon and on the orders of the Emperor Jahangir, they were also released from the prison. It is on this account that Guru Sahib is defied as 'Bandi-Chhor'.

Guru Sahib fought four battles with the Mughals during the reign of Shah Jahan against —

1. Mukhlis Khan at Amritsar in 1628 A.D.

2. Abdullah Khan at Sri Hargobindpur in the year 1630 A.D.

3. Qamar Beg near Gurusar in 1631 A.D.

4. Kale Khan and Painde Khan at Kartarpur in District Jalandhar in 1634 A.D. Guru Hargobind expired on March 3, 1644 at Kiratpur.[17]

As stated earlier Jahangir was a fanatic muslim. He was the man who rebelled against his father—Akbar the Great. When failed, started slow poisoning with the connivance of his family physician and got him killed and occupied the Mughal throne. Though he was famous for his *'insaf'* Adel called Adel-e-Jahangir but he tortured to death Guru Arjun Dev and imprisoned his son—the Sixth Guru of the Sikhs Guru Hargobind, got killed Abul Fazal—one of the Nav Rattan of Akbar the great, killed husband of Nur Jahan (Ali Quli Khan/Sher Afghan) and married her. Martyrdom of Veer Haqiqat Rai took place during his regime, so on and so far. . . and the end of the Pathetic story of Anarkali is known to everyone. His first wife Man Bai committed suicide on 6th May 1605, due to his indifferent attitude towards her. During his life time he married more than 1600 women.

As recorded by Muni Lal—Though the seraglio (Ranwas) of Akbar had grown to the dimension of a fair size township, he was not a happy man. He yearned for the gift of a son. Non of his many hundred bed companions had so far been able to oblige him. The twins born to Jodha Bai in the year 1564 died in infancy. What was the use of all the conquests, he lamented one day, if there was no one to succeed him? Like Babar and Humayun, he was obsessed early death, and often shared his gloomy thought with Hindu and Muslim holy men whom he invited for discussion in his palace. The Yogi-seat was instituted by Akbar after the capture of Chitor close to the royal throne in Diwan-i-Khas, it was occupied by spiritual teachers invited for discussions. This seat in Diwan-i-Khas was occupied always by a specially invited divine with whom Akbar conversed directly on such spiritual problems as baffled him. One day the Emperor asked his honoured guest (a Hindu Sanyasi of Mathura) about the duties of a king. The reply saddened Akbar.... Akbar listened to the discourse with rapt attention. When the Yogi raised his right hand to bless and to indicate that he had finished, the Padshah stepped down the Vishnu throne, walked up to the aged preceptor, stood deferentially before him for a few seconds, and then left with the abruptness of a sacred charger. For two days he did not come out of his private chambers. Neither did he allow any of the Begums to intrude on his self-imposed seclusion.

On the third day, Akbar announced his decision to travel to Sikri on foot. There resided, amidst rocks and beasts, Sheikh Salim Chishti, a man of God known for his piety and spiritual attainments. He had neither money nor contacts with the outside world. Alms by a few devout persons kept the saints body and soul together. Not unoften was the Sheikh found in deep meditation completely oblivious of what was happening around him. His equation with God was said to be of total submission to His will. He was loth to meet kings and men of wealth lest his mind be distracted and the totality of his merger with the Absolute compromised.

The news of Akbar's decision to visit him aroused his curiosity. What could a penniless darvesh do to help a world conquering monarch? There was not even a wooden stool in his hut for the Emperor to sit on. For drink he had nothing to offer except water from a nearby spring. Of food and fruit he had none with which to welcome the King. The Sheikh swept his cottage, spread on the floor a piece of time-worn cloth, and waited for Akbar's arrival.

The twenty-three dusty miles to the west of Agra were covered by Akbar and his small entourage, which included Sheikh Muhammad Bokhari and Hakim Ain-ul Mulk, in one and a half days. It was near noon when the Emperor dressed simply in white cotton and without wearing any insignia of royalty, walked up the rough-cut fight of stairs leading to the Sheikh's hut. The latter, out of humility that comes from proximity to God, rushed out of his humble dwilling to meet the royal visitor. The ensuing scene has been attempted to be captured by many artists, but none has been able to fully depict the emotional depth of the meeting. Akbar leaned forward to bow to and touch the knees of the preceptor. The latter drew back and held out his arms to welcome and embrace the monarch. For a moment, it seemed the world had come to a stand still and that the holy spirit had descended on the rocks of Sikri.

Preliminaries over, the Sheikh recited a couple of ayats from the Quran, and led the shahinshah to his hut about fifty yards away. At the thresholds, he stopped as if to apologise for the bareness of his dwelling. Akbar read his thoughts, gave a knowing smile, stepped inside, and proclaimed aloud that God be thanked for giving him access to "this abode of peace". How I wish I could live here for ever. This place is heaven, heaven, heaven. Allah Himself seems to be in residence here. Permit me, revered Sheikh, to share your lodging for at least a few days. My soul years to merge with the infinite, and it is only here that I can attain the much longed for peace of mind.

The Sheikh was embarrassed. He did not know how to react to the kingly request. Hymns from the holy book, wherein are recorded the virtues of humility, readily came to his mind. He recited them in low tone, and then stood motionless, not daring to ask the Emperor to squat on the seat he had prepared for him. Akbar came to his rescue not waiting to be invited, he downed himself to sit crossed-legged on the dusty floor, and requested the Sheikh to sit on the piece of cloth on his right. He said:

I have come to do you homage, to sit at your feet and seek your blessings in the performance of my duties. For many years I have been wanting to come on a pilgrimage to this hallowed abode. In the fulfilment of my wish, I see a design of Destiny, a command of Allah, a coming together of all the unseen forces to my rescue. I solicit your benediction, my Master! Bless me, and initiate me into the secrets that sustain the facade of this material world. Though I am a king: yet I consider myself the loweiest of all mankind, an humble scrubber of floors of the Divine Court, an instrument of His will, an insignificant moth in search of the light of His beneficence. I have come to sit at your blessed feet, and learn first hand the mystiques of life and death. I depend on your generosity and your solicitation to the great God on my behalf. No more shall I say for the present. I beg to be permitted, O, however of the ultimate, to bask in the sunshine of your company for a few days. Turn me not away. I am a humble seeker after Truth.

The Sheikh was touched. Tears, not words came out in response to Akbar's submission. He rushed out to collect whatever food he lay his hands upon. A royal guest, he felt, could not be welcomed with verses from the Quran alone. Akbar came out too. He sat pensively on a boulder, and waited for the Sheikh's return when he saw his host coming hutward with a leaf full of black berries in his hand, Akbar rose, stood his ground respectfully and when the Sheikh offered him the freshly picked fruit, he accepted the fare with expression of deep gratitude. A party of the Emperor's entourage stood at a distance watching the proceedings with a certain degree of awe. Akbar beckoned them to come over and pay their respects to the holy man. He also ordered that the construction of a masque and a school in the vicinity of the hut should be taken in hand immediately. Food for the entire population of Sikri was to be prepared in the royal kitchen for as long as he remained in the township. An all-weather cottage was to be put up for the Sheikh's residence, and ample provisions made for his comfort and also for the upkeep of the institutions proposed to be set up.

A man of few words, the Sheikh hung down his head in submission to Allah and said:

Your Majesty, poverty is my most valued asset. I beg not to be deprived of my riches. The ancients say that God makes ready to go out of the window as soon as affluence comes in through the door. I would request your Majesty to leave me alone with my poverty and my God. Thereupon hinges my happiness and the self-realization that I am constantly in search of. For whatever they are worth, my prayers and blessings will always be with you. I shall invoke the Creator of the Universe for fulfilment of your inward desires. In His mercy, He may respond with favour. My faith in Him is total. Let us all pray here and now, and remind ourselves that not a leaf of tree moves without His will, and that what he does not do is all for the good of mankind.

The small assemblage raised their hands, and praised God for His bounties. Akbar was overwhelmed. He spent the next few hours in the Sheikhs hut sharing in full measures the saints worldly indigence as also his spiritual affluence. When the time came for the Emperor to leave, Sheikh Salim bid him farewell with a prophecy that God would bless him *with three sons*, and that succession to the house of Timur was assured for many generations. Salim also prophesied a long life for the Emperor, and told him that his conquests would dazzle the eyes of the world. Insofar as these readings of the future presaged the fulfilment of his in most wishes Akbar was elated and he left Sikri with the conviction that his place in history was pre-ordained... Salim was born on 30th August 1569 at Fatehpur Sikri.[18]

Khawaja Sheikh Salim Chishti

He was a pious man known all over the Muslim world for his learning and spiritual powers. No less than twenty five years of his life had been spent at the feet of renowned scholars of theology in Arabia, Syria, Asia Minor and

Mesopotamia. Mecca and Madina were the "sanctum sanctorum" he returned to frequently after his travels. In all he spent nine years in these holy cities, and became famous for his enunciations of the Quaranic way of life.

A descendant of King Farakh Shah of Kabul, Sheikh Salim spurned riches and spent whatever he happened to possess for meeting the needs of the poor. Come hail, come high wind, he never wore anything more than a cotton shirt and a piece of cloth around his waist. For food he cared still less and subsisted for the most part on what was brought to him by his disciples. It was in 1564 at the age of 85, that he returned to Hindustan to spend the remaining years of his life in the country of his birth. Khawaja Salim Chishti was born in Delhi in 1479. The quiet of Sikri attracted him. There on a rock surrounded by a dense forest he built for himself a simple dwelling berefit of any suggestion of luxury. People from all over Hindustan came there to do him homage. It soon became widely known that a silent wish made in the presence of the Shaikh never remained unfulfilled. When Akbar came to know about the Shaikh's equation with God, he decided to go on a pilgrimage to Sikri.[19]

Shaikhu Baba/Salim/Jahangir was a child of many prayers. He was born with the blessings of Godly saint Khawaja Salim Chishti of Fatehpur Sikri. He was named after him. It is shocking that this man in his practical life proved most ungrateful, cruel and cunning. He did not spare even his father Akbar the Great, his son Khusrau, wife Man Bai, teacher; Khan-i-Khana.. He remained silent when Khusru was done to the death treacherously by a rebellious Khurrum/ Shah Jahan.

It is difficult to assess with any certainty the number of children Jahangir fathered in the first decade of his adolescence. They perhaps ran into three figures. However, most of them died in infacy. Jahangir is not known to have expressed any great grief at the demise of his children. Pleasures of the flesh had perhaps blunted his finer sensitivities. Alchohal had even shifted his conscience. Blood-letting for its own sake was his hobby. The pages of his diary are full of lists of hundreds of animals and birds he killed every day on his hunting expeditions. There was fire in his eyes at the slightest provocation. Even the slightest rebuff to his will sent him into paralysisms of wild rage. His wrath was terrible. The type of grusome tortures he is known to have invented bespoke of a disease of a diseased, perverted genius. Akbar was horrified at the stories of his son's heartlessness. What was worse, his Shaikhu Baba was impervious to advice or threat. Akbar was disillusioned was it for this that Shaikh Salim had interceded on his behalf with God? Fatehpur Sikri repelled him. This was the political condition of the country when Jahangir died midway between Rajouri and Bhimbar on 28th October 1627.[20]

Baba Sri Chand was of about 133 years old at that time.

Chronology of Events—1494 A.D. —1643 A.D.
(Baba Sri Chand's life time)

1494	-	Birth of Baba Sri Chand (elder son of Guru Nanak)
1494	-	Accession of Babur in Farghana
1496	-	Birth of Baba Lakhmi Das (younger son of Guru Nanak)
1496-1567	-	The Narsinga dynasty of Vijayanagar
1497	-	Babur at Samarkand
1498	-	Vasco de Gama at Calicut
1504	-	Babur occupied Kabul
1505	-	Beginning of the rule of the Tuluva Dynasty in Vijayanagar
1507-1527	-	Rana Sanga
1509	-	Alburquerque, Portuguese Governor of India
1509	-	Accession of Krishna Deva Raya
1510	-	The Portuguese capture Goa

1510-1686	-	Bijapur Kingdom
1511	-	Babur captures Samarkand again
1512-1687	-	Kutab Shahi Dynasty of Golconda
1513	-	Death of Alburquerque
1517-1526	-	Reign of Ibrahim Lodi
1518	-	Establishment of Kutub Shahi dynasty of Golconda
1522	-	Visit of Domingo Paes, a Portuguese merchant
1526	-	First battle of Panipat—Babur defeated Ibrahim Lodi
1527	-	Battle of Khanua - defeat of Rajputs
1529	-	Battle of Gogra
1529	-	Death of Krishnadeva Raya
1530-1540	-	Reign of Humayun
1533	-	Bahadur Shah of Gujarat captures Chittor
1533	-	Chaitanya Mahaprabhu, the Vaishnav Saint, passed away
1534	-	Humayun marches to Malwa
1535	-	Defeat of Bahadur Shah of Gujarat and his flight to Mandu
1537	-	Death of Bahadur Shah of Gujarat
1538	-	Sher Khan defeats Mohammad Shah of Bengal
1538	-	Humayun enters Gaur
1539	-	Death of Guru Nanak
1539	-	Sher Khan defeats Humayun at Chaunsa and assumes sovereignty

1540   -   Humayun's defeat near Kanauj—he flees to Rajputana

1540   -   Inquisition establishment in Goa

1540-1545   -   Reign of Sher Shah Suri

1542   -   Birth of Akbar

1542   -   Ramaraja usurps power in Vijayanagar

1543   -   Alliance of Bijapur and Vijayanagar against Ahmadnagar

1544   -   Humayun arrives in Persia

1545   -   Death of Guru Angad

1554   -   Death of Islam Shah

1554   -   Accession of Muhammad Adil Shah

1554   -   Sikandar Suri in the Punjab

1555   -   Humayun recovers the throne of Delhi

1556   -   Death of Humayun and accession of Akbar

1556   -   Second battle of Panipat

1556-1605   -   Reign of Akbar

1558   -   Death of Ibrahim Sur, End of Sur Dynasty

1560   -   Fall of Bairam Khan—Akbar assumes full power

1561   -   Mughal invasion of Malwa

1562   -   Akbar marries a Princess of Amber. End of Peticoat Government

1564   -   Abolition of the Jaziya

1564   -   Death of Rani Durgawati and annexation of the Gond Kingdom

1565   -   Battle of Talikota. Abolition of toll tax

1568   -   Fall of Chittor

1569   -   Capture of Ranthambhor and Kalinjar

1569   -   Birth of Salim/Sheikhu/Jahangir

1571   -   Foundation of Fatehpur Sikri

1572   -   Akbar Annexes Gujarat

1573   -   Surat surrenders to Akbar. Understanding with the Portuguese

1574   -   Goswami Tulsidas commences writing his Rama-Charitamanas

1574   -   Death of Guru Amar Das

1574   -   Abul Fazal comes to Court

1574   -   Bidar and Berar—annexation by Ahmadnagar

1574-1581   -   Guru Ram Das

1576   -   Subjugation of Bengal. Death of Daud near Rajmahal

1576   -   The battle of Golcund or Haldighati

1577   -   Akbar's troops invades Khandesh; Akbar grants the site of Amritsar to the Sikhs

1579   -   Infallibility Decree promulgated

1579   -   Akbar becomes Head of Din-e-Ilahi

1580   -   Accession of Ibrahim Adil Shah II in Bijapur

1580   -   First Jesuit mission at Agra

1581   -   Rebellion in Bihar and Bengal

1581   -   Akbar's march against Mirza Muhammad Hakim and reconciliation with him

1581   -   Death of Guru Ram Das

1581-1606	-	Guru Arjun Dev the fifth Guru of the Sikhs (born 1563)
1582	-	Divine Faith promulgated
1585	-	Death of Mohammad Hakim and annexation of Kabul
1586	-	Annexation of Kashmir
1589	-	Death of Todar Mal and Bhagwan Das
1591	-	Mughal conquest of Sind (by Abd-ur-Rahim, the Khan-e-Khana)
1592	-	Annexation of Orissa
1595	-	Seige of Ahmadnagar—Acquisition of Kandhar
1595	-	Annexation of Baluchistan—Death of Faizi
1597	-	Death of Rana Pratap
1600	-	Charter to the London East India Company
1600	-	Ahmadnagar stormed
1600	-	Death of Chand Bibi
1601	-	Capture of Asirgarh
1602	-	Rebellion of Prince Saleem
1602	-	Death of Abul Fazl
1602	-	Formation of the United East India Company of the Netherlands
1604	-	First compilation of the Guru Granth Sahib
1605	-	Death of Akbar
1605-1627	-	Reign of Jahangir
1606	-	Rebellion of Khusru
1606	-	Qandhar invested by the Persians

1606	-	Execution of the Fifth Sikh Guru, Arjun
1606	-	Guru Hargobind forms the Sikhs into a brotherhood
1607	-	Qandhar relieved by the Mughals
1607	-	Sher Afghan (Ali Quli Khan), first husband of Nur Jahan, killed
1608	-	Malik Ambar takes Ahmadnagar
1609	-	Williams Hawkins arrives at Agra
1609	-	The Dutch open a factory at Calicut
1611	-	Jahangir marries Nur Jahan
1611	-	Hawkins leaves Agra
1611	-	The English establish factory at Masulipatam
1612	-	Prince Khurram (Shah Jahan) marries Anjumand Banu Begam (Mumtaz Mahal) daughter of Nur Jahan's brother
1612	-	First English factory at Surat
1612	-	The Mughal Governor of Bengal defeats the rebellious Agra
1612	-	Danish East India Company founded
1615	-	Submission of Mewar to the Mughals
1615-1619	-	Sir Thomas Roe in India as Ambassador of James I of England to Jahangir
1616	-	Jahangir receives Roe. The Dutch establish a factory at Surat
1617	-	Prince Khurram makes peace in Deccan and receives title of Shah Jahan
1618	-	Roe, after obtaining 'firman' for English trade, leaves the Imperial court

1619	-	Jahangir visits Kashmir. Campaign in Kishtwar
1620	-	Capture of the Kangra Fort
1620	-	Prince Shahryar, brother of Khurram betrothed to Nur Jahan's daughter, Ladli Begum (by Sher Afghan)
1622	-	Death of Prince Khusru, brother of Khurram. Shah Abbas of Persia besieges and takes Qandhar. Prince Khurram ordered to recover Qandhar but rebels. Malik Ambar takes Bidari
1624	-	Suppression of Prince Khurram's rebellion
1625	-	Dutch factory at Chinsura, Khurram retires to Balaghat and offers submission
1626	-	Death of Malik Ambar, Rebellion of Mahabat Khan
1627	-	Death of Jahangir
1627	-	Birth of Shivaji (1630 according to some scholars)
1628	-	Khurram proclaimed Emperor as Shah Jahan
1629	-	Rebellion of Khan Jahan Lodi
1631	-	Death of Mumtaz Mahal. Defeat and death of Khan Jahan Lodi
1632	-	Mughal invasion of Bijapur. Sack of Portuguese Hoogly by Mughal Governor of Bengal
1634	-	'Firman' permitting English to trade in Bengal. Abdal of Baltistan submits
1636	-	Treaties with Bijapur and Golconda. Shahji enters the service of Bijapur. Prince Aurangzeb appointed Viceroy of the Deccan
1638	-	Peace between the Mughals and the Ahoms
1638	-	Qandhar recovered by the Mughals

| 1639 | - | Foundation laid of Shahjahanabad at Delhi and of Fort Saint Geogre at Madras |

| 1641 | - | Revolt in Kangra |

| 1643 A.D. | - | (Vikram Samvat 1700)—Bhagwan Shri Shri Chandra arrived at Chamba when he was 149 years old and declared his end. He gave Sahansarnama and Shri Arta to Baba Mehra Chand Ji, son of Baba Dharam Chand Ji (son of Lakshmi Das), and advised the Sangat to read them as part of their continuing worship of Guru Nanak. He made farewell to Bhai Kamalia, his life long companion, and gave his last message to his followers:- |

"Those who wished to remain brahamchari and keep the Udasi symbols must maintain very high character and renunciation and direct the sadhu samaj on correct lines. Those who wished to adopt Udasi symbols while remaining with families must follow Udasi teaching sincerely.

Thus saying, he crossed the river standing on a slab of stone which moved like a boat and in the twinkling of an eye disappeared. Babaji's body could not be found. (Source—Living by the example of Baba Sri Chand, "Baba Sri Chand's spiritual example"—A talk by Baba Virsa Singh page 1 "Baba Sri Chand's Life and Teaching's Bhai Kirpal Singh, p. 8—Gobind Sadan Publications Gadaipur, Via Mehrauli, New Delhi -110020)

| 1645 | - | Death of Nur Jahan |

| 1645 | - | Death of Guru Hargobind |

Courtesy: Source of Chronology except 1643 - Encyclopaedia of India,[21] volume 2 by P.N. Chopra and Prabhu Chopra.

Notes and References

1. Guru Nanak Dev—contemporary events

2. Guru Nanak Dev—The life of Guru Nanak according to the Puratan Janam Sakhis.

3. Life and Times—The Sikh Gurus (Guru Nanak and Babur)— Madhuban Educational Books, New Delhi, 1992.

4. Ibid.

5. History of the Sikh people (1469-1978) by Dr. Gopal Singh (Guru Angads p. 151—World Sikh University Press, New Delhi, 1979.

6. Ibid.—pp.164-165.

7. The Sikh Religion—Macauliffe?

8. Life and Times—The Sikh Gurus—Mrs. Mridula Oberoi— Madhuban Educational Books, New Delhi.

9. Ibid.

10. The Sikh Religion—M. Macauliffe etc.

11. Ibid.

12. Life and Times—The Sikh Gurus by Shrimati Mridula Oberoi— Madhuban Education Books—a division of Vikas Publishing House Pvt. Ltd. 1997.

13. The Sikh Gurus—Harcharan Singh Sobti—Perfect Press Pvt. Ltd. 1996.

14. A History of the Sikh People (1469-1978) by Doctor Gopal Singh, World Sikh University Press, New Delhi, 1979.

15. A History of the Sikh People 1469-1978 by Dr. Gopal Singh pp.187-195.

16. The Sikh Religion—M. Macauliffe.

17. The Sikh Gurus—Harcharan Singh Sobti and Arahat Inderjeet Singh. Perfect Press, Noida 1996.

18. Akbar—Muni Lal—Vikas Publishing House Pvt. Ltd. 1980, pp. 154-159.

19. Jahangir—Muni Lal, Vikas Publishing House Pvt. Ltd. 1983 pp. 2.

20. Ibid.

21. Encyclopaedia of India Vol. 2 by P.N. Chopra .

2

The Religious Conditions (1494-1643)

The Prime Minister of India Shrimati Indira Gandhi in a Foreword to Doctor Vivek Bhattacharya's book entitled "The Spirit of Indian—culture—Saints of India, wrotes—India has its ages of silver and gold but the highest honour has always been reserved for the sage and the ascetic rather than for the king. And even among temporal rulers, those who exemplified wisdom and obedience to Dharma have ranked above mere warriors. Ranunciation and not acquisition, restraint not indulgence, is the essence of Indian culture.[1]

It was an epoch making period during which Guru Nanak was born and lived (1469-1539). Events of great significance took place then both in Europe and India.

The establishment of Tudor rule in England in 1485 heralded the Modern Age, not only in England but also in Europe generally. It was an age of renaissance, adventure and discovery and of religious reformation. In India too, there was religious renaissance. The Bhakti movement was at its height. Prominent leaders had done commendable work in various parts of the country. Ramanand and Kabir in Uttar Pardesh, Namdev and Eknath in Maharashtra, who had given to the people their message of the Unity of God, Love and Peace.

Among Guru Nanak's contemporaries may be mentioned (1) Vallabhacharya, born in 1449, with a large following in

Gujarat and Rajasthan; (2) Chaitanya Maha Prabhu, who flourished in Bengal from 1486 to 1533. He was a great saint of Bengal and a great devotee of Krishna. Through his faith and devotion to God, he inspired among the people a great religious fervour. Through songs and kirtan accompanied by dance his followers went into ecstasy to see the vision of God; (2) Mira Bai a Rajput Princess born in Jodhpur in 1449— became a devotee of Lord Krishna and a great saint, composer and singer of devotional songs which are popular till today and are sung in all parts of the country, and (4) the Poet Tulsidas who was born in 1532 and was a great exponent of the Rama cult—the author of the immortal Ramacharitmanas— a book read and listened to by the largest number of persons in the world till the present day.

Contemporary Saints and Sikh Votaries of Baba Sri Chand

Kabir (1440 A.D.-1508 A.D.) was the most outstanding of the disciples of Ramananda. The son of a Muslim weaver, completely illiterate, he composed poems spontaneously in glory of God. He was a dominant force in shunning caste system, the most poisonous ulcer in Indian social order. He struck the death-knell to the existing system of caste according to birth and preached unity of man in all his thousands of songs which are on the lips of the rich and the poor even today.

Kabir's equally talented contemporary colleague and a disciple of Ramanand, Ravidas was by birth a cobbler but he rose to be a saint by dint of high spiritual attainment. His spiritual power was so predominent that Rani Jhali of Chittor became his disciple and one of the most outstanding figures in medieval India. Meerabai, was also one of his disciples who left the royal throne to preach the message of God.[2]

Mahapurush Sankar Deva (1449 A.D.-1569 A.D.)--In Assam a new voice was heard from Mahapurush Sankar Deva (1449 A.D.-1569 A.D.) who joined them in a place where *Sakta* because of popularity of Tantra cult was the prevalent religion. Mahapurush Sankar Deva has got even today millions of devoted disciples who worship Vishnu. He lived for 120 years and devoted himself solely to spreading his divine message.[3]

Mahaprabhu Srikrishna Chaitanya (1486 A.D.-1553 A.D.) was an incarnation of love. According to great historians, Chaitanya was the greatest and most popular of the Vaishnava saints. He came with a new message of universal brotherhood of man and humility and renunciation. A great learned person, in fact the most learned among the saints of contemporary, India. Mahaprabhu was an incarnation of humility Chaitanya's main message was --

"Be humbler than a blade of grass

Be patient and forbearing like the tree,

Take no honour to thyself

Give Honour to all,

Chant unceasingly the Name of the Lord."

The disciples of Chaitanya Mahaprabhu started the Gauriya Math throughout the country to carry on the message of universal brotherhood of man. The Krishna cult is now quite familiar and popular in some of the Western countries. Now there are millions of western disciples of Chaitanya also.[4]

Vallabhacharya (1471 A.D.-1539 A.D.)

Acharya Vallabha was born in Varanasi of a Telugu Brahmin family. Through his 84 eminent disciples known popularly *Chourasya Sampradaya* he spread the message of God in Northern India. He insisted on the complete identity of both soul and world with the supreme spirit."[5]

Surdas (1478 A.D.-1585 A.D.) the poet singer and devotee, carries under his name several thousand of poems in Brijbhasha. They are mostly lyrical, originally sung as an integral part of the poet's devotion. Even if one ignores the religious aspects of Surdas, that he was a worshipper of Lord

Krishna and completely dedicated to him, body soul and mind, or that it was a part of his commitment to sing about Krishna's life and divine sports, the fact remains that he holds a very high place in medieval Hindi poetry, based just on the literary merits of his lyrics. The most commonly quoted verse about Surdas, in the tradition of Hindi poetry, is Sur soor. Tulsi sasi, Udngan Keshavdas—Surdas is the Sun, Tulsidas is moon and Keshavdas a star thus giving him the highest ranking even above Tulsidas, another great Hindi Poet and devotee.[6]

Purandar Das (1484 A.D.-1564 A.D.)

Purandar Das was a great poet and saint of Karnataka. He was a great musician as well. He composed thrilling music as he could hear the divine music his Saint Purandara Das is equalled with the great saints like Kabir, Surdas, Gauranga, Tukaram and Tyagaraja. He lived during the glorious days of the Karnatic Empire of Vijayanagar in the sixteenth century. In fact, Gauranga Vallabhacharaya and Purandara Das were contemporaries.

He was born in a rich Brahmin family in 1484 A.D. at Purandargiri, a town about fifteen miles from the modern city of Pune. He was known by the name Srinivasa Naik before he became a devotee of Sri Krishna. He married Saraswati Bai a pious and rich lady. He had intense love for music and cultivated that art to a great proficiency. He was a jeweller and carried on the business of money lending as well and lived a luxurious life. He was known as Navakoti Narayana on account of his extreme wealth. However, he was also a great miser and never spent any money on charity. He would never entertain brahmins, sanyasis and poor people. This made Naik's wife greatly grieved at heart on account of the materialistic and impious nature of her husband.

One day an old Brahmin who wanted to perform the thread ceremony of his son approached Purandara Das and asked for some money. Saraswati Bai told the brahmin that she had no money of her own. But the old brahmin told the woman that the diamond nose ring she was wearing was given to her own wishes. Saraswati gladly gave the nose ring to the brahmin. In turn, the brahmin gave the nose ring to Srinivasa Naik and asked for a loan on its security. The Naik at once found out that it was his wife's nose ring but the brahmin bluntly refused. He left the shop saying that he would return shortly for his money. The Naik put the nose ring in the safe and immediately ran to his house. He asked Saraswati to bring her nose ring. Saraswati was in great dilemma. She thought her husband would rebuke and chastise her severely. So she wanted to commit suicide by taking poison. As she was about to drink the poison, she felt something falling into the cup. She removed it and found to her great surprise that it was her own nose ring which she had given in charity to the old brahmin. She thanked the Lord for his benign mercy and grace and showed the nose ring to her husband. The Naik was struck with amazement. He immediately went to the shop and did not find the jewel in his iron safe. He asked his wife to narrate the whole story about the nose ring. Saraswati related all that happened. Naik realised that the old Brahmin who never turned up later was none but the God himself who had come to teach him a lesson. The incident changed him completely. The spirit of renunciation filled his heart and he left for Vijayanagar, the capital of Karnatic empire on the bank of Tungbhadra. Krishnadev Raja was the emperor. Vyasaraja a scholar and a mystic was the patron saint of the empire. Naik became a disciple of Vyasraja.

Father of Carnatic Music

Purandara Das is regarded as an avatara of Narad Rishi and he is considered as the father of Carnatic system of music. He had perfound knowledge of Raga and Tula. Purandara Das combined in himself command of language, beauty of expression, poetic genius, vast learning and scholarship of ancient writings in sanskrit. In addition, he had a sound knowledge of music in respect of both harmony and rythem. He was familiar with Nartya or rythmic movements with expressive Bhavas. Above all he had aparoksha anubhuti or the realisation of the self.

Purandara Das initiated a line of saints who spread the message of spiritualism and bhakti throughout Karnataka. Purandara Das sang:-

"In youth I was proud and ignorant

There is no limit to my desire

My desire for woman is still unquenched

Not once, have I remembered you, O Lord

Make me thy servant

And give me peace of mind

Forgive my sins

He spent nearly forty years in dissimination of bhakti all over the land through his songs. He died at the age of eighty at Vijayanagar in 1564 A.D.[7]

Mira Bai (1498-1547A.D.)— was the famous saint, singer of Rajasthan, whose life is become a legend of devotion of Krishna. Mira Bai belongs to the great glaxy of medieval saint. Poets and spiritual lyricists like Surdas and Vidyapati.[8]

Dadu Dayal (1544-1603)— Dadu was born in Ahmedabad in a Brahman family. Before Dadu, Kabir and Nanak had started the work of reform among the Hindus. Dadu was strongly influenced by their teachings and started the work of reform in North India from Ahmedabad to Delhi. Dadu was originally from Amber—the old capital of Jaipur. He preached the message of Bhakti to God all over North India.[9]

Bhai Gurdas (1551-1635 A.D.)—Contemporary of five Gurus namely, Guru Angad (1504-1552), Guru Amar Das (1479-1574), Guru Ram Das (1534-1581), Guru Arjun Dev (1563-1606) and Guru Hargobind (1595-1644) and contemporary of Eight Emperors:--

Zahiruddin Babar (1483-1530), Humayun (1503-1556)

Sur dynasty--Sher Shah Suri (died 1545) Islam Shah (died 1553), Feroz Khan etc. etc. Humayun (1530-1540) Akbar (1542-1605), Jahangir (1605-1627) and Shah Jahan (1627-1658).

He is well known for his poetic universalization of the religious beliefs and practices of the Sikh faith in Punjabi and Braji languages.

The Bhai views Guru Nanak and his faith as the natural and inevitable culmination of the long history of Indian religious thought.

Steeped in Indian lore, the Bhai's poetry is characterized by his suggestive diction, impeccable idiom and illustrative imagination.

Bhai Gurdas's work provides valuable source material to regional and national historiographers, especially those interested in such fields of human activity as religion, philosophy, hermaneutics, sociology, economics, agriculture and literature.

He holds a very interesting mirror to the rural activities of medieval Punjab.[10]

Tulsi Das (A.D. 1543-1623 A.D.)

There are no authentic records to throw light on the date or the place of birth of Tulsi Das, or even his parentage scholars have drawn upon accounts left by his disciples or his disciples or friends, or contemporary saints, or such highly placed personages as Rajas or Mughal Viceroys. Data provided by one scholar is at variance with the data provided by others.

One disciple Beni Madhav Das the author of Mool Gosain Charita (circa 1630 A.D.) places the date of birth of Tulsi Das around 1497 A.D. others at different points of time during the following 46 years i.e. till 1543 A.D. There is however, unanimity that he died in 1623.

The fame and popularity that Tulsi Das got one such that scholars have devoted volumes in support of their claims regarding his birth place, be it Raipur in Banda district, Soron in Etah district, Hastinapur in Meerut district or Ayodhya. Similarly, many a scholar has dealt at length with the caste to which Tulsi Das belonged. It is now generally agreed that Tulsi Das was born at Rajapur to mother Hulasi and father Atma Ram around 1543 A.D. There seem to have been the usual festivities in the village. Family astrologers said that abuktamul the constellation of stars, under which the child was born was extremely unlucky for the parents. Legend says that the child was unusual, that he was born a year after conception, that he was "as big as a child of five," that it had 32 teeth and that, instead of crying, it uttered the word "Rama", (Hence his original name, "Rambola" i.e. one that uttered the name Rama).

The mother of the new born heard the whispers. She feared the worst and asked her devoted maid, Muniya to whisk away the child at the dead of night to maids in-laws across the river and thus save him from death. The maid obliged. Three days after, Hulasi, the mother died. After five year's the maid's mother-in-law, Chuniya also died of snake bite. The child was again left uncared for.

His father Atma Ram was requested to take his son back. He, however, declined "This child brings bad luck to whosoever takes care of him," he is reported to have said, "what would I do with him! In so far as I am concerned, he is as good as dead."

The child roamed in the streets aimlessly within five years, it is said, the father also died. He begged for alms for his survival and used to sleep at night in the mosque.[11]

At this time a wandering saint named Naraharyanand took pity on the poor boy and adopted him as his disciple. Rambola went with him to a place on the bank of Saraju river. There he was initiated by his guru, and a new name 'Tulsidas' was given to him.

Tulsidas heard from his guru the story of Sri Ramachandra, which fascinated him. Soon after he visited with his guru, Ayodhya, Kashi, Dandakaranya, Mithila and other places where Lord Rama had gone. But Kashi attracted his mind, as it was known as the holy seat of ancient Indian knowledge. There he met Shesh Sanatan alias Sanatandas, the most respected South Indian teacher of sanskrit of his time. Naraharayanand asked Tulsidas to stay with Shesh Sanatan to study the religious scriptures under the great scholar and he himself left for pilgrimage. Tulsidas had studied the Vedas, the Puranas and other ancient religious scriptures. He used to attend the philosophical discourses and debates of the scholars of vast Hindu mythology.

Fifteen years after Tulsidas had become a disciple of Shesh Sanatan, the veteran saint died. Tulsidas performed the last rites of his teacher, as a son would do for the father. Now he returned to his native place where he could not trace his family or even their house where his ancestors had lived. He was, however, welcomed by the villagers as the 'son of the soil'. They offered him a plot of land and a small house to live in. His vast knowledge of ancient Hindu lore brought him fame and people would flock to hear him.

Tulsidas married Ratnavali, the daughter of Dinabandhu Patnaik, a pious Brahmin living in a neighbouring village. Ratna's youthful beauty and charming nature pleased Tulsidas and he was in deep love with his beloved wife. He was so involved in his conjugal life that he could not bear the thought of seperation from his wife for a single moment.

Once Tulsidas had gone to a distant place to attend a religious seminar when Ratna's brother accompanied her to their parent's house, finding her homesick. Tulsidas returned home late in the evening. He searched for Ratnavati in every corner of his house, but was disappointed. Then his neighbours informed him that Ratna left for her parents house with her brother. Tulsidas became sad and depressed in absence of his wife. He sat silently for hours together without any food or even a drop of water. Pangs of separation had been burning his heart. He grew restless as the night advanced. At last at the dead of the night which was stormy and rainy, he left home in his single piece of loin cloth, forgetful of the time and wheather, swam across the village river which became turbulent by the storm and heavy showers, and reached the house of his father-in-law during the later part of the dark night having been fully drenched in rain and in torn clothes. He knocked at the door of the room where Ratnavali was sleeping. Ratnavali came out and seeing him in that pitiable condition at that odd hours of the night, she scolded him by saying that he must be merely in love with her physical charms and so he had come to her, but if he could love God with the same intensity he would have achieved salvation. By saying so, she closed her door upon her husband who had been shivering in cold outside in darkness.

Ratnavali's door was closed upon him, but the door of the heart of Tulsidas was opened to receive Lord Rama within. This was a turning point of the life of Tulsidas. He turned his back on the life of a house holder. At that particular hour of dawn, when the sky became clear with the new rays light of the day, Tulsidas left the place and went to Allahabad, Ayodhya, Rameshwaram, Chitrakut, Dwarka, Jagannathpuri, Brindaban, Kashi and places with which the name of Sri Ramchandra was associated.

In her parent's house, Ratnavali also could not sleep during the night, after misbehaving with her husband. She waited for the morning to come when she wanted to apologise to her husband and receive him well. She opened the door and found none. Shri broke into tears and called her brother to fetch her husband. The brother looked for him in his village, but he found the door of the house of Tulsidas opened, and the house empty. He was not to be found any where. The brother did not know how to console his repented sister.

Tulsidas now become a different man—a holy heart full of philosophical and devotional thoughts. He was a free traveller and a meditator of Lord Rama. Wherever he went, he felt, as if his Lord was with him. He was very eager to have a vision of his Ishatdev (Bhagwan Rama). He settled at Kashi and there under a tree on the bank of the river Ganga, he took his seat for meditation. Everyday he used to sprinkle water from his pot at the root of a tree and pray to it for a vision of his deity. He believed that the tree was an embodiment of a holy spirit.

During recitation of Ramayana at Dashaswamedh Ghat he happened to meet Hanumanji who promised to have darshan of Lord Rama to Tulsidas.

Once at Chitrakoot Ghat when Tulsidas was preparing sandal paste for decorating the idol before worship, suddenly a most beautiful boy appeared before him and wanted Tulsidas to put the sandal paste on his forehead. Tulsidas was in a dilemma, as to whether the sandal paste meant for the deity, should be applied on the boy's forehead. Finding the holyman perplexed, the boy insisted on his putting it on his forehead. Tulsidas became charmed with the boys innocent nature and as if bearing hypnotised by him, he agreed to put the sandal paste on his forehead. As soon as he had put the paste with love and care, the boy assumed his full form of a young man by standing in front of him with a bow in his hand. He smiled at Tulsidas with his right hand raised with blessings. Tulsidas now recognized Lord Shri Ramchandra, for whose sight he waited for years in agony and anxiety. He prostrated before the Lord with devotion and joy. The Lord then commanded him to write for the common people the Ramayana, and disappeared.

So Tulsidas composed Ramcharitmanas, popularly known as 'Tulsi Ramayan, which was completed in the year 1576 A.D. The popularity of Tulsidas for his Ramcharitmanas roused jealousy in the minds of the so called orthodox Pandits of Kashi. Tulsidas was upset and depressed on the suggestion of Mahavir to write a petition to Shri Ramchandra explaining his position. Tulsidas composed *Vinay Patrika*.

Some orthodox Pandits of Kashi wanted to test Tulsidas. They demanded that Tulsidas made the temple bull (made of stone) of the adjacent Shiva temple come to life and graze in the green field which was nearby. By the grace of Lord Rama, the stone bull came to life, walked out of the temple and grazed in the field to the utter surprise of the said Pandit. They fell on the feet of Tulsidas and asked for his pardon. The sage took them in his arms with love. There is a long long list of other legends and miracles about the supernatural powers of Tulsidas.

Tulsidas was also tested by the Mughal Emperor Akbar the Great. He breathed his last on the bank of river Assi in the year 1623.[12]

Mardana (1459-1529)

Mardana was the first disciple and life long companion of Guru Nanak and his reback player. He was born in 1450 A.D. at Talwandi Rae Bhoe Ki, the home town of Guru Nanak. His father was Badra and mother Lakho. In the year 1497 Nanak and Mardana started on a journey to the east. Guru Nanak undertook several journeys. His last journey was made to West Asia from 1517 to 1521. Mardana was with him. Mardana was a master reback player. He sang devotional songs of Kabir, Ravidas, Trilochan, Bani Dhanna and Guru Nanak. He composed verses also, three of which are included in the Adi Granth in Biharge Ki Var. He died in the year 1524 while his homeword journey.[14]

Baba Budha (1506-1628)

Baba Budha occupies a unique position in Sikh history. He applied tilak of guruship to five Gurus, saw seven Gurus and remained in close association with first six Sikh Gurus from 1521 to 1628 for over 100 years. He was the first priest of Hari Mandir, and laid the foundations of Dera Baba Nanak and most of the holy buildings at Amritsar. His original name was Bura. He was born on October 22, 1506 A.D. His father's name was Sugha Randhawa and mother's Gauran. They lived in Kathu Nangal village of Amritsar District.

In 1524 A.D. Guru Nanak alongwith Bala was returning to Kartarpur on the western bank of river Ravi where he was living. On the way in the jungle the Guru sat under a tree to take rest. Nearly he saw a boy grazing cattle. The Guru called him, and asked him about his village and parents etc. Then he told him to go and look after his cattle. The boy enquired if he could do him any service. The Guru said there was nothing to be done by him and he had called him by the way while talking with him Guru remarked that though he was young in age but great in wisdom and was not Bura but Bura or Budha, because he talked like an old man. Since then Burha came to be called Bhai Budha. He became a sincere devotee of the Guru, spent a good deal of his time with him, and lived like a hermit. He passed away in 1628 A.D. at the age of 122 years. His son Bhana erected Budha's tomb in 1629 at Ramdaspura.[15]

Mian Mir (1550-1635)

Mian Mir was a renowned Sufi saint of Lahore. He belonged to Sistan in Central Asia. His original name was Shaikh Muhammad. He was born about 1550 A.D. He had a religious bent of mind. As a child he attentively listened to religious sermons. He became a disciple of Shaikh Khizr of the Qadiri order of Sufis. Sufis believed in spreading Islam by peaceful means. As India was a great field for conversion, Mian Mir decided to come here. He was then about 25 years old. He settled at Lahore. He resides in his suburbs of the city called Begampura. The whole area is now called after him Mian Mir.

Mian Mir was such a holy man of God that the boons granted by him turned into reality. People thronged to him in large number from far and wide. Guru Arjun often visited Lahore to see the birth place of his father and meet his relatives. On the occasion of one of such visits he called on the Pir. The two men of God met and became life long friends. Mian Mir was thirteen years older than Guru Arjun.

Guru Arjun was responsible for the construction of many tanks and buildings. In the year 1589 he planned to build a temple in the centre of the holy tank called Amritsar or the tank of nectar. As the temple was to be thrown open to people of all castes, creeds, he invited Mian Mir to lay the foundation stone of the Hari Mandir. He came to Amritsar wearing a religious mendicants long cloak made up of patches of coarse wool and a cone cap made of a number of gores with rose flower on top.

Jahangir held Mian Mir in high esteem and had a meeting with him. In Tuzuk-e-Jahangiri he writes:

"I had heard so much about the sound scholarship, greatness and piety of Shaikh Mohammad Mir Lahori, popularly known as Hazrat Mian Mir, that I had a great urge to see him, but I was at Agra then, and the situation was such that I could not proceed to Lahore. Therefore in the 14th year of my reign, 1620, I invited him to Agra. He was kind enough to accept my invitation and came along to oblige me.

The emperor recorded his impressions of the holy man thus:-

"This great man is unique today in his unblemished spiritualism and purity of heart. I go to him after, and he favours me with religious and worldy guidance. I wanted to present some cash but he does not accept it from anybody. I, therefore, did send the prayermat made of stag's skin which he very kindly agreed to accept and then left for Lahore."

Jahangir was so highly impressed with the holy man's discourses that he asked him for any service. The saint replied: "Then I request you not to disturb me again". Afterwards Jahangir maintained contact with Mian Mir through correspondence. It seems probable that on this occasion Guru Hargobind was released from Gwalior Jail on Mian Mir's recommendations.

When the saint's end drew near, he fell seriously ill. The famous Physician Wazir Khan offered his services. Mian Mir replied he was under the treatment of the Great Physician. A little before his death he instructed his disciples not to sell his bones, meaning they should not accept offerings on his grave. He passed away on 11th August 1635. Guru Tegh Bahadur as a child met Mian Mir who blessed him.[16]

Dadu Dayal (1544-1603 A.D.)

Dadu a Muslim cotton cleaner, whose original name was Daaood, was born in 1544 in Ahmedabad, he lived mostly in Rajasthan. His compassionate and generous disposition earned him the little of Dadu Dayal. He was an advatin, who worshipped Rama and founded the Dadu Panthi Sect. At the age of 11, he was initiated by Bridhanand. During his second visit, eight years later, his preceptor directed him to go to Rajasthan and preach the truth revealed to him. He travelled place to place between Gujarat and Rajasthan. After meeting him, Emperor Akbar became all the more tolerant and secular. He died in 1603.

Dadu spoke not with any assumed authority, but from his personal spiritual experience. According to him, God, who is within each of us, can be realised only by controlling and studying the mind through devotion to Nam, under the guidance of a living master who prescribes the path of love and devotion, austere life and a company of saints. He dubs all rituals and externals of religion as futile and recommends internal practices for God realisation and salvation. All his hymns are collected in Dadubani.[17]

Jahangir and Rishi Jadrup

A few miles out of Ujjain there resided Rishi Jadrup in a cave. An ascetic, he sought self-realization in self-denial. Never did he wear anything more than a piece of cloth around his waist. Neither intense cold nor scorching heat induced a change in his sartorial style. He subsisted on four morsels of food a week, and these he received in turn as alms from his disciples in Ujjain. He swallowed his food to defeat the lure of taste. Chewing, according to him, was an avoidable concession to the senses. A bundle of unshapely bones, Jadrup was an intellectual colossus, well versed in metaphysics and the Hindu code of moral values. Akbar used to hold along discussions with him whenever he happened to pass by Ujjain. He even invited him to partake in religious debates at Agra, but the saint begged to be left alone. Jahangir (then Salim had also visited him once with his father).

The urge to call on Jadrup seized Jahangir when he was in Ujjain on way to Mandu. Like his father he walked barefoot to the saints cave, and remained closeted with him for over two hours. "The experience" he wrote in the Tuzk, "Chastened me", and went on to record.

The place he (Jadrup) had chosen to live in was a hole on the side of a hill which had been dug out and door made. At the entrance there is an opening in the shape of mihrab, which is in length one gaz (A gaz = 36 inches; a gira = 2.25 inches) and in breadth ten gira and the distance from this door to a hole which is his real abode is two gaz and five gira in length and in breadth about twelve gira. The height from the ground to the roof is one gaz and three gira. The hole whence is the entrance to the abode is in length five and a half gira and its breadth three and a half gira. A lean person can only enter it with a hundred difficulties. It has no mat and no straw. In this narrow and dark hole he passes his time in soltitude. In the cold days of winter though he is quite naked, with the exception of a piece of rag that he has in front and behind, he never lights a fire.

He bathes twice a day in a pool of water near his abode, and once a day goes into the city of Ujjain, and nowhere but to the houses of three Brahmins whom he has selected out of seven, who have wives and children and whom he believes to have religious feelings and contentment.

He takes by way of alms four mouthfuls of food out of what they have prepared for their own eatings, which he swallows without chewing, in order that he may not enjoy their flavour, always provided that no misfortune has happened to their three houses, that there has been no birth, and there be no monstrous woman in the house. This is his method of living just as it is now written.

He does not desire to associate with me, but as he has obtained great fame, people go to see him. He is not devoid of knowledge, for he has thoroughly mastered the science of the Vedanta, which is the science of Sufism. I conversed with him for six gharis; he spoke well, so much so as to make a great impression on me. My society also suited him. At the time when my revered father conquered the fort of Asir, in the province of Khandesh, and was returning to Agra, he saw him in the very same place and always remembered him well.

On Saturday, for the second time, my desire for the company of Jadrup increased. After performing the midday devotions, I embarked in a boat and hastened to meet him, and at the close of day I went and enjoyed his society in the retirement of his cell. I heard many sublime words of religious duties and knowledge of Divine things without immoderate praise, he sets forth clearly the doctrines of wholesome Sufism, and one can find delight in his society. He is sixty years old.

He was twenty two years of age when forsaking all external attachments, he placed the foot of determination on the high road of asceticism and for thirty eight years he had lived in the garment of nakedness. When I took leave he said: In what language can I return thanks for this gift of Allah that I am engaged in the reign of such a just king in the worship of my own deity in ease and contentment. Sublime words were spoken between us. God Almighty has granted him an unusual grace, a lofty understanding, an exalted nature, and sharp intellectual powers, with God given knowledge and a heart free from the attachment of the world so that, ignoring the world and all that is in it, he sits content in the corner of soltitude and without wants.

He has chosen of worldly goods, half a gaz of old cotton cloth, and a piece of earthenware for drinking water. This tribute of a pleasure loving monarch to one who shunned all sensory enjoyments is illustrative of the quality in Jahangir's character. He was perhaps more than a mere hedonist (आनन्दजीवी) interested only in catering to the flesh. It seems he yearned inwardly for knowledge and a place among men of the spirit. This is a surmise difficult to substantiate. In the

Tuzk there are no other references to Jahangir's search for the Divine. He remained bogged down in wine and women throughout his youth, and when old age came he was too ill to bother about the abstractions of spirituality.

Once, Jahangir alongwith Nur Jahan visited Muttra (Mathura) and also called on Sanyasi Jadrup who had shifted from Ujjain to a deserted cave outside Muttra.

Jahangir records in the Tuzk an interesting note about his meeting with Jadrup. Paying high tribute to the ascetic's knowledge of Hindu scriptures and his conquest of the self, the Emperor wrote that, as always, it was a rare privilege to spend some hours with that holy man of God. Jahangir first invited Jadrup to accompany him to Kashmir. The latter apologised profusely for his inability to comply with the Emperor's wishes. At this, Jahangir suggested that he might consider transferring his residence to Agra. Jadrup replied: "Your Majesty, it might have been easy for me to migrate to Agra from Ujjain. To retrace my step from here will be like tearing away flesh from the nails of my fingers. Let me Sire, breathe the air of Muttra and Brindaban for the remaining few years of my life." Jahangir was pleased with Jadrup's faith and words of touching devotion to his deity. He never broached the subjected again.[18]

There are five leading sects of Sikhs:

1. The Udasis, or those who are "in different" to the world

2. The Suthra, or the "Pure"

3. The Diwane, or "mad" saints

4. The Nirmala Sadhu or "spotless saints"

5. The Akalis or worshippers of the "Eternal One".[19]

Sikhs Gurus

Sl. No.	Name	Date of Birth	Installation as Guru	Date of Death
1.	Guru Nanak (1469-1539)	15.4.1469	-	22.9.1539
2.	Guru Angad (1504-1522)	31.3.1504	14.6.1539	29.3.1552
3.	Guru Amardas (1479-1574)	5.5.1479	29.3.1552	1.9.1574
4.	Guru Ramdas (1534-1581)	24.9.1534	1.9.1574	1.9.1581
5.	Guru Arjun Dev (1563-1606)	15.4.1563	1.9.1581	30.5.1606
6.	Guru Hargobind (1505-1644)	14.6.1595	25.5.1606	3.3.1644
7.	Guru Har Rai (1630-1661)	26.2.1630	8.3.1644	6.10.1661
8.	Guru Har Kishan (1656-1664)	7.7.1656	7.10.1661	30.3.1664
9.	Guru Tegh Bahadur (1621-1675)	1.4.1621	20.3.1665	11.11.1675
10.	Guru Gobind Singh (1666-1708)	22.12.1666	11.11.1675	7.10.1708[20]

Sl.No.	Date of birth	Date of death	Duration of Guruship
1.	Guru Nanak	1538	34 years
2.	Guru Angad	1552	14 years
3.	Guru Amar Das	1574	22 years
4.	Guru Ram Das	1581	7 years
5..	Guru Arjun	1606	25 years
6.	Guru Har Gobind	1638	32 years
7.	Guru Hari Rai	1660	22 years
8.	Guru Hari Krishan	1664	4 years
9.	Guru Tegh Bahadur	1675	11 years
10.	Guru Gobind Singh	1708	33 years[21]

Contemporary Sikh Gurus

1. Guru Nanak Dev (Date of birth 15th April 1469 A.D.) at Nankana Sahib

   Date of death   22 Sept. 1539.

2. Guru Angad Dev (Date of birth 31st March 1504 A.D.) at Mattedi Sarai, Distt.Ferozpur.

   Accession to Guru gaddi   1539 A.D. (Kartarpur)

   Date of death   29th March 1552 A.D. at Khadur Sahib.

3. Guru Amar Das (Date of birth 5th May 1479 at Basarke Distt. Amritsar)

   Accession to Guru Gaddi   1552 A.D. (Khadur Sahib)

   Date of death   1st September 1574 at Goindwal, Distt. Amritsar.

4. Guru Ram Das (Date of birth 1534 A.D.)

   Accession to Guru Gaddi   1574 A.D. (Goindwal)

   Date of death   1581 at Goindwal

5. Guru Arjun Dev (Date of birth 15th April 1563 A.D.) at Goindwal

   Accession to Guru Gaddi   1st Sept. 1581 A.D. at Goindwal

   Date of Martyrdom   May 30, 1606 at Lahore

6. Guru Hargobind (Date of birth 14th June 1595 A.D.)

   Accession to Guru Gaddi   25th May 1606 A.D. (Guru Ki Vadali Distt. Amritsar)

   Date of death   3rd March 1644 at Kiratpur

7. Guru Hari Rai (Date of birth 26th Feb. 1630) at Kiratpur

   Accession to Guru Gaddi   8th March 1644 A.D. at Kiratpur

   Date of death   6th Oct. 1661 at Kiratpur

8. Guru Hari Krishan (Date of birth 7th July 1656 A.D.) at Kiratpur

   Accession to Guru Gaddi   7th October 1661 A.D.) at Kiratpur at the age of 5 years

   Date of death   30th March 1664 A.D. at Delhi

9. Guru Tegh Bahadur (Date of birth 1st April 1621 A.D.) at Guru ke Mahal at Amritsar

   Accession to Guru Gaddi   20th March 1665 at Baba Bakala in Distt. Amritsar

   Date of Martyrdom   Nov. 11, 1675 A.D. at Delhi.

Sikh Guru and Contemporary Rulers

1. Guru Nanak Dev (1469-1539 A.D.)

    1. Bahlol Lodhi (r. 1451-1489 A.D.)

    2. Sikandar Lodhi (r. 1489-1517 A.D.)

    3. Ibrahim Lodhi (r. 1517-1526 A.D.)

    4. Emperor Babur (r. 1526-1530 A.D.)

    5. Emperor Humayun (1530-1540 A.D.)

2. Guru Angad Dev (1504-1552 A.D.)

    1. Emperor Humayun (r. 1530-1540)

    2. Sher Shah Suri (r. 1542-1545 A.D.)

    3.. Islam Shah (r. 1545-1553 A.D.)

3. Guru Amar Das (1479-1574 A.D.)

    = Emperor Akbar (r. 1556-1605 A.D.)

4. Guru Ram Das (1534-1581 A.D.)

    = Emperor Akbar (r. 1556-1605 A.D.)

5. Guru Arjun Dev (1563-1606 A.D.)

    = Emperor Akbar (r. 1556-1605 A.D.)

6. Guru Hargobind (1595-1644 A.D.)

    = Emperor Jahangir (r. 1605-1626 A.D.)

7. Guru Harirai (1630-1661 A.D.)

    = Emperor Aurangzeb (r. 1658-1707 A.D.)

8. Guru Harikrishan (1656-1664 A.D.)

    = Emperor Aurangzeb (r. 1658-1707 A.D.)

9. Guru Tegh Bahadur (1621-1675 A.D.)

    = Emperor Aurangzeb (r. 1658-1707 A.D.)

10. Guru Gobind Singh (1666-1708)

    = Emperor Aurangzeb (r. 1658-1707 A.D.)

    Emperor Bahadur Shah (r. 1707-1708 A.D.)

Contemporary Sikh Gurus of Baba Sri Chand

1. Baba Sri Chand (1494-1643 A.D.)

    1. Guru Nanak Dev (1469-1539 A.D.)

    2. Guru Angad Dev (1504-1552 A.D.)

    3. Guru Amar Das (1479-1574 A.D.)

    4. Guru Ram Das (1534-1581 A.D.)

    5. Guru Arjun Dev (1563-1606 A.D.)

    6. Guru Hargobind (1595-1644 A.D.)

    7. Guru Harirai (1630-1661 A.D.)

    8. Guru Hari Krishan (1656-1661 A.D.)

    9. Guru Tegh Bahadur (1621-1675 A.D.)

Contemporary Rulers

1. Baba Sri Chand (1494-1643 A.D.)

    1. Sikandar Lodhi (r. 1489-1517 A.D.)

    2. Ibrahim Lodhi (r. 1517-1526 A.D.)

    3. Emperor Babur (r. 1526-1530 A.D.)

    4. Emperor Humayun (r. 1530-1540 A.D.)

    5. Sher Shah Suri (r. 1542-1545 A.D.)

6. Islam Shah (r. 1545-1553 A.D.)

7. Emperor Akbar (r. 1556-1605 A.D.)

8. Emperor Jahangir (r. 1605-1626 A.D.)

9. Emperor Shahjahan (r. 1627-1658 A.D.)

Appointments for Guruship

1. Guru Nanak appointed his disciple Lehna (Guru Angad) as second Guru, ignoring his sons, Baba Srichand and Lakhmi Das.

2. Guru Angad appointed his disciple Amar Das as Third Guru (aged 73)

3. Guru Amar Das appointed Bhai Jetha his son-in-law as Fourth Guru and hence forward Guruship became hereditary—under the name of Ram Das (ignoring his sons—Baba Mohan and Baba Mohari).

4. Guru Ram Das nominated his youngest son Arjun Dev as the 5th Guru ignoring his eldest son Baba Pirthi Chand and 2nd son Baba Maha Dev.

5. Guru Arjun Dev the 5th Guru nominated his son Hargobind as the 6th Guru.

6. Guru Hargobind the 6th Guru nominated his grandson Harirai son of Gurditta—as the 7th Guru ignoring his sons—Baba Gurditta and Baba Suraj Mal.

7. Guru Harirai the 7th Guru nominated his 2nd son (younger son) Hari Krishan as 8th Guru ignoring his eldest son Baba Ram Rai.

8. Guru Hari Krishan died at the early age of 8 years due to the attack of smallpox and named Tegh Bahadur's name who was meditating at Baba Bakala. He was the youngest son of Guru Hari Gobind.

9. Guru Tegh Bahadur accessioned to Guru Gaddi on 20th March 1665 and was martyed at Delhi on 11th November 1675. He nominated his son.

10.   Gobind Rai as 10th Guru (Died on 7th October 1708) at Mandu.

Details of Adi Granth

The following list collects the totals in the foregoing tabular statement; and it shows at a glance the amount which each writer contributed to the book. The Fifth Guru Arjun was the collector and arranger of the Adi Granth; and we see from this list that he actually himself wrote nearly half the book he was engaged on arranging:-

Author	Number of Stanzas
Fifth Guru	6204
First Guru	2949 (including the Japji)
Third Guru	2522
Fourth Guru	1730
Kabir	1146
Namdev	239
Ninth Guru	196
Sheikh Farid	149
Ravidas	134
Second Guru	57
Trilochan	20
Beni	19
Dhanna	13
Rai Balvandi	8
Jaidev	7
Bhikhan	5
Sainu	4
Sadhana	4
Surdas	4
Mardana	3
Paramanand	3

Mira Bai	3
Pipa	2
Tenth Guru	1
Various Bhatts	122

Unnamed Bhagat at end of Rag

Jaitsari	6
Rag Mala, etc.	25
Total Stanza	15,575[22]

The followers of Gobind Singh, the tenth and last Guru are as previously stated called Singhs or lions. The followers of Nanak and of his eight successors are known simply as Sikhs. These are subdivided into Udasis, Nanak Shahis, Adan Shahis and Suthra Sahis, minor sects which it is not necessary to present to fully describe. They all believes in the "Adi Granth" or first Granth compiled by Arjun, but not in the volumes compiled by Guru Gobind. For this reason Gobind's followers consider Nanak's followers heterodox. Nanak's followers in return despise the imputation, avoid contact with Gobind's followers and sometimes lead an ascetic life like Hindu mendicants.

There are three classes in the Sikhs:-

1. Akalis

2. Nihangs and

3. Nirmillas[23]

Mughal Empire (1526-1858)

Babur 1526-1530	=	4 years
Humayun 1530-1536	=	6 years
Akbar 1566-1605	=	49 years
Jahangir 1605-1627	=	22 years
Shah Jahan 1628-1657	=	39 years

Aurangzeb 1658-1707	=	49 years
Bahadur Shah I 1707-1712	=	5 years
Farukhsiyar 1713-1719	=	9 years
Muhammad Shah 1719-1748	=	29 years
Ahmad Shah 1748-1757	=	6 years
Shah Alam II 1759-1806	=	47 years
Akbar Shah II 1806-1837	=	31 years
Bahadur Shah II 1837-1858	=	21 years

Notes and References

1. Foreword to Dr. Vivek Bhattacharya's book 'The Spirit of Indian Culture' Saints of India-by the Prime Minister of India Shrimati Indira Gandhi.

2. The spirit of Indian Culture—Saints of India (Introduction XIV) by Dr. Vivek Bhattacharya Metropolitan.

3. Ibid.

4. Ibid.

5. Ibid.

6. Surdas by Usha S. Nilsson (Makers of Indian Literature Series). Sahitya Akadami, Rabindra Bhavan, 35, Ferozeshah Road, New Delhi 110001. 1997.

7. Saints Gurus and Mystics of India by Dr. Giri Raj Singh vol. 2.

8. Mira Bai by Pritam Singh and S. Nilsson

9. Dadu Dayal: Sujatha Nayak—Poet Saints of India ed. by M. Sivarama Krishna and Sunita Roy 1996.

10. Bhai Gurdas by Pritam Singh etc. (Makers of Indian Literature New Delhi, Sahitya Academy in 1992).

11. Tulsidas—by Madan Gopal (Ramayan, Mahabharat and Bhagavata writers—General Editors V. Raghvan - Publication Division 1978.

12. Tulsi Das from Great Indian Saints—Bandyopadhyay.

13. History of the Sikhs. Hari Ram Gupta

14. Ibid.

15.   Ibid.

16.   Ibid.

17.   Dadu-Singer saints of India by Rajindra Singh Verma

18.   Jahangir by Muni Lal, New Delhi, Vikas Publishing House, 5, Ansari Road, 1983 pp.170-172 and 242.

14.   Sikhism by Fredric Pincott from the book Western Image of the Sikh Religion—A source Book, New Delhi, NBO, 1999 ed. by Darshan Singh, p. 184.

20.   Encyclopaedia of Sikh Religion and Culture.

21.   Sikhism by Fredric Pincott from the book Western Image of the Sikh Religion—A source Book ed. by Darshan Singh, New Delhi, NBO, 1999 - p.178.

22.   The Arrangement of the Hymns of the Adi Granth by Fredric Pincott—from the book Western Image of the Sikh Religion. A source book ed. by Darshan Singh, New Delhi 1999 pp. 209-210.

23.   The Sikh Religion under Banda and its present condition by M.A. Macauliffe from the book—Western Image of the Sikh Religion ed. by Darshan Singh, New Delhi, NBO199 pp. 276-277.

3

Family Background

Shri Jeevan Prakash Jeevan in his book entitled Avnashi Chandra has written that before leaving the world, Lord Rama founded the capital cities of Kushawati near Vindhiya mountains Lovepore in the name of his two sons Kusha and Lova. Their decendants ruled from these cities for centuries together and helped each other in the times of adversity. As time passed away, they also developed some fights. The chief of Kushawati raided the fort of Lovepore and the chief of the fallen kingdom was driven out of his area. He fled towards South to save his life. In his way he met another Rajpoot chief by the name of Amrit who married his daughter to this fallen hero. As he was totally pennyless he thought it prudent to reside with his in-laws. After some years he was blessed with a son who was named as Sadeev Rao upon attaining majorhood Sadeev Rao after learning all the facts about his family, attacked Kushawati with the help of armies of his maternal grandfather, defeated the King of Kushawati and gained control of both the kingdoms of Kushawati and Lovepore. This defeat had such an effect upon the fallen king of Kushawati that he renounced his Kshatriya traits and went to Varanasi to learn four vedas. He started teaching Vedas and by doing so his decendents gained the family surname of Vedi; that deformed as Bedi.

In this Bedi clan of Kshatriyas, Kalyan Dass was born in the 15th century. He was a renowned Patwari, Revenue official of Talwandi, Kalyan Dass was a devout Hindu having deep faith in God. He had a small family, Himself, his wife Tripta and one daughter Nanaki. He and his wife were absorbed in the religious ceremonies all the year and served the public feeling God in the service of mankind; They served with all their might sadhus and saints who ever had a time to visit their place. They had everything in their household except a male child. So they always asked for this favour from every religious figure.

Ultimately the prayers of Mother Tripta bore fruit and she was blessed with a son in 1526 Vik. on Vaishakha Sudi 3 at Talwandi; who in the long run came to be adorned as Guru Nanak Dev in the religious world.

Guru Nanak (1469 A.D.-1538 A.D.) was one of the pioneers of the Bhakti movement of medieval India, founder of Sikhism, an incarnation of love. He boldly practised and preached equality of man before God. God is all-prevading "One Great and True Being". Nanak rebelled against the age-old caste system and defied the Brahmanical rituals. He was a great prophet with a vision of finding God in man.

Born in April 1469 in a village Talwandi in Punjab the Guru was a Khatri by caste. Like other great saints he had shown the signs of spiritual inclination right in his childhood. He was a gifted poet, a talented student with a mind deeply absorbed in mysticism. His father Kalu Bedi was an accountant by profession. His mothers' name was Tripta. Both were deeply religious.[1]

At the age of five, Nanak was sent to school, where he studied under the guidance of a Hindu teacher the language, literature, arithmetic and religious scriptures in Sanskrit and also under a Muslim teacher the texts of Arabic and Persian literature. Thus at an early age, he had earned the elementary knowledge. But Nanak did not like a regular confinement in the school for hours. He used to went out very often to wander into the woods where he meditated upon God in solitude.

As Nanak lacked interest in his studies, his father gave

him the cattle to graze. One day he sat under the tree meditating on God, while the cattle grazed another's farm to destroy his crops. Nanak's father got angry with his son for the complaint, and had however compensated the loss of the neighbour by paying money to him. But he did not allow Nanak to graze the cattle any more.

On the day of his sacred thread ceremony, Nanak refused to wear the sacred thread. He said "What is the use of wearing the thread which is soiled, and may be broken or burnt, and which goes not with one into the beyond.

On being asked by the priest what kind of thread he would wish to wear, he said", -

> If compassion be the cotton,
>
> contentment the thread,
>
> continuence the knot,
>
> Truth the twist.

these would weave an ideal thread for the soul. This thread will neither break nor burn, neither be soiled, nor be wasted and lost. Such a thread is worn only by the blessed ones of God.[2]

He was married to Sulakhani, daughter of Moola, a pious Chona Khatri merchant of Batala (now in the district of Gurdaspur). He had two sons from this marriage Sri Chand and Lakhmi Das.

There is some difference of opinion regarding the age of his marriage. Bhai Mani Singh in his Gyan Ratnavali avers that Nanak married at the age of 14, when he was at Talwandi (page 123). Ganda Singh (A History of the Sikhs) suggests 18 to be his age at marriage, when he had according to him, shifted to Sultanpur. Says the *Puratan Janam Sakhi* at the age of 12, Nanak was married". (page 6). Meharvan's *Janamsakhi* gives the date of the betrothal ceremony as the first day of the dark half of Vaisakh (Vaisakh Vadi Ekam) Samvat 1542 i.e. "when he was 15-16 years of age", and that the marriage took place at Talwandi (page 33). If Nanak finished his schooling at 13, it must have taken quite some time for his parents to persuade him to marry. Meharvan gives the name of Nanak's mother as Tipara and of his wife, Ghumi, Malcolm quoting some nameless Sikh authors gives the date of marriage as Asarh (June-July) of Samvat 1545 i.e. at the age of 19.

Similarly no one is clear about the dates of his sons birth, though were alive at the time of their father's demise.

Meharvan gives their dates of birth when Nanak was 27 and 28 i.e. in 1496 and 1497 A.D. i.e. twelve years after his marriage according to this author when Nanak was still at Talwandi (page 66). According to Kahan Singh, Lakhmi Das was born on 19 Phagun, Samvat 1553 (1496 A.D.) at Sultanpur and died on 13 Vaishakh, Samvat 1612 (1555 A.D.) at Kartarpur (Mahakosh Page 3162). The dates of Sri Chand given by him are: Birth: Bhadon Sudi 9, Samvat 1551 (1494 A.D.) at Sultanpur and death on 15 Asuj, Samvat 1669 (1612 A.D.) at the age of 118 years. Lakhmi Das was a married householder and the Bedis of the present day claim their descent from him, even though, as we shall learn later, he was disinherited by his father for his impudence and excessive display of worldly outlook. Sri Chand became an Udasi reclue, and his Akharas or Maths did a lot to propagate the faith of Nanak in their own Vedantic light even during the darkest days of the persecution of the Sikhs by the Moghals. The orthodox Sikhs, however have never identified themselves with the Udas's calling them a heretical sect, disapproved of by Guru Nanak himself.

"A History of the Sikhs", by Ganda Singh and Teja Singh affirms that Nanak was married at the age of 18 while in the service of the Nawab at Sultanpur, and left service at the age of 27 to launch upon his divine mission. The *Purantan Janam Sakhi* is silent as to how many years Nanak stayed at Sultanpur. However, it is stated here that after his marriage and the birth of his two sons at Talwandi, Nanak joined the service at Sultanpur, leaving his family behind and assuring them that he would call them when he felt settled. From the respect and trust of the Nawab that he enjoyed, it can be safely conjectured that it must have been a reasonably long period of stay here. Meharvan, however says Nanak went to Sultanpur at the age of 35 years, 6 months and 15 days and stayed there only for 2 years. According to him (p. 73), Mardana accompanied him alongwith ten servants and that Nanak rode on a horseback took another one along together with two camel, loads of goods, tents, clothes, linens carpets and furniture (a paraphernalia wholly alien to Nanak's way of life).[3]

He would frequently leave his house and go to the jungles and concentrate peacefully there in meditation. He was fond of solitude. Whenever he was in company of many he would divert their entire attention to group singing in praise of the Lord. By and by people came to know about his spiritual bent of mind. The father lost all hopes of the child's getting settled as a householder. It is said that sometime he would give Him money for trade purposes. The son would be meditating on the way and spend the whole money on feeding the poor. The feudal Lord of the village of Talwandi was an admirer of the Guru. He wanted to save Him from the clutches of His father, the promising yogin and sent Him to Sultanpur, with an offer of a job.

The father-in-law was a senior official of the rank of a Collector of Revenue under the Governor and wanted to settle Him at Sultanpur. Both the feudal Lord and the father-in-law Jai Ram sent the young man to an official of the Governor Daulat Khan. He was appointed as a Store Keeper. During these days salary was paid in kind and Nanak was getting quite a substantial quantity. He was keeping for Himself only a very minor portion and distribute the rest to the Sadhus around Him. He was extremely popular among the poor and the needy. One of His most trusted disciples, Mardana joined Him as "Private servant, friend and companion in devotion.

He devoted Himself completely in divine thoughts and spent all his time in meditation. In this long journey His only companion was Mardana, the trusted servant and the disciple. Mardana followed them like a shadow in all His pilgrimages.[4] He travelled for 14 years. His first and second journey took place during the year 1507-1515 and visited East and South of India, Sri Lanka etc. and covered approximately distance of 6400 miles. His third journey took place between the year 1515-1517; visited Himalayas and Tibet. His fourth journey took place between 1517-1521; visited West Asia-Bagdad, Mecca and Medina and covered about 6000 miles.

Guru Sahib undertook five Udasis for the benefit of one and all and travelled extensively throughout Indian sub-continent apart from visiting Sri Lanka, Mecca (Saudi Arabia), Iraq, Iran and Afghanistan and other places.

God's Realization

While living at Sultanpur Lodhi, one morning he went to the rivulet vein to take his usual bath. Therefrom he went to the nearby forest for Nama-Simran and suddenly fell into trance. He was blessed with Divine vision. His first serman was:

"Na Ko Hindu hai

no ko Musalman hai"

Neither there is any Hindu nor Muslim.[5]

While in the employment of the Nawab, Nanak became extremely popular with him and his servants to whom he would issue rations from the imperial stores. "He worked so well that everyone was pleased with him and said 'what a man, what a man". Every one commended him to the Nawab who also became enamoured of him." Whatever rations he got for himself, he would offer these to others in the name of God, himself being content with the barest minimum for his upkeep." It is also said when he would weigh up the stores and reached at the figure '13' (in Hindustan Tera, which also means Thine) he would enter an ecstasy and continue endlessly to repeat: "Tera, main Tera" (Thine O God, I am Thine) (says Malcolm in his "Sketch of the Sikhs" (p. 15) that on reports reaching the Nawab that Nanak was squandering his stores on unauthorised persons, he arrested Jairam. But on the account being taken, a balance was found in his favour on which Jairam was not only released but re-instated in the employment and the favour of his master.

About Daulat Khan Lodhi, Dr. Gopal Singh has recorded 'All historians are agreed that Nawab Daulat Khan Lodhi (died 1526) was appointed Governor of Punjab by Ibrahim Lodhi in or about 1502 A.D. and remained at his post for over 20 years, giving the Punjab comparative peace and prosperity. But, later due to the maltreatment of himself and his son, he turned against Ibrahim and invited Babur to invade India in 1523 (Oxford History of India, V. Smith, third edition, page 321). Later on he turned against Babur as well, for the emperor not having kept his word for restoring Punjab's Governorship to him (which he had lost in an expedition against him by Bihar Khan, a general of Ibrahim Lodhi) but instead arrested him, though he was later released and put incharge of Sultanpur (Bannerjee, Evolution of Khalsa page 39), which according to Kahan Singh, was his ancestoral estate (Mahan Kosh, p. 1958). Sultanpur then was also the capital of a province Jullundar-Doab. So we know that Daulat Khan had something to do with Sultanpur, where the ruins of his fort can still be seen. Babur in his Babur-Nama mentions Daulat Khan's father, Tatar Khan, "as having been appointed by Bahlol Lodhi to the Governorship of a country north of Satluj and Sarhind and that on his death, Sikandar Lodi took over these territories and gave only Lahore to Daulat Khan one or two years before I came into Kabul (910 A.H. i.e. in 1502 or 1503) (A.S. Beveridge's translation, vol. I, page 383).[6]

There are innumerable accounts giving the details of the biographical events of this great master. Among the great Western scholars who devoted their research on the Guru, the works of Cunningham (History of the Sikhs) Macauliffe (The Sikh Religion), Scot, George Batley (Religion and short History of the Sikhs 1479-1930 and Archar John Clark (The Sikhs) are only a few to mention. Research work has also been conducted at the level of the UNESCO to popularise the universal message of love as preached and practised by Guru Nanak.

Guru Nanak had miraculous power. There are many instances associated with the life of the Guru which are not only legends but historic facts. He never wanted to show this power to anybody but they were revealed in face of circumstances.

Once the Guru was passing through a place known as Syedpur. This was during the pilgrimage. The Saint was showering his blessing to one and all. In Syedpur there was a pious man, Lallo. He was a poor carpenter but a deeply religious man. He was living from hand to mouth but he was keen to have Nanak as his guest. With his long yellow robe, handsome feature and a glow on his face, the Saint became soon quite known in the neighbourhood.

Malik Bhaggo was a Dewan of the Pathan Subedar. He was known for his philanthropy and pious deeds. He used to feed monks and fakir regularly. His invitation to the monks was a standing one.

Nanak liked Lallo, the carpenter. He was living with him. Poor man could offer him only a meager diet. But his heart was warm with divine affection and Nanak enjoyed his company. The Saint did not care for the food. A good man eats to live others live to eat.

Malik Bhaggo heard the name of the new monk whom he expected every day in his community lunch. The invitation being general he did not care to extend any special one to the Saint. When Bhaggo could not see Nanak in his rich community lunch, his pride was touched. He thought, "how is it?" All the monks, big and small, are participating in the community lunch thrown by him. How is it that the new monk does not even care to join them even for once? He went to the carpenter's house and found the Saint surrounded by a couple of men who were fortunate enough to listen to the golden voice of the Guru. He was showering divine nectar. This rich proud man approached the Saint and, more or less, on a point of explanation asked him why he never joined his community lunch. Is it that you do not know me? Do you not know I am a powerful man?

Yes I know you. And that is exactly the reason why I do not join you.

The Dewan got enraged.

"What do you mean?" The Dewan roared.

"It is very clear. I know you. I know you so well that I do not feel like touching your *Halwa Puri*".

I am quite happy with the dry piece of bread from Lallo.

The rich Dewan lost his temper. The Saint's words touched his vanity.

"You mean to say you know me".

"Yes"

But how is it? You never saw my face.

Nanak kept quiet. His smile provoked the Dewan.

Bhaggo said, "You must explain,"

Nanak called the Dewan near him and calmly told him. "You want to see why I accept Lallo as a host and not you.

Alright please do me a favour. Get the *Puri Halwa* that you want to offer me.

The Saint asked Lallo, the carpenter, also to get him the dry piece of bread that he normally offers him.

Then a miracle happened.

The details are given in the most authentic biography of the Master *Janam Sakhi*.

Nanak placed Lallo's piece of dry bread side by side with Dewan's *Puri Halwa*. Just to teach a lesson to the proud rich man the Saint showed his miracle. He squeezed the *Halwa Puri* of Dewan. Everybody saw pure red blood pouring out of his hand.

Then the saint kept the dry bread of Lallo, the carpenter. He squeezed this too. Everybody saw pure white milk pouring out of his hand.

So you see why I do not join your lunch.

The Dewan's vanity dashed against the ground. He fell down at the feet of the Guru and asked for his blessings and pardon. By and by the story got spread Hundreds of people started thronging the Saint. So the next dawn the Guru left Syedpur alongwith Balla and Mardana.[7]

Travels of Guru Nanak

Having realised that the age of ignorance and strife requires the message of truth and peace, Nanak took the momentous decision of spreading it. To do so, he undertook orduous and extensive tours in the North, South, East and West and visited the important centres of the Hindus, Muslims, Buddhist and Jains, Sufis, Jogis etc. and met people of different races, different tribes, diverse culture patterns. His travels covered a period nearly thirty years.

In his first Udasi, he traversed in terms of the modern political geography of India and Pakistan, Haryana, Delhi, Uttar Pradesh, Bihar, Bengal, Orissa, Madras, Kerala, Mysore, Andhra Pradesh, Maharashtra, Gujarat, Madhya Pradesh, Rajasthan and West Pakistan. He also visited Ceylon. He went there from Nagapathinam, and returned via Rameshwaram. The second Udasi (tour) took the Guru into the interior of the Himalayan region where he visited the Kangra valley, the spiti, Western Tibet, Ladakh, Kashmir and West Punjab (Pakistan).

After this, the Guru undertook his third missionary journey to the Muslim countries of West Africa wearing the dress of a muslim devotee. Some prominent places connected with this tour of the Guru were Multan, Lakhpat, Hinglay, Mecca, Madina, Baghdad, Mashad, Herat, Kandhar, Kabul Para Chinnar and Gorakh-Hatri (Peshawar).

Guru Nanak and Babur

Towards the end of their travels, Guru Nanak and Bhai Mardana happened to visit Eminabad a second time. As was their practice they went to Bhai Laloo's house and stayed with them.

Around that time Emperor Babur had defeated and imprisoned the people of Eminabad. Many of them had been killed. Their houses were looted and the poor unhappy people were made to carry their own looted property to Babur's camp.

Guru Nanak and Bhai Mardana were also taken prisoners and given a heavy load to carry. Guru Nanak's heart ached with sorrow at the misery of the people around him. He began to sing sweet, holy songs in praise of God, which brought great solace to the sufferers.

Babur's men reported this incident to him. Babur decided to visit the prison and see things for himself. When he reached the prison, he found Guru Nanak sitting peacefully with his eyes closed. He was singing a melodious voice while all the prisoners sat with folded hands. Even though he could not follow the words, Babur too joined the crowd. He seemed to be under a magic spell.

When Guru Nanak stopped singing, Babur asked him the meaning of the hymn. Guru Nanak boldly explained to him that he was singing about the Emperor's cruelty and the plight of the victims:

> Babur ruled over Khurasan and hath terrified Hindustan
>
> The Creator taketh no blame to Himself; it was death disguised as a Mughal who made war on us
>
> When there was such slaughter and lamentation didst not thou,
>
> O God, feel pain?
>
> Creator, Thou belongest to all....

Babur was impressed by Guru Nanak's courage and truthfulnes. He said to him, What can I do for you? Guru Nanak at once said, Set the prisoners free and return their property and wealth which your man have so mercilessly plundered. Babur readily agreed to his request.

After a long journey Guru Nanak settled at Kartarpur. On September 22, 1539 he laid himself on a bed and asked his followers to sing 'sohila', the praise of God. He closed his eyes and went into a 'samadhi' and soon his spirit left the body. He was at that time seventy years, five months and seven days old.[8]

Bani of Guru Nanak

Total number of hymns 947 in Ragas e.g. Asa, Basantu, Dhanasari, Gauri, Majh, Ramakali, Sorathi, Sri Rag, and Suhi etc. He also recited Japu which is not in any Rag. His Bani under various headings in various Ragas, e.g. Sidh Gosati, Arti, Patti, and Onkaru etc. is included in Guru Granth Sahib.

His message: He enjoined the Sikhs as—

1. Kirat Karo

2. Nama Japo

3. Vend Ke Chhako

4. To shed away caste-prejudices, because all human beings are equal

5. To imbibe the spirit of Service and Humility.[9]

Guru Nanak's life and times
At a Glance

A.D.

1469	Born at Talwandi
1474-1482	Education at Talwandi
1485-1505	Work at home with father
1487	Marriage with Mata Sulakhni

1494	Birth of Sri Chand
1497	Birth of Lakhmi Chand
1504	Employment at Sultanpur (where sister Nanki and brother-in-law Jai Ram Uppal lived.)
1507	Resigned from the job
1507 Aug. 23	Angels took Nanak to the house of God from river Bein
1507 Aug. 26	Came back from God—First Commandment at Sultanpur
1507-1521	Travels for 14 years
1507-1510	First journey accompanied by Bhai Mardana

Multan—conversion of Sheikh Sajjan

Panipat—discourses with Shah Sharif

Delhi—revived a dead elephant; meeting with Sultan Ibrahim

Banaras—discourse with Pandit Chatur Das

Nanakmatta—discourse with yogis

Assam (Kamrup)—Conversion of Nur Shah

Puri (Orissa)—Hymn of Aarti

Talwandi—meeting with parents

Goindwal—healing of a leper

Saidpur—(Eminabad), Babur's attack and arrest Mallick Bhago and Lalo

1510-1515	Second journey (5 years) South of India and Ceylon. Madhya Pradesh—conversion of Kanda. Ceylon. Enlightenment of Raja Shivnabn.
1515-1517	Third journey (2 years). North of India

Kashmir—discourse with Pandit Brahma Das

	Mount Summer—discourse with Siddhs. Achal, festival of Shivratri; discourse with yogis.
1517-1521	Fourth journey (West of Asia)
	Mecca—discourse with Qazi Bukundin
	Baghdad—discourse with Pir Dastgir
	Hasan Abdala—discourse with Wali Qandhari
1521	End of missionary journeys. Settlement at Kartarpur, on the banks of river Ravi.
1532	Meeting with Bhai Lehna
1539-July 14	Appointment of Lehna as the Second Guru of the Sikhs
1539-Sept. 22	Death of Guru Nanak (2 months and 8 days after the appointment of Guru Angad).

Notes and References

1. Guru Nanak (1469 A.D. 1538 A.D.)—The spirit of Indian Culture—Saints of India by Vivek Bhattacharya.

2. Guru Nanak (1469 A.D.-1538 A.D.) From Great Indian Saints by Bandyopadhyay.

3. A History of the Sikh People - 1469-1978 by Dr. Gopal Singh, New Delhi, World Sikh University Press, 1979.

4. Guru Nanak—The spirit of Indian Culture—Saints of India by Vivek Bhattacharya.

5. The Sikh Gurus. Harcharan Singh Sobti and Arahat Inderjeet Singh, New Delhi, Perfect Press Pvt. Ltd. 1996.

6. A History of the Sikh People 1469-1978 by Dr. Gopal Singh, New Delhi, World Sikh University Press, 1979.

7. Guru Nanak (The Spirit of Indian Culture—Saints of India by Vivek Bhattacharya).

8. Life and Times—The Sikh Gurus. New Delhi, Vikas Publishing House 1997.

9. The Sikh Gurus by Harcharan Singh Sobti and A. Inderjeet Singh, New Delhi, Perfect Press 1996.

4

Baba Sri Chand—An Early Phase

"Yogis (mystics) who are full of dispassion and are wholly detached from God's creation keep awake (in the daylight of wisdom) muttering the name with their tongue, and enjoy the felicity of Brahma (the Absolute) which is incomparable unspeakable, unmixed with sorrow and devoid of name and form. Even those (seekers of truth) who aspire to know the mysterious ways of Providence are able to comprehend them by muttering the name. Strivers (hankering after worldly achievements) repeat the Name, absorbed in contemplation, and become accomplished, acquiring superhuman powers such as that of becoming infinitely small in size.* If devotees in distress mutter the Name, their worst calamities of the gravest type disappear and they become happy. In this world there are four kinds of devotees† of Sri Rama; all the four of them are virtuous, sinless and noble. All the four, clever as they are, rely upon the name. Of these the enlightened devotee is specially dear to the Lord. The glory of the Name is supreme in all the four Yugas and all the four Vedas, particularly in the Kaliage, in which there is no other means of salvation (1-4)."

---

* Works on Yoga enumerate the following eight kinds of miraculous powers acquired by yogies :

1. Anima (the faculty of reducing one's body to the size of an atom. 2. Mahima (the power of expanding one's body to an infinitely large size. 3. Garima (the power of becoming infinitely heavy. 4. Laghima (the power of becoming infinitely light in body. 5. Prapti (unrestricted access to all places). 6. Prakarma (realizing whatever one desires). 7. Isitva (absolute lordship) and 8. Vasitva (subjugating all).

† Srimad Bhagavadgita mentions four kinds of devotees, viz., 1. Arta (the afflicted), 2. Jijnasu (the seeker of truth), 3. Artharthi (the seeker of worldly riches), and 4. Jnani (the enlightened) and speaks of them all as virtuous and benevolent. Of course, the enlightened devotee, it is pointed out, is the most beloved of the Lord and constitutes this way self (vide VII-16-18).

Birth of Baba Sri Chand

History records that whenever a human being became a slave to carnal desires got scorched by avarice and attachment, forgot his real self veiled by illusion, and thus the truth, righteousness, devotion and all the noble virtues are annihilated; only then the Great Souls reincarnate themselves to set right the conditions of the whole world according to the needs of the times. For example, Great Saints like Shri Kabir Sahib Ji, Shri Guru Nanak Dev Ji, Saint Paltu Das Ji, Saint Dadu Dayal Ji, Saint Sahjo Bai Ji, Saint Daya Bai Ji and numerous other highly realized souls, who were the embodiments of spiritual knowledge and devotion unto God appeared to meet the demands of the times. They infused a new rejuvenating spirit in the almost lifeless world by preaching love, Bhakti, renunciation detachment, spiritual knowledge, meditation and enlightening the path of self-realization.

Lord Krishna says in Shrimad Bhagwad Gita:

।।श्लोक।।

यदा यदा हि धर्मस्य ग्लानिर्भवति भारत।
अभ्युत्थानमधर्मस्य तदात्मानं सृजाम्यहम्।।

परित्राणाम साधूनां विनाशय च दुष्कृताम्।
धर्मसस्थापनार्थाय सम्भवामि युगे युगे।।

Whenever declines righteousness,
> And the Power of evil increases
O Scion of Bharata, I embody forth,
> Myself then to defend the truth
I come back for the good to protect
> And the wicked to annihilate
From age to age I come into being
> To establish what is right and sterling.

(Gita IV/7-8)

Lord Krishan Chandra Ji says "In every age, whenever there is decay of righteousness and the unrighteousness prevails, the wicked torture the good and the devotees, truth, noble virtues, religion and devotion decline, spiritual light dims, evil forces rule the earth, then I manifest myself in human form in such critical times for the protection of the good and noble for the destruction of the wicked and to re-establish righteousness.

Shri Ramayana also testifies the same truth in the following verse:

||चौपाई||

जब जब होय धर्म की हानी। बाढ़हि असुर अधम अभिमानी॥

करहिं अनीति जाय नहिं वरणी। सीदहिं विप्र घेनुसुर धरणी॥

तब तब प्रभु धरि विविध शरीरा। हरहिं कृपानिधि सज्जन पीरा॥

Whenever there is decline of goodness,

Rise of evil, demons haughty and unrighteous

Whose acts are utterly vile and treacherous

The Brahamans, Cows, gods and the earth they harass;

Then God incarnates in times of such distress

To relieve sorrow of the good and virtuous

(Baal Kand)

Lord Shiva explains to Parvati Ji the theory of Lords incarnation thus—'O Parvati! God incarnates Himself according to the need of times to protect His devotees. Just as Lord Vishnu had to assume Narsinhas form to save Prahlada and again become a barber for the sake of His devotee "Sen", similarly God incarnates Himself in every age, in every nation and in every community (in the garb of the most venerable Great Saint). Sometimes He appears in usual form, at another in special form for a set purpose. Special incarnations are perfect armed with full powers to bring about special changes in a particular age or Yuga. Lord's usual forms are those of Great Saints, Perfect Masters, the Sadgurus.

They appear on this earth to warn the people caught in the clutches of illusion, to comfort the troubled minds, to inspire the selfish worldly people to take up the service of the humanity, to rekindle the glimmering light of spiritual knowledge, to teach the people the art of self-realization, to infuse the sweet melody of love into every one's life, to make every body stead fast on the path of righteousness and duty, to liberate them from the worldly fetters and to make them an embodiment of Truth and happiness. There is no difference between them and God, for they are embodiments of God.

Lord Shri Ram, Lord Shri Krishan, Maharishi Gautam, Shri Ved Vyasa and Braham Rishi Vashishtha incarnated themselves on this very soil of Bharata to reveal the glory of devotion to the Lord and glorified this country. The various Great Saints who have been mentioned above appeared in India itself at different times. All the four ages:

Satya Yuga

Dwapra

Treta and earlier part of

Kali Yuga

are a witness to this immoral truth. The entire world has been benefitted from this reservoir of devotion and spirituality and continues to do so even in present times. This is evident from the following Shaloka of Manu Smriti.

एतद देश प्रसूतस्य सकाशादग्रजन्मन: ।
स्वं स्वं चरित्रं रिक्षिरन् पृथिण्याँ सर्वमानवा ।।

All the nations of the world used to build up their character by learning from the ancestors, scholars and great teachers of this country. From this point of view, it will not be improper to call India the Guru (Guide) and the teacher that enlightens the path for the whole world. In the present scientific age, the credit for all the scientific advancement must go to the Vedas, which disclosed the basic principles and knowledge of various sciences, soul and God and the technique of Yoga. Atharva Ved particularly contains special instructions as to how to conquer nature.

The names and forms of the reformers and the Saints of the world may have been different but their aim has always been one and the same

Acharya Shri Srichandra who was an incarnation of Lord Shiva came on earth to safeguard the Sanatan Dharam. During the Muslim rule in India, the citizens of India, particularly Hindus were deprived from their religious rights and worshipping of their God especially idol worship. This was due to the efforts and encouragement of Acharya Shri who enabled and encouraged the Hindu community to perform their religious duties. Before his arrival the Hindus of the area were horrified by the atrocities of Mughal rulers. Knowing this that area administrator naming Acharya Shri as a mad man. Acharya Ji replied that every deranged person consider others as mad man. The day Acharya said this on same night the area administrator started behaving like a mad person and the very night he pushed his own sword in his stomach and died.[1]

Guru Nanak was 32 years old when he was blessed with a son on Bhadrapad Shukla Nawami of 1551 Bik Samat (1494 A.D.). The baby was born to mother Sulakshani Devi at Talwandi.[2]

It is told that he was busy in a spiritual discourse with some of his friends in the outer sitting room, when the news was delivered to him by his elder sister Nanaki. She also informed him that the new born baby, first appeared as Lord Shiva, then disappeared and now he his wearing a Karan Kundal, in his ear a natural ring of flesh and the holy ashes. (Vibhuti) adorn his body. Hearing this, all present, got excited and congratulated Shri Nanak. He also felt and saw during his meditation and told the whole story to Bebe Nanaki that Lord Shiva, has incarnated himself in the form of that child.

Sri Chandra was the founder of Udasin sect who carved his path for himself and did not follow the beaten track.

The sixth day or the Chhati was observed with pomp and show in the house of Baba Nanak. All and one came to see the new born; Shiva incarnate. They observed locks of hair on his head, Tripund; (त्रिपुण्ड) Tilak on his forehead and Vibhuti (Sacred ash) all over his body. His father Nanak believed that he was the incarnation of Shiva himself. He invited the famous Astrologist. Pandit Hardyalu Sharma to prepare the Janam Kundili of the new born child. He was delighted to find the strange arrangement of Nine planets in the horoscope. People were anxious to hear the outcome of the horoscope. Keeping in view their anxiety, Pandit Hardyalu told the gathering and the father of the newborn; "Nanakji, you are lucky enough, who are blessed with such a glorious son. This boy will glorify the parent's name with his miraculous powers and the yogic and meditative enchants. He will observe ultimate celibasy (Akhand Brahamcharya) and will protect Vedic religious traditions and the down trodden Hindu society. He will fly the flag of Hinduism high in the skies of Indian religious and will infuse new blood in the body of Hinduism. He will bring a revolution in this country. He will destroy the false-hood and the oppressors. He will usher a new dawn in India. I salute such a divine child.

Controversy over Date of Birth and Place of Birth

According to Dr. Harbans Singh

Sri Chand, Baba (1494-1629), the elder son of Guru Nanak and the founder of the ascetic sect of Udasis, was born to Mata Sulakkhani on Bhadon sudi 9, 1551 Bk/8 September 1494 at Sultanpur Lodhi, now in Kapurthala district of the Punjab. After Guru Nanak left home on his travels to distant parts, Sri Chand's mother took him and his younger brother, Lakhmi Das, to her parents' home at Pakkhoke Randhave on the left bank of the River Ravi. Sri Chand from the very beginning loved solitude and as he grew up, he developed indifference to worldly affairs. At the tender age of eleven he left for Kashmir where he studied Sanskrit texts under Pandit

Purushottam Kaul and later studied and practised yoga under Avinashi Muni. When Guru Nanak, after his travels, had settled down at Kartarpur on the right bank of Ravi and not far from Pakkhoke, Sri Chand rejoined the family. He however retained his preference for the life of an ascetic. Guru Nanak having chosen one of his disciples as his spiritual successor, passed away at Kartarpur on 7 September 1539 and a monument was raised over the site where his ashes were buried. As the monument was washed away by floods in the river, Sri Chand had the urn containing the ashes salvaged, reburied it at some distance close to the well of Ajitta Randhava, a devotee of the late Guru, and built a mud hut over it. The place came to be revered as dehra or samadh (mausoleum) of Guru Nanak around which grew up the present town of Dera Baba Nanak.

Baba Sri Chand stayed on at Pakkhoke Randhave for some time. He gathered around him a band of his own disciples who like him shunned the householder's life and practised austerities. With his disciples he travelled throughout the length and breadth of India, initiating more converts to his Udasin or Udasi (lit. indifferent, stoic) sect who functioned as itinerant preachers and established missionary centres at different places in the country and beyond. Through them Guru Nanak's word was also carried to far corners of the land. Baba Sri Chand's own main centre was at Barath, 8 km southwest of Pathankot in Gurdaspur district of the Punjab. Baba Sri Chand also kept in touch with successive Guru's during his long life of well over a century. The Gurus held him in high esteem in view of his holy descent, old age and piety. In 1626, when at the behest of Guru Hargobind, his eldest son, Baba Gurditta, proceeded to found the town of Kiratpur in the lower Sivalik hills, he had the ground broken by Baba Sri Chand. According to the Bhatt Vahis, Baba Sri Chand died at Kiratpur on Magh *sudi* 1, 1685 Bk/ 13 January 1629. Before that he had, with Guru Hargobind's approval, appointed Baba Gurditta to succeed him as head of the Udasi sect.

According to Baba Virsa Singh

Baba Sri Chand was born in 1494 as the elder son of Guru Nanak, the First Sikh Guru. As a child, he was of contemplative nature, and he became the first person to whom Guru Nanak prescribed the life of an Udasi. In contrast to ascetics who leave the world in order to meditate, an Udasi is a renunciate who lives in the world, maintaining everyday life as well as practicing meditation.

Baba Sri Chand was a renunciate--self denying, celibate, and dedicated to meditation--but he was also a farmer. His father asked him not to leave the world but to take responsibility for the community farm at Kartarpur while he, Guru Nanak, was away. When Guru Nanak returned from his travels, the whole village happily told him that they had learned from Baba Sri Chand how to combine hard work on the farm and meditation.

Baba Sri Chand had an extensive and dedicated following. When the Emperor Jahangir asked Mian Mir his own darvesh (Muslim term for a powerful, truthful, God-intoxicated holy person), who is the greatest darvesh today?'' Mian Mir replied, "At this time the elder son of Guru Nanak is the king of the darveshes."

Baba Sri Chand lived to the great age of 149, and his guidance was revered by the first six Sikh Gurus. Although his followers numbered in the millions, he encouraged them to be devotees of Guru Nanak rather than of himself. He never married but he took responsibility for raising his brother's son, Dharm Chand, and then arranged the boy's marriage.

When Baba Sri Chand left the visible world in 1643, he left with his body intact. He has existed for thousands of years and he is the same now. We cannot see him with our external eyes but he has not gone anywhere. He is proof of what is written by Guru Ram Das: *Satguru mera sada sada, na avay na ja-ay. Oh Abnasi Purakh hai, sab me reha samaye*--My Guru is the Eternal One. He is for all times. He neither comes nor goes. He is the Eternal Lord who pervades all of Creation."[5]

According to Professor Teja Singh

Baba Sri Chand the eldest son of Guru Nanak was born at Sultanpur in the year 1494. Lakhmidas was his younger brother. Siri Chand was only three years old when his father, Guru Nanak went to the foreign countries to preach religion.

In the absence of Guru Nanak Dev Sri Chand was looked after by Bibi Nanki, the sister of Guru Nanak. She loved him like his son. She was a religious minded and God fearing lady. Being brought under his guardianship, Sri Chand inherited God fearing spirit from her. When Guru Nanak Dev returned from his religious tours he set up a permanent home at Kartarpur. Sri Chand also reached there in the year 1522 to stay with his parents.

Guru Nanak started agricultural farm there. He wished that his sons help him in this work. Though he was quite happy with their learning towards religion but he did not want to see them non-working. Lakhmidas was very proud due to his father's towering personality and he did not want to undertake any work. Sri Chand was a religious person. He always devoted himself in the memory of God and have no time to think about the worldly affairs.

Being a eldest amongst the two brothers he was supposed to take over the thrown of his father. But his father declined his claim. Guru Nanak never wished that his followers may follow such a person who has no time to think about worldly affairs. Consequently he appointed Bhai Lehna as his successor.

Sri Chand was very much annoyed by his father's decision and left his house and become a Udasi sadhu. He adopted to wear a long 'Kalindari' cap and Lotus mala. After touring for a short time he settled in a village named Barth in Gurdaspur district of Punjab.

For years together he did not like to meet the decendents of his father. But daring his old age he forgive them and have cordial relations with them.

Once he went to Guru Ramdas to meet him at Goindwal. Guru Ramdas welcomed him with a smile. Baba Sri Chand touched long beard of the Guru with his hands and asked him why do you keep such a long beard ? Guruji replied "This has been kept to clean the feet of the people of high stature like you". Baba Sri Chand was very much impressed and pleased to listen this reply and said Oh! this is due to your such type of humility which enabled you to have thrown of a Guru".

Afterwards Guru Arjun Deva called on him and later on Guru Hargovind also went to him. When Guru Hargovind met him in Barth then his eldest son Gurditta was also accompanied him. Baba Sri Chand asked him, "how many sons you have?" Guruji replied. "Five"!

Will you keep all your sons with you? Won't you give me even one"?

"Yes! I can give you my eldest son, who is with me at the moment".

Baba Sri Chand blessed him by keeping his kind hand on his head. Pointing towards Guruji he said, "You are already occupying the thrown of Guru with you. I have only one Kalindari Cap and a Lotus Rosary with me. I am handing over both these articles to you". While saying so he handed over symbol of a sage to Baba Gurditta. After this incident the difference between Baba Sri Chand and the decendents of his father came to an end.

After this historic event Baba Sri Chand left towards the mountains of Chamba. He was seen lastly in the year 1612 while crossing river Ravi. Afterwards nothing could be traced out about him.[6]

Srichand and Lakhmi Das

No one is clear about the dates of their birth, though both

were alive at the time of their father's demise. Meharvan gives
their dates of birth when Nanak was 27 and 28 i.e. in 1496 and
1497 A.D. i.e. twelve years after his marriage according to this
author when Nanak was still at Talwandi. According to
Kahan Singh, Lakhmi Das was born on 19 Phagun, Samvat
1553 (1496 A.D.) at Sultanpur and died on 13 Vaisakh, Samvat
1612 (1555 A.D.) at Kartarpur. The dates for Srichand given
by him are—Birth: Bhadon Sudi 9, Samvat 1551 (1494 A.D.)
at Sultanpur and death on 15 Asuj, Samvat 1669 (1612 A.D.)
at the age of 118 years. Lakhmi Das was a married
householder and the Bedis of the present day claim their
descent from him, even though, as we shall learn later, he was
disinherited by his father for his impudence and excessive
display of worldly outlook. Srichand became an udasi recluse,
and his Akharas or Maths did a lot to propagate the faith of
Nanak in their own Vedantic light even during the darkest
days of the persecutions of the Sikhs by the Moghuls. The
orthodox Sikhs, however, have never identified themselves
with the Udasis, calling them a heretical sect, disapproved by
Guru Nanak himself.

The ascetic son of Guru Nanak, Sri Chand though
disinherited by the father, was still alive and preaching his
gospel of renunciation as an Udasis though he was mature
and disinterested enough not to come actively in the way of
the third Guru. But, it was really hard for the common run
of the Sikhs "too choose between Guru Nanak's son and the
nominee of his nominee".[7]

Mehant Baba Janki Das Ji has related an interesting
story about the birth of Baba Sri Chand. He has written at the
birth of Baba Sri Chand, Guru Nanak's elder sister Bibi Nanki
came to congratulate Him. Shri Nanak Dev Ji said—sister !
This is not an ordinary child. This is incarnation of Lord Shiva
Shankar who has born in our house. You may recall that after
seeing my meditation Lord Shiva was much impressed and
pleased and had promised to born in my house as a son of
mine.

It would not be out of place to mention here that mother

Sulakshna used to visit Shiv Temple daily. One day Shri Sri Chand insisted to accompany his mother to Shiv Temple. When he did not acceded to the requests of his mother, then she put Him in one of rooms of the house and closed the doors from outside and reached the temple. When she reached there she was stunned to see the Sri Chand sitting near the Shivling in the guise of Lord Shiva and followers of Lord Shiva were garlanding Him. She was over joyed to see this and had the firm belief that his son virtually is not any ordinary person but incarnation of Lord Shiva in the real sense. As similarly mother Kaushalya had seen his son Rama sleeping in the craddle and taking food in the kitchen at one time in two positions, she immediately came to know that his son Rama is not an ordinary person but incarnation of Lord Vishnu. In the same manner mother Sulakshna came to know the secret of his son Sri Chand.[8]

Bhai Kirpal Singh says that:

Baba Sri Chand Ji was a great Udasi saint, as described by Hazrat Mian Mir in his conversation with Emperor Jehangir. Mir referred to Babaji as the "Emperor of all Fakirs". Eldest son as well as the disciple of Guru Nanak Dev Ji, Baba Sri Chand Ji was highly respected by kings, saints, yogis, Sikh Gurus, and the common people of all sects and religions. Babaji devoted his long life (149 years) to meditation, preaching Nam, and to moral, spiritual, and religious uplift of society, helping the poor, the downtrodden, and those in need. As directed by his father and Master, Baba Sri Chand Ji played a unique role of setting the sadhu samaj on the right path.

Birth

Babaji was born on Bhadon Sudi 9 of Samat 1551 (1494 A.D.) in Sultanpur Lodhi District Kapurthala, Punjab. His mother Sulakhni Ji was a great lady who did all she could to help him achieve his goal.

There were several highly unusual circumstances surrounding his birth. Instead of crying, he emerged laughing. The room was filled with light and fragrance. A thin layer of ashes covered his body and the small curly knots of his hair were shining brightly. His right ear lobe was extended in a ring of flesh, leaving no doubt that he was a born "yogi".

Early life

Guru Nanak Dev Ji started Babaji's training at a very early age, mostly by personal example. Thus, as a child he formed habits of rising early, bathing, and spending long hours in meditation. He was told religious stories and sermons to which he listened attentively. Babaji did not play like other children of his age; on the other hand he collected them and taught them meditation whenever they called upon him to play.

There are several miracles associated with his childhood, for instance. Once when people got anxious over the delay in his return from the jungle where he had gone, a search party was organized. It found, to its great surprise, Babaji in deep meditation surrounded by wild animals of all sorts such as elephants, tigers, and leopards. All were sitting at his feet motionless, perfectly silent, with eyes closed, enamoured by his mystical powers and in service of their master.

With Bebe Nanaki

In 1558, when Babaji was seven, Guru Nanak Dev Ji left for his first *Udasi* (long preaching journey as a renunciate). Babaji was placed in the care of Bebe Nanaki, Guru Ji's elder sister. "Respected sister," said Guru Nanak Dev Ji, "this is no ordinary child. He will grow to be a great saint, with a large following. He will have a long life and lead a separate seat. He will not marry but his younger brother Baba Lakhmi Chand will have a family and provide a link with our future generation."

Babaji visited Pakhoke and Talwandi also to meet his grandparents. Though he was a child, Babaji's face was glowing with friendliness and his wide knowledge, sharp intelligence, and spiritual achievements at such a tender age made him popular everwhere. The Nawabs at these places especially paid homage, as they did to Guru Nanak.

When Guru Ji returned from his first Udasi, he found his son, a lad of fifteen, very firm in his principles and fully devoted to meditation. Guru Ji during his brief stay at Sultanpur and before leaving for the second Udasi, gave maximum time to Babaji and blessed him with NAAM as his first disciple.

On return from the second Udasi, Guru Ji advised him to study Vedas and other Shastras to continue his religious education, even though both sets of grandparents wanted him to enter business, in accordance with the family tradition.

Namkaran Sanskar

When Pandit Hardyalu prepared the horoscope on the Chhati festival, then relatives requested the learned pandit to suggest a befitting name for the newly born. After some pondering, he suggested the name as Sri Chandra, according to the lagan in which this miraculous child was born. He also told the gathering Sri Chandra will dispel the darkness of ignorance. When grown up, Sri Chandra proved that Pandit Hardyalu was right in his prediction.

Balyogi Sri Chandra was in his fourth year of age when the second son Lakshmi Chandra was born in the house of Guru Nanak Dev. After the birth of his second son, Guru Nanak Dev adorned the Sanyasi clothes and left his house hold to tour the various countries. Father Kalyan Das and Father-in-law Sh. Mul Chand both of them were shocked to hear the news of Guru Nanak's leaving the household. Now they pinned their hopes over two sons of Guru Nanak that they may handle the household responsibilities well after him. So both the families showered their full love and attention upon these two children. But as it said

"Only the will of almighty prevails."

"Wahi hota hai Jo Manzoore-Khuda hota hai"

Nobody knew that the Shiv incarnate Sri Chandra was not made for a limited family as he was to look after the whole of humanity as his family members and as such he will testify the saying. "*Wasudhev Katumbhkam*" i.e. let the whole of humanity become one large family. In the very childhood Sri Chandra inculcated the thoughts of world brotherlihood and aversion towards self pleasures.[10]

Bal Lila of Bhagwan Srichandra Ji

Bhagwan Srichandra whose name the astrologers have proposed as Srichandra Mauli" due to his childhood miracles put the people in a surprise. Pandit Haridayal Sharma after seeing the face of this dynamic personality has predicted that this boy one day will become a world fame personality with his spiritual powers, and will become a great religious reformer and will play a historic role to propagate the ideals of Sanatam Dharam.

It is said the face of Srichandra Mauli always remain fresh like a Lotus flower. Whosover see him in a smiling pose always forget his or her griefs, and feels a current of happiness in their bodies. Bhagwan Sri Chandra was an incarnation of Lord Shiva. His darshan had a mericulous effects on the visitor. He always used to play a role of meditator among the waring groups of children. Off and on he used to go to a Mandir to participate discussion of the life and deeds of Bhagwan Ram. He used to sit under the shadow of trees to reply the questions put to him by a group of people gathered there. Often he used to go under a deep smadhi for hours together. Sometimes his actions put the people in a strange position. As mentioned in a Sanskrit Sloka:-

कदापि वनमासाद्य बालकैः सह तउग तान।
नागान्नगानिव प्रेरणा स्पर्श घृत कींतुकः।।

(Kadapi Vanmasadhya Balke Seh Tadag Tan
Naganaganiv Prumna Sparsh Dharit Kaulak)

Sometimes alongwith other children he used to go in a nearby jungle and start playing with Cobras.

कब चिद नेदर व्याप्त भीमनाद विनार्देनाम।
नवं केसरिणः सूनूं प्रपच्छ कुशलं मुनि।।

(Kab Chid Nedar Vyapat Bhimnad Vinodinam l
Navam Kesrin Sunn Prapachh Kushlam Muni l l

Sometimes in a dense jungle approach the cubs to ask about their health and happiness.

कदाचिद गृहनागत्य याचन्तं कमापि द्विजम्।
मौक्तिकै: प्राणे यामास बाल भाव गतः शिवः।।

(Kadachild Grahangatya Yachantam Kampi Duajam!
Mautike pron Yamas Bal Bhav Gat Shiva)

Sometimes he gave pearls to please a Sanyasi/Sadhu whosoever visit his house.

मन्दिरो दर माविश्य कदाचित बालकै: सह।
भगवन्तमुमानाथ मनाथ समपूज्यत।।
(Mandro Dar Mavishya Kadachit Balke Sah!
Bhagvantmunath Manath Sampoojayate

Sometimes alongwith his friends seems worshipping Shivshankar in a temple.

वनोदर मुपागत्य तरूच्छाया समाश्रितान्।
कदाचित बालकनिष बालकोत्यन्च शिक्षयत्।।
(Vanodar Mupagatya Taruchaya Samishartan
Kadachit Balaknish Balkotayanav Shikshayat

And some time along with children go to jungle and sitting under the shade of the trees used to give sermons to them.[11]

Sri Srichandra Mauli and Pandit Vishnudas

When Pandit Vishnudas reached Pakhoke and happened to see childhood miracle he was surprised to note. After witnessing Bhagwan's miracle Pandit Vishnu Das asked some spiritual questions. He was fully satisfied by the replies given by Chandra Mauli. Pandit Vishnu Das was so impressed that he acknowledged Chandra Mauli as the incarnation of Lord Shiva. Pandit Vishnu Das alongwith his colleagues paid their obcisance with a'Sashtang Dandvat".[12]

Childhood of Baba Sri Chand Ji

At Guru's house (Guru Nanak Dev), Bhai Budha served with utmost devotion. He rose early under the light of stars, cleaned the house, polished the hearth with sticky mud, filled the pitchers with water, milked cows and buffaloes, worked in the fields and served in the langar. He attended all the sermons of the Guru, and was always at the Guru's back and call. Whenever Guru Nanak went on a preaching tour in the neighbouring villages, Bhai Budha took care of the Guru's household and served Mata Sulakhani, Sri Chand and Lakhmi Das like a true devotee.

Later on Nanak decided to nominate his successor. He chose Bhai Lehna for this purpose. One day the Guru held a special langar and then a darbar. He placed a coconut and five paise before Bhai Lehna, called him Angad and appointed him the next Guru. At the Guru's bidding Bhai Budha applied the tilak on Angad's forehead.

On Guru Nanak's death in 1539, Guru Angad left Kartarpur and established his seat at Khadur near river Beas. Bhai Budha lived at Kartarpur. Guru Nanak's elder son Sri Chand, was not happy at his supersession in favour of Angad. The new Guru did not like to give any offence to Nanak's family. He shut himself up in the house of an old woman named Bhirai at village Sanghar, and told her not to disclose his identity. The Guru spent his time in meditation, and for a year and six months Sikhs could not trace him. They approached Bhai Budha, who led them first to Khadur and then to Sanghar. He prevailed upon the Guru to give up seclusion and resume his duties.

Once there was heavy rains in summer. The river Ravi was heavily flooded. It ate away a lot of land. Nanak's tomb situated on the river bank stood in great danger. Sri Chand and Lakshmi Das dug up the brass pitcher containing Guru's ashes. At some distance they decided to bury ashes in a new village. The foundation stone of the first building there was laid by Bhai Budha and the place was called Dera Baba Nanak.[13]

Balyogi's pleasure was out of bound having obtained the permission of her mother to move to attain knowledge from whatever corner of the world it was possible. He bowed his head on her lotus feet, filled his heart with highest kind of reverence and promised her that he would come to see her whenever she remembered and ordered him to do so. You have obliged me by giving your permission to go to Kashmir. It is impossible to free oneself from the debt of one's mother. The position and status of mother is much higher than other relationships. Her heart starts yearning when her children are away from her sight.

But today you are sending me away to a foreign land to attain higher education, after making yourself free from all the bandages of love and affection. It is the evident proof of your great sacrifice. It is not with in my limits to repay this debt. Balyogi had attained and fulfilled his desire. His heart started to bloom like a flower as the bud of his heart was ready to open its developed mouth.

That person only can fully understand the pain of the pangs of separation. Who himself has felt and faced such a situation. It is much painful to part from such a child who by his chrismatic conduct gained love and affection not of his relatives and near ones but of the whole village.

JIS TAN LAGEY VEY HI JANE
KON JANE PEED PARAYI!

जिस तन लागे वे ही जाने
क्रौन जाने पीड़ पराई।

[He who has himself been hurt can only guess the pain of others; none else can do so.]

This way leaving behind the whole family and the village, one fine morning, Balyogi Shri Sri Chandra set on his destined tour of Kashmir after touching the lotus feet of her dear mother.

Those days it was not a child's play to set upon such a long journey. One had to face odds at every step. There was a swear shortage of means of transportation. Those who have to do something miraculous do not fear anything. They always put their feet forward. To stop; this word does not find any place in their dictionary. Moving forward is synonymus of life and to stop is just equal to death for them.

Yogiraja Sri Chandra moved on and finally the land of Kashmir got obliged and sanctified by the touch of lotus feet of this strange Balyogi. It was full of joy to see its dreams come true. In those days Kashmir was one of the centres of Vedic learning where Brahmans of high character, having no greed and fully contented, parted with their knowledge of worldly and spiritual affairs to their students. These learned Brahmins looked after the foreign students well like their own children and cared for their boarding and lodging.

The name of Pundit Purshotam Kaul stood on number one in the list of such, suffers full of pure feelings having no greed. His personal life was a visible example of selfless service. His name was famous in the airs of Kashmir. Balyogi Sri Chandra turned up as a student at the doorstep of such a learned teacher. In fact, no teachner shrinks to impart knowledge to his students as per the tradition as it is considered highest order of donation. That is why in olden days it costed nothing to gain knowledge, Rishis and Munis imparted teaching and training to their students with open mind.

They had no distinction such as rich or poor students. These days education costs are so high that a student of poor family can do nothing except going from pillar to post to gain knowledge. The past teachers felt themselves debt free after imparting education to deserving candidates. Kaul Ji found himself lucky to have a competent student in the body of Sri Chandra; and hoped to free himself from the *Rishi rin* or the Rishi debt. He started imparting education to Sri Chandra with all his might. Sri Chandra as a student also tried his level best to learn everything by heart. He was named as Chandra Mauli by his fellow classmates with affection. Many of the students envied with him and lost no chance to complain against him to the Guru Kaul Ji, but they failed everytime to gain their objective. Kaul rebuked them all as he understood the whole situation.

During his study period, Balyogi did not change his habit of moving into the nearby jungles after attending his daily classes. He used to go to the jungle after his class was over, sat there with his eyes shut and went deep into the meditation.[13A]

A Lion and Cobra at His Service

Boy Chandra Mauli, when he was hardly about five years old went to jungle alongwith a group of his friends. When they reached there they heard roaring of a lion. His colleagues fled the spot but Chandra Mauli advanced towards the roaring voice. In the jungle near the den he went into meditation. Reaching his home the children related the whole story to his parents. Knowing this incident they were badly upset. His father approached Rai Bullar and requested for help. This news spread like jungle fire in the town. People rushed towards the scene to help and save him. They were suspicious that the lion must have killed him till now.

In the mean time Rai Bullar alongwith his force advanced towards the place where Chandra Mauli had gone into deep meditation/Samadhi. Reaching there they witnessed that boy under a shady tree on the grassy ground unaware of the big black cobra beside him and a lion is sitting near him. It was, indeed, an alarming sight to behold. They thought perhaps the Cobra had bitten and killed Shri Srichandra. When the cobra and a lion saw a group of people advancing towards them, the cobra folded his hood and the lion awakened from his sleep and quietly went towards the jungle and disappeared from the scene. Every body took a sigh of relief. In the meantime Srichandra Mauli broke his samadhi and stared at them. Seeing this Rai Bullar and his colleagues filled with joy and wonder. He said to himself, Srichandra is very dear to God Almighty. It was God who made the cobra shade his face from the hot sun and lion to protect him. He alighted from his horse, bowed his head before him and touched his feet. The people acknowledged him as an incarnation of God.[14]

As an incarnation of Shiva

When Srichandra Mauli was eight years old he alongwith his grandfather (Nana) Shri Mool Chandra and his mother Sulakshna went to his maternal town Pakhoke. Reaching there Srichandra delivered spiritual sermons which had a great impact on the heart and soul of the people. Knowing about his miracles the people of the town acknowledged him as an incarnation of Shiva.[15]

Rai Bullar and Baba Sri Chand

Even poison is turned into nectar by the touch of sacred hearts. Anger subsides and burning hearts are blamed. Following the above quote all the violent animals present in that jungle, shunning their violent attitude turned docile due to the sacred smadhi of this child Sri Chandra and gathered round him. It looked as if on the banks of Mansarovar lake Lions and Goats were drinking water. But Sri Chandra was unaware of the span of time for he had been contemplating in that violent atmosphere.

When all the city dwellers, who have come with Rai Bullar and Kalyandass had a glimpse of Sri Chandra escorted by the lion and the deadly snakes round his neck and fore arm; and other violent animals of that jungle sitting like faithful disciples around Sri Chandra with their faces turned towards the moon like face of their master. When he opened his eyes everybody wandered to find the absence of all those animals, walking away to their respective places.

Sri Chandra, upon seeing the worried faces of his grand father the landlord Rai Bullar and others he spoke to them in a low voice.

You were worrying unnecessarily, you would have rested in your respective homes. I was just to return to the village after my daily prayer. He gave such a befitting advice to Rai Bullar that he felt obliged and bending upon the lotus feet of Sri Chandra he promised to follow his advice in future and would look after his subjects like his own children. I would try to serve my people without the barriers of caste, creed or religion and do justice to every citizen. He escorted the child to the village.[16]

Call of Beggars

He was a born ascetic and yogi and still enjoying in the household of his parents. Once some beggars came to their door and asked for alms. It was a practice amongst the well behaved householders that they try to entertain the beggars with an open mind, taking them as the embodiment of God itself. As his mother was busy in the household work she could not respond to the call of the beggar. Sri Chandra came running into the house store, brought a hand full of grams and poured these into the bag of the beggar. The beggar was surprised to find diamonds instead of grams. He refused to accept the alms for the fear of being caught as a thief. Sri Chandra requested to accept the grams and the beggar insisted otherwise. On hearing the altercation the mother of Sri Chandra came and was charmed to see diamonds held in the palms of

Sri Chandra. She saw the image of lord Shiva in the shape of Sri Chandra and was enlightened. She requested the beggar to receive the alms from the hands of her child. The beggar accepted the alms of precious stones and left blessing the little child.[17]

Education at Kashmir

When Sri Chandra was hardly about seven years old he visited his maternal home at Pakhoke for the first time alongwith his younger brother and mother. He stayed there for about three years and came back to his village. After his thread ceremony he proceeded to Kashmir to join Pandit Purshottam Kaul for studies. At that time there were two famous education centres in India namely 'Kashiji and Kashmir. Within a short period he completed studies of all the religious books. During his stay in Kashmir he happened to meet Shri Guru Avinashi Muni Ji Maharaj. After staying with him for a short period he became his disciple.[18]

Dr. Gyan Inder Singh is also of the opinion that Baba Sri Chand studied the Hindu scriptures from a Kashmiri Pandit Purshottam Kaul of Srinagar and was initiated into the Udasin fold by a Sadhu Avinashi Muni in Srinagar, Kashmir. Bhagwan Sri Chandra initiated four of his early disciples in Srinagar, who are considered to be the incarnation of four sons of Brahma.

These four greatmen are named as four Dhuna's of Udasin Sect.

1. First Dhuna or Holy fire of Bawa Almast Ji

2. Second Dhuna or Holy fire of Bawa Govind Sahib Ji

3. Third Dhuna or Holy fire of Bawa Phool Sahib Ji

4. Fourth Dhuna or Holy fire of Bawa Balu Hasan Ji.

Besides these four Dhunas there are six Bakhsheeshs and ten Up-Bakhsheeshs:-

1. First Bakhsheesh of Bawa Mihan Sahib Ji

2. Second Bakhsheesh of Bawa Sangat Sahib Ji

3. Third Bakhsheesh of Bawa Bhagat Bhagwan Ji

4. Fourth Bakhsheesh of Bawa Suthere Shah Ji

5. Fifth Bakhsheesh of Bawa Bakhat Mal Ji

6. Sixth Bakhsheesh of Bawa Ajit Mal Ji.

Ten Up-Bakhsheeshs or Secondary Bakhsheesh are also counted such as:-

1. Ramdass Ke

2. Sodhi Dakhni Rai Ke

3. Sadhu Nand Lal Ke

4. Diwane Sadhu

5. Hira Dasiye

6. Ram Rai Ke

7. Hindaliya or Niranjaniye

8. Meharban Ke (Miney)

9. Gahar gambhiriey

10. Nirankariey.[19]

Child Chandra Mauli and Pandit Somnath Tripathi

During childhood Chandra Mauli's student days he has had to participate in a discourse on Hindu shastras with renowned intellectual of Kashi Pandit Somnath Tripathi when he reached Kashmir. Pandit Somnath Tripathi was very proud of his knowledge, on reaching Kashmir he challenged the intelligentsia of Kashmiri Pandits for discourse on Hindu shastras. The head of the Kashmiri Vidvat Parishad and the President of the College Pandit Purushottam Lal Kaul, under whose guidance Chandra Mauli was a student of Sanskrit literature. The challenge of Pandit Somnath Tripathi upset Shri Kaul badly. When Chandra Mauli asked his guru the reasons of his disappointment, he apprised Chandra Mauli about his anxiety. He stared at his guru and requested with folded hands, if you may kindly permit me, I myself would like to have discourses with Pandit Somnath Tripathi. Having a green signal from his guru Chandra Mauli got ready for discourse.

Next day in the compound of the college in the presence of Kashmiri intelligentsia discourse was started between Pandit Somnath Tripathi and child Chandra Mauli. Both the great men expressed and stressed their view point in fluent Sanskrit. Kashmiri Pandits were stunned to see the debating personalities, but child Mauli Chandra put his spiritual questions in such a fashion, it seemed that 'Saraswati' herself had come down to earth to participate in the discussion. Pandit Somnath miserably failed to reply His Lords questions and had to cut a sorry figure. Seeing the defeat of a Kashi Pandit in the hands of a small child the lecture hall which was full to capacity greeted Mauli with thunderous applause. Entire Kashmir valley plunged in excitement.

Consequently Pandit Somnath Tripathi greeted Mauli with folded hands and paid his obeisance to the Avtar of Shivji Maharaj, and prayed as under:

असित गिरी समंस्यात् कज्जलं सिंधु पात्रे ।
सुरतरुवर शाखा लेखिनी पत्रमुवी ।
लिखति यदि गृहीत्वा शारदा सर्व कालम् ।
तदपि तव गुणानाम् ईश पारं न याति ।।

(Asit Giri Samsyat Kanjaam Sindhu Patre
Surtaruvar Shakha Lakhani Patramoovi.
Likhati yadi grihtva sharda sarv kalam,
Tadpi tab gunanam Eish param na yati.)

If the Ink weighing equal to black mountain, and a pot is equal to Vast Sea and a Pen is made of from the branches of Kalptaru and paper of the size of length and breadth of the whole earth, if Saraswati herself may start recording your merits. O Lord! to understand you is very difficult.

देव देव विरूपाक्ष,
नीलकण्ट नमोस्तुते।
तत्क्षमस्व महादेव,
पाहिमाम् करूणनिधे।।

Oh! Lord of Lords Neelkanth (incarnation of Lord Shiva - Shrichandra) I bow my head before you. O Mahadev you are a treasure of love and mercy. Please forgive us and protect us.

In this manner child Chandra Mauli defeated Pandit Somnath Tripathi in the discourses and became a hero in the student community.

Some one has said truly like this:-

गुरूःब्रह्मा गुरूःविष्णु गुरूःदेवो महेश्वरः
गुरूः साक्षात् परब्रह्मा तस्मै श्री गुरूवे नमः

(Guru Brahma, Guru Vishnu, Guru Dev Maheshwar, Guru Sakshat Parbrahma Tasmei Shri Gurve Namah!)

Child Maulichandra was blessed by his Guru in such a fashion that during his student life he showed exemplary miracles.

एवं आदर्श चरितो ब्रह्मचारी हठव्रत: ।
श्रीचन्द्र मौलिरेकान्ते ध्यान यागे प्ररोड़ भ्यवत ।।

(Evam Adarsh Charito Brahmchari Hath varata
Shrichandra Maulirkante Dhyanyog Prod Bhayavat)

In this manner celibate Shrichandra completing reading
of all the four Vedas devoted himself in the deep dedication.[20]

Jeevan Prakash Jeevan has related this incident in the
following words:

Balyogi was in his 14th spring and his study was still
going on. A famous learned man of Kashi Pundit Somnath
Tripathi after defeating so many learned men of the country
in discourses came to Kashmir for dialogue with the Kashmiri
Pundits. Those days Pundit Kaul was leader of the Kashmiri
learned society. Tripathi challenged all the Kashmiri Pundits
to come and beat him in philosophical discourses. Though
Pt. Kaul was himself an expert in Hindu religious scriptures,
he was afraid of Pt. Tripathi's fame and shirked to have a
debate with him. Because Sastrarth (debate) was not based
on the learning but it was the technique of debating that
counted. He who was more apt in the art of oration, could
win easily over his counterpart. This thought made Pt. Kaul
sick of the situation. In the meantime, Chandra Mauli happened
to be there. He saw his teacher in deep worry and asked the
reason of his concern by saying How it is possible that my
teacher was worried for something, was there anything that
he could do for him?

Guru Kaul replied, "My son! problem is so complex that
it is not easy to solve it. World renowned Pandit Tripathi has
challenged all the learned men of Kashmir to have a debate
with him and the anchor is going to fall on me."

Chandra Mauli replied, "Rest assure Sir, *till* your servant
is here. I need your blessing only. You will watch that this

student of yours returns with flying colours. This miracle is going to happen very soon, Sir!

One of the students who was sitting by the side of Pandit Kaul remarks, "Sir it would be suicidal to depend upon an apperentice in the debate with a learned man of such a caliber. It may not darken the face of Kashmiri intellect." But the perfect teacher had full faith in his student Chandramauli. However he ordered all of his students to put questions to Chandramauli so as to test his metal. If he is able to give satisfying replies than we will certainly be victorious. Upon this all the students gathered round Chandramauli and started questioning him. Chandramauli satisfied all of them, so Pandit Kaul got assured and sent a messanger to Pt. Tripathi that we accept your challenge with open hands.

The very next morning Tripathi arrived at the door step of the school of Pandit Kaul with his party and was received in a befitting manner. They were given some fruits to eat and made to rest for a while seated upon their respective places. Pandit Tripathi was impressed by the sublimation, greatness and egoless attitude of Pandit Kaul and his followers so he said, "I have seen and visited lot of institutions through out India but Pandit Kaul's institution is of a different nature. It has earned a reputation for itself. If others follow its traditions then in a short span of time, the age old great Indian culture will rule all the world over."

Pandit Diwakar was declared as the mediator of the discourse. He ordered the debate to start as the time was moving fast. Tripathi was setting his moustaches with his hand as if he had already won. He started with his points of discussion after having a green signal from Pandit Diwakar. Kashmiri Pundits were agog to hear his well placed logical questions. They feared that their counterpart was no match to his learning and he may loose the battle. Pandit Kaul also feared and worried. He had thought that Tripathi would ask something from logic or grammar and it would not be difficult for Chandramauli to satisfy him. But Tripathi was asking such questions of philosophic nature that Chandramauli had not studied A, B, C of such subjects at the school of Pandit Kaul, on the other hand, there was no sign of tension over the face of Chandramauli. He started giving replies as soon as Pandit Tripathi completed his question part, in such a poised manner that all the doubts were settled in a twinkle of the eyes. The House was full of praises for our Chandramauli. He destroyed all the citadels of Pandit Tripathi's shallow logic point by point he contradicted them and put forward his own solution to the problems projected by Pandit Tripathi. A ray of hope came over the faces of Pandit Kaul's party and gloom spread over the faces of everyone in Pandit Tripathi's camp.

Tripathi tried to intrude but he was stopped there and then by Pandit Diwakar who said, "Look here Pandit Ji it is against the rules of the game. You have no right to stop him during his turn. You will be free to comment upon his deliberations when your turn comes. It is against the rules to stop the other party during a discussion. Kashmiri Pundits were happy over the oratory of Chandramauli. They were spell bound. Sri Chandra dashed to the ground all the hypothetical propositions of Tripathi. Pandit Tripathi accepted his defeat and the discourse came to a close.

Tripathi wanted to revenge this defeat. He decided to have a new series of debate so as to bring forth new points for discussion, so as to bring down the other side. Although the string had got burned but its twist was still there. False pride when it is hurt, makes a man blind to the real situation and it becomes difficult for him decide the right course of action. His state of mind turns like that of a gambler who after loosing one game staked double the money in another round to win back his lost money. He was busy in the thoughts of a second round of debate when he was empowered by a double doze of sleep. He had a dream during his sleep. He found him performing puja in a Shiva temple of Kashi. He bowed before Lord Shiva and prayed for his success. He said "O God ! Bhole Nath ! what have you done to my scheme of conquering the world over all the learned men but today a young lad of Kashmir have dashed all my plans to the ground. I am much troubled at my heart crushing defeat at the hands of that boy. Please do some miracle so that my defeat may turn into my success to sooth my hurt ego." When he turned his head towards the idol of Lord Shiva he was surprised to see the face of smiling Chandramauli in place of Lord Shiva. After he woke up he again started thinking on the same old line. God himself had tried to make him understand but he whose intellect is covered with the clouds of ego and false pride of being highly educated can not understand such signs of the ultimate truth. Really pride hath a fall. Ravana was a great scholar and supreme warrior but was razed to the ground due to his ego. The golden Lanka was turned into ashes by the fire.

He could not take any clue from last night's dream. It proved like a line on the waters of a stream. He again sent an invitation for another round of deliberations of the debate for a second time. It was accepted and the debate started the next day. Pandit Tripathi tried to keep his pace but stumbled many times during his lecture. Chandramauli replied like clouds making gentle rain over the sandy desert. Satoguni thoughts were received like dew drops of nectar by audience. After the debate was over Tripathi accepted his defeat. He desired to pay his tributes at the lotus feet of Sri Chandra Ji guessing his intentions, yogiraj quietly stood up and left his place and went away. Tripathi followed him, ran after him but soon Sri Chandra Ji got disappeared. He tried to find him but all in vain. So he sat under a tree deeply thinking of Chandramauli and requested him to appear before him. He vowed not to take a drop of water till he does not have a darshan of Sri Chandra. He will not move from that place. As we know god is always at the command of his lovers. Whosoever remembers him and calls him, is visited by him at his own place. Sri Chandra Ji, observing the deep devotion and firm decision of his bhakat Tripathi, decided to visit him. So Tripathi's thoughts were disrupted by the murmur of lotus like feet of the lord Sri Chandra, he open his eyes and found yogiraj smiling before him. He touched his lotus feet and beg his pardon. Yogiraj picked him up and embraced him saying "You are my dear devotee. I tried in so many different ways to bring you on the right track but there was a thin veil of false pride over your wisdom so you could not follow those indications. Well if somebody returns home in the evening he is not taken as a lost person. Drop the wall of false pride i.e. ego with one firm hand than you will find victory herself waiting for you." After this episode the whole trend of his life was changed. He started praying, "Hey Lord! please keep me near your lotus feet." Upon this lord ordered him to return to Kashi. I will initiate you there when I visit Kashi during my tour of India. Upon receiving this order Tripathi Ji touched the lotus feet, picked up the sacred earth the place, where Sri Chandra Ji was just standing and marched towards Kashi along with his disciples.[21]

Mauli Chandra and Maulvi Noor-ud-Uddin

When child Chandra Mauli was busy in Question-Answer session with the children, Maulvi Noor-ud-Uddin happened to pass from there and having witness the occasion, he dared to put some spiritulistic questions just to test him:

Maulvi	:	Whom do you called Hari?
Chandra Mauli	:	Rahim is Hari.
Maulvi	:	Whom do you called Rahim?

Chandra Mauli : Rahim is a urdu word which means mercy, and he who has mercy on others, he is called Rahim.

Maulvi : Whether God is justiciable or unjusticiable?

Chandra Mauli : God is justiciable and always rewards his devotee according to his karm.

Maulvi : Then how God could be a justiciable? Justiciable never punish anybody. If God never penalise a person how He could be a justiciable?

Chandra Mauli : God is always justiciable for those who believe in hard work. He is kind to those who devote themselves in his work. For example, cow always hates its dung. If ever grass is even touched by dung cow never take it. But it licks its newly born calf with its tongue even if its body is full of dung. Like this the God Almighty even tuff but always kind to his devotees.

After listening such philosophical answers from child Chandra Mauli the Maulvi was impressed a lot. He acknowledged him as an incarnation of God and paid his obeisance and appreciated him among Muslim community. Consequently they started attending His sermons and followed him. It had great effect on both the communities and succeeded to integrate them. He taught them that Hindu, Muslim, Sikh and Christian all are His children. They are one and they are all brothers. Every one is equal and there is no disparity among any one. A person in the light of his 'Karmas' gains or loose in his/her personal life.

Goswami Tulsidas Ji has very rightly said:

ईश्वर अंश जीव अविनाशी।

(Ishwar Ansh Jeev Avinashi)

God remains in every soul.

करहि जो करम पाप फल सोई।
निगम नीति यह कह सब कोई।।

(Karhi Jo Karm Pap Phal Soi
Nigam Niti Yeh Keh Sab Koi)

A person whatsoever practise in his personal life, he gets the same result in the same coin. It has been clearly mentioned in the Vedas, Shruti and Niti. It can be said without any doubt that child Chandra Mauli role in those very critical times was of a very good Social Reformer. He gave a new direction to equality and Karma Philosophy. In the real sense he was an incarnation of God.[22]

Avinashi Muni and Baba Sri Chand

Balyogi Sri Chandra's guru Vishnu Kaul was now fully convinced about the special abilities of his student who had in such an early age, learned all the sacred books with their deepest possible understanding. He observed that he would have been some yogi or a mendicant of olden times. This sharp minded lad had saved the pride of Kashmir by defeating a great vizard in spiritual debate.

Now Yogiraj decided to leave his school and devoted whole of his time in contemplating the name of god in a nearby jungle by the side of sacred fire i.e. dhuna. He visited his guru Pandit Kaul in the evening for a while to collect some eatables, to keep himself fit and returned to the jungle for the night stay. Regular devotion resulted in the advancement of the spirit of detachment from the worldly affairs.

He came to this conclusion that it was the proper time to be initiated into the fourth part of Indian style of religious living, i.e. time to take sanyas.

This dream of Yogiraj Sri Chandra turned to take shape when he learned about the arrival of Avinashi Muni, the great sage on Pilgrimage of Amarnath in Sri Nagar in 1575 Bikarmi. The public of Kashmir was delighted to have this news. Daily satsang was attended by the public in great strength and they enjoyed his lecture.

One day when as per his schedule Sri Chandra arrived at the door of Pandit Kaul from his jungle abode, he was informed about the arrival and importance of Avinashi Muni. This news delighted Sri Chandra and his heart was filled with joy. He reached the specified place to hear the discourse of Shri Avinashi Muni. He found him seated on a raised platform amidst a large gathering in a calm and poised state of mind. This first sight of the famous muni deeply impressed the heart and he submitted himself with full determination and devotion like a faithful disciple in his mind and took his seat silently like an ordinary visitor.

Mahamuni started his speech, and after one hour of heart touching pour out of nectar spells he demanded of the large crowd that they should not indulge in petty family feuds and have full faith in their age old Vedic religion, should pray, with fullness of mind, words and deeds; in the court of god that he may send some great warrior to revitalize the Hindu society removing all its rust-worn parts for its revival and welfare. You should march towards ethical reforms. Then and only then you may attain spiritual advancement. The audience was spell bound to hear those sweet and stimulating thoughts. Sri Chandra Ji's heart got stirred and it came to his mind that Muniji has earmarked my future line of action. People returned to their respective places after applauding Avinashi Muni. Sri Chandra moved to his jungle abode.

Next day Sri Chandra could not reach in time to hear the discourse but he was able to find some time to talk to Avinashi Muni Ji after his lecture came to an end. He bowed his head and sat close to his feet. One of the disciple of Muni Ji, who used to serve him daily asked him to explain for him the rights and duties of a fourth ashramite, a Sanyasi. Muni Ji told him in detail that it did not mean that a Sanyasi should leave behind the society in following the path of self-realization. The seeker should take a vow to work for the all round betterment of his society. In reality the service of mankind is the real service of Almighty. Sri Chandra returned to his jungle site after bowing his head to the learned Muni Ji. He was so impressed by his words that he decided to become his disciple. He could not sleep that night. Next morning after attending to his puja etc. he took some fruits and flowers and reached the place where Muni Avinashi was staying. Muni Ji blessed and said, "Oh son ! Enjoy Life ! Sri Chandra humbly submitted, I need your kind blessings only.

After that Sri Chandra asked some questions about the attainment of real and eternal peace, and after receiving satisfactory replies he was much pleased. He requested Shri Avinashi Muni to take him under his protective cover and he at once, understanding his real quest, initiated him into the Udasin fold.

As the Chakor (bird) upon seeing the poonam moon, peacock on the sight of dark clouds and a little bird who sings sweet songs, (Paphiya - Cuckoo) after receiving Swati bindu, that is the first drop of rain water in a special moment of time are pleased to find the above situations like that Avinashi Muni was fully pleased to have a pupil like Sri Chandra.

Just after initiation ceremony, Sri Chandra asked his mentor about his future course of action. Avinashi Muni smilingly remarked, "My son at the moment all the four sections of Hindu society are in a state of mess. Tantrik Sidhas and Vaam margis (Hindu cults) are misguiding the simple public and are busy in corrupt practices. People are also facing the worst type of tyranny of the Mughal invaders. Our sacred scriptures are being burnt and our religion attacked from all sides. Everyone is praying to God for putting an end to all this highhandedness. So to solve all these problems faced by our public, you will have to shoulder the responsibility of doing this life consuming task. I am fully convinced that you are capable of taking up this responsibility. Muni became silent after saying that much and after bowing his head and touching his sacred lotus feet, Sri Chandra asked his permission to leave for a long tour of India.

When Sri Chandra stepped out for a long journey of the sacred tirathas of India, the political atmosphere of the country was in a mess. In Mewar the great warlord Maharana Sanga had emerged over the throne. He, due to his apt policies, was able to capture Mewar, Bikaner, Amer and other areas of Rajputana.

In 1519 Daulat Khan Lodhi, the then Governor of Punjab invited Babar to invade India. In 1526, Babar in collision with the forces of Rana Sanga defeated the armies of Ibrahim Lodhi, a descendant of Sikandar Lodhi on April 21st. In 1528 Sanga was poisoned to death by one of his relatives. These days yogiraj Sri Chandra was touring India. He found that Tantrik Siddhas were misguiding and corrupting the religious-minded Hindus through the corrupt practices of their Vam marga.

Tantriks and Shakts, both were spoiling the social fabric of Hindus by indulging them in five M's such as Matsya (fish), Madya (wine), Maithun (sexual intercourse), Mansa (meat) and Mudra (women). Sri Chandra had seen with his own eyes their misdeeds in Tibet, Bhutan and Nepal etc. So he tried to counter their propaganda through the propagation of the true Hindu religion for five long years and thus the simple public was saved from the cruel clutches of Vammargis. He reached Mathura after paying a visit to the Tirthas situated upon the banks of Ganga and Yamuna rivers. Then he proceeded to Gokul, Vrindavan, Govardhan and Barsana etc. for many months and reformed people with his teachings.[23]

Notes and References

1. *Udasin Kalptaru* (Hindi, p. 34).

2. This village Talwandi is 30° west to Lahore and is known as Nankana Sahib. (Page 11th of old *Janam Sakhi*, first published by Wazir Hind Press, Amritsar).

   Some writers have given Sultanpur (Distt. Kapurthala) as his birth place which is not correct. Bebe Nanaki, paternal Aunt of the new born baby, who loved and cared for him the most, had taken a painting of this child with him and the place where this painting was kept and adorned came to be known as the birth place of Sri Chandra. This created the confusion. The younger brother of Shri Sri Chandra and four of his descendants resided in Talwandi. The fifth descendant Lajpat Rai, shifted to Dera Baba Nanak as he found Talwandi a deserted place. His descendants are still residing at Dera Baba Nanak. In 1738 AD Sadhu Hanuman Dass had a chance to visit Talwandi and was shocked to find the birth place of Bhagwan Sri Chandra deserted; constructed a Mandir in his memory and name it Janam Asthan. The descendants of Hanuman Ji progressed well here and in the time of his eighth descendant Mahant Sadhu Ram: this place progressed all round, 10th Mahant Mahant Narayan Dass faced stiff opposition, and tried to save this place of Udasin worship with all his might, but failed to save it from the clutches of opponents, due to the apathy and short-sightedness of the Hindus and diplomacy of the rulers. He had to undergo Jail for Ten years without any fault.

   (i) *Short Muni Shariamint* (Swami Gangeshwara Nand, p. 131).

   (ii) *Bharat ke Sant Mahatma* (Ram Lal, p. 350).

   (iii) *Shri Shri Chandracharya* (Acharya Sita Ram, p. 14).

   (iv) *Bharat ke udasin Sant* (p. 174).

3. *Avinashi Chandra*, Jeevan Prakash Jeevan, published by Mahant Anantanandji Maharaj "Udasin" Akhara Sangalwal, Bazar Mai Sewan, Amritsar, 1995, p. 24.

4. *Encyclopaedia of Sikhs*, Dr. Harbans Singh, Punjabi University, Patiala.

5. *Living by the Example of Baba Sri Chand*, "Baba Sri Chand's spiritual example." A talk by Baba Virsa Singh, page 1. Gobind Sadan Publications, Gadai, Via Mehrauli, New Delhi.

6. *Sikh Itihas Ke Jhalkiyan* by Teja Singh, Part second. Publication Bureau, Punjabi University, Patiala 1994, pp. 7-9.

7. *A History of the Sikh People 1469-1978* by Dr. Gopal Singh, World Sikh University Press, 12/3, Asaf Ali Road, New Delhi, 1979, page 41.

8. *Shri Shri 1108 Yogiraj Balyatti Shri Chandra Bhagwan Udasin Acharya Ji Ka Sanchhipat Jeevan Charittar* by Mahant Baba Jankidas Ji, Udasin Badi Sangat Baba Bhagat Ram Ji, Gurusthan-Purthiya Tola, Etawah (UP).

9. *Baba Sri Chandra's Life and Teachings* by Bhai Kirpal Singh (Living by the Example of Baba Sri Chand, New Delhi, Gobind Sadan Publications, Gadaipur, via Mehrauli, New Delhi.

10. *Avinashi Chandra* by Jeevan Prakash Jeevan translated by Dr. Gyaninder Singh, Published by Mahant Anantanand Udasin, Akhara Sangalwala, Bazar Mai Sewan, Amritsar, Samvat 2054.

11. Translated from a Hindi article entitled "Bhagwan Shrichandra Ke Bal Lila" appeared in the Periodical, *Udasin Kalptaru*, ed. by Mahant Brahm Rishi Ji Maharaj and Published by Shri Panchayati Akhara Bada, Udasin-Prayag, Vikarmi Samvat 2045, pp. 19-20).

12. *Ibid.*, p. 21.

13. *Eminent Votaries of Sikh Gurus—Baba Budha (1506-1628)*. From *History of the Sikhs* by Dr. Hari Ram Gupta.

14. Translated from *Udasin Kalptaru*, p. 20.

15. Translated from *Udasin Kalptaru*, p. 20.

16. *Avinashi Chandra* by Jeevan Prakash Jeevan (pp. 29-30).

17. *Avinashi Chandra* by Jeevan Prakash Jeevan (p. 17).

18. *Nirvan Priyatam Charit* by Mahant Anantanand Udasin, Amritsar, President Priyatam Prakashan, Akhara Sangalwala, Bazar Mai Sewan, Amritsar, Samvat 2048.

19. *A Brief History of Shri Nirvan Akhara Sangalwala*, Bazar Mai Sewan, Amritsar by Dr. Gyan Inder Singh (Guru Ramdass School of Planning, Guru Nanak Dev University, Amritsar, 1994).

20. *Udasin Kalptaru* (Hindi), pp. 23-24.

21. Jeevan Prakash Jeevan, *Avinashi Chandra*.

22. *Udasin Kalptaru* (Hindi), pp. 21-22.

23. JPJ, *Avinashi Chandra*.

Bibliography

1. Nara, Ishar Singh, *Itihas Baba Sri Chand Ji Sahib ata Udasin Sampardai*, Amritsar, 1975.

2. Randhir Singh, *Udasi Sikhan di Vithia*, Amritsar, 1959.

3. Macauliffe, Max Arthur, *The Sikh Religion*, Oxford, 1909.

4. Harbans Singh, *Guru Nanak and Origins of the Sikh Faith*, Bombay, 1969.

5

Meeting with Avinashi Muni and His Initiation

Avinashi muni was born into the house of a learned Brahmin family of Ajmer (Rajasthan). He had learned vedas and puranas alongwith other sacred books right in his childhood due to the environment of the household.

Avinashi muni was always busy in finding solution of strange problems. He could not be satisfied with the stereotype explanations put forth by the learned people around him. He wanted to solve the real mystery behind the circle of birth and death.

Some fine morning he left his home in search of a real teacher who could set at rest all his questions and reached the top of Abu mountain. Abu parvat as it was known and famous for the meeting place of sadhus, Rishi-munis and sages-saints since times immemorable. There he had a chance meeting with Ved muni.

He was much impressed by the divine presence of Ved muni. He asked him many questions and got satisfying replies. He touched his lotus feet and requested him to initiate him into the udasin fold.

There he saw the remains of those Agnikunds, which were lighted by the famous learned Brahmins to give birth to four Kshatriya warriors Parmar, Parhar, Solanki and Chauhan to get rid of the dirty Malechhas, the foreign invaders. These four Kshatriya Rajput clans fought for the freedom of India from the clutches of muslim invaders.

After having a darshan of these fire-bath tubs or pits, Avinashi muni got such an inspiration that he started pondering over the complex question, "it is a question of shame for us to be under the yoke of foreign invaders and to bear with the insults showered by them upon people. We are subjected to such a tyrany that we are unable to give birth to such a real warrior who could make our land free from the clutches of dirty (Malechh) invaders. He got inspired by his inner soul, It is cowardness to leave this work for some body other. We should follow the saying.

"Apna Hath Jagannath"

I should myself take upon this challenge; and do the needful. God will certainly help me in this venture of religious nature. So he took the vow just, like the "Bhesham partigya" to serve the country and to enlighten his fellow countrymen to take up the arms for the protection of their motherland. He promised himself to practice celebasy, the life long Brahmacharya. Nothing can stand in the way of a person who owns a firm determination. That is, why some one has said.

Banta Udham Hi Bidhi Hai
Milti Jisse Sukh Ki Nidhi Hai

"बनता उधम ही बिधि है।
मिलती जिस से सुख की निधि है"।।

One can only find its way to success through hard labour. It is the master key to the treasurers of happiness.

So this way Avinashi muni got himself busy in the hard work of national reconstruction and propagation of true religion after being initiated by Shri Ved Muni into the udasin fold. Avinashi muni was always in search of a befitting worker who could materialise his dreams.

His sacred desire was fulfilled by the almighty with a

strange style. He found that valuable stone from the earth of Punjab, for which he was wandering from pillar to post in whole of this country. He felt himself rewarded to find scion of the Suryavansh—Bedi Vanshi family, a Kshatriya lad in the form of Balyogi Sri Chandra. This so happened that during his search throughout India he had a chance to visit Punjab. He made people aware of the great tradition their sacred Vedic religion and asked them to come forward to help themselves to dispel the existing dismay. He was passing through the way where the relatives of Sri Chandra were searching for him.

When he came across these people, he asked them the cause of their concern. Upon learning the disappearance of Balyogi Sri Chandra, he contemplated for a while and then asked them to rest assure; as they had no reason to worry about the person who has been sent by the almighty to worry for them. So you must not worry for him. He is of a Charismatic personality, sent for inculcating new vigour in the near-dead Hindu society. So you should not worry for him and return to your respective places. No body can harm him. He is all right and soon will be back in his home. But there is one bet, you will have to donate me both of your children in case he returns safe and sound. Upon hearing this the grandmother kept mum but mother Sulakshna remarked, "Sir ! what to say of these two children, the whole of the world belongs to you. These two are also within the orbit of this world. As wave from ocean, smell from the flower, coolness from the moon, heat from the sun; can not be separated these two children are also inseparable from the world. They are part and parcel of this world. So when all of the world is yours, who are we to give these two to you. As Kabir has said-

Mera Mujh Men Kuchh Nahin Jo Kuchh Hai So Tor
Tera Tujh Ko Sonpte Kiya Lagat Hai Mor

मेरा मुझ में कुछ नहीं जो कुछ है सो तोर।
तेरा तुझ को सौंपते क्या लागत है मोर।।

I have nothing of myself in me and all belongs to you

alone. So what goes of mine if you ask for the thing that belongs to you.

"We will submit both the boys when we return home. But there is one thought; scriptures point out that it is a great sin to stop the linage of ones family. That was the reason for which param satguru Rain Dass did not allow my husband to leave the household before having male children to hold the linage of the family".

Muni Raj was pleased to hear the logical reply of Sulakhsna and said, "well if not two then give me one of your children". The mother happily agreed to the proposal and asked his choice. Muni Raj said is there any need to ask such a question he who belongs to me will follow me."

The saying of Avinashi Muni proved true as Sri Chandra reached home before the arrival of Sri Mul Chand. The whole of the village was delighted to hear that news. Mother's happiness knew no bounds and the grandmother embraced the child. In a twinkle of an eye the whole family was delighted as if Lord Shiva had showered bliss from the Kailash.

His grandfather worried about him as he had seen the ways and means of his father. A thought came to his mind that he may also leave the house like his father. So he tried to bring him home but all in vain.

He told Sri Chandra that he was yet a small child and cannot decide for himself as he knows not good or bad for his future life. You must not move deep into the jungle. It may happen some day that you come across any violent maneater and we may have to repent afterwards. He wanted to frighten him but Sri Chandra knew no fear.

When the grandfather could not break any ice with this fellow he tried to bring home his daughter. So as to divert the attention of her ward towards money making. One needs much of money to start ones business. Mother Sulakshna told his father that her child was not a general child. He was Shiva-in-carnate, an expert yogi. He has come to emancipate the whole world, how he could be bound in the strings of family. He will never opt for a personal family so it will be of no use to tie him up in any wed lock.[1]

Details of the Tours of Baba Sri Chand

According to Bakhshi Singh Adil (Jeevani Baba Sri Chand page 92) Baba Sri Chand during his life time travelled about 16000 miles journey on foot. In those days when transport facility was not available and to go on a pilgrimage passing through the dense jungles full of wild animals and to cross rivers and high mountains was a most dangerous and tiresome job. To face ups and downs of the wheather and to face burning sun and cold and rainy seasons is not an easy thing. Facing all these difficulties Baba Sri Chand devoted his every nerve to propagate the Vedic religion and reformed the anti-hindu elements was a tremendous work which was undertake by that yogi. Jungle Raj was prevailing in India Mullas and Maulvis words were orders which every citizens was supposed to comply. There was no rule of law, no vakil, no dalil, no court etc. Religious places were being demolished women's were treated like goats. Hindus were brutally murdered and their heads were displayed on the outer walls of the city. No Hindu was allowed to perform any religious ritual, neither pooja could be performed. Ringing of Bells, shells, counchs were prohibited.[2]

Pilgrimages of Bhagwan Shri Srichandra Maharaj

Bhagwan Shri Srichandra chalked out 11 years long programme for the pilgrimage of entire India. Secondly, the study of ancient places of pilgrimage and thirdly, to revive the study of Vedic religion. Lord Shri Srichandra had made up his mind to tour all the four directions of India.

Bhagwan Shri Srichandra visited Nepal, Tibet, Bhutan and propagated Hindu religion and cautioned the people to safeguard Sanatan Dharam. After this he visited Gangotri, Yamnotri, Kedarnath, Badrinath and reached Haridwar wherever he visited the religious places of ancient Rishis and

Munis he set up centres for the propagation of Sanatan Dharam and by his miracles he win over the hearts of the people. During Vikrami Samvat 1581 he reached Delhi from Haridwar, and in Kartik Shukal second reached Mathura and took bath in the river Yamuna. Lord Srichandra delivered lectures on Sanatan Dharam in Vrindavan, Barsana and Gokul and visited ancient Ashrams of Rishis.

During his journey when in the month of Magh Sankranti Lord Srichandra reached 'Tapat Gram.' There he saw a temple of Lord Krishna. After paying his obeisance to Lord Krishna he sat there and recited Bhagvadgita. A number of village kids assembled there to listen the recitation of Gita. In that gathering there was a boy named Dhanroy. He was very keen to listen Gita recitation from Bhagwan Shri Srichandra. When Bhagwan finished recitation of Gita, he inquired from the said boy his name and address. The boy told Lord Srichandra about his whereabouts. He was blessed by Lord and consequently he used to come daily to attend the sermon and devoted his heart and soul in the meditation of God.

One day that boy determined to have 'darshan' of the Lord and did not taken even meal and water throughout the day. In spite of his best efforts he failed to have a glimpse of the Lord. He felt humiliated and in a rage of despair and anger to made up his mind to burn himself alive. He failed in his venture as by the grace of God a fast wind started blowing and all the pieces of burning logs of wood blown in the air. In the end he tried to cut his bally with a sword, and in a moment the Lord Shri Srichandra appeared on the spot at once and catch hold of sword from his hand and saved him. Seeing this miracle he fell on the pious feet of Lord Shri Srichandra Ji Maharaj. Then Bhagwan consoled him and asked him to take food. As advised by the Lord he took food.

From that place His Excellency reached Agra and from there to Etawaha and then reached Ayudhya. After visiting Ayudhya he reached Prayag. During Vikrami Samvat 1582 on the occasion of Shivratri he reached Kashi.[3]

In the year 1524 A.D. (Vikrami Samvat 1581) Baba Sri Chand set out for his First Udasi (tour) alongwith his colleagues of student life, residents of Faizabad District. He visited Haridwar, Kankhal, Rishikesh, Lachman Jhoola, Hemkund and reached Tapat; a village in Uttar Pradesh. Stayed in this village temple and met Dhanna Bhagat. After staying in the village Tapat's Krishna Temple, Baba Sri Chand proceeded towards Mathura, Agra, Kanpur, Lucknow, Faizabad, Ayodhya, Prayag (Allahabad).

In the year 1525 A.D. (Vikrami Samvat 1582) from Kashi alongwith Pandit Somnath Tripathi via Gaya visited Patna, Mokamah across the river Ganga Hari Chhattar Fair. After staying there for few days he went to visit Kamrup, Kamakhya Temple, Assam and from there reached Bengal's 24 Pargana, Murshidabad, Midnapur and Orissa's Balasore district and reached Cuttack.

In the year 1525 A.D. (Vikrami Samvat 1582) reached Kashi and visited Vishwanath and other temples there. (This was the same temple which was demolished by Mughal Emperor Aurangzeb (1658-1707 A.D.) and a Mosque was constructed at that place.

In the year 1526 A.D. (Vikrami Samvat 1580). After staying for few days in Cuttack, reached Jagannathpuri. Raja of Jagannathpuri alongwith his wife called on Baba Sri Chand for his blessing for a son. Due to the kind blessing of Baba Ji— Raja and Rani were blessed with a handsome son after a year.

On his return journey from Jagannathpuri via Orissa Babaji reached 'Amarkantak' Pilgrimage of Satyuga times in the dense jungles and horrible mountain of Madhya Pradesh. It is situated at about 7 miles west to Pindara Road Station at the top of a mountain. It is a historical temple. From this pilgrimage there is a source of Four Rivers namely:-

1.   Sone river towards Bihar

2.   Maha Nadi river towards Orissa

3. Godawari river towards Andhra Pradesh and

4. Narbada river towards Gujarat and Maharashtra.

It is said that in the ancient period great sages of India used to came to this place for meditation to this pilgrimage named Amarkantak. There is an ancient Shiva-Temple at this place.

After staying for few days in Cuttack (Sangalbad Udasin Math) Baba Ji reached Jagannathpuri. In the memory of Babaji's visit a Math namely Mangu Math of Balu Hasan has been established. The Raja of Puri has donated 3000 Bighas of land to this Math.

In the year 1526 A.D. Baba Sri Chand had attained the age of 32 years when he met his father Guru Nanak Dev. It was to be pointed out that when Guru Nanak Dev left for his first Udasi (tour) Baba Sri Chand was only 3 years old.

During the year 1526-1527 A.D. (Vikrami Samvat 1583-1584) Baba Sri Chand was about 32-33 years old when he travelled about 400 miles on foot and visited various places.

In the year 1527 Baba Ji visited Kashmir, Bohd Wadala, Galdi, Barath, Memoon and Achal Batala. In the year 1538 A.D. Baba Sri Chand came back to Kartarpur and stayed with his parents. During his tours between 1527-1538 A.D. he travelled for about 1200 miles journey. In the year 1540 A.D. he visited Kandhar. Also visited Kashmir, stayed there for few months and came back to Kartarpur. After few days stay there he proceeded towards Pakhoke and proceeded towards Amritsar, Sultanwind and reached Lahore.

After few days stay reached Multan and then to Peshawar. In the same year he also visited Haridwar and other religious places.

In the year 1543 A.D. he again visited Haridwar, stayed at Kankhal and on a urgent call proceeded towards Sindh.

From Haridwar he reached Bathinda, then Multan and ultimately reached Thadda. Meeting with Bhagat Giri from

Thadda via Kachh visited Dwarkapuri and Sudamapuri in Gujarat.

In the year 1545 Baba Sri Chand reached Baghdad, had religious discourses with the Maulvis and via Baluchistan and Peshawar reached Kartarpur.

In the year 1564 A.D. (Vikrami Samvat 1621) Baba Sri Chand proceeded on the tour of Western side of the country. From Barath he reached Dera Baba Nanak, from there to Lahore and reached Multan. After staying there for few days he reached Sindh. In this tour Somdev, Virdas and Kamalia also accompanied Him. He stayed at Hinglaj Devi Temple (Hinglaj is the sacred place where Palate (Talu) had fallen of Mother Parvati. Hinglaj Temple is situated on the Hinglaj mountain, district Hyderabad Sind. From Thatta via Dwarka, Gujarat and Abu, Babaji reached Barath.

From Thatta or Thadda reached Devi Hinglaj's temple proceeded towards Dwarka, Sudamapuri in Gujarat and Kathiawad. Thatta in Sindh district was the capital of Nawab Isakhan who was a fanatic muslim. Thatta is the place where Sher Shah Suri defeated Humayun and he fled away and approached Baba Sri Chand for his blessings.

In the same year at the sea shore near Dwarka when Babaji failed to get a drop of drinking water and on the sarcastic remarks of the local woman Babaji put his Shankh in the earth then mericulously a powerful shower of water came rushing from the earth. This place is known as 'Sankheshwar Dham'.

In the year 1608 A.D. (Vikrami Samvat 1665) Baba Chand stayed at Barath and Dera Baba Nanak for a long time. For a short while he went to Nanak Chak and—discussion with Sidhs.

In the year 1609-1623 A.D. (Vikrami Samvat 1668-1680) Babaji visted Southern India and made Samrath Ram Das His disciple.

In the year 1628 A.D. (Vikrami Samvat 1685) when Baba

Sri Chand from Dera Baba Nanak Chak, Kadrabad, Galdi Sahib and Barath was going to Kashmir he stayed at Charan Paduka for few days.[4]

Southern Tour of Baba Sri Chand (1609-1623 A.D.)

During the year 1609 A.D. Baba Ji used to stay at Barath. After staying here for some time he went to Kashmir (Srinagar) and stayed there for a long time. In His stay at Srinagar Baba Ji composed Matra Shastra and authored a few books of Vedas and Gita. Unfortunately any of these sacred books nothing has been traced out.

From Srinagar reached Pakhoke. There was a Thumb (Tomer) and Tahli (Sheesham tree) whosoever used to go there for darshan and presents 'Rot Prashad' he or she get rid of fever.

From Kartarpur, Dera Baba Nanak, Dalam Nangal, Ratta Abdal, Dhuan, Jangli, Jaurian, Bohd, Wadala, Sidhwa, Kilanaur he came back to Nanak Chak and from there he proceeded towards South India tour. Kamalia accompanied Baba Ji.

From Nanak Chak to Ajmer, Ujjain and Chanda visit he proceeded towards Ramkumari, Rameshwaram. While going towards Rameshwaram Baba Ji stayed at the Dera of Dasu son of Guru Angad, near the Fort of Chanda. Learned readers of this book may recall that first of all Guru Angad had presented his son Dasu to Baba Sri Chand who thus became his first disciple even before Baba Gurditta. On this very place Dasu had set up a big Ashram for Udasi saints. On His way back from Rameshwaram via Dharwar Baba Ji reached Takli Gram near Nasik. He stayed there for few days. On this place one person named Narayan served Baba Ji with full devotion. Baba Ji was so pleased with his sincerity and service that he was admitted one of His disciple and renamed him as Smrath Ramdas. At that time he was only 18 years old. He was the same Smrath Ramdas who became Guru of Chhattarpati Shivaji Maharaj. After completing His South India tour Baba Ji reached Dera Baba Nanak in the year 1623 A.D. (Approximately Vikrami Samvat 1680).[5]

Foreign Countries visits

Mahant Purshottam Das Ji in his book entitled, 'Bhagwan Shri Sri Chandra Ji Avam Harihar Udasin Ashram Ke Mahapurshon Ke Pawan Sansmaran (Hindi) 'has record that Acharya Sri Chandra Bhagwan while touring entire India and propagating for the spiritual awakening. He not only visited India from East to West and from North to South. He preached His message in the foreign countries like France, Germany, Castuntunia, Kabul, Kandhar, Sinhaldweep, Baluchistan etc. etc.[6]

In Udasin Kalptaru it is mentioned that Baba Ji also visited Nepal, Bhutan and Tibet also.[7]

MORE DETAILS OF HISTORICAL VISITS

Sweet Water Tank at Dwarka

When the great saint and yogi Lord Sri Chand alongwith Kamaliya and Dharam Chand (son of Lakhmi Chand) during his Bharat Darshan programme reached at the Seashore of Gujarat near Dwarka. There is a paucity of drinking water in that area. The child Dharam Chand was very much thirsty. Unfortunately drinking water was not available anywhere. On the request of women folk and other residents of the area Bhagwan Baba Sri Chand put his 'Shankh' in the earth and pressed it, and the people saw a great flow of sweet water started flowing from there. Even today on that very place there is a small tank of sweet water exists there and a temple in the memory of Baba Sri Chand's visit has been erected.

Gujarat Visit

When he was admist his Gujarat tour Moghuls had expanded their rule over Rajasthan also. Akbar, by founding his religion of Din-i-Illahi, had started to bring Hindus into his clutches. A number of Hindu Rajas had given their daughters to him in wedlock. To win over the Hindus, he got their sacred scriputures like Geeta, Ramayana and Mahabharata translated into the persian language. He appointed Birbal,

Faizy and others as Navrattans (Nine gems). Through the diplomacy of Tohid-i-Illahi he won so many simple Rajput families towards his side.

Famous Rajput princes like Raja Man Singh also turned traitors. This weakened the fabric of Indian society. Yet there was a great son of India in Rajasthan who did not bow his head before Akbar. He was 'Mewad Kesri Maharana Pratap'. He did not allow the flag of Hinduism dragged on the ground. He fought Akbar admist several hardships. In that period so many saintly people like Surdas and Tulsidas were trying hard to wake up the slumbering Hindu society. When a person is helpless from all sides then he turns toward the almighty God for help. That was the reason, why saints and saintly poets were giving voice to the otherwise helpless Hindu sentiments. It is true God is remembered only when we are in a fix.

"Dukh men sumiran sab karen

Sukh men kare na koye

Jo Sukh men sumiran karen

Dukh kahe ko hoye".

This way where on one side Bhakta poets were giving philip to their hurt feelings, in the political field Maharana Pratap was holding the flag of Indian dignity with his sacrifices in his life for the freedom of this country. When he came to know about the arrival of a great man and great scholar of Sanskrit of the caliber of Yogiraj Sri Chandra in the temple of Ekling, he along with his home minister Bhama Shah came upon his lotus feet. They were fully pleased to meet him. Bhagwan Sri Chandra was also pleased to have a look upon the impressive personality of Maharana Pratap. Yogiraj encouraged him with those words, "You are a trusted dewan (minister) of Bhagwan Ekling and a true son of mother India. The prestige of mother India is dependent over the muscular power of your arms. You are from the family of that Lord Rama, who being a jungle resident, had won over the great warrior Ravana. You know, how much difficult it is to construct a bridge over the sea to reach the country of an aline king and kill the opposing Rakshashas.

You are from the clan of brave people like Bappa Raval and Samrar Singh whose bravery is still alive in the memory of those invaders. They used to shiver upon hearing their names. These brave people have cut opponents like the farmers cut their harvest in the season. You are a brave son of those brave people, so keep up your struggle against these foreign invaders and put out their roots from our mother land. Bhagwan Ekling is your protector. The goddess of victory will embrace your feet. So what to worry? Just remember your grandfather Maharana Sangha who had 80 wounds on his body still he was fighting his enemy. Who can forget the name of Maharana Luxman Singh who died with his eleven sons fighting his enemy for the freedom of his mother land. The flame of fire of Johar by Maharani Padmini along with sixteen thousand brave ladies to save their Rajput dignity. They saved their dignity and the dignity of Indian women in the whole of the world. I hope that you will be able to save the Hindu religion and other communities. My blessings are with you, God will help you in such a religious task.

The inspiring voice of Yogiraj filled new spirit in the body of Maharana Pratap. Every nerve was ready to take revenge from the enemies. He touched the feet of Yogiraj and said, "I swear by the name of Mahadev Ekling Bhagwan, I will keep the flag of Bappa Rawal's name flying till the last drop of my blood. I may have to face unbearable situations but I will put everything on the alter of country and community. Yogiraj Sri Chandra's heart was over filled with joy on hearing such talk of bravery. He prophessed that you would be victorious and the kingdom of Mughals perish very soon. Maharana Pratap once again touched the sacred feet of Yogiraj and requested, "Do remember me Sir I believe your blessing will certainly prove right in the near future." Shri Sri Chandra said with love, "I am worried about everybody of Suryavanshi clan. You are also an offspring of that clan, you must bloom like that of a full grown flower, I again bless you to be successful in your mission," saying so Yogiraj proceeded towards Sindh.[8]

Haridwar visit of Acharya Shri (1543 A.D.)

After consoling his mother, for the purpose of preaching Sanatan Dharam in the Vikrami Samvat 1600 reached Haridwar and in the land of Daksha Prajapati's "Yagnabhoomi", Kankhal. Here after performing the ritual, worshipped Lord Shiva and started deep meditation. Due to this reasons this place is known as Siddh Sthan. Udasin Sant Kumar after following the `Nivriti Marg' started meditation impressed by his surmons their disciples constructed a temple in which Acharya Srichandra's is worshipped.[9]

Jagannath Puri visit

The story of disappearance of Bhog Samagri took round the Kashi city for several days. Tripathi was already waiting for Bhagwan Shri. When he heard the upper story he was convinced about the arrival of Yogiraj Sri Chandra, because he was the only greatman of that time. He reached the Mandir to see him after enquiring from so many people about him. After having a glimpse of him he was very happy and his mind wanted to dance and sing with joy, like a peacock on seeing the dark clouds of the month of Sawan. With this whole of the city dwellers started coming to pay a visit to this strange yogi. Yogiraj kept on thinking without making a speech but when a sufficient gathering was there he did say some noble words for the welfare of the gathering. He used to talk about renunication of worldly pleasures and pains and advised them to lead a contented life. Everybody should think about society at large and the mother land. May it come to sacrifice one's life for the defence of the country, one should not lag behind on such a time. If our country is happy and prosperous than only we could progress. Dependence is a curse. If the king is of the same religion and society than and only then he can think about the welfare of the country. The defence of religion is based upon the defence of the country.

When Yogiraj talked about moving out of Kashi for some other place then Somnath requested him to kindly remember his promise given in the jungle of Kashmir. Antaryami Bhagwan knew each and everything so he asked him to follow. After passing through many cities they reached Jagan Nath Puri. Somnath took the responsibility of caring for Acharaya Ji upon himself. Bhagwan Sri Chandra initiated him after seeing his doubtless submission and named him Somdev in place of Somnath. In Jagan Nath Puri people got mouth full of nector from Bhagwan in the shape of his teachings. The dust gathered for years over their hearts was washed away with the nector sprinkles. He had a meting with Chaitanya Maha Prabhu in Puri. It is said that a Sadhu named Mangudass of the Balhass order of Udasin sadhus got a beautiful place developed at the site where Bhagwan Sri first stayed and gave his sacred sermons. This place is now called Mangu Math. Those who go to visit Jagan Nath Puri, do stay at Mangu Math.[10]

Kabul Visit

Bhagwan Sri Chandra Ji Maharaj reached Kabul during their Bhakti yatra. His sacred teaching had a positive effect over Hindus in general and some of the muslims also, resulting in so many muslims turning towards Lord Rama and Shri Krishna. In those muslims one Wazir Khan was also there. He started meditating upon the name of Rama. When the Maulvis came to know about his activities of anti-islamic order, they termed him 'Kafir'. Some of the Maulvis tried to divert him from that path but all in vain.

One day Wazir Khan came before the main gate of Mosque, reciting Ram Nam, where muslim devotees were performing their Namaz. Maulvis got furious hearing the name of Rama and upon their instigation some of the people gathered there came to blows with poor Wazir Khan. Here Wazir Khan being a true devotee of Lord Rama had no fear of death or any injury so he kept on singing Ram Nam without stopping for a moment. By the grace of Bhagwan Sri Chandra, one of his pupils Kshemdev reached there and saved Wazir

Khan from the fury of those muslims; and look him safely to Bhagwan Sri Chandra. The muslim fanatics ran after him and reached the place where Yogiraj was staying under a canopy. They wanted to kill 'Kafir' Wazir Khan. But to their great dismay they found their feet stuck to the ground firmly when they tried to enter the place where he was seated near the Yogiraj. They tried to move forward but could not do so and found themselves as idols of stone unable to move about a single step. So they requested Yogiraj to forgive them and they would not do such a thing in future. But Bhagwan told them that they must make such request to Wazir Khan who was capable of forgiving. Hearing this Wazir Khan appeared on the scene repeating the names of Rama and Krishna and with his arrival all of them came to motion and their state of inertia ended there and then. They all started repeating the sacred name of Rama and Krishna. Uptil today that sacred canopy under which Yogiraj stayed is revered by the people of Kabul. They have a firm opinion that who so ever comes under that canopy (chhappar) with a firm belief, is relieved of all the grief and pain.[11]

Punishment for a Sin

It was in 1590 when Sri Chandra Ji was still in Kandhar. He was mediitating sitting on a huge stone slab in the mountaineous region. Nearby was a beautiful valley in which deer and other jungle animals were freely moving about. Its beauty was beyond words. Where ever one tries to go it finds greenary alround. Cool breeze was flowing. Birds were chirping as if they were singing songs in praise of God. Trees used to dance to the tune of winds as if they were dancing and singing in the praise of God. In that beautiful valley the King, Kamran used to come for hunting. One day he killed a deer with his arrow and brought out its beautiful eyes as a memoir.

Bhagwan was in his smadhi at that time but his pupil Somdev was looking at this heart breaking scene. His eyes started dropping tears. He said to the king, Sir ! you have done a great sin. This place has been sanctified by the touch of lotus feet of Bhagwan Sri Chandra so one should not commit such a sin over here. Kamran, the king was full of proud of his kingdom. Though he had already seen the miracles of Bhagwan and had admitted his spiritual superiority but now in his vain of royalty he said ! do not recognise the power of your Bhagwan could he make alive this dead dear. If he does this miracle than I would never go for hunting in future.

Somdev and Kamran were still busy in their conversation, Yogiraj came out of his trance. Somdev narrated the whole story to Yogiraj. Yogiraj said as he has picked out the eyes of this simple deer in the same way some one will snatch his eyes. God is watching everybody and his justice is blind. He loves everybody alike. If some one hurts his creatures, it hurts God himself; so he disliked such an activity. Hence we should not do any such work that goes against the wishes of God. Any deed that harms the fabric of the society is a seed of sin. A work done to grind our own axe will lead to painful result towards. To kill a person not at fault is just to kill one's own self. The result of bad deeds one had to face afterwards. He can never escape from these and sin never dies.

On the other hand who is kind to helpless and in pain fellows qualities for the kindness of god. It is no bravery to kill living beings. Real bravery is to kill the passions.

Such heart touching words of Bhagwan went direct into the mind of Kamran and he started trembling due to fear of fate. He was much impressed by the miracles of Bhagwan Sri Chandra his heart started working like the bellow of a blacksmith he fell on the lotus feet of Bhagwan and requested for his grace. He also asked the way out. Bhagwan went into deep Smadhi and Kamran lost his senses in fear of future. He lost all need of food and water for 15 long hours. When Sri Chandra came out of his smadhi; Somdev told the whole story and his state of mind. Bhagwan said, "Som ! Nobody can change the rules of nature. What have I said is going to happen in future. God has himself said it through my tongue. So it can not be changed. No body can fight against his fate. Kamran was puzzled to hear such words from Bhagwan. He requested, "please save me my lord. I will not repeat such a thing in future." Watching his pitiable condition Bhagwan's heart also melted and he said, "If you decide with true heart not to hurt and kill living beings, you could be saved but if you repeat such an act in future then you will have to face the music. "Kamran said with folded hands, "My Lord ! I will not repeat such a thing in future but my doubts will only be removed if you make the dead deer alive again." The kindhearted lord took some water from his Karmandalu (water pot held in hand) and sprinkled it over the dead deer and the dead deer got up from its slumber and went running into jungle, soon becoming out of sight. Kamran stood motionless for a while, watching this miracle and went towards his palace after bowing over the lotus feet of Lord Sri Chandra.

It is said that Kamran struck to his promise for sometime, but soon he again started hunting in his royal way. And in 1611 Humayun attacked him. He fought bravely but lost the battle. He was captured and blinded by his brother Humayun. Both of his eyes were blinded and then extracted.

This way Bhagwan's curse came to be true.[12]

Kashi Visit 1525 A.D. (Vikram Samvat 1582)

Once Shri Srichandra reached Kashi and attempted to have 'darshan' at Vishavanath temple. The priest of the temple did not allow Bhagwan Srichandra to enter the temple. Udasinacharya left the temple and sat at a high place at a distance of the temple and started reciting 'Sohang Mantar'. The priests of the temple were surprised to note that all the material kept in the temple automatically reached to Baba Srichand and the temple was found entirely empty of all the belongings.

Seeing this miracle with their own eyes all the priests of Vishavnath temple rushed towards Bhagwan Sri Chandra and paid dandvat pranam and plead for pardon. This news spread like wild fire in the city.

Bhagwan Sri Chandra stayed in Kashi for over a year.

From their He visited Patna, Gaya, Magadh and after visiting Baba Baijnath Dham reached Navdweep. From there after visiting Bengal and Assam in the Vikrami Samvat 1584 on the occasion of Chet Shukla Panchami reached Jagdishpuri. Where-ever he went, was greeted by thousands of people and that place was converted into a pilgrimage. At Jagannathpuri there was a disciple of Bhagwan Sri Shrichandra named Mangaldas. He was so impressed by the sermons of the Acharya that he constructed a building which is known as Mangu Math. He also visited Janakpur, Hari Har Om, Gorakhpur, Nemaimishayaranya and after that reached Jalandhar where he explained to Nawab Daulat Khan Lodhi the definition of 'dan' (charity). Consequently he started spending his entire wealth in the service of the poor and down trodden. Afterwards explained the secrets of 'Shastras'.

Visit to Vishwanath Temple Kashi

In 1582 Bhagwan reached Kashi to pay a visit to Vishwa Nath Temple. It was time to feed the deity so the attendent did not allow him to get in. Being asked he replied that during the feeding period no visitors are allowed so please wait for a while. Bhagwan seated himself near the entrance of the Vishwanath temple and passed into deep trance. Pujaris, who had gathered and placed the feeding material near the idol of Shri Vishwanath Ji were surprised not to find the material there. Where it could move about without anybody entering in? They again brought new material but that also disappeared. Pujaris got surprised and started thinking about the whole phenomenon. They thought that it might have been due to our not paying due respect to that strange naked sadhu who had come at that odd hours to have a darshan. So they tried to locate that sadhu and found him sitting in smadhi near the main gate. When they approached him they were doubly surprised to find those trays full of puja samagri etc. before him. They bowed their heads on the lotus feet of that sadhu. This news spread like a lightening in the whole of Kashi city and devotees gathered round Bhagwan Sri. He stayed for a while there preached the public to do good deeds and then marched towards Assi ghat.[14]

Human Sacrifice at Madhya Pradesh for Rain and Baba Sri Chand

Bakshi Singh 'Aadil' in his Punjabi book entitled Jeevan Baba Sri Chand (Naveen Prakashan, Amritsar 1978) at page 77 has mentioned an interesting miraculous story when Baba Sri Chand was coming back from Amar Kantak Temple pilgramage in Madhya Pradesh in the year 1526 A.D. It is said that this is the place where Shivji Maharaj had meditated for years together and whenever Rawan used to go from Lanka to Kailash Parbat he used to stay here. Amar Kantak is a source of four rivers namely: Sone river, Maha Nadi river, Godawari river and Narbada river.

After the pilgrimage of Amar Kantak, Baba Sri Chand proceeded towards Jabalpur. This is the same area of Madhya Pradesh which was occupied by man eaters tribals and to whom Guru Nanak Dev had once through his sermons apprised them of true path of humanity which helped them to get rid of this most hernions crime. Human sacrifice had become a part and parcle of the religious life of the tribals of this area. Baba Ji was travelling between Amarkantak to Jabalpur. He had to stay in a village temple at night. This was such a backward area the residents of which have never seen such a yogi like Baba Sri Chand. It was a badly drought hit area—To please the God of rain.

To please the rain of God these tribals used to sacrifice their beloved ones in the presence of the entire population. Fortunately on that night Baba Sri Chand Ji was staying in the village temple. At the dead of night he was woken up by the shinks of a poor woman who's son they were going to sacrifice. Baba Ji sent one of his disciple to find out the cause of disturbance. On his return he apprised Baba Ji as the area is in the grip of acute draught, the tribals as per their custom have brought a widow's son to sacrifice to please the God of rain. To know this Baba Ji become teribly upset and rushed to that place. Addressing the gathering he said--you need not sacrifice this innocent chap. I will pray for you for rain provided you promise to release this kid after the rain. They noted their heads. Consequently Baba Ji went into deep samadhi. . . and as a result of this it started raining heavily. They were all amused, bowed their heads before him and let that boy go home with his widow mother.[15]

Miracle at Mamoon

Yogiraj reached Mamoon and in the morning time he was cleaning his teeth with the help of a datun, near his sacred fire, dhuni. He saw some of the village girls carrying water pitchers ove their heads from a nearby water spring. He requested the young ladies to pour some water into his Kamandalu so that he may be able to wash his face and hands. Village girls took Yogiraj as a simple Sadhu. They replied, we have brought water with much labour, if we give water to you, we will have to go again for fetching water. Please go to the water body yourself. You will have the water and a morning walk also." saying so they marched towards the village cracking jokes with one another. They had gone some steps away only when Bhagwan picked up his iron tongs (chimta) and put it with force on the ground with touching the earth and there appeared a stream of water. Observing this miracle of yogiraj girls were surprised. They put down their pitchers on the ground, requested with folded hands to forgive them. But Sri Chandra Ji replied, "you are goddesses so you need not request for forgiveness. You are the maternal force. Even gods submit to your powers, you have given birth to all the great men of this world. Rishis, munis, Tapis, Tapishwaras, yogis and even god incarnates. Vedas have sung your praises "There reside Gods where ladies are worshipped." Because there was a shortage of water over here so this spring will serve for ever. Those ladies then thanked Bhagwan and left for their homes. There was a dried tree of Peepal where Bhagwan affixed his `aasan' for meditation; that also became green and is still verdant.

There is a temple at that place and managed by Akhara Sangalwala, Amritsar under the stewardship of Mahant Anantanand Ji Maharaj. He sends his representative to manage the affairs of this temple.

Staying for some more days at Mamoon, Bhagwan reached Chamba with Gurditta. He was not prepared to return but obeyed his master and returned after some days. When he was returning home he met another pupil of Bhagwan, Brahmaketu by name in search of Sri Chandra Ji so Gurditta told about the whereabouts of Bhagwan in Chamba. Brahmaketu was pleased to hear all this. He marched towards and reached Chamba. He remained for 12 long years at Chamba.

Gurditta returned to Kiratpur and meditated for five years over a small hillock near by. He passed away in 1693 Vikrami at Kiratpur. Udasin circles respect Gurditta like four dhunas because he was with Bhagwan uptill he was asked to return from Chamba. He is considered more respectable due to his association with Bhagwan. Udasin sadhus give great importance to restrain and Gurditta Ji was an embodiment of restrain so he was revered for that.

Miraculous Pillar at Pakhoke Village

Yogiraj was staying outside Pakhoke village and the residents of that village tried to get maximum benefit out of his preachings. One of his pupils got fever of Chauth (that comes after fourth day). But he had so much faith in Bhagwan that he used to take food after paying his respects to Bhagwan first. Due to the attack of this fever he could not come to see him. He was down with fever, wanted to see Bhagwan but the physician had ordered him to be in his bed all the time. But he could not stop himself from going and with the help of one of his relatives went to meet Bhagwan. He was still shivering with fever. He bowed over the feet of Bhagwan. Antaryami Prabhu the supreme spirit who could pervade the interior self, knew each and every details of the heart of his follower. He had created this whole play for testing the dedication of the Bhakat. So he asked him, "Bhakat what is the matter today. Why you are trembling? What is the cause of your worry?" Bhakat said, "Sir ! you know each and everything what can I tell you? However, I do not want to disobey you and become a sinner. Last night fever has caught

me and it does not subsides". Bhagwan smiled and said to
the fever. "Oh ! stupid ! why are you bothering him?" Hearing
this the fever left that Bhakat and entered into a nearby
(thumbh) pillar that started to shiver badly.

Seeing the pillar trembling everyone present, was
surprised and started applausive shouts. Bhagwan said in a
blessing tone, who so ever suffers from this fourthday fever
and comes at this place; places the 'Rot Prasad' (the udasin
offering of a sweet meat) He would be relieved of that fever.
That pillar still stands in an Udasin temple in Pakhoke near
Dera Baba Nanak. Bhagat people believe who prays over here
get rids of his fourth day fever near to this pillar stands a
sheesham Tree. It is said that Bhagwan dropped his datun (a
fibrous twing used to brush teeth) after cleansing his teeth.
One of his pupils picked it up and sowed it in the earth near
that pillar. That Datun sprouted after somedays and developed
into a big tree. It is still there and tells the story of Bhagwan's
miracles. All the followers of Udasin faith come to pay their
tributes every year here with offerings and enjoy the pleasures
of eternal bliss.

Saviour of Sindh

Sri Chandra Ji had a great liking for Kankhal as the
founder Acharya of Udasin cult Shri Sanat Kumar lived here.

This place has great historical importance. After staying
for some time in Kankhal, Bhagwan along with his pupils
Somdev and Veer Dass were ready to leave for Uttar Kashi,
when a sindhi disciple of Bhagwan came to pay his respects.
He told about the anarchy let loose by muslim invaders in
Sindh. Bhagwan's heart was much disturbed. Telling his
pitiable plight, he told about the Arabs who believed that
Adams foot prints are available in Lanka. Those went to see
these foot prints had to pass through Sindh. After preaching
Islam in Arabia, Mohamad Bin Kasim invaded Sindh in 7th
century AD and captured Sindh due to the selflessness of the
pujari community. King Dahar was killed fighting to save his
kingdom. After murdering the queen, her beautiful daughters

and other ladies of the house were sent to the Khalifa and they ended their life, jumping down from the roof of the royal residence.

Kasim looted and let loose such a reign of terror that one trembles to hear the pitiable tales of agony. This way Sindh was changed into a sanctuary for Islam and later on it became a citadel of muslim missionaries.

Those who were brave enough fought for the dignity of their motherland and gave their lives for it and those with weak minds were subjected and submitted to Islamic or muslim religion. In the 7th century many Hindu kings had gained control over a large portion of Indian territory, but no body bothered about Sindh. So many Saints and Mahatmas were there they also kept quite about the plight of Hindus of Sindh. Wammargi sect of Hindus had developed there big centre and they used to practice freely their sectarian ideologies and usage of meat and wine gained popularity in Sindh.

Ram Chandra told his story with tears rolling down his eyes and he wept bitterly placing his head over the lotus feet of Lord Sri Chandra. A stream of kindness began to flow from the kind heart of Yogiraj Srichandra. He consoled Ram Chandra by saying "Dear Ram ! this Hindu creed can not be wiped out from the surface of this earth. Those who tried to finish it were themselves finished as the saying goes.

Yunano Misra Roma Sab mit gaya jahan Se

Baki Magar hai ab Tak namo nishan Hamara

They left the idea of going to uttar Kashi and marched towards Multan to reach Sindh and the city of Thatha after some time.

Thatha city was a major spot of Sindhi Muslims but in those days it was a big stop over place for the people who used to visit Hinglaj Devi. All the passengers used to stay for a night or two entourage to Hinglaj. So Muslims and Tantriks had utilized it as their halting place. By being here Bhagwan could perform both of his tasks well from here; one to smash the false pride of the muslims and secondly the purification of the hearts of the rulers. So Yogiraj got lit his sacred fire over there. Whenever Tantriks passed that way, he used to have a dialogue with them and convert them to his fold of udasin sect. They were so impressed by his teachings that they got initiated into the forth ashram and to work for the welfare of the Hindu Society.[16]

References

1. Courtsey Shri Jeevan Prakash Jeevan.

2. Bakhshi Singh Adil, Jeevani Baba Sri Chand, p. 92.

3. Translated from an Article in Hindi, "Bhagwan Ki Bharat Yatra appeared in Periodical 'Udasin Kalptaru' ed. by Mahant Brahmrishi Ji Maharaj and published by Shri Panchayati Akhara, Bada Udasin, Prayag, Vikrami Samvat 2045, pp. 27-28.

4. Bakhshi Singh Adil, Jeevani Baba Sri Chand (Punjabi).

5. Bakhshi Singh Adil, Jeevani Baba Sri Chand (Punjabi).

6. Mahant Purshottam Dat Ji, Baghwan Sri Shri Chandra Ji Avam Harihar Udasin Ashram Ke Mahapurshaon Ke Pawan Sansmaran.

7. Udasin Kalptaru.

8. Abnashi Chandra, Jeeven Prakash Jeevan.

9. Hindi, Udasin Kalptaru, p. 30.

10. Abnashi Chandra, Jeevan Prakash Jeevan.

11. Ibid.

12. Ibid.

13. Hindi, Udasin Kalptaru, p. 20

14. Ibid.

15. Bakhshi Singh Adil, Jeevan Baba Sri Chand, Naveen Prakashan, Amritsar, 1978.

16. Abnashi Chandra, Jeeven Prakash Jeevan.

6

Baba Sri Chand
and Mughal Emperor

Emperor Humayun and Baba Sri Chand

Once Emperor Humayun alongwith his Queen and other high officials of the government called on Acharya Shiromani Lord Baba Srichand at the bank of river Ravi in his Ashram situated at Kartarpur. The Emperor presented precious gifts to Baba Sri Chand and listened to his sermons with full devotion. Those were the days when Humayun had been ousted from Delhi by Sher Shah Suri (1542-1545) and occupied his throne. He was running from pillar to post and was greatly upset and disappointed person on earth. After listening the sermon of great Yogi of those times Lord Srichand, Humayun was encouraged to gain his lost empire. Baba Srichand blessed him to defeat Sher Shah Suri and occupy the Delhi throne shortly.[1]

Kamran The Cruel Creature

Kamran the son of Babur was very cruel person. He was very fond of hunting. One day while hunting he killed a beautiful deer and mercilessly pulled out its eyes. This unbearable scene Yogiraj Baba Srichand could not tolerate. He summoned Kamran and told him that one day due to your inhuman behaviour towards innocent animals your eyes will also be pulled out from your face. Thus he cursed him. Kamran assured the great Yogi not to do such mischief in future. Baba Sri Chand sprinkled a few drops of water from his 'chippi' (water container) and revived the dead deer.[2]

Kamran—The King of Kabul

Kamran the King of Kabul was very cruel towards Hindus. He imposed certain taxes and restrictions on them. When Baba Srichand visited Kabul, he did not enter the city and refused to pay any tax and sat down outside the boundary walls of the city. One Wazir Khan after becoming his follower joined the Kirtan there. The opponent Mughals and Pathans when dared to attack Baba Srichand and his followers after listening his sermons fail to move towards him and bowed before him.[3]

84 Followers of Guru Gorakhnath and Baba Sri Chand

The 84 Siddh Yogis follower of Guru Gorakhnath who used to live in the dense jungles of Himalaya—one day through sky route reached at Nanakchak to test the yogic powers of Baba Sri Chand where Acharya Shiromani was sitting before a Dhoona (burning wood fire) in deep devotion. At the time of lungar, the great saint served 84 kinds of delicious food to these Siddh yogis; which they relished. They were very much surprised to see this miracle and impressed immensly. Instead of testing his ability and yogic powers all the 84 Siddhs vowed their heads in the feet of Baba Sri Chand.[4]

Pathan of Peshawar and Baba Sri Chand

The Pathans of Peshawar had imposed numerous restrictions on the religious functions of the Hindu community. To console the Hindus of Peshawar and to encourage them Baba Sri Chand reached Peshawar. The Pathans of Peshawar were impressed by his sermons and persuaded them to withdraw all the restrictions imposed on the Hindus of the area. A devotee of Baba Sri Chand named Praga converted his home into a temple and lighted five lights (Jyotiyan) of Ghee. A person named Mirkhor after demolishing the temple converted it into a House shed. Thereafter his horses started dying every day. Seeing this Mirkhor fell at the feet of Baba Sri Chand for pardon. He was consoled and he promised to reconstruct the temple.[5]

Revival's of Jahangir's Son

It is said that in Lahore the son of Emperor Jahangir fell down from the palace and lost his life when he was flying kites. This matter was brought to the notice of Lord Sri Chand who with his kind blessing revived him. To say thanks the Emperor alongwith his family members reached Kadrabad (Nanakchak) to present gifts and pay his obeisance. On this occasion Jahangir offered 700 Bighas of land in the name of Dharam Chand the son of Sri Chand's younger brother Lakhmi Chand.[6]

Jahangir's Elephant fail to carry the weight of Baba Sri Chand's Loi/Kambal

Emperor Jahangir was much impressed to learn the popularity and miracles done by Baba Sri Chand. He was eager to meet and have his darshan. He deputed high officials of his darbar to fetch Baba Sri Chand to Lahore. At the time of departure to Lahore where Yogiraj's Loi (Shawl) was kept on the elephant, it failed to bear the burden of the Shawl. Pointing towards the miserable condition of the elephant Baba Sri Chand said to the Royal carvan, Look ! if this elephant could not carry even the weight of my Shawl how can it carry me to Lahore.[7]

Humayun and Guru Angad

It will not be out of place to mention here that during Guru Angad's time (1539-1552 A.D.) Emperor Humayun came to the throne of India. He had to fight two consecutive battles against Sher Shah Suri and was defeated in the second battle. Near Kanauj, he suffered yet another defeat and was obliged to flee from India (Humayun took over from his father Babur in the year 1530 and ruled upto 1540 in the first instance). He made his way to Lahore. Reaching Lahore he enquired for some priests who could perform miracles and help him to regain his lost empire. He was informed of the greatness of the late Guru Nanak and his successor Guru Angad and advised to seek the latter's assistance.

Humayun then proceeded to Khadur Sahib to meet the Guru. At that time the Guru was in deep meditation while his minstrees were playing and singing the Guru's Hymns. The Emperor was kept standing. He was offended and in a fit of rage, put his hand on the hirt of the sword and drew it out of the scabbard. He wanted to cut off the Guru's head with the sword.

The Guru opened his eyes and looked at Humayun. Then he smiled and said "when you should have used your sword against Sher Shah, you failed to do so. Now when you came amongst the man of God, instead of saluting them respectfully you desire to draw your sword on them. You fled from the battlefield in a cowardly manner and now you are posing as a hero who wishes to attack religious men".

Humayun hung his head in shame and craved the Guru's spiritual assistance. The Guru said "I shall pray for you. You will get back your kingdom after sometime. But do not forget God even then. Be a just and kind ruler. Such were the Great Sikh Gurus ![8]

Blessing to Humayun and Akbar

When during the year 1540 A.D. Sher Shah Suri ousted Humayun from India, and when he was fleeing from one place to another he reached Sindh Province. There he met Bhagwan Shri Srichandra Ji Maharaj and requested him for his help to take over his lost empire once again. Acharya Shri was much impressed the way he most humbly requested and blessed him, Don't worry. Not only you will rule India again, but also your descendents will also rule this country, but the condition is that in future you will not harass and torture the followers of Sanatan Dharam. Listening the advice of the great Lord Humayun touched his feet and advanced towards Amarkot. This was the same place where God Almighty blessed him with a son who later on ruled India under the name of Akbar the Great. From Amarkot he returned to Delhi with a big force and attacked Sikandar Lodhi and won the battle and again became the Emperor of India. His son also followed him. It has been recorded in "Udasin Mat Pradeep" while Akbar was coming back from Kabul he visited Nankana Sahib and paid his obeisance to Acharya Sri Chandra. There he was astonished to see long ques of saints taking food and enquired that who met the expenses. The moment Akbar thought to help the Acharya by giving 12 villages as a `dan' Acharya Shri told him that every body takes food according to his or her previous doings. So whatsoever you want to donate, please distribute among the poor people. As you know Akbar is known the best well wisher of Hindus and always protected their rights.[9]

Jahangir and Baba Sri Chand

After saving the people of Kashmir from the claws of Yakub, he visited village Kadirabad in Punjab, Prince Saleem had taken over the name of Jahangir and captured the throne of Delhi after the death of Akbar in 1662 A.D. He had heard the stories of miracles performed by Yogiraj from his courtiers and was much impressed. He reached Kadirabad from Lahore. The emperor of India fell at the sacred feet of ash smeared Fakir. He was all pleased to meet Yogiraj. He requested Yogiraj to kindly visit him at his capital city of Delhi. Delhi would feel obliged with such an visit. But how could a person like Sri Chandra accept such an invitation who was trying to free everybody from all types of bondages. Actually who does not have worries is the real emperor and worries are caused by unfulfilled desires.

Chah gayi Chinta Miti Manuae Beparwah

Jisko Kachu Na chahiye weh Shahen ke Sha

Jahangir could not fulfil his desire. Bhagwan did not grant his prayer. But Jahangir when reached Lahore, the eye catching heart bewitching Godly figure of yogiraj got deep entry into the eyes of his heart and his dedication for him increased. He started to remain disturbed for him. This news of his unrest of mind reached the court of yogiraj. He started sending his courtiers to yogiraj for requesting him to visit him at Lahore. Yogiraj had to accept his invitation watching his deep dedication. Jahangir's joy new no bounds when he was informed about the visit of Bhagwan. He stepped down from his seat and with his crown over his head bowed it upon the lotus feet of yogiraj and made him to sit near him over the pearl decked throne. At that time Kamalasn was also with Bhagwan. Yogiraj stayed for sometime in the court, promised to come again next day and went into the near by Jungle. The king announced that a diwan-i-aam would be held tomorrow in honour of Yogiraj; so that public could also enjoy his sight and hear his preachings.

The other day, when everybody was in their seats, Yogiraj reached the court. Jahangir welcomed him in and offered him a suitable seat. Kamalasn also got a seat near Yogiraj. He had kept his gudri nearby. It was trembling and doing some acrobatic like exercises. Jahangir was much surprised to note all this. He requested Yogiraj to tell him what was hidden in that cloth as the gudri was breathing heavily as it some animal was hidden in that gudri. Bhagwan upon their querry order his gudri to bring out the thing that was hidden inside it. He had spoken these words and at once Jahangir started to tremble like that gudri and it stopped doing those actions. Jahangir's face turned pale and could not speak even a word. Bhagwan said to him; "Have you watched what in this gudri. The thing that made it to dance had entered your body and you are now trembling like that gudri. Jahangir requested with folded hands, "O God save me from this bolt from the blue ! otherwise I would die due to this disease."

Bhagwan ordered the fever to re-enter the gudri and leave aside the king. At once Jahangir was relieved of his problem and he was alright in a twinkle of an eye. Jahangir got a new span of life. Bhagwan gave a sermon to all present and asked them to try for their spiritual uplift. They were all impressed by the knowledge possessed by Yogiraj. He stayed for some days in Lahore.[10]

Imprisonment of Sikh Gurus By Muslim rulers

In the year 1497 Nanak and Mardana started on a journey to the east. They went as far as Dhaka, now capital of Bangladesh and returned through Central India to Punjab in 1509 after twelve years. At Delhi Nanak and Mardana were both imprisoned by Sikandar Lodhi for preaching in Public in violation of his orders. In Jail both sang songs while Mardana played upon reback also. This was a fascinating performance, and the prisoners thronged to listen to them. Such a scene was rare in jail. As this disturbed the normal routine of the place, the Guru and the disciple were set free.[11]

When Guru Hargobind was imprisoned in the Gwalior Fort, Mata Ganga sent Baba Budha there to bring the news about the Guru. Budha visited the place 768 kilometres away at the head of many Sikhs.

In 1606 Guru Arjun was implicated in the affairs of Khusrau, the rebel son of Jahangir. He was imprisoned in the Lahore Fort and was barbarously tortured. When Mian Mir heard about it, he came to see the Guru. He found Guru Arjun calm and serene having completely resigned himself to the will of God. Mian Mir suggested to the Guru whether he should intercede with Emperor Jahangir on his behalf. Guru forbade him saying that Gods will must have its course unchecked, as it was not proper to interfere with its working. He only asked for the Saints blessings for his son Hargobind. It seems probable that on the recommendation of Mian Mir to Jahangir, Guru Hargobind was released from Gwalior Jail.

Guru Hargobind became Guru in 1606 A.D. The tilak of succession was applied by Bhai Budha who adorned the Guru with two swords of Miri and Piri. The Holy Granth was recited by Bhai Gurdas when the Guru was imprisoned in the fort of Gwalior. Mata Ganga the Guru's mother, sent Bhai Gurdas there to bring news about Hargobind.

At Delhi the Guru (Tegh Bahadur) and his four companions (Bhai Mati Das, Bhai Sati Das, Bhai Dayala and Bhai Gurditta) were summoned into the Council chamber of the Red Fort. After a few days Guru Tegh Bahadur and three of his companions were produced before the Qazi of the city. Gurditta had managed to escape. Qazi first of all turned to Mati Das and asked him to embrace Islam. He replied that Sikhism was true and Islam was false, and he would not renounce virtue for vice. If God had created only Islam, all men would have been born circumcised, he said. He was condemned to instaneous death.

The executioners were called and the Guru and all the three of his companions were made to sit at the place of execution. Bhai Mati Das approached the Guru with folded hands and asked for his blessings saying that he was happy to be the first to achieve martyrdom. The Guru blessed him telling that they must resign themselves cheerfully to the will of the Lord. He praised him for his life long single minded devotion to him and his cause with tears in his eyes he bade him farewell saying his sacrifice would occupy an abiding place in history. Mati Das touched the Guru's feet, embraced his friend and brother and came to his place.

Mati Das while standing erect was tied between two posts. Two executioners placed a double handed saw on his head. Mati Das serenely uttered "Om" and started repeating the Japji. He was sawn across from head to lions. Dayal Das abused the Emperor and his courtiers for this unfernal act. He was tied up like a round bundle and thrown into a huge cauldron of boiling oil. He was roasted alive into a block of charcoal. Sati Das condemned these brutalities. He was hacked to pieces limb by limb. The Guru witnessed this savagery with divine coolness. The world history does not offer anything worse than this halal butchery of human beings.[12]

References

1. Sri Chandra Jyotsna, edited by Shravan Das Shastri and Dr. Gian Singh, Pritam Prakashan, Akhara Sandalwala, Bazar Mai Sewan, Amritsar, 1997.

2. Ibid.

3. Ibid.

4. Ibid.

5. Ibid.

6. Ibid.

7. Ibid.

8. Sobti, The Sikh Guru.

9. Udasin Kalptaru.

10. Abnashi Chandra, Jeevan Prakash Jeevani.

11. Eminent Votaries of Sikh Gurus--History of the Sikhs by Hari Ram Gupta.

7

Mir Ayub Khan of Kashmir and Baba Sri Chand (1585 A.D.)

Due to the atrocities of Mir Ayub Khan the Kashmiri Brahmins were converted to Islam. To fight for their cause and to safeguard their interests when Bhagwan Baba Sri Chand reached Kashmir, a big number of Kashmiri Pandits called on the great spiritual yogi of that time to relate their tales of woe to Him. After attending the touching sermons of Baba Sri Chand all the converted Kashmiri Brahmans came back to their Hindu fold. Seeing the reaction of Baba Sri Chand's sermons Mir Ayub Khan lost his temper and said to Baba Sri Chand sarcastically:

The Fakir who himself is sitting in the sun, how can he can provide shelter to others? Baba Sri Chand who was sitting around his Dhoona (burning fire wood) took out one small burning log of chinar wood and put it in the earth, and in a moments time that burning piece of chinar tree converted into a green tree. Seeing this miracle Mir Ayub Khan fell on the feet of Lord Sri Chand and begged for pardon. After this incident Ayub Khan stopped harassment and conversion of Kashmiri Pandits in Kashmir valley.[1]

Yakub and Baba Sri Chand

The Brahmin delegation went to Yakub and reported the episode of Sri Chand to him. Hearing that Yakub was much disturbed, he proudly asked his Wazir to produce before him the so called guru of the Brahmins. Let us see what type of power he owns. If he disobeys than bring him in chains before me. The Wazir took some soldiers and went to bring him. He was surprised to see the glow over the face of Bhagwan. He was stunned and looked like a stone statute who could not move in any direction. He forget all about his aim and the orders of his master. He did not speek even a word and sat before him quietly.

Bhagwan Sri Chandra took out a burning wood from his dhuni (sacred fire) and put it into the earth nearby. It rose to a great height and turn into a flourishing Chinar tree. The Wazir was much surprised to watch this miracle. It is said that this huge Chinar tree is still there in Sri Nagar city.

When Yakub had sent his men to capture Sri Chandra, there rose a great pain in his leg. No body could find the reason of such an ailment. His men tried in so many ways but all in vain. In the mean time Wazir returned to the durbar. He narrated the whole story of the miracle he had observed in the presence of Yogiraj Sri Chandra. He also advised Yakub to pray in the durbar of Baba Sri Chandra to grant him relief in his pain.

Yakub repented with a true heart and requested Bhagwan to forgive him. With in no time his pain vanished. Then he visited Bhagwan Sri Chandra with his Malika (wife) and after bowing at his lotus feet promised not to let loose the tyrany over Brahmans and Hindus.[2]

Advice to National Hero and Minister Bhama Shah

This was the time when Arya Hindu states had been captured by Muslim rulers. Maharana Pratap was a shattered and disappointed person and hiding himself in a jungle. He was a follower of Bhagwan Sri Shrichandra. When the great Acharya came to know the miserable condition of his disciple, he appeared in his dream. He was pleased to see him and paid his obeisance (Dandvat Pranam). He related his story of

Acharya Shri. Acharya Ji blessed him and for the fulfilment of his dreams summoned disciple Bhama Shah. Bhagwan Shri Srichandra advise him to help Maharana Pratap in his time of crisis. On his guru's advice Bhama Shah handed over his property to Maharana Pratap. After receiving sufficient amount Rana reorganised his army and fought against the Mughal army to defend Mother India.[3]

Bhana Shah Saudagar (1540)

In the year 1540 A.D. a businessman named Bhana Shah came to India in a ship, which was full of various goods. He had to face a strong storm in the sea. All the passengers were frightened and of the firm belief that the ship must drowned in the sea alongwith the goods. Bhana Shah was also terribly upset. He with his firm belief and faith hung his head with folded hands in the name of Baba Sri Chand and started reciting his pious name and humbly requested to come to his help and to save the ship and all the passengers. Miraculously his humble request was acceded by Baba Sri Chand. The storm gradually lessened its speed and the danger was over and the ship reached the coast safely. All the passengers thanked the Almighty for His timely help. Their leaps had no bounds.

Bhana Shah reached Peshawar with his goods safe and sound. Reaching there he came to know about Baba Sri Chand's presence in the town. He was much delighted to learn about this good news. He immediately reached Baba Ji and presented entire amount in the lotus feet of his Guru and related the whole story to Baba Sri Chand. Baba Ji refused to accept the offering made by Bhana Shah. But Bhana Shah was adamant to offer everything to his Guru. Keeping in mind the sincere desires of his disciple Baba said, Bhana ! if you want to give this amount to me, please don't offer this huge amount to me, instead construct a Dharamsala on this place for the pilgrims. After staying for few days at Peshawar Baba Ji proceeded towards Kabul and from Kabul to Kandhar. At that time Humayun's brother Kamaran was ruling that State.[4]

Blessing to Raja of Jagannath Puri

Everybody is fully aware that Baba Sri Chand Ji was an incarnation of Lord Shiva. He was blessed with full spiritual power. He was a great saint and spiritual power.

Once Raja of Jagannath Puri Udaysen approached him and requested him to be blessed with a son. On his request Lord Sri Chand not only blessed him with a son but also blessed him with a long life of 111 years instead of 11 days or 11 months or 11 years.

Maharana Pratap and Baba Sri Chand

Yogiraj went away and Maharana Pratap got himself busy in mustering support of his armies. In 1632, he fought with such a gallantry in the field of Haldi Ghati riding on his famous horse 'Chetak' that the pages of Indian history still remember his brave deeds.

In the battle of Haldi Ghati, one of Maharana Pratap's bodyguards Jhalmana gave his life to save his lord in such a way that histories recall his sacrifice with pride. After the historic fight of Haldi Ghati, Rana Pratap fought for 11 long years. All of his brave men fell fighting one by one and he remained all alone and had to play a hide and seek game with the forces of the enemy. He had nothing to eat. Sometimes he had to feed himself on a bread made of grass roots. He did not loose heart and rose again to fight. He decided to meet Yogiraj who was in Sindh. He was just on the borders of Rajasthan when one of his old minister Bhama Shah met with him with his treasures and asked him to utilize that money for the sake of purchasing the armaments for his army to fight the enemy. It is said that behind this sacrifice of Bhama Shah was the inspiration of Bhagwan Sri Chandra. He had given this inspiration in a dream to the old Bhamashah. With that much money 25 thousand soldiers could fight for almost 12 years.

The details of the dream that changed the mind of Bhamashah is given like that-

One night Bhamashah had a dream of a Paramyogi who had a glow over his face lightening all the ten directions. He could not bear that glow. He tried to recollect and found that he was the same person seen by him in the Ekling temple with Maharana Pratap. Bhamashah bowed his head over his feet respectfully and asked what he could do for him? Bhagwan then smiled and said, "Sastras have allowed the Vaishya to collect money but this does not mean that he should dig a pit in the earth and put all that treasure into it. This is a crime to keep money like that if it is not utilized at the time of its need. You have lot of money with the grace of God, earned by your forefathers so please denote it to Maharana Pratap for using it in the defence of our country as he needs it badly. He is short of sources due to 11 years of exile. Go and donate this money to him, so that he may again try to free his country. If the country is saved, money could be again accumulated. If we become dependent than this money may go into the hands of the enemy. After saying so much Yogiraj disappeared. Bhamashah got up at the termination of the dream and started to think. His innerself cautioned him about the invariable death that may come any moment. Money will not go with him. So he decided to donate all the money with him to Maharana Pratap.

It is said that very night Maharana also was visited in his dream by Bhagwan Sri Chand. He said to him, "Do not worry. You have done well in your test. Now you will soon find the Vijay Luxmi (Victory). For whose sight you have decided to go to Sindh is always with you. Maharana could not make sense of the above dream. When he was given money in the morning by Bhamashah, the reality of the dream was clear before him. With that money he again made all the preparations and was victorious over all the lost area.

He had been fighting the battles for years together that showed upon his health. Every inch of his body had wounds. So he left for his heavenly abode in 1653 and went to rest in the lap of almighty.

This was with Sri Chandra's grace, Maharana attained

victory. Bhagwan Sri Chandra after saving the Hindus from the tyrany of Muslim rulers and passing through the cities of Rajasthan and Punjab reached Kashmir. At that time Yakub was the ruler of Kashmir. He was very cruel and Tyrant and die-hard muslim. The die hard core maulvis started poisoning the ears of Yakub against Hindus and asked him to convert them to Islam. They told him that it were the Pundits that should first be converted to Islam as they were responsible for leading the Hindus in their religions matters. They held Islam degraded in their eyes. So they should be taught a lesson. Geeta is their sacred book, from there they learn a lesson to fight for their genuine cause. So you must first try to convert them and if they do not oblige than they should be made to taste the sword's edge.

There is a magic like effect in their speech. Whosoever hears them, come to take death as a toy. Yakub was much convinced by this argument and he called the Kashmiri Brahmins. They were given many promises if they turned back toward Hindu religion and if they did not oblige then be ready to face death. This did not work so he angerly told them in clear words either to embrace Islam or death, the choice was theirs'. Hearing this pendimonium prevailed in the Hall. Some of them left Kashmir in the darkness of night. Those who were firm in their belief in Hinduism decided to face death. Much hue and cry was created but all in vain. Hindus were left with no choice but to pray in the court of God for relief. They cried, "Oh God save us from the cruelities of these rulers ! to whom we should pray if not to you. Oh God save us !

It is said love begets love. As Draupdi, in time of need called for Lord Krishna, and he also turned towards her, and ran to save her modesity. Similarly hearing the cries of Kashmiri Hindus, Bhagwan Sri Chandra marched towards Kashmir. He had known their plight through Dhyan Yoga. He decided to save the Hindus from the cruel clutches of Yakub. Cancelling all his programmes he reached Kashmir. When the Kashmiri Hindus came to know about his arrival, they came to pay him their respect and told him the details of their lot. Now they were relieved but Sri Chandra was worried. He told them to rest assure. God will save them.

Maharaja Nepal and Baba Sri Chand

Once in the dense jungles of Nepal Baba Sri Chand was putting up at 'Dhooni Sahib' alongwith a group of Sadhus. Knowing this the king of Nepal alongwith his Maharani came to the darshan of Lord Sri Chand. The Raja and Rani attended the Kirtan and listened the sermons of Lord Sri Chand.[7]

Maharana Pratap and Baba Sri Chand Ji

When the king of Mewar Maharana Pratap was disappointed while fighting with the Mughals, on the advice of his Prime Minister Bhama Shah he called on Lord Sri Chand for his blessing at Udaipur. Reminding the Maharana the Lord said that remember you are the descendant of Raghuvanshis Ram who killed Ravana to save this earth from his misrule. Don't be disheartened and carry on with your mission and continue your fight against Mughal mite. With a new spirit the Maharana started his fight against Akbar and sacrificed his life for the motherland.[8]

Miracle of Ram Nam

He was consoling the Brahmins when some persons came crying with a pyre. Behind them was an old lady Prabhawati. She was crying bitterly plucking her hair, beating her breasts and weeping loudly. Sri Chandra enquired about the whole story.

One devotee, Vishnu Kaul told Bhagwan that she was the mother of the dead child. He was her only child and support of her old age. Please do something, bless her with the life of her son. Bhagwan smiled and said who says he is dead. He is only in deep sleep. Please say Ram Nam in his ears and he will be all right. Vishnu Kaul did the same and everybody was surprised to see him getting up saying Ram Ram !

Everybody present was delighted to find him alive. All of them bowed their heads on the feet of Bhagwan Sri Chandra.

The news of this miracle spread over far off places like the fire of the jungle. All of the Kashmiri Brahmins in the leadership of Vishnu Kaul came to him and asked the way out of their ills. Bhagwan said, "Do not worry ! There is no body who could destroy the Hindu religion from the land of Kashmir. God came to save his subjects whenever there rose a occasion to do so. God that had put to an end bloody demon kings like Hrinyakahyapp, Ravana, Kansa, Madhu, Kaltabh and others from time to time. He will certainly come to do away this demon Yakub also, so rest assure. You go and tell Yakub that our Guru is in Sri Nagar these days. Ask him to accept Islam we will all embrace Islam if he does so.[9]

Yusuf Pashori and Baba Sri Chand (1540)

Yusuf was a staunch Muslim ruler of Peshawar. During His tour when Baba Sri Chand reached Peshawar he stayed near his house. Being a narrow minded person he could not tolerate the presence of a Hindu saint near his haveli. He conveyed to Baba Ji as there is a stable of horses near your camp and will create inconvenience to you. Baba Ji without any hesitation left that place and put up his camp elsewhere. Mericulously after the departure of Baba Ji a mysterious disease engulfed the horses which up-set Yusuf. He approached Baba Ji, requested for pardon his ill treatment and took Babaji in his haveli. The place where Baba Sri Chand stayed, a temple was constructed, a light (lamp) kept bearning 24 hours and moments of Baba Sri Chand were kept there for public darshan.[10]

References

1.   Shrichandra Jyotsna edited by Shravan Das Shastri and Dr. Gyan Singh, Pritam Prakashan, Akhara Sangalwala, Bazar Mai Sewan, Amritsar, 1997.

2.   Abnashi Chandra, Jeevan Prakash Jeevan.

3. Udasin Kalptaru (Hindi).

4. Bakhshi Singh Adil, p. 96.

5. Shrichandra Jyotsna, 1997.

6. Abinashi Chandra, Jeevan Prakash Jeevan.

7. Shrichandra Jyotsna, 1997.

8. Ibid.

9. Abinashi Chandra, Jeevan Prakash Jeevan.

10. Bakhshi Singh Adi., p. 96.

1. Shri Almast Ji

2. Shri Balhasan Ji younger brother of Shri Almast (Brahman)

3. Shri Goend Ji

4. Shri Phull younger brother of Shri Goend Ji

8

Sikh Gurus and Baba Sri Chand

Babaji and Sikh Gurus

The most noteworthy feature of Babaji's long life and great mission was his utmost respect and love for the Sikh Gurus, who in turn had looked upon him as not only the son of Guru Nanak but as a perfect saint and an elder and very respectable member of the family, so much so that they visited him with their followers, sought his advice, sent regular offerings, and willingly accept making their children Babaji's disciples.

Guru Amar Dassji

The *sangat* (spiritual congregation) once asked Guru Amar Dasji what was the best way to pay respect to Baba Sri Chandji. Guruji's answer was his own personal example: He was went to village Barath with his sons in a humble and friendly way bowed before Babaji and sangat. He said, "Baba Sri Chand Maharajji you are great, you are doing meditation, you have compassion for the sufferers, you have all good qualities. Guru Amar Dass Ji also gave his son Baba Mohanji to Babaji as his disciple. Mohanji was given NAAM and returned to Goindwal Sahib with instructions to fully devote himself to meditation. Baba Mohanji was also trusted with some handwritten collections of Gurbani and was told to keep these in safe custody till required.

Guru Ram Dass Ji

Guru Ram Dassji visited Barath in 1634 and waited for two days for the opening of Babaji's *samadhi*, where he was sitting in deep meditation. Guru Sahib then made an offering of five hundred rupees and clothes and sweets. On Babaji's suggestions, Guruji changed the name of the town which he was building from "Ramdaspur" to "Amritsar". A return visit by Babaji to Amritsar in 1636 was welcomed with great enthusiasm and ceremony. Babaji was seated on a high throne and his advice was sought on Guruji's plan for the holy tank and Harmandir Sahib.

Guru Arjan Devji

Baba Sri Chand used to sit in meditation not for one or two or three hours, but continuously for weeks at a time. He sat in a room, closed the door from inside, and then carried out meditation without eating, without leaving for any reason. When Guru Arjan Devji came to visit Babaji in 1635 he had to wait because Babaji was in deep samadhi from which he did not emerge for a long time. Two places exist at Barath today which mark the visit of Guruji. One is a pillar where Guruji waited daily, and the second is gurdwara, "Manji Sahib," about a mile away where Guruji rested for the night.

When he at last met Babaji, Guru Arjan Devji recited sixteen astpadis of his composition Sukhmani Sahib, but Babaji advised completing them up to twenty-four. The opening stanza of the seventeenth astpadi was given by Babaji on Guruji's request.

Guruji discussed many subjects such as his brother Prithia's mischievous behaviour, the collecting of writings for the Guru Granth Sahib, and the instability of the water supply in Tarn Tarn Tank which he was constructing for the removal of the afflictions and worries of those who bathed there. Babaji blessed him with success, gave some handwritten holy scriptures and told him to take others from his maternal uncle Baba Mohanji. Although Guruji had requested Babaji to give some of his own writings for inclusion in the Guru Granth Sahib, Babaji said, "I do not want to write anything. I just repeat what Guru Nanak has said, "Out of his compassion for the suffering people, Babaji gave a vessel of water from his own *baoli* to be poured into the Taran Taran Tank. Guru Arjan Devji carried that water on his own head from Barath to Tarn Taran, and since then the Tarn Taran Tank has never become dry.

Guru Hargobind Sahib

When the Emperor Jahangir imprisoned Guru Hargobind Sahib and suggested that Babaji assume his seat, Baba Sri Chand firmly told the Emperor that all his power and loyalty was in support of the lineage of the Sikh Gurus and that Guru Hargobind Sahib was the rightful heir to his father's seat. Released by the Emperor, Guru Hargobind Sahib visited Babaji with his sons and followers. When asked by Babaji, he readily gave his eldest son Tika Gurditta, who was eleven and already married and handsome. Tikka Gurditta was left there to serve Babaji, which he did with great love and devotion. Babaji gave him all his secrets, and finding him fit, declared him as his successor. It surprised people how a young man was given a position of such high rank by such a great personality.

Babaji completed his mission and proved that as with his father, his *gaddi* was not the prerogative of his clan or nephew, though they were worthy in all respects and that for the Udasi sect, the distinction between *grasthis* or brahmcharis had no meaning.[1]

Regards of Sikh Gurus towards Baba Sri Chand

1. Guru Angad Dev presented his son Dasu to Baba Sri Chand.

2. Guru Amar Das presented his son Mohan to Baba Sri Chand.

3. Guru Ram Das presented his son Mahadev to Baba Sri Chand.

4. Guru Hargobind presented his son Gurditta to Baba Sri Chand.

5. Guru Hari Rai who discarded his son Ram Rai due to wrong interpretation of "Mittee Musalman Ki Pede Paye Ghumar (मिट्टी मुस्लिमान की पेडे पई धुमार) to please Emperor Aurangzeb. He went to Baba Sri Chand who after great persuation permitted him (as desired by his father) to go to Dehradun.

It is ironical that the son of most defamed Mahant of Nankana Sahib Tragedy (1921) Mahant Narain Das's son Mahant Indresh Das is heading Darbar Sahib, Dehradun. He belongs to Balu Hasan Dhuna. According to Bakhshi Singh Adil he is a great scholar and well read person.

Note: As there was only one son of Guru Arjun Dev named Guru Hargobind. He could not present his son to Baba Sri Chand.

During the period 1527 A.D. to 1539 A.D. Baba Sri Chand visited Kashmir, Bohad, Wadala, Galdi, Barath, Mamoon and Achal Batala.

After the year 1528 A.D. Baba Sri Chand started his tour from Peshawar. After visiting several places he stayed at Bartha for a long time.

Meeting with Guru Arjan Dev and Guru Hargobind

When Baba Sri Chand was staying at Bartha; most probably in the year 1528 A.D. both the above quoted Sikh Gurus called on him. This is the place where Guru Harbobind handed over his eldest son Baba Gurditta to Baba Sri Chand. This place is being managed by Udasi Sadhus. Barth Sahib, is situated at Amritsar Pathankot Railway Line and is about 5 kilometres from Sarna Railway Station.

After staying for some time at Bartha Baba Sri Chand via Mamoon reached Kashmir.[2]

Udasis and Guru Gobind Singh

The Guru's scouts who had been sent to Bhangani, reported that the enemy were marching to attack. He must therefore proceed at once to intercept them, otherwise they would enter Paunta on the morrow. The Guru sent orders to a body of Udasis to put on their turbans, take their arms, and prepare for defence. The Udasis too did not wish to lose their lives. They said that there were other countries where they might beg for their living and that the Guru's kitchen from which they used to eat, was not the only one in the world which remained to them. It was not for the purpose of fighting they had left their homes and become pilgrims. They accordingly resolved to abscond during the night one by one, so that their departure might be unobserved.

Next morning the Guru was informed that the Udasis had all fled except their Mahant Kripal, who remained in a state of abstraction. The Guru smiled and said, `The root at any rate is left, and since there is the root the tree shall bear blossom and fruit. If the mahant had gone, the Udasis would have been totally extirpated, and excommunicated from Sikhism.' The Guru then ordered the mahant to be sent for, and thus addressed him; O'-mahant, whether have thy Udasis fled ! Hearken to me. Thy disciples eat our sacred food, but when they see a green field elsewhere, they go to graze on it like cattle. They have all absconded in the present hour of need. The mahant calmly replied, All disciples of the Gurus are made by thee, and thou thyself canst pardon them.

Kirpal, the mahant of the Udasis, now advanced on horseback, and asked the Guru's permission to engage Haiyat Khan. The Guru replied O holy saint, thou canst kill him with thy words. Pray that I may be victorious. Kirpal the Guru's uncle, over hearing this conversation, and seeing that the mahant was filled with martial enthusiasm, prayed the Guru to let him engage Haiyat Khan. The Guru inquired with what weapon the mahant was going to contend with his adversary. The mahant replied 'with this club'. The Guru smiled and said, 'Go and engage thine enemy. It was a spectacle to see the mahant with his matted hair twisted round his head, his body only clothed with a thin plaster of ashes, and his belly projecting for in front of his saddle, proceeding to engage a practised warrior armed with the latest weapons of destruction.

When the mahant approached and challenged Haiyat Khan, the latter saw that he had no warlike weapon and consequently retreated from him, scorning to attack, defenceless man. The onlookers were amused and said, 'How can that Faqir contend with a Pathan? The mahant, however, continued to challenge Haiyat Khan. As when a snake is escaping into its hole it will come forth if its tail be trodden on and attack the aggressor, so Haiyat Khan who had been retiring before the mahant, now advanced against him goaded by his taunts. He aimed a blow of his sword at the mahant, which the latter received on his club, when la ! Haiyat Khan's sword fell to pieces. The mahant then addressed him, 'Now hold thy ground and defend thyself from me'. The mahant rose on his stirrups and wielding his club with both hands struck Haiyat Khan with such force on the head that his skull broke, and his brains issued forth and stained the battle-field.

The mahant continued to display his skill and bravery to the Pathans, but was at last surrounded by them and placed in a very hazardous position. When Jit Mal, one of the Guru's cousins, saw this, he rained such a shower of arrows on the Pathans, that they retreated and left the mahant unmolested. He then made his way to the Guru, and received his approbation.

The Guru thence proceeded to Mehar, also in Ludhiana district, where lived Kirpal, the Udasi Mahant who had so distinguished himself in the battle of Bhangani. The Guru on meeting him dismissed Ghani Khan and Nabi Khan, after giving them presents and a letter recommending them to the consideration of the faithful. Though Kripal had been previously so devoted to the Guru, he now feared to entertain him lest the Muhammadans should be informed that he was sheltering on outlaw. He accordingly advised the Guru to move on towards the villages of Lamma and Jatpura.[3]

Guru Arjan and Sri Chand

After the Lahore visit Guru (Arjan Dev) went to the shrine of Guru Nanak at Dera Baba Nanak in the Gurdaspur district, Punjab. Thence he proceeded to Barath in the same district to visit Sri Chand, Guru Nanak's son. After mutual salutations they held a conversation. Sri Chand asked why the Guru wandered hither and thither and did not reside in Amritsar. The Guru replied that Prithia (Prithi Chand) was distressed at his residence and so he travelled to propagate his religion. After some further conversation, in the course of which Sri Chand censured the conduct of Pirthia (Pirthi Chand), and said it would be the cause of his damnation, the Guru took his departure for Amritsar, and thus consulted the wishes of his Sikhs and of Sri Chand.[4]

Balwand and Satta and Guru Angad

Balwand and Satta continued to please the Guru's visitors with their songs and music; but on seeing his glory increase, their pride and greed increased in the same ratio. They boasted that it was on account of their music the Guru had become renowned. One day an elderly Sikh asked them to sing him a hymn. They made a rude reply, saying 'Shall be sing hymns for peasants?' The Guru on hearing this was not pleased, and when the minstrels came to sing at the evening prayer, turned his back on them. They went so round so as to catch his eye, but he again avoided their salutation. They asked what offence they had committed. He informed them and said that, as they would not sing to a Sikh of his, they must not sing to him. They fell at his feet and begged his pardon, which he good-naturally granted. Their pride, however, was not totally humbled. They determined to sing for the future only on condition that they received high wages. After a short time they told the Guru that one of their daughters was to be marraied, and they asked for five hundred rupees to meet the expenses. The Guru desired them to wait for two months, and he would settle their accounts at the yearly Baisakhi fair. Balwand said they could not wait so long, they wanted money at once, and pressed him to borrow it for them. The Guru replied that it was not a good thing to borrow and he asked them to have patience and see what God would do. They then began to address him in an insolent tone: 'It is we who by singing thy praises have made thee famous. Did we not sing the Guru's hymns the Sikh would never make thee offerings. Therefore refuse not our request. If thou choose not to give the money we require, we will go to our homes and sing our hymns there.'

The quarrel was not adjusted, and next morning they did not present themselves. The Guru sent for them, but they failed to answer his summons. He again sent a special messenger to tell them not to delay but come to him at once. The more, however, the Guru humbled himself, the prouder they became. They replied, 'The Guru knoweth not our worth. His court shall have no splendour without us. Even Guru Nanak's court would not have been known without the music of Mardana.' The Guru could endure the ingratitude of the minstrels who owed everything to him, but he could not endure the disrespect shown to Guru Nanak's court, so he cursed them and said, 'Their children shall wander forlorn, and none shall cherish them.' The Guru then assigned the duty of singing the hymns to his Sikhs. For a good cause enthusiasts are sometimes found Bhai Ramu, Bhai Dipa, Bhai Ugarsain, and Bhai Nagauri came from Dalla with two stringed violins and cymbals, and took the places of the faithless Balwand and Satta. It soon began to rain showers of melody and devotion, and the audiences were delighted Balwand and Satta on reaching their homes continued to sing the Guru's hymns with the object of withdrawing the Sikhs from the Guru, but in this they completely failed. No one would go to them or listen to their minstrely. They found themselves without corn or money to buy it, and then they began to repent of their inpudence and imprudence. They said to some Sikhs whom they expected to perform the office of mediators between them and the Guru, that they would return to their duties, if they even received food and clothes as remuneration. The Sikhs mentioned this to the Guru, but he sternly forbade them to make any representation again on behalf of man who showed disrespect to the house of Guru Nanak. He said he would have the beared and moustaches of any one who again spoke in their favour cut off and his face blackened, and he would then have him mounted on a donkey and led in disgrace through the city.

Two months after this, Balwand and Satta went to Lahore to visit one Bhai Ladha, whom they knew to possess great influence with the Guru. They told him all the circumstances connected with their quarrel with the Guru, and begged him to intercede for them. Bhai Ladha said to himself, 'Here is a chance of doing good. The body and wealth abide not for ever'. The only gain is for him who doeth a good action. He sent Balwand and Satta on before him, and having shaved his head, blackened his face, and mounted a donkey with his face turned to the tail, went round the city of Khadur, and finally arrived in the Guru's presence. The Guru asked him what guise he had assumed. He said he was merely obeying the Guru's order and prayed him to be good enough to pardon and reinstate the reback players. The Sikhs err, `said Bhai Ladha, `but the Guru can pardon and mend what is broken.'

The Guru granted Bhai Ladha's request and commanding his self-devotion, took the opportunity of expitiating on the merits of Philanthropy: `The best devotion is the remembrance of the True Name; the best act is Philanthropy: without both of these accursed is man's human birth. He merely vegetateth and heedeth not what is best for him. He is a beast without a tail or horn, and vain is his advent into the world. At the last moment they myrmidous of Death shall firmly seize him, and he shall depart grieving with empty hands. Alms gifts, penance, and sacrifices are not equal to philanthropy of the various sins that man commits none is worse than selfishness.

When the reback-players came, they fell at the Guru's feet, but they were too much abashed to lift their eyes to his. He put rebacks into their hands, and ordered them to sing with the same mouths and to the same instruments the praises of Guru Nanak whom they had reviled. They then composed

and sang in Guru Nanak and Guru Angad's praises five
pauris in the Ramkali Ki War, which when completed by three
pauris more, Guru Arjan subsequently included in the Granth
Sahib. The composition is known among the Sikhs as the
Coronation Ode. (Tikke di war).[5]

Sri Chand and Guru Ram Das

Sri Chand, the elder son of Baba Nanak, wore long hair,
wandered a naked hermit and established the sect of the
Udasis. He would not go to meet either Guru Angad or Guru
Amar Das, but, now that a long time had elapsed since his
father's death, and he had partially forgotten his imaginary
grievances, he thought he would visit Guru Ram Dass. When
he arrived in the suburbs of Goindwal, the Guru went and
took him, as the son of Guru Nanak, an offerings of sweets
and five hundred rupees in money. Sri Chand on beholding
Guru Ram Das, thought him the very image of Guru Nanak.
In the course of conversation Sri Chand remarked to him that
he had grown a long beard. The Guru replied, Yes, I have
grown a long beard that I may wipe the feet therewith,
whereupon the Guru proceeded to suit the action to the word.
Sri Chand felt abashed, drew back his feet from the Guru, and
said ," O great King, thou art senior, thou art in my father's
place. It is magic like this which hath made thee a Guru. I
possess no such power, and therefore was I superseded. I
cannot express thy greatness. The Sikhs who come to behold
thee shall be saved.[6]

Guru Ram Das and Baba Sri Chand

Guru Ram Das the Fourth Sikh Guru (1534-1581), whose
original name was Jetha, was born at Lahore on September 24,
1534. He was a pious soul. Once he went to pay his respects
to Guru Amardas and was so impressed by his teaching that
he became his disciple.

Guru Amardas had two daughters. The elder, Bibi Dani
was married to Sri Ram while his younger daughter, Bibi
Bhani was not yet married. By virtue of his piety Jetha had
won the heart of Guru Amardas, who married his daughter
Bibi Bhani to him.

Even after his marriage to the Guru's daughter Ramdas continued to work in the langar with all humility and sincerity. Not for a moment did he considered himself a son-in-law. His relationship with him was strictly one of Guru and his Sikh.

When the Guru began to construct a 'baoli' (a well with steps leading to the level of the water), Ramdas began to work there as a labourer. He carried basket full of mud on his head. He did not mind sailing his fine clothes. Some people even laughed at him saying that he worked as a coolie in his own father-in-law's house.

Before his death, Guru Amardas appointed Jetha as his successor and gave him the name, Guru Ramdas. He did this after putting both of his sons-in-law through a trial. Since both were pious, people wondered who would make the next Guru out of the two.

One day Guru Amardas came to the place where baoli was being constructed. He asked Sri Ram and Shri Ramdas to erect a platform each. When the platform were ready the Guru rejected them and ordered new ones to be made. Sri Ram demolished his platform reluctantly while Sri Ramdas brought his platform down without uttering a word. This process of rejection and reconstruction carried on several times. Sri Ram ran out of patience and questioned the Guru irritably as to what was wrong with the platform while Shri Ramdas fell at the Guru's feet and confessed that he had failed to understand his Guru's orders. He added that he would try once again in the hope of succeeding in carrying out the assignment.

Guru Amardas embraced him and declared him the successful candidate for guruship. He called his sons and his Principal Sikhs and addressed them thus: "Guru Nanak made the rule that guruship should go to the best person. I have found Sri Ramdas to be the next worthy upon whom I bestow guruship".

It was the devotion, patience and humility of Guru

Ramdas which won him the Guruship. Even Guru Nanak's elder son, Baba Sri Chand, who bore a grudge against his father for not nominating him as his successor, sccumbed to his sweet humility.

Baba Sri Chand was an 'Udasi', one who has given up worldly life. He wore long hair and wandered about as a naked hermit. He refused to meet Guru Angad and Guru Amardas but now that a long time had elapsed since his father's death, and he had partially forgotten his imaginary grievances, he decided to visit Guru Ramdas (Guru Nanak expired on 22 September 1530 A.D. He was at that time seventy years, five months and seven days old).

When he arrived in the suburbs of Goindwal, Guru Ramdas went out to receive and welcome the holy visitors. He made him an offering of a beautiful horse and five hundred rupees in cash. Baba Sri Chand found in Guru Ramdas the very image of his father Guru Nanak. During their conversation Baba Sri Chand remarked that he had grown a very long beard and asked the purpose for doing so. Guru Ramdas replied in a humble voice, "O Holy Sir, I have grown this long beard in order to wipe with it the feet of holy men like you". Saying this the Guru actually started wiping Baba Sri Chand's feet with his long black beard, Baba Sri Chand was overwhelmed. He drew back his feet and said, "You are in my father's place, I should show respect to you. Because of your sweetness and humility you have taken my father's place. I have non of these virtues. I now understand and appreciate my father's gesture in not nominating me as his successor." (From the book entitled, Life and Times—The Sikh Gurus by Shrimati Mridula Oberoi—Madhuban Educational Books—a division of Vikas Publishing House, Private Limited, 1997).[7]

The other incident has been narrated in Shrichandra Jyotsna 1997 as under:

Guru Ramdas accompanied by a group of his followers went to Baba Sri Chand to pay his obeisance and darshan reached Barth. He presented clothes and Rupees Five Hundred as cash to Baba Sri Chand. When Baba Sri Chand asked the name of the colony and the Sarovar constructed by Guru Ramdas. He apprised him that the name of the city has been proposed as Ramdas chak and the name of the Sarovar is "Ramdas Sar". Then Lord Sri Chand suggested the name for the city and Sarovar as "Amritsar". (For more details please see Shri Chand Itihas by Ishar Singh Nahra, pp. 368, 370).[8]

Guru Amardas and Baba Sri Chand

The third Sikh Guru Amardas alongwith his both the sons namely Mohanji and Jethaji and other followers called on Baba Sri Chand to pay his regards reached Barth. After the exchange of presents they exchanged their views on various topics. During their discussion Yogiraj noticed great qualities of a suprerman and gentle habits of Mohanji and was impressed by his personality. He requested Guru Amardas to give Mohan to him. Guru Amardas immediately acceded his request and handed over his son Mohan to Baba Sri Chand Ji.

Guruship

Guru Nanak Dev appointed Bhai Lehna, a devoted disciple, as his successor in preference to his sons (Sri Chand and Lakhmi Das), who were found wanting for the sacred office of Guruship. The nomination of a successor by the Guru proved an important landmark in the growth of the Sikh religious organization.

One side from which reaction could come was the Udasi sect founded by Guru Nanak's son Sri Chand. Sri Chand had founded his own creed after being deprive of Guruship. But Guru Angad through his sweetness of personality and devotion put the true creed of Guru Nanak on a firm footing against which no reaction could succeed.

The second Guru during his life time, had nominated Amardas, a venerable old disciple as his successor. The new Guru had, however, also to face the opposition of Sri Chand and the sons of Guru Angad, especially Datu the elder of the two.[10]

Devotion and Humility

Once Guru Nanak had collected three bundles of grass for his cows and buffaloes; and he desired to have them taken home. The grass was wet and muddy. Since no one was willing for the task, the Guru asked his sons Sri Chand and Lakshmi Das to carry the bundles. They too evaded the duty, saying that labourer could do the job. Lehna, who had just arrived there, bowed before the Guru and said most humbly consider me as your labourer and give me this job to do.

The Guru said he might take as many as his strength permitted Lehna, gathering strength from his enthusiasm and devotion, picked up all the bundles and walked towards Guru Nanak's house.

On reaching home, the Guru's wife asked him: Is it proper for you to impose such menial labour on a guest and soil his new clothes? See from head to toe, he is dripping with muddy water!

The Guru replied, "This is not mud but `saffrron of God's court which marketh the elects". On looking again, the Guru's wife observed that the mud on Lehna's clothes had really changed to saffrron!

On another occasion, Guru Nanak sent for his sons at the dead of night and asked them to wash his soiled clothes. His sons protested in a chorus, "There is no water around. Even if we manage to wash your clothes, how are they ever going to dry at this unearthly hour?"

Guru Nanak repeated his request. His sons replied in differently. "At the break of the day we shall have your clothes delivered to the Washerman to wash. Why don't you wear a new set of clothes until then.

The Guru made the same request to Lehnaji. He at once set out for doing the assigned task with all sincerity. Early next morning he presented his master with clean, washed and dried clothes.

One winter night it poured so heavily that a part of the wall of the Guru's house collapsed. Around midnight he asked his sons to repair it. They said, it is dark and bitterly cold. Besides, it is not our job to build or repair walls. Tomorrow morning we shall summon masons and labourers to do the work.

The Guru said to his sons, "Since it is the Guru's work, it must only be done by his Sikhs; and it must be done immediately, without any further delay".

Lehnaji who happened to be standing next to the Guru, offered his services. He started building the wall. When he was nearly half way through, the Guru said that the wall was not straight. He asked him to demolish the half built wall and build it again. Lehnaji obeyed his master and started rebuilding the wall with utmost care. But the Guru was still not satisfied. He had to pull it down once more. This carried on several times.

The Guru's own sons tried to discourage Lehnaji against this task assigned to him. They said, "You can never please him. Give up the work".

But Lehnaji said, "A servant must do his master's work. It is for the master to decide what work he should assign to his servant".

Guru Nanak used to get up every morning to bathe in the river Ravi, Lehnaji would go along with him and sit near the Guru's clothes while he bathed. By now Guru Nanak had become so fond of him that he had come to be known as Baba Lehna. Some of the Guru's disciples had become jealous of Baba Lehna. One day three of these jealous Sikhs decided to do what Baba Lehna was doing for the Guru. They thought this would please their master.

It was a cold dark morning. The sky was overcast and soon it began to hail. The three Sikhs could not bear the chill and returned home. But Baba Lehna waited for the Guru to step out of the river.

When Guru Nanak reached the bank of the river where Baba Lehna was sitting by himself, he said to him, "The other Sikhs deserted me on this chilly morning. Why didn't you follow suit"?

Baba Lehna bowed humbly to his Guru and said, "A servant must never desert his master, How could I do that?"

All these trials fully convinced Guru Nanak that in Baba Lehnaji had found a true successor. He addressed Baba Lehnaji, "You have become so dear to me that you seem a part of me. You are my Angad, a part of my 'ang' or body."

Thus his name was changed to Guru Angad and he became the second Sikh Guru in preference to Guru Nanak's own sons. Guru Nanak told his unhappy sons that Angad alone had proved himself worthy of the guruship.[11]

Humility wins over an enemy

It was Guru Ramdas's devotion, patience and humility which won him the guruship. Even Guru Nanak's son Baba Sri Chand who bore a grudge against his father for not nominating him as his successor, succumbed to his sweet humility.

Baba Sri Chand was an 'Udasi', one who has given up worldly life. He wore long hair and wandered about as a naked hermit. He refused to meet Guru Angad or Guru Amardas, but now that a long time had elapsed since his father's death, and he had partially forgotten his imaginary grievances, he decided to visit Guru Ramdas.

When he arrived in the suburbs of Goindwal, Guru Ramdas went out to receive and welcome the holy visitor. He made him an offering of a beautiful horse and five hundred rupees in cash. Sri Chand found in Guru Ramdas the very image of his father Guru Nanak. During their conversation, Sri Chand remarked that he had grown a very long beard and asked the purpose for doing so. Guru Ramdas replied in a humble voice, "O Holy Sir, I have grown this long beard in order to wipe with it the feet of holy man like you". Saying this the Guru actually started wiping Baba Sri Chand's feet with his long black beard. Baba Sri Chand was overwhelmed. He draw back his feet and said, "You are in my father's place. I should show respect to you. Because of your sweetness and humility you have taken my father's place. I have none of these virtues. I now understand and appreciate my father's gesture in not nominating me as his successor".

The ascetic son of Guru Nanak, Sri Chand, though disinherited by the father, was still alive and preaching his gospel of renunciation as an Udasi though he was mature and disinterested enough not to come actively in the way of the third Guru. But, it was really hard for the common run of the Sikhs "to choose between Guru Nanak's son and the nominee of his nominee".[12]

References

1. Baba Sri Chands Life and Teachings by Bhai Kirpal Singh.

2. Bakhshi Singh Adil, Jeevan Baba Sri Chand, 208315, Gali Punjab Singh, Chak Prag Das, Amritsar, 1978, p. 93.

3. The Sikh Gurus, Macauliffe, Vol, 5-6, pp. 34, 39, 193 (Vol. 5).

4. The Sikh Religion (Life of Guru Arjun) Max Arthur, Macauliffe, Vol. 6, pp. 27-28.

5. The Sikh Religion, Max Arthur, Macauliffe, Vol. 2, pp. 21-25.

6. Ibid.

7. Life and Times, The Sikh Gurus by Shrimati Mridula Oberoi, Madhuban Educational Books, A division of Vikas Publishing House, Pvt., Ltd., 1997.

8. Shrichandra Jyotsna, 1997.

9. Shrichandra Itihas, Ishan Singh Nahra, p. 380.

10. Growth of the Sikh Faith (1460-1708), Gurcharan Singh.

11. Life and Times, The Sikh Gurus by Mridula Oberoi, Vikas Publishing House, 1992.

12. History of the Sikh People, Dr. Gopal Singh, p. 162.

9

Great Departure

It was in Vikrami Samvat 1700 (1643 A.D.) when one day Bhagwan Sri Chand got up from his samadhi, marched towards the Bank of Ravi River and thought of going across it. It was a bit dark at that time. Moon had gone home and Sun was yet to rise. Boatsmen were still asleep, who would sail the boat? Brahmaketu, a dedicated worshipper was with him. He caught the idea and awakened one of the boatsmen and said to him come with your boat and take us to the other bank at once. An other person wanting to go to the other side was also sitting there. He planted a joke over Bhagwan Sri Chandra who was looking just like Bhagwan Shiva with the ash smeared body. He said, "Mahatman, you are from the clan of Bhagwan Ram who build a stone bridge over the sea to reach Lanka, can not you ask a small stone to swim across the Ravi. Bhagwan smilingly thought there has come an iota of suspicion in his mind about the power of Ram nam So ! must ask a stone slab to swim. And he picked up a stone slab lying near by and placed it in the water, made himself sit on it in Kamalasn (a posture of yoga) and ordered the slab to swim. Lo! it started moving like a boat driven by an expert boatsman. In a twinkle of an eye it reached the other bank. Bhagwan got off the slab and disappeared in the dense forest. His pupil Brahmaketu, Boat man and the third non believer man watched this miracle without a twinkle of an eye. Nobody saw Bhagwan after that day.

This is a biography of that great yogi who saved Hindus and their religion in the rule of Muslim kings.

Yogiraj was an incarnation of Lord Shiva. He had come to reform the Hindu society. There is a great debt over the Hindus. Who so ever came in his contact became gold with his 'paras' touch. Yogiraj was an apt scholar of Vedas and Sastras. He visited every nook and corner of the country to spread his message of real religion and awakened Indians into a new era of vedic culture. In his personality got developed the finest elements of Hindu culture. His life was an embodiment of penance, renunciation and meditation. Even followers of other religions had to bow upon his lotus feet due to his spiritual powers. The creeper planted by Bhagwan is still green and is perfuming all the directions with its fragrance. After him his disciples carried on his mission of vedic regeneration. Udasin sadhus are well spread in all directions in this country and abroad and are busy in the works of religious upliftment and social welfare. It is our sacred duty to follow in the footsteps of Bhagwan Sri Chandra and to work with our full capacity for the redemption of our community and our country.

The end

Babaji arrived at Chamba in Samvat 1700 (1643 A.D.) when he was 149 years old and declared his end. He gave Sahansarnama and Shri Arta to Baba Mehar Chand Ji, son of Baba Dharm Chand Ji, and advised the sangat to read them as part of their continuing worship of Guru Nanak. He bade farewell to Bhai Kamalia, his life-long companion, and gave his last message to his followers: Those who wished to remain brahmchari and keep the Udasi symbols must maintain very high character and renunciation and direct the sadhu samaj on correct lines. Those who wished to adopt Udasi symbols while remaining with families must follow Udasi teaching sincerely.

Thus saying, he crossed the river standing on a slab of

stone which moved like a boat and in the twinkling of an eye disappeared.

Babaji's body could not be found.

References

1.   Ahnashi Chandra by Jeevan Prakash Jeevan.

2.   Baba Sri Chand's Life and Teachings by Bhai Kirpal Singh.

10

Udasin Bhagats

Almast—The Udasi Sikh Priest

Almast, the Udasi Sikh Priest (either he or his name sake) was also, it is said, deputed by Guru Hargobind to go to Shujatpur, near Dacca, and take charge of the Sangat there. This Sangat was known after Natha Sahib, third in succession to Almast, and according to the inscription on the well, its forwarding is ascribed to Almast, and its priests were appointed and removed by the High Priest of Nankana (vide G.B. Singh's article, Sikh relics in Eastern Bengal. Dacca Review, 1916 p. 228). Thus under Guru Hargobind the seat of Sikhism were consolidated from Kabul on the one hand to Dacca on the other, first sanctified by the visit of Guru Nanak. Under his son, Baba Gurditta, the system of Sangats and Masands was supplemented by four Dhunas (hearths or consecrated seats supervised by Balu Hasna, Almast, Phul Shah and Gonda) under the Udasi Sikhs who though living celibate and ascetic lives, as enjoined by Baba Srichand, their founder, in no other way departed from the Sikh doctrine. The Guru's eldest son, Baba Gurditta's, father of the seventh Guru was adopted and appointed successor by Srichand and in token thereof "put on Gurditta's head a Persian hat (topi) and on his neck a string of lotus seeds." Under Gurus Hari Rai, Tegh Bahadur and Gobind Singh, six Bakhishes (Bounties) were added to their order, which included the Suthrashahis, Sangat Sahibis, Jitmalias, Bakhat, malias, Bhagat Bhagwanias and Miranshahis. The Udasis have played a most notable part for the propagation of the Sikh faith in times of worst crises in its history, but the Akali movement of the present century for the control of the Sikh historic shrines has disrupted the existing cordial relations almost permanently between the two. Earlier, the Udasis wore a crown of long hair on their head, covered by a tall, cony cap, but many of them are now shaved and though the majority still wear the ochri robes (earlier they were deep red), some even smear their naked bodies with ashes and even wear matted hair. However, they all believe in the Sikh scripture, the Guru Granth Sahib.[1]

Bakta Nand (1634 A.D.)

He was known as Baba Bakta. He was born in the year 1634 A.D. (Vikrami Samvat 1691) in a Sarswat Brahman family in a village named Daroli in district Ferozpur, Punjab. Learn three R's from Kashi and studied from a Mahatma of Assam. He became disciple of Swami Karta Rai and joined Udasi Sampardai. He was also named as Swami Ajita Nand but was famous as Ajit Mal.[2]

Shri Baba Hasan Ji (1654 - 1660 A.D.)

Was younger brother of Shri Almast Ji. He was born in the year 1564 A.D. (Vikrami Samvat 1621, Maghar 10) in Kashmir. He used to stay at Dehradun. Shri Ram Rai Ji used to stay with him. He was the stannch follower of Guru Hargobind. He used to look after as a chief of the horse Brigade of Guru Hargobind. He expired in Dehradun in the year 1660 A.D. (Vikrami Samvat 1717). The mahants of the Dera of Baba Ram Rai are the descents of his sect. He also set up Dera of Moolwali.[3]

Bhagat Bhagwan Ji (1497 A.D.)

Was born in the year 1497 A.D. (Vikrami Samvat 1554, Maghar Vadi 4). He was a saint like nature from his very childhood. For a short period he followed as a Sadhu'Sanyasi Sect' and became a mahant in Gaya. He was known as Bhagat Giri at that time. He was going for the pilgrimage of Hinglaj Devi, he happened to meet Baba Sri Chand at Thatta and became His disciple.[4]

Bhana Bhagat

Once Udasin Shiromani Baba Sri Chand alongwith Kamaliya was attending a Kirtan. The people notice that great saint disappeared for a moment. When he again appeared on the persistant demands of his followers the Yogiraj apprised them that the ship of Bhanu Bhagat which was full of precious goods was about to sink in the sea. Bhanu Bhagat remembered his Lord Baba Sri Chand and on his request Baba Sri Chand reached on the spot and with his spiritual powers managed to rescue the sinking ship.[5]

Dhanna Bhagat

In 1581, Bhagwan Sri Chandra reached in a village named TAPTA and stayed in the famous temple of Lord Krishna. Some Cow-boys used to visit that temple for having a look of the idol of Lord Krishna daily during their beat, with their cows. That day also, they came and were astonished to find one naked fakir, having smashed ashes all over his body. One of the cow-boys did sit near him while he was reading some passages from the sacred Geeta. When he stopped the reading; he asked the boy his name. The boy replied that his name was Dhanna Ray. But the village folk called him Dhanna with love.

He told that he was 10 years of age and asked the name of the book he was reading. Bhagwan Sri Chandra replied that as he was himself a yadav vanshi (from the clan of Lord Krishna) he must know that this is the book in which Lord Krishna has given Arjuna that sacred sermon upon hearing which he lost all his ignorance and cowardness. The boy was delighted to know that he belonged to the clan of Lord Krishna so he danced with a fit of supreme joy; and said well he would not accept a drop of water, what to say of food till Lord Krishna does not pay a personal visit to him right in that temple. He sung a song like that

AB DIJO DARASH GIRDHARI

JAN DHANE KO DARAS DIKHAO

PAKDI OT TUMHARI

अब दीजो दर्श गिरधारी
जन धन्ने को दर्श दिखायो
पकडी ओट तुम्हारी।

Come oh Girdhari and give me your sacred darshan as
I have come to your assylum, under your protection come and
show me your lotus face.

Other cow-boys when returned back with their hoard of
cows, found Dhanna sitting and singing the songs in the
praise of lord. He had no sense of his where abouts. His
friends tried to pursuade him to accompany them but failed
to do so. The sun got set but this beloved of Lord Krishna kept
on saying, "Oh Lord do come please!"

When he did not reach home, then family members
worried about him. They were informed about his where
abouts by his friends. His mother went to fetch him from the
temple but he told his mother to return as he had taken a vow
not to touch water and food till Lord Krishna did not come
to sooth him. She returned home without him. Dhanna did
not bother about food and hunger. As the saying goes-

RAGHUKUL RITI SADA CHALI AYI
PRAN JAYEN PAR VACHAN NA JAYI

रघुकुल रीत सदा चली आई।
प्राण जाये पर वचन न जाई।।

It is the custom of the decendents of Lord Rama. That
one may die but does not run from his word.

So he decided either he meets the Lord or face the death
but will not go home. Two days lapsed but he could not see
the sacred face of the Lord. The dhuni sacred fire lighted by
Sri Chandra was still having some burning wood pieces; so
he decided to make a fire bed for him and end his useless life.
He lighted a big fire taking a burning wood from the fire of
Mahatma Trilochan. The flames rose high in the sky and as
he tried to end his life by jumping into that fire a miracle
happened. A big wind blew and took away those burning

wood with it. Watching this, Dhanna got into rages and tried to kill himself with the help of his sackle (drati) and said lo! the wind has taken away the fire, who will stop me from ending my life now and who will snatch this cutter from my hand. Let the wind blow and take away this cutter also with it.

As soon as he tried to do away with himself some hidden force stopped him to do so by holding his hand. He saw with wide open eyes that Lord Krishna was holding his hand, in his full attire. The Lord was smiling over his Bhakta. He was hungry and his throat was dry due to want of water. The food left by her mother was still there and Lord Krishna tried to feed him with his own hands but he refused to eat; until and unless Lord himself would not take that food from his hands. So Lord had to acceed to his demand. Lord Krishna took half of the bread made of Bajra (a coarse food).[6]

Dodha Jat

One day Baba Sri Chand was sitting in a deep meditation. There came Dodha Jat who was a staunch follower of Guru Nanak. He was the same person who had donated major portion of his land to Guru Nanak for the setting up of Kartarpur. Once Dodha Jat requested Guru Nanak for a blessing that he wants to become immortal and never to die. Guru Nanak did not acceded his request and said—Dodha-one has to die ultimately but it would be within your power you would die when you like to do so.

When Baba Sri Chand opened his eyes and saw Dodha-Baba Ji asked him, "Dodha, tell me now you wish to die or not? knowing this Dodha fell on the feet of Baba Ji and said— I want to die but I have one wish in my mind that if you could bless me as Guru Nanak, then I will die. In the twinkling of an eye Dodha witnessed Baba Sri Chand in incarnation of Guru Nanak Dev Ji. Thus his last desire was fulfilled and he expired there and then.[7]

Bhagat Giri and Hinglaj Devi

Once upon a time Mahatma Bhagat Giri alongwith Ram

Giri Tantrik, both alongwith a group of their disciples were going to pay their obeisance to Mata Hinglaj. When they reached at Kartarpur they heard about the greatness of Acharya Srichandra Bhagwan. They determined to test him because both these persons were proud of their spiritual power.

From Kartarpur they reached Nankana Sahib and stayed in the Ashram of Acharya Srichandra Ji Maharaj. They were greeted there with due regards by the Mahant of the Ashram. When they reached there it was a lunch time. The Mahant requested them to take meals. Then Bhagat Giri replied that there is a lot of saints and sewaks with us. Mahant said, nothing to worry ! it is a 'guru ka langar'. On Mahant's request Bhagat Giri and his associates participated in the lunch. When the Langar incharge started distributing food among the people, Bhagat Giri just to test the spiritual powers of Acharya Shri Chandra put his 'Khappar' before him and requested him to fill it up and we will be satisfied. When the Mahant of the Ashram came to know about this incident, he remembered Acharya Srichandra and put a mouth full of grain in his 'khappar', which was filled to capacity. On seeing this strange miracle Bhagat Giri made up his mind to have a glimpse of Acharya Srichandra Ji Maharaj. He asked the Mahant about the whereabouts of Acharya Shri and said that I am eager to have his 'darshan'. Mahant told him that our esteemed Acharya Ji is touring territory of Sindh these days.

The Hinglaj Devi for whose darshan you are going that Devi used to come everyday to serve Acharya Srichandra Ji Maharaj. Knowing about this incident they rushed to have darshan of great Acharya. Gradually they reached in the village named Thatha in the Sindh Pradesh. There they met Acharya Shri and did 'Dandvat Pranam'. After exchange of greetings Acharya asked them about their journey and future programme. Bhagwan Sri Chandra told them that you would be able to have darshan of the devi here itself and you people need not to go anywhere.

One day in the morning Bhagat Giri noticed an old lady

cleaning 'Dhoona'. Bhagat Giri's intution told him that this old lady is 'Hingalaj Mata'—he fell on her feet and request her to bless him in her real position. She acceded his request and fulfilled his desire. Then Mother Hingalaj told him that Acharya Srichandra is nothing else but an incarnation of Lord Shiva. To strength and propagate the ideals of Udasin saints to safeguard the interests of his followers he has born in this Kaliyuga. Owing to this reason I used to come to serve Him daily. If you also want success in your life, please follow him saying this Devi Hinglaj vanished from there. Bhagat Giri's happiness have no bounds. He laid down in the feet of Acharya Srichandra and request Him to enroll him as one of his disciple. Seeing his affection and love Bhagwan Shrichandra during Vikrami Samvat 1601, Kartik Shudi 15 enrolled him as his disciple and gave a 'Saile Topi' and marked Babhut renamed him as Bhagat Bhagwan and blessed him with 'Ridhi' and 'Siddhi' Vardan and said, "Dargah Parwan". Owing to this blessing Bhagat Bhagwan is known as the first 'Bakhshish' in guise of a Udasi Saint. "Dargh" means the pious place of God 'Parwan' means certified or sanctioned by the God Almighty.[8]

Jeevan Prakash Jeevan has related this incident in the following words:

Bhagat Giri born in a utkal Brahman family of Gaya, was a learned pundit of Bodh religion and incharge of the Bodh Gaya temple complex. He along with his 360 disciples was going on the pilgrimage to Hinglaj Devi. He passed with his retinue through Thatha and had a chance to be with Sri Chandraji in a lovely jungle away from the city. Bhagwan was in his smadhi at that time. He was much impressed by the glimpse of Sri Bhagwan and sat near him. When he was up from his samadhi, he asked Giriji about his future plans. Giriji told Bhagwan that they were going to pay their homage at Hinglaj Devi. Bhagwan replied, "what for you are facing such a hazard of your pilgrimage in these lonely and fearful jungles. Devi comes hear daily to give her darshan. Bhagat Giri was surprised to hear such words from the lotus mouth of Bhagwan. He was proud of his Bhakti and a Sidha yogi himself. It is said that he had such diamond with him that due to it he had not to bother about thirst and hunger. When Sri Chandra asked him about some thing for drinking or eating he replied that it was his time to take milk. So if it is possible for you to procure a kamandlu full of milk at this time, I would be much obliged. Sri Chandra asked one of his pupils to fetch some milk. He brought some milk and tried to pour it into the Kamandlu of Bhagat Giri but he was surprised to find that it was not possible to fulfil his Kamandlu as the milk disappeared from the pot. Giri said till you not fill my pot I will not take a drop of milk. When Sri Chandra came to know the happening he ordered that not only of the Bhagat Giri but all other Kamandals of his fellow travellers may please be filled with milk. Yogiraj through his spiritual power, learned that Bhagat Giri used to drink milk by his miracle and that was the reason behind the non-fulfilment of his Kamandlu. So by his spiritual power, Bhagwan Sri Chandra matched his miraculous expertise and see all the pots were now overflowing with milk. Bhagat Giri exhaused all his powers but failed to consume his Kamandlu of milk. All the night passed. In the early morning Giri Ji found Hinglaj Devi at the ashram of Sri Chandra Ji. When he tried to bow his head upon the feet of devi, she turned into the full form of Asta bhuja (with eight hands) and riding on her famous lion before him. Enjoying her divine appearance, Bhagat Giri was full of eternal Bliss and started dancing and singing. In the mean time devi disappeared. Yogiraj Sri Chandra asked Bhagat Giri and his followers to wake up if you want to attain your desired destination. Having this Bhagat Giri opened up his eyes and along with his pupils got initiated into the udasin sect from the hands of Bhagwan Sri Chandra Ji. He was named Bhagat Bhagwan in place of Bhagat Giri. He was blessed by Bhagwan with these words. "Who so ever will become your pupil will be accepted at the door step of Bhagwan by him. All his 360 disciples after being initiated into the udasin sect were asked to leave for various places for the propagation of Vedic Hindu religion. Bhagwan Sri Chandra advised him to oppose everywhere the misdeeds of Tantriks and Shakats so that people like him though being wise enough not to fall into the clutches of Tantriks and Shaktas again. He was then informed about the daily routine of a sidh udasin sadhu. He was also told to follow panchdeva puja as such a practice saves people of all faiths from quarreling with each other. This could bring comradeship amongst Shaivas and Vaishnavas. Such sermons transformed the life style of Bhagat Bhagwan. One of his followers Ramgiri who refused to accept the new order was expelled from the group by him. When Bhagat Bhagwan was about to leave, yogiraj requested him to oppose with all his might the ever increasing tyranny of the muslims so as to weaken the foundation of their misrule. You should try to save the simple public from going into the clutches of Tantriks and to give them guide-lines to follow in a better way the age old Vedic way of Hindu religion. You should take my message to every nook and corner of India. Religious brave-men go into their field with full courage, God helps those who help themselves. He helps courageous people always. So be brave and come forward as to march is the real life:-

> *Those who work with full force-*
> *always are rewarded-*
> *They earn everything and are blessed*
> *by god, who never sit with folded hands.*

Leave aside all inactivity. Have faith in God and start working for the fulfilment of your mission. I am fully confident that God will help you to fulfil your desires. Such an advice of Bhagwan Sri Chandra had a great effect over Bhagat Bhagwan so he bowed his head over the divine feet of his preceptor and left for his mission to be fulfilled by hard work and determination.

Bhagat Bhagwan had 360 mathas (temples) under him, all those were turned into the udasin centres of learning. With the grace of God, the dream of muni Avinashi Ji turned to take concrete shape. His sacred concept started heavily over Tantriks and muslims. Their activities started to be curtailed.

In one part of India Bhagat Bhagwan started his activities of religious reforms. On the other hand Sindh, Punjab, Kashmir, Afghanistan and the frontier province areas were covered by Yogiraj Bhagwan himself. He established religious centres at various places such as Srinagar in Kashmir, Thatha in Sindh, Barath in Punjab, Peshawar in frontier province and Kabul in Afghanistan. In those days Muslim propaganda was in full swing in frontier province. So it was not a childs' play to handle the situation in that province. His missionary work in these muslim populated areas will always be written in Golden letters. Udasin missionary work was in full swing in all parts of the country, but Bhagwan Sri Chandra gave more attention on Muslim populated areas. Udasin sadhus never feared Muslim mussle power and they worked with determination with their coffins tied upon their heads. This gave much spiritual upliftment to the down trodden Hindus and they started living with dignity following their age old religion with peace. His idea got roots in Punjab also. Udasin (Chaturth ashrims) fourth ashmites worked day and night to bring new revival amongst the Hindus of this country.[9]

Bakhshi Singh Adil quoted this incident as under:

Bakhshi Singh Adil has mentioned an interesting incident in his book that when Baba Sri Chand during his tour in the year 1564 A.D. (Vikrami Samvat 1625) reached at the Temple of Hinglaj Devi (Hyderabad Sind). He happened to meet Bhagat Giri who was also going for darshan of Devi Hinglaj alongwith his 360 disciples. Bhagat Giri was great Saint and was the chief of Budh Gaya Math (Orissa) and was a renowned scholar. When he saw Baba Sri Chand Ji in his deep meditation he advised his disciples to halt there. When Baba Sri Chand came out of his samadhi then Bhagat Giri told that he is going for the pilgrimage of the Devi. Baba Sri Chand told him that why you are taking trouble to go there, as Devi usually comes to me daily. During discussion Bhagat Giri expressed his desire to have milk. Babaji advised his disciple to arrange for milk. When they came and poured milk in the pot of Bhagat Giri, it was never filled up. Baba Sri Chand immediately sensed that Giri wants to test his spiritual powers. Baba Sri Chand exercised His powers and in no time the pot was filled to capacity. Seeing this that Baba Sri Chand is more powerful than me, he fell down on the feet of Babaji. On the same night Bhagat Giri has darshan of Devi Hinglaji at the Dera of Baba Sri Chand. Seeing this miracle Bhagat Giri and all his followers became disciple of Baba Sri Chand. Babaji changed his name from Bhagat Giri to Bhagat Bhagwan and all his 360 Maths were converted into the Udasin Centres.[10]

Shri Goend Ji (1569 A.D.-1649 A.D.)

Was born in the year 1569 A.D. (Vikrami Samvat 1626, Asuj 5) in a Khatri family of Kashmir. He stayed for a long time in Hyderabad but at the time of his demise he was in Lahore. He became disciple of Baba Gurditta in the year 1634 A.D. (Vikrami Samvat 1691). He was known as Sadhu of `Tahli Wale'. In Lucknow his disciple known as disciple of Mehan Sahib sect had a well known Gaddi. He expired in Phillaur in the year 1649 A.D. (Vikrami Samvat 1706). Previously Bakshi Singh Adil has mentioned that he expired in Lahore? He also set up Dera Tahli Sahib at Pakhoke.[11]

Baba Gurditta Ji

Was born in the year 1613 A.D. (Vikrami Samvat 1670, Kartik Sudi 15). His father's name was Guru Hargobind and mother's name was Damodari. He had four brothers namely— Baba Surajmal Ji, Baba Aney Roy Ji, Baba Atal Roy Ji, and Guru Tegh Bahadur and one sister named Viran. He was married at the age of 11 years in the year 1624 A.D. (Vikrami Samvat 1681, Baisakh 21) with Ananti daughter of Rama Mal Khatri of Batala. He had two sons namely Baba Dhir Mal and Guru Hari Ray Ji. It is said that he blessed Sai Buddhan Shah in the incarnation of Guru Nanak Dev Ji. He became disciple of Baba Sri Chand in the year 1625 A.D. (Vikrami Samvat 1681, Baisakh Sudi 3). He expired in the year 1638 (Vikrami Samvat 1694-Asu Shudi 10) at the age of about 25 years at Kiratpur. He nominated his following four disciples:-

1. Shri Almast Ji

2. Shri Balhasan Ji younger brother of Shri Almast (Brahman)

3. Shri Goend Ji

4. Shri Phull younger brother of Shri Goend Ji.

Shri Guru Hargobind Ji was blessed with a son by the blessing of Baba Buddha Ji and Baba Sri Chand Ji. Once, Guru Hargobind Ji alongwith his five sons went to Barath to have darshan of Baba Sri Chand Ji. Guru Ji presented a sum of Rupees five hundred and a horse to Baba Sri Chand. He requested Baba pointing towards his five sons. Bhagwan! You can take any one out of my five sons as your disciple. Baba Ji name Gurditta. This happened in the year 1622 A.D. (Vikrami Samvat 1679).

Once Baba Sri Chand alongwith Baba Gurditta went to Mamoon near Pathankot and stayed outside the village. The village girls passed near their Dhuna having pitcher full of water on their heads. Baba Gurditta requested them to give some water for drinking which was refused. Baba Gurditta related this incident to Baba Sri Chand. Hearing this Baba Sri Chand put his chimta in the ground with his full force and in no time a showering fountain of water started coming out the ground and the Peepal tree under which Baba Ji was sitting in the twinkling of an eye became green. To see this miracle hundred and thousands of people assembled there which were addressed by Baba Sri Chandji.[12]

Gyandra of Ganauli and Miracle of Baba Nirbandhan Dev Ji

In Srimad Bhagavad Gita Bhagwan (Lord) Krishna has said that: The Yogi who is ever content, steady in meditation, self controlled, is of firm resolve with mind and understanding given up to Me - he, My devotee, is dear to Me... and also said:- He by whom the world, is not agitated, and who cannot be agitated by the world and who is freed from joy, envy, fear and anxiety—he is dear to Me... and have also said that:- He who has no expectations, is pure, skilful impartial and untroubled and who renounces the feeling of doorship in all undertakings—he My devotee is dear to me.

Before we turn to Gyandraji of Ganauli, let us first apprise the learned scholars and readers of this book about the great Udasin saint Baba Nirbandhan Devji who was the incarnation of Baba Sri Chand Ji Maharaj.

He was born in a village named Faizpur near Lahore (now in Pakistan). Date of birth has not been traced out. He belonged to a respectable Khatri family knew Punjabi only. Details of educational qualification also not known. Worked in a shop named Sacha Sauda as an assistant. Earned lot of money while working in that shop. Being a celibate and a man of high character he was a man of very simple habits. The money which he had earned due to his hard and sincere efforts does not know how and where to spent. He started weeping at night due to excess of money. Ironically everthing was lost within a period of one month. He left Faizpur and reached village Baneke, Tehsil Hafizabad, District Gujranwala (now in Pakistan). There he happened to meet Pandit Girdhari Lal Punj, a renowned leader of Arya Samaj. He was a great scholar. One day he (Girdhari Lal) was meditating in a dense jungle and happened to meet Baba Nirbandhan Dev and inquired whereabouts of Pandit Girdhari Lal. He told him that he is a Brahman by caste. Don't you know this? You are not a Brahmin. But now onwards you would become Brahmin. Girdhari Lal stared at him and touch his feet and took Baba Ji to his home and there on his request blessed him with darshan as Vishnu. After this incident Girdhari Lal alongwith one Hem Raj of the same village remained with Babaji for about 40 years.

There was a dera of Udasin Sadhus at Hafizabad. During partition days that dera was attacked by the local Mohammadens. Baba Nirbandhan Dev was there. He encouraged the sadhus to face the situation boldly and convinced the locals not to harm these sadhus. The miscreants looted the dera but permitted the sadhus to leave the place.

All the occupants of that dera reached Amritsar safely in the company of Baba Nirbandhan Dev.

After staying in Amritsar for a few days Babaji alongwith Girdhari Lal came to Delhi and settled in Okhla (Village Matela) and put up a hut in the agricultural land of Shri Balamkand father of Sardar Jagir Singh and stayed there till he left for his heavenly abode. Our hero Gyandraji of Ganauli called on Baba Nirbandhan Dev Ji in the year 1968 two days before the Diwali festival. Since 1968 Gyandraji continuously remained attached with Baba Ji because he was impressed by his dynamic personality. Baba Ji also loved Gyandraji due to his selfless services and sincerity. As Gyandraji was in the teaching profession Baba Ji assigned the job of translation of "Shrimukh Vivek" granth which was written in Punjabi to translate in Hindi in June 1970. Gyandraji completed the translation work of "Shrimukh Vivek" in the year 1971. When this job was assigned to him Baba Ji sounded him Look Gyandra! You have had to undergo a very difficult test of your life. You have had to lay down your life for this service but you will regain everything miraculously and that miracle took place on 24th September 1972 which you will read in the next pages.

Baba Nirbandhan Dev breathed his last on Akadashi—11 days after Diwali in the year 1973.

Before I disclose the most interesting and unbelievable hidden character of Udasin Sampardaya's most thrilling and full of miracle of Baba Nirbandhan Dev Ji performed on one of his most trusted disciple Master Gyandra Ji of Ganauli, District Ghaziabad, Uttar Pradesh, I wish to introduce my life long most trusted friend and guide Choudhary Chup Singh Ji, who has been a close contemporary of (C.K. Nair, who was one of the 14 Jewels of Mahatma Gandhi; who was nominated by the father of the Nation to arrange, manage and look after the Congress affairs of Delhi State. He was the man who set up Gandhi Ashram, Narela, Dr. Sukh Dev Ji, the grand old man of Delhi, Lala Onkarnathji, Lala Sham Nath Ji, Lala Deshbandhu Gupta, Choudhary Braham Prakash Ji, Maharaja

Naunihal Singh Ji (Namdhari) member of Parliament, brother of Maharaj Pratap Singh, Mehar Chand Ji Khanna and Shri Jag Pravesh Chandra) visited my hut one day. He accompanied a beautiful person with a dynamic personality dressed in pure Khadi introduced with him with the following words:-

Ralhan Sahib !!! Please meet my friend Master Gyandra Ji; who is a teacher in Government High School, Tilpat. He belongs to village Ganauli, Post Office Charodi, District Ghaziabad (U.P.). His father Chaudhari Hari Singh was a renowned person in the area due to his contribution in the social, cultural , religious and political fields. His family has a great regards and reputation in the area. Gyandra Ji has inherited the spirit of social service and help to suffering mankind in his very childhood. He was born on 1.7.1929, graduated from Punjab University in 1973 and took teacher training from Delhi in the year 1953-54 and was appointed as a teacher in the Govt. School, Bhondsi Punjab and later on posted as a teacher in the year 1958 in Govt. High School, Tilpat.

From Bhondsi Primary School he was transferred to Government Primary School, Anangpur in August 1957. As he was well-known social worker and eager to educate Gujar Community, there he also made selfless service and was succeeded in upgrading that Primary School to Government Middle School. As Anangpur was selected as model village by Chaudhary Ram Narain, President Gram Sahyog Samaj previously General Secretary Bharat Sewak Samaj. He was very close to Pandit Jawaharlal Nehru. Pandit Nehru spoke to Punjab Chief Minister Sardar Pratap Singh Kairon to help Chaudhary Ram Narain in his venture to develop the village and other rural areas in Punjab.

Due to the tireless efforts of Gyandraji, the School upgraded. The village Panchayat was grateful of Gyandraji, they donated Rupees Twenty Five Thousand in cash and a new Jeep to Chaudhary Ram Narain.

Sardar Pratap Singh Kairon alongwith his cabinet

colleagues visited Anangpur in the year 1960 and was fully impressed to see the contribution of Choudhary Ram Narain and Master Gyandraji and his colleagues Choudhary Tunda Ram, member Block Samiti and other colleagues.

On this occasion, the Chief Minister Sardar Pratap Singh Kairon upgraded this Middle School to Government Higher Secondary School, Anangpur. Not ony that the Chief Minister, awarded Master Gyandra Ji due to his showing excellent results of the School by giving two advance increments and was honoured publically.

In the present day political leadership; Shri Avtar Singh Bhadana, member Parliament, Kartar Singh Bhadana, Minister Haryana Government, both these brothers has been students of Master Gyandra Ji. They are worthy son of Chaudhary Nahar Singh; a brave, honest and religious person of village Anangpur.

In the year 1965 Gyandra was transferred to Government Middle School, Sarai Khawaja, District Faridabad. There he also devoted his every nerve to coach the students. In this school, there was a student named Sat Pal who topped Middle School examination in the district. He was such a brilliant student that he topped from Middle to M.Sc. examination. Now a days he is devoting full time as a sanyasi and heading Jiwaji Institute, Sheetal Chchaya, Brindaban, U.P.

As his Gujar Bradari was very backward in the educational fields he pledged to change that situation and to implement his ideals he went door to door to collect one brick from every person whom he approached for this purpose. It took years to him to collect sufficient bricks, land and other material to set up a college in the area. Ultimately his tireless efforts bore fruit and he succeeded to set up a Janata Inter College at village Saroli, Ghaziabad. He not only set up this college he also started two schools, Primary School and Senior Secondary School at his village which are being run and looked after by his both the sons. The setting up of a College and two Schools in the area when he was in Government service. As he is a man of action and a real social worker he devoted his every nerve for the upliftment of the oppressed and depressed in his area. While he was in service he came in contact with a Udasin Yogi named Nirbandhan Dev at his Ashram situated in Abul Fazal Enclave, Okhla Delhi. He was so impressed by the dynamic personality of the saint that he became his follower whole heartedly. Now after meeting his Guru there were only two motives of his life—Teaching and Devotion to his Guru and meditation. One day when he was in the Ashram he recited 'Mukhuwak of his Guru in the presence of Shri Hem Raj who was a close associate of Baba Nirbandhan Dev Ji—He said: in Hindi

'Nam Rup Sab Atma Guru Mukh Jane Gyan'
Ullu Ko Samjhe Nahi Prakate Prakash-e-Bhan

Shri Hem Raj asked Guruji who is this gentleman? Shri Maharaj Ji said, Don't you know, this is the same Gyandra who remains always with me in the past and now in the present will also be with me in the future. Hem Raj was stunned to learn.

One day Gyandra Ji informed Baba Nirbandhandev Ji that "Maharaj Ji our school has been closed for summer vacations and I humbly offer my services at your disposal. Guru Ji advised him to devote his spare time in your family affairs. Gyandraji apprised Guru Ji that he never undertake any domestic job. My first and last service is dedicated to the lotus feet of my Guru. Guru Ji was pleased to know and advised him to come on coming Sunday to collect one sacred book to be translated in Hindi. Gyandraji was over-whelmed to know the faith of his beloved Guru in him. Because he was happy on his good fortune as he was selected by his Guru for a noble cause ignoring his two old disciples who had been living with him for the last about forty years.

On the appointed Sunday Guru Ji handed over that sacred book to Gyandra Ji. The hand written manuscript was in Gurmukhi script; which he never read. Miraculously when he opened the book and with the blessing of his Guru he started reading the manuscript quite easily and without any difficulty. He gone through the book twice—understood the hidden message and chalked out the programme to translate it in Devnagari (Hindi). When he was undertaking this historical project he was putting up at the Farm House of Rao Tofa Singh of Sarai Khawja, district Faridabad. He completed the job within 1½ months time and handed over to Guruji. Occasionally Guru Ji used to say that whosoever undertook the translation of this Granth has to die publically without fail. When Gyandra Ji was busy in translating the sacred Granth Guruji used to said to the gatherings at his Ashram that some mericulous thing is going to happen very soon! He asked? Can you believe that if a person is cremted by his family members and that person reached his home safely? Hearing this one person named Mangaldas from the gatherings asked Guruji—Guruji how it is possible? When a person is cremated it is next to impossible to see him as a living human being.

Guru Maharaj Ji replied—Kabhi Na Man-e- Guru Ki Kahni - Jab tak Na Dikhe Apne Naini (Don't believe Guru's saying until and unless one sees with is own eyes).

On 24th October 1972 when Gyandra Ji reached Ashram there was no body in the Ashram. Seeing Gyandra Guruji advised him to bring one cup of tea with some snacks. He did the needful and sat near the lotus feet of his Guru. Babaji said— Gyandra! you know both the gentlemen who are with me like my shadow—know nothing about me—Gyandra replied—Bhagwan I know all about you. I have always witnessed the glimpse of my Lord in you. Babaji said this is due to your belief in me. Gyandra Ji replied—this is all due to your blessings. He requested that Prabhu I do not want any worldly thing from you. I wish to breathe my last breath in your lotus feet. This is my final request.

After this meeting one day Guru Ji with his spiritual powers created a duplicate Gyandra and put him on a bench in a Verandah of Irwin Hospital as a sinking patient. The patient was in a critical position—though he was breathing but was not in a position to speak. Treating him as a hopeless patient he was admitted in the Emergency Ward of the Hospital. He was kept on Gulucose and Oxygen, but after midnight he expired and body was kept in the Mortury as an un-identified person. Next day when body was brought to the Postmortem table of Dr. Vishnu Kumar and his assistant Dr. Yash Pal Rana (village Kheda Kalan, Delhi), he recognised him as he was a close relative of one Shri Jogindra Malik of Sonepat; who has been a teacher and posted at Bapu Park, Kotla Mubarakpur, New Delhi's MCD Primary School. Dr. Rana requested his senior Doctor Vishnu Kumar to delay and wait as he has recognised Shri Gyandra Bansal. Shri Jogindra Malik conveyed the message to his family members at Ganauli. When the messenger reached his home his father was reading Sukh Sagar and his wife was looking after the animals. He informed his father Choudhary Hari Singh that Baba Ji, Master Ji had met with an accident—he had died and body is lying in the Irwin Hospital.

On hearing this news hell broke out—father stunned and his wife wept bitterly. Entire population of the village flocked at his house to know the sad and sudden demise of a prominent person and renowned educationist and well known social worker of the area. He was beloved of all. He commanded a great regards among the common people and particularly among the Gujar Community of the area. About 50 persons alongwith his nearers and dearer ones rushed towards Irwin Hospital to bring his dead body.

As Gyandra was the founding father of Janata Inter College, Saroli, he was beloved leader of the villagers. Hundreds and thousands of people participated in his cremation ceremony. Being a well wisher of Gujar community he was a known figure of the area and beloved and worshipped by every one. There was a pin drop silence on that occasion. His dear ones were unconsolable. All the prominent persons from all shades of life came to his father to express their heart felt condolenses and to console them.

When the news of his demise reached in the village of

Anangpur to his son-in-law (Damad) then he sent a person to Government High School, Tilpat to find out whereabouts of his father-in-law. When the person concerned reached there he saw Gyandra Ji devoted in the translation work assigned by his Master "Mukh Vivek" and was reciting:-

Hari Om Nirankar Parmatma !

Tum he ho Tum he ho Tum he ho

Sarv Sarishti Ke Karta Purshottam

Tum he ho Tum he ho Tum he ho

The said person came, stayed with him, inquired about his well being and left to Anangpur and reported the matter to Shri Jaya Prakash and requested him to immediately rush to village Ganauli to find out the facts. When he reached there he saw a sea of humanity assembled there to express their sympathies and condolenses and to console family members of Gyandra. He did not expressed his condolenses to any one and straight away reached his elder brother and asked what you have done ! He told him that Gyandra has passed away. He informed him what do you talking about. He is very much alive and busy in rewriting his Guru's Granth at Tilpat. He did not believe him.

At about 9 p.m. his son-in-law (Damad) Jayaprakash and his nephew Narindra Kumar reached Tilpat. When they reached there he was busy in reciting the 'Name' of his Lord. Jayaprakash and Narendra related the whole incident to him. When asked why don't you come to me first? They said when everything was recognised which resembled you then we deemed fit to reach Ganauli first instead of coming to Tilpat.

After the exchange of views all the three persons proceeded towards Ganauli. At about 12.30 at night they reached Ganauli. Reaching at his door steps he called to his father and elder brother in raised voice, but no body responded. After few moments his elder brother who had cremated him came out of the house and stared at him. Others also followed him and a number of people came out of the house. No body dared to approach him or to touch him. He simply said—God knows better what is happening? Everybody was quite mum and shivering—When Gyandra named them they rushed towards him weeping bitterly and fell down on his feet. Every one was wonder struck and did not believe that Gyandra had virtually come. Every one was murmuring 'Bhagwan Teri Maya'.

One person named Harcharn pointing towards Gyandra said! brother! you are an exception in the world as you are the only person on earth who have seen the widowhood of your wife with your own eyes... when he saw his wife 'Shrimati Ram Rati'—she was badly shattered and was in a miserable condition.

Those person who had attended his cremation in the morning rushed to see him alive. The number of visitors was increasing gradually. On this occasion the sweat meats were distributed among the people and the sad occasion changed into a happy one.

In the morning his elder brother told him that I am at a loss to understand that whether you are the real person or he was real person whom we have cremated? He requested Gyandra to make haste to go to that Baba who has done this unbelievable miracle. He told his brother—perhaps you could not be in a position to recognize him as he is the incarnation of Lord Shiva himself. He insisted to meet Babaji without any delay, so that I may come out of the grief and shock of this incident.

When both the brothers reached Okhla in the Babaji's Ashram he was in deep meditation. After a while when Babaji opened his smadhi, He asked why you have brought him here. His brother questioned Baba Ji—Baba Ji what you have done with us"? We have never done any harm to you? Maharaj Ji said why are you asking this question to me? I have done nothing. Neither I know anything nor Gyandra, whatsoever is done is done by the Doctors of Irwin Hospital, or the Police or you have done it. Ask them. Men of God have always played such miracles?

In the Capital City—where President of India, Prime Minister of India, Home Minister of India, CBI, IB, CID, Radio, Television and Newspapers offices are there ask them who was that man who expired in a Government Hospital and body was handed over to his dependents by Darya Ganj Police.

Babaji further said, If you think that this miracle has been done by me and you have had to spent about Rupees 800-900 hundred. If you wish I can refund you the said amount. You see such miracle could not take place in crores of rupees. Ever you heard that anybody which had been cremated by thousands of people came back alive—Tell me !!!

After the demise of Baba Nirbandhan Dev Ji, Gyandra Ji looking after 'Shri Baba Nirbandhan Dev Ashram Trust (Registered) which is situated a few yards away from Okhla Police Post, Abul Fazal Enclave near God's Grace Public School), Okhla, New Delhi-110025 (Phone No. 6327360).

It will not be out of place to mention here that when whom after quitting Bharat Sewak Samaj in 1960 Chaudhary Ram Narayan founded Akhil Bhartiya Gram Sahyog Sewak Samaj and adopted one village named Anangpur in District Ghaziabad, Uttar Pradesh, our hero Gyandra Ji was working as a teacher in the Primary School of that village. With the help of Chaudhary Ram Narayan and active support of Gyandra Ji, that school was upgraded first of all as Middle School and later on as High School. Sardar Pratap Singh Kairon, the then Chief Minister of Punjab and Pandit Jawaharlal Nehru, the Prime Minister of India appreciated the efforts made by these two stalwarts in the field of education.

Note: 'Mukhwak' written by Baba Sri Chand was in the possession of Baba Nirbandhan Dev Ji which is now in the safe custody of Gyandra Ji. This is one of the original works of Baba Sri Chand Ji Maharaj.[13]

Karta Ram

Karta Ram was one of the audience who used to come everyday before the start of the discourse and went away after everybody else had left. He had deep faith in Bhagwan. Bhagwan also had full benedictions for him. His father was Raja Ram and mother Ratan Devi. She was realy a jem and Raja Ram was a true devotee of Raghupati Raja Ram.

He was so impressed by his teachings that he developed apathy from this world in his mind. His mother thought that he may not leave this world as he had no love for wordly allurements. He was engaged and date of his marriage was fixed. On the fixed day he was made to wear very lovely clothes and seated over a *ghori* (mare) marriage procession (Bharat) was to pass through a spot nearly a cemetry (Shamshan Bhoomi). They saw an Arthi (dead body over the shoulders of four persons).

Karta Ram asked one of his friends about the episode. He was informed that it was of Lala Des Raj who was returning from his shop when a nearby wall fell upon him and he died instantly. Des Raj was a fast friend of Karta Ram. Karta Ram was much grieved to hear about the death of his friend. He was so disillusioned from his life that he came down the Ghori, torn his wedding clothes and ran away to the court of Bhagwan Sri Chandra requested him to initiate him into the udasin sect and renounced this immaterial world.[14]

Lakhmi Chand (Controversy on date of birth): Dr. Gopal Singh mentioned in his book 'History of the Sikh People' that there is no one is clear about the dates of their birth, though both were alive at the time of their father's demise. Meharvan gives their dates of birth when Nanak was 27 and 28 i.e. in 1496 and 1497 A.D. (Baba Sri Chand 1496 A.D. and Baba Lakhmi Chand 1497 A.D.), i.e. twelve years after his marriage according to this author when Nanak was still at Talwandi (p.66). According to Kahn Singh, Lakhmi Das was born on19 Phagun Samvat 1553 (1496 A.D.) at Sultanpur and died on 13 Vaisakh, Samvat 1612 (1555 A.D.) at Kartarpur (Mahan Kosh, p. 3162). The dates for Sri Chand given by him are:- Birth, Bhadon Sudi 9, Samvat 1551 (1494 A.D.) at Sultanpur and death on 15 Asuj, Samvat 1669 (1612 A.D.) at the age of 118 years. Lakhmi Das was a married householder and Bedis of the present day claim their descent from him, even though, as we shall learn later, he was disinherited by his father for his impudence and excessive display of worldly outlook. Sri Chand became an Udasi recluse and his Akharas or Maths did a lot to propagate the faith of Nanak in their own Vedantic light even during the darkest days of the persecution of the Sikhs by the Moghals. The orthodox Sikhs, however, have never identified themselves with the Udasis, calling them a heretical sect, disapproved of by Guru Nanak himself.)[15]

Bhai Gurdas—who has in his Vars (See Var 26) denounced all detractors of the Gurus, particularly Sri Chand and Lakhmi Das (sons of Guru Nanak), Dasu and Datu (Sons of Guru Angad), Mohan and Mohri (Sons of Guru Amar Das) and Prithi Chand and Mahadev (Sons of Guru Ram Das) has not at all mentioned in the name of Maharvan, Kesar Singh Chhibar, author of Bansavalinama, however, suggests that Meharvan also compiled a Granth of his own in opposition to the one completed by Guru Arjan in which he included only the hymns of the first four Gurus but not of the fifth one, the influence deducible there from being that he did not acknowledge Arjan as the fifty Guru.[16]

Mihan Dev Ji/Mihan Sahib (1643 A.D.)

His real name was Ram Dev later on Ram Singh. He was known as Mihan Sahib. He was born in the year 1643 A.D. (Vikram Samvat 1700) in a Rajput family of Bilaspur in Himachal Pradesh. He was very clever, visionary and an intellectual. He was named as Ram Dev by his Guru Nirban Nand. He always travel in a procession like a Maharaja. He preached the ideals of Udasi sect near about in the entire India.[17]

Shri Pehul Ji (1573 A.D.-1673 A.D.)

He was younger brother of Shri Goend Ji. He was born in the year 1573 A.D. (Vikram Samvat 1630) in Srinagar. He stayed for a long time in Peshawar. He became disciple of Baba Gurditta in the year 1631 (Vikrami Samvat 1688). He expired in the year 1673 A.D. (Vikrami Samvat 1730) in Hoshiarpur (Punjab). He set up Dera of Lohare. According to book, Jogeshwar Guru the following are the six Bakhshishes:-

1. Bhagat Bhagwan Ji

2. Mihan Sahib Ji

3. Guru Sangat Sahib Ji

4. Suthre Shah Ji

5. Dewana Ji

6. Ajit Mal Ji

According to `Udasi Sikhan Di Vikhya' these are the six Bakhshishes:-

1. Bhagat Bhagwan Ji

2. Suthre Shah Ji

3. Sangat Sahib Ji

4. Mihan Sahib Ji

5. Bakhat Mal Ji

6. Jim Mal Ji[18]

Sangat Dev Ji (1640 A.D.)

He was born in the year 1640 A.D. (Vikrami Samvat 1697) in a Uppal Khatri family of village Daroli, district Ferozpur, Punjab. He was a soft spoken person. He was very kind to the down trodden. He became disciple of Karta Rai. Alongwith his Guru he travelled a lot, and visit near about all the historical religious places. In the year 1603 A.D. (Vikrami Samvat 1720) he took over as a Mahant of his village Dera. He was a great Yogi.[19]

Sanyasi Bhagwan Gir

There was a Sanyasi called Bhagwan Gir, who in order to obtain spiritual consolation, went to visit the Guru (Guru Har Rai) at Kiratpur. The Guru advised him to proceed to

Dehra Baba Nanak and join the Udasis there. This was tantamount to ordering Bhagwan Gir to relinquish his sect for the Sanyasis worship Dattatre, while the Udasis have as their Guru Sri Chand, the eldest son of Guru Nanak.

The Mahant at Dehra Baba Nanak at that time was Mihar Chand, the great-grandson of Guru Nanak. The Guru commended Mihar Chand as a man of piety. Bhagwan Gir acted on the Guru's advice. He prostrated himself before Mihar Chand, and received from him initiation, and the name Bhagat Bhagwan, or saint of God. Bhagwan Gir then travelled in various countries as a missionary, but without any success. He was not wanting in energy or eloquence, but no one would heed him or listen to his exhortations. Disheartened he returned to Mihar Chand to report his failure.

Mihar Chand told him, that if he had desired to become a priest, he ought to have received initiation from Guru Hari Rai who was the real Guru, and to have solicited his orders before proceeding on his mission. It was, however, not yet too late. Bhagat Bhagwan might even now go to the Guru and crave his blessing. On appearing before the Guru, Bhagat Bhagwan began to weep and repent of his error in not having asked his permission before he had set up as a teacher. The Guru cheerfully pardoned him, and said that he had now become acceptable in God's court. The Guru directed him to go to Hindustan and reform its people. He was not to hide his light, but put it in a conspicuous place to illumine men's minds. The Guru promised that he should be everywhere well received, and that his preaching should be heartily accepted. Bhagat Bhagwan proceeded on his mission and irrigated with the water of his instruction the dried and shrivelled hearts of his Hindustani hearers. His disciples are now prosperous land owners in the north of India.[20]

Suthre Shah (1581 A.D.)

was born in the year 1581 A.D. (Vikrami Samvat 1638) in a Khatri family in village Behirampur. He became disciple of Baba Natha Sahib who was the follower of Almast line of Udasi sect. He was blessed with so many spiritual powers.

Dere Shah, Rajala Shah and Andher Shah were his followers.[21]

Baba Wadbhag Singh Ji Maharaj

This greatman of Kartarpur was a descendent of Baba Dhir Singh's family. He was the man who cremated the dead body of Faujdar of Nasir Ali of Jalandhar after digging from his tomb. This Faujdar was responsible who set on fire 'the Thum Sahib' of Kartarpur, Baba Wadbhag Singh expired in the year 1762. A big fair is held every year at Dera Wadbhag Singh on the occasion of Holi.

Family Tree of Baba Wadbhag Singh

1. Baba Gurditta Ji

2. Baba Dhir Mal Ji

3. Baba Bahar Chand Ji

4. Baba Niranjan Rai Ji

5. Baba Bikram Singh Ji

6. Baba Ram Singh Ji

7. Baba Wadhbag Singh Ji.[22]

References

1. A History of the Sikh People, 1469-1978, by Dr. Gopal Singh, 1979.

2. Bakshi Singh Adil.

3. Ibid.

4. Ibid.

5. Shrichandra Jyotsna, 1997.

6. Avinashi Chandra, Jeevan Prakash Jeewan.

7. Bakhshi Singh Adil.

8. Udasin Kalptaru, p. 32.

9. Avinashi Chandra, Jeevan Prakash Jeevan.

10. Bakhshi Singh Adil, pp. 102-103.

11.   Ibid.

12.   Ibid.

13.   Gyanendra Ji's interview with the author.

14.   Avinashi Chandra, Jeevan Prakash Jeevan.

15.   A History of the Sikh People by Dr. Gopal Singh.

16.   Ibid.

17.   Bakhshi Singh Adil.

18.   Ibid.

19.   Ibid.

20.   The Sikh Religious—Its Gurus, Sacrad Writings and Authors by Max Arthau Macauliffe, Vol. 4, pp. 288-289.

21.   Bakhshi Singh Adil.

22.   Ibid.

11

Vani of Baba Sri Chand

Affection

One of the major teachings of Bhagwan Sri Chandra is that we should treat every human being affectionately. This affection only can establish the world-wide peace and tranquility. Love for the Universe is taken as the love for God. All the living beings are parts of the same God.

"Ishwar Ansh-Jeev Avinashi"

If we love his creatures, he will certainly love us. It is an universal law. In Sanskrit, sneh has two meanings, such as Oil and love. The earthen lamp will light till it is full of oil. Similarly, love keeps the life lamp burning. Darkness spreads all around when this love goes out of our life. Brothers become enemies of each other, father and son do not see eye with each other. Turmoil spreads all around.

"Bhagwan describes in one of the stanzas of Srimatra"

"Nirver Sandhya Darshan Chhaapaa

Vaad Vivaad Mitavey Aapaa"

"निर्वेर सन्ध्या दर्शन छापा वाद विवाद मिटावे आपा"

That is, we should enjoy life leaving aside all the petty differences and conflicts, attachment and malevolence and the feelings of enmity towards others. We should feed the lamp of life with the oil of love, affection and goodwill. He considers loving each other the highest kind of service to the God. That is why he has said.

Pooja Prem Bhog Maha Ras

"पूजा प्रेम भोग महारस।।"

Contentment

Bhagwan Sri Chandra, through his life style, has given us a lesson in contentment, we must lead a contented life. Patience is bitter but its fruit sweet. Contented mind is a contented feast. It is such a treasure that a contented life has nothing to do with pains and pleasures, attachment/detachment, grace or disgrace etc. He is at peace all the time.

Bhagwan says in his matra.

Santosh Soot Vivek Dhagey.

संतोष सूत विवेक धागे

In my Godri, pallet/tattered garment warp is of contentment and the wood is of reasoning (wisdom). I have styled my life-style on the basis of contentment and wisdom. He tries to make us understand that without these two faculties of mind, we cannot attain knowledge. Because the material cause of cloth is its warp and woof made of cotton thread. Suppose if there had been no cotton, then there would have been no thread, no thread then no warp and no-woof-no warp, no woof then no cloth, no cloth then no Godri, so as to say we can't live peacefully without contentment. We cannot enjoy life without knowledge. Bhagwan has told us that contentment and reasoning are the material cause of knowledge, we cannot decide correctly without the help of reasoning. That is why all the greatmen have talked about contentment being more than a kingdom.

They have said

GODHAN, GAJDHAN, BAJIDHAN AUR RATAN DHAN KHAN,

JAB AVEY SANTOSH DHAN, SABDHAN DHURI SMAAN

Bhagwan tries to make us understand discontentment is the root cause of all disputes, scrambles and altercations. Everybody, every family, every country is busy in worst kind of illegal activities, atrocities, injustice, violence, corruption, misconduct and cruelities. Discontentment simmers lust, lure and desire in the mind of human beings. That is why Bhagwan has asked us to beware of all these bad habits and to lead a life full of contentment. He opines.

TOPI HARI CHIT SANTOSH VICHAARM
DHARE SEES SO UTRE PAARM

टोपी हरि चित्त संतोष विचारं। धरे सीस से उतरे पारं।।

that who shuns desires and lust and leads a contented life, engrossing his mind in the memory of his God, enjoys the divine shelter of the almighty God.

Bhagwan himself was a contented soul right from his early childhood. He was satisfied with whatever was given to him for eating, drinking and clothing. He never insisted for any thing speical for him like many other children. Sometimes he had to live without food and shelter and was ticked of by her mother Sulakshini on coming home (returning).

He had no lust for mundane articles, had he desired so he would have lived a settled family life like many other worldly beings. But he knew well the part he was destined to play in this world, for that reason he abandoned all the mundane desires and worked for the uplift of suffering fellow-beings.

He was a contented soul in real sense of the word. He had subdued all his passions.

Courage

"We must be courageous", is one of the teachings of Bhagwan Sri Chandra. If you think that your stand is right, then you must stand boldly for your cause, come what may. We must not fear the opponent however strong and sourceful he may be. Inferiorty complex must not enter our thoughts. One who is on the right track and who is bold enough, can never fail. He wins in the long run.

Ruler of Kandhar, Kamran and Yaqub, the ruler of Kashmir were oppressing their Hindu citizens. It was not easy to stand against them. Injustice, tyranny, outrage, corruption and immorality were the ruling factor. No religion was safe other than the Islam (Muslim).There was no rule of law; instead of law, the writ of the religious bigots of Islam ran large. Hindus were not allowed to blow the conch-shell or to strike the bell according to their style of worship. There were daily forced conversions to Islam. It was not an easy job to speak against such rulers. Bhagwan Sri Chandra decided to fight against these odds to end their misdeeds. This was an act of sheer courage and boldness.

Desireless Deeds

Bhagwan Sri Chandra has taught us to practice Karma Yoga alongwith Gyan Yoga and Bhakti Yoga. According to a Shloka of Geeta, Karamanevadhi Karastey Ma Phaleshu Kadachana; Bhagwan tells us to indulge in desireless deeds; meaning that you should do your work as if you are performing your duty without caring for the results; as we are free to do our work,we have control over our deeds, not on its results. Some understand it in a wrong way, saving that why should we work at all if we have no control over their results. But they are unable to understand the purport of (hidden design/meaning) and shun work. It simply means that you should not waste your valuable time thinking about the outcome of the deeds, utilise your time in doing your work whole-heartedly with full devotion. If the work is done perfectly, the outcome will certainly fall in line. It must lead to success, so it is not advisable to shun doing your duty.

We are told that there are three different routes to reach the citadel of God. Gyan (Knowledge), Karma (deeds) and

Sadhna (worship) that is through Gyan Yoga, Karma Yoga and Bhakti Yoga. Sri Sankracharya, a monoistic believed that the path of knowledge is the only way to the attainment of God. Sri Ramanuja and Sri Madhva-Charya opine in favour of Bhakti, as the way of worship is the only way to reach the door of God.

They say it is not necessary to profess knowledge and do work for the attainment of the Lord. Bhakti or the worship is the only way by which a worsnipper can have the Lord. When the Lord showers his kindness on the be:ng, he attains salvation.

Bhagwan Sri Chandra's views on Gyan, Karma and Bhakti are quite different from other Sects. He takes all the three elements as different faces of the same.

Whereas Gyan and Bhakti help a person, who is pious of attaining salvation, to get riddance of the mundane attachments and progress on the path of spiritualism, then the same aim can be achieved through the practice of selfless deeds.

It does not behave of a true Udasin shunning Karma. Work is essential but one should not be disturbed, worried or anxious about the good or bad reward of ones deeds. It should go on working completely free of concern about the result.

Bhagwan Sri Chandra was gifted with an unshakable mental equilibrium. He was equally disposed towards all the conditions like thick and thin, joy or sorrow, delight or grief, respect or disrespect and so on. Such a person could only indulge in detached deeds, because a person with unstable mind or a wishful man could not bear any unfavourable result, however, minute it might be.

So whereas Bhagwan by saying in his Matra "AKAL SANOJH PREET KE BAN" establishes the supremacy of knowledge (Gyan) and Devotion (Bhakti) by quoting NIKARAM JEAN TATVA KA JOURA tries to tell us about essentiality of NISHKAM KARAM detached deeds alongwith knowledge and devotion to achieve the God. Thus Sri Chandra recognises all the three elements knowledge, devotion and unattached deeds, so as to gain the God.

Bhagwan Sri Chandra had explained the unattached deeds to the enquiring Sidhas by saying that this question was related with both the spiritualism as well as materialism. He demonstrated the practical aspect of this desireless deed theory to the world through his own life style. For example, his moving from pillar to post on foot to relieve the sufferings of the depressed and aggrieved people, to inspire Bhamashah to help and support Rana Pratap fighting for the honour of the motherland; to inspire samrath Guru Ramdass to prepare some able disciple, to stand against the oppression of Yaqub and Kamran; are some of the glaring examples of selfless and desireless work in the service of mankind.

He had no interest of his own in such deeds. Had he desired a settled life, he could have done so, but he did not do so.

Bhagwan Sri Chandra was a true Karam Yogi and a staunch Udasin in the real sense of the word. Every deed of his was selfless. He was an contented soul and a Sobre Yogi having full control over his passions. He did not aspired for any material article. He used to live without food and sleep for a number of days. Throughout his life he managed no shelter for himself. He was stable through heat-cold, grief-pleasure, respect-disrespect, gain-loss etc. He considered every human being as his own self and had malice towards none. He was always absorbed in his inner self and lived an unattached life, free from the bonds of Maya, illusion and attachment.

Sundar Kavi, a poet, has described the qualities of such a great soul in the following way.

Kaam hi na Krodh jaake, Lobh hi na moh taake.
Mad hi na matsra, Na kou hi vikaari hai.

Dukh hi na sukh maaney, Paap hi na punya jaane.

Harash na shok aaney, deh hi te nyaari hai.

Ninda na prashansha kare, Raag hi na dwesh dharey.
Len hi na den jaake, kachhu na pasaari hai.

Sunder kahat, taki Agam agaadh gati.
Aiso koyu Saadhu, hi to braham urdhaari hai.

काम ही न क्रोध जा के, लोभ ही न मोह ताके
मद ही न मत्सर, न कोऊ ही विकारी है।।

दुःख ही न सुख माने, पाप ही न पुन्य जाने
हर्ष न शोक आने, देह ही ते न्यारी है।।

निन्दा न प्रशंसा करे, राग ही न द्वेष धरे
लेन ही न देन जाके, कछु न पसारी है।।

सुन्दर कहत, ताकी अगम अगाध गति
एसो कोऊ साधु, ही तो ब्रह्म उरधारी है।।

Eternal Bliss

The biographical details from the life span of Bhagwan
Sri Chandra tell us to strive for the attainment of pleasure,
peace, contentment and Bliss. Such a state of mind is achieved
only by the stability, while our mind is indulged in the service
of the God, worshipping him with utmost devotion. Bhagwan
replying to a question asked by a sidh, says

Sharam Ki Mudraa, Shiv Vibbuta

श्रम की मुद्रा शिव विभूता

Sharam is the eternal bliss, for which everybody in this
world is in search of. But unfortuntely, due to misconception,
it desires to attain it through the wordly treasures, those are
material cause of all human sufferings, are destructible and
do not lead to eternal bliss. It tries to find out the bliss in those
things which do not contain it. Only a very small number of
seekers opt for the real road to permanent happiness. That
eternal bliss could only be obtained through knowledge and
true devotion.

In a stanza, of Sri Matra

HARI BHAKTI MRIGANI LAI PAHIRE GURUPUTA

Bhagwan tries to bring it to our notice that true devotion towards God is the fountain head of real pleasure or eternal bliss. So in the eyes of Bhagwan Sri Chandra, worship and devotion to the God is the only way to achieve eternal bliss.

There exists not a single person in this world who desires giref and sorrow, everybody wants pleasure and is busy like a bee to attain its goal. In search of pleasure, he goes for the construction of a house, earns lot of money, collects more and more property and buys large bungalows (mansions) installed with all the gadgets of modern facilities. What for he tries to do all this? Because he likes to have maximum pleasure and bliss. But why is he in so much agony although he owns each and every material of this world? Because the real pleasure is not within those materials.

This eternal bliss resides hidden under the fifth sheeth, that is Anandmay Kosh, out of the five sheeths within this human body. Unknowingly, this person tries to search this eternal bliss in perishable articles. The eternal bliss, covered under the blissful sheeth, (आनन्दमय कोश) can be attained through pure sentiments of devotion, penance and knowledge. Bhagwan Sri Chandra warned every devotee saying "ALAKH PURASH KA SUMIRAHO NAAM" that is you should try to locate that eternal bliss within yourself rather to go in its search in property and family members.

All these visible wordly things are the root cause of all the sufferings; either find the locale of the wanted pleasures or be drowned in the whirlpool of worldly affairs.

Bhagwan is warning the fellows drowned in materialism, not to go far into the pathless dense jungle of mundane sentiments lest you become harmful to your fellow citizens. No doubt money is essential for the fulfilment of basic needs like food, clothes and shelter, but it is not everything, it is not the fountain head of eternal pleasure. You can reach this fountain head only with the help of your guide (Guru) and with the grace of almighty, the God. So leaving aside the bondages of Maya from your heart, come into the protection of the omnipotent who is giver of the eternal bliss. If you waste your time and energy in the bewitching web of worldly illusion, you may loose your hard earned human body, which is called rare and scared i.e. not easily available and difficult to achieve or attain.

So he advises us to shun all the shades of this delusive ignorance.

"MAYA MOHINI SAKAL TIYAG"

He does not mean that you should leave all your personal belongings, all your property move into the dense jungle and meditate there. He only desires us to keep control over ours emotions. These should not gain an upper hand and subdue over higher pursuit for eternal bliss.

This can be more easily understood through the following examples. A bird can fly only with both wings intact. It cannot fly with one wing wounded or lost. In the same way a human being can enjoy the fight of eternal bliss only if it has both of its wings of materialism and spiritualism healthy and balanced. We need both worldly affairs and spiritual pursuits in a balanced way to enjoy pleasure and perfection in the shelter of the master of this universe.

For this very reason, Bhagwan repeatedly warns us about this transitory world, it is not for ever, we have a very short span of life and have a lot of things to do like play, study (read and write) marriage, worship, pilgrimage, eat, sleep, convalesce after an illness etc., before this life comes to an abrupt end. It is possible only if we start thinking in this direction right now without wasting more time.

We have to do many things but have a limited span of life, half of our life is spent in sleeping and most of the remaining period we have to do our daily work for a fine living. One is left with a very small amount of time to be utilised in the higher values of worship and selfless service to humanity and we ourselves are our own judge to see how we adjust and utilise our time.

Equanimity

We should try to follow the doctrine of Vasudhev Katumbhkam and should take every human being as our own friend, relative and well wisher. Bhagwan's heart was full of pure feelings for the whole of mankind. He considered none his enemy of opponent whatever his/her cast, creed or religion may be, he took everbody as his own friend.

Violent beasts such as snakes and lions, considered dangerous for human beings, were found sitting by the side of Sri Bhagwan, leaving behind their inherent animity. He considered the pleasures and pains of all the beings as his own. He took all the creatures as his own self.

He had imbibed in his innerself such a fire by the interaction of continuous Yogic exercises and three-fold qualities of mind viz. Satogun Purity and Goodness, *Rajogun*, luxuriousness, marry making, exhibition and *tamogun*, darkness and ignorance, that all such passions like sorrow, sufferings, pleasure and pain, Heat and Cold, Prestige, respect, disrespect were completely burned. Sri Chandra Bhagwan tries to bring home the above said feelings to the equising Sidha's in his Sri Matra Sastra.

> Trai gun Chakmak Agni Mathi Payi
> Dukh Sukh dhuni dai jalayi (Sri Matra)

> त्रैगुण चकमक अग्नि मथि पाई।
> दुःख सुख धूनी देहि जलाई।। (श्री मात्रा)

that we need fire to keep warm the innerself also alongwith the outer body composed of five elements, such as air, water, fire, earth and void (Sky) as the inner body is the real basis of the outer body. So the inner fire is far more important than our outer fire (dhuni).

All the mundane feelings such as pleasures and pains,

Heat and Cold, happiness and sorrow, loss and gain, censure and praise, respect and disrespect are reduced to ashes when the inner fire is set aglow.

Bhagwan desired the highest degree of purity and progress for India. For this reason, he tried to evolve an ideal model of communism five centuries ago. In his sight nobody was of higher or lower grade. He told that all human beings are equal and inter-related. He opined so in the 26th Stanza of his Matra:-

Sayah Safaid Zard surkhayi jo lai pahrey so gurbhai "26"

स्याह सफैद जरद सुरखाई जो लै पहरे सो गुरभाई ॥२६॥

In fact, he wanted to revitalize the wornout Vedic religion. The Hindu religion was torn into pieces due to its rules of regimentation of the Indian society. Due to this bickering they were subjected daily to the atrocities of Mughal Rulers. To bring together these bickering factions of the society, he wrote in the above stanza. In fact, Bhagwan was not against the intruders, but he was certainly against their injustice and atrocities. He was fighting on dual fronts; on the one hand against the internal bickerings and on the other hand against the misrule of Mughal invaders.

Besides this, Black, White, Yellow and Red colours symbolize Sudra, Brahman, Vaishya and Kshatriya casts according to the Hindu religious scriptures.

Bhagwan wants to bring home the fact that any body who wears robes of any one of the above quoted colours is our Brother-in-religion. He may belong to any of the four castes/VARNAS, it makes no difference. We take him as our Guru Bhai or Brother in religion. He opines in one of his matras. RAKTA, PEETA, SYAMA RANG SAFAID. Sidh Dekh Sisya Kariyo Het. Rank Bhoop Sabek Saman, Yeh Vairag Udaas Gyan.

Varna has been described of dress clothes, cover, cladding, Sheath, form, appearance etc.

The Brahman (white) Kshatriya (red), Vaishya (yellow)/ Sudra (black), all the four divisions of Indian Society and their covering (clothes) material earth, water, air, sky, fire and the spirit (aatma) is the same in all the cases.

As there is no difference in their making, so there should be no divisions on these lines. So, please end all this conflict, be one and think everybody as your own brother.

He says:

"DWAIT BHED UDAIYE EHO SIDH DHUNI LAIYE"

"द्वैत भेद उड़.इये, एहो सिद्ध धूनी लाइये।।"

This quotation engulfs in itself the spiritual message and it also conveys the wordly meaning as such that leaving aside the concepts of low, high, kshatriya, Brahman etc., all human beings are just brothers.

Patriotism

Bhagwan Sri Chandra's life shows us the glorious path of loving one's motherland. Every citizen, whatever his/her religion, caste, creed, state, party or community may be, should have full faith, devotion and feelings of love and affection towards his/her country and fellow countrymen. Everybody should be ready to sacrifice everything for its unity and integrity. One should contribute one's might for the defence of motherland and its citizens. We, our family, our wealth is secure, if our country is safe.

These sentiments moved this Yogi renouncer recluse, rough and rugged religious mendicant Sri Chandra to help Maharana Pratap, defeated and humiliated at the hands of Mughals, to regain his self-confidence and prepared him to fight again with the help of money and arsenal supplied by a famous moneylender. Bhamashah inspired by Bhagwan Sri Chandra to help Rana Pratap.

He also inspired Samrath Guru Ramdass to find and prepare a befitting fighter and warrior who could free the motherland from the clutches of foreign invadors. (आचार्य श्री चन्द्र साधना, सिद्धांत और साहित्य तथा उदासीन मुनि परिचय पृ–११)

Selfless Service

It is fair of the teachings of this great teacher that we should indulge in the selfless service of mankind to attain higher values in our life. We should not shun service. Through service one can attain power. Nothing can be achieved without service. Wealth, property, respect, prosperity and even God could be achieved while doing service selflessly.

Patriots like Mahatma Gandhi, Jawaharlal Nehru, Vallabh Bhai Patel, Subhash Chandra, Saheed Bhagat Singh, Chandra Shekhar Azad etc., who are remembered respectfully, were devoted to their motherland and served her with all their might.

This sentiment of service can be found in the Gods category also. It has been told that different parts of our body are governed by different Gods who look after their proper functioning such as Sun God for eyes, Ashwini Kumar for nose, Indra for hands, Vishnu for feet etc. If thought deeply, Vishnu, the supreme God, cares for feet, the humblest and foremost to bear the burnt of coming troubles and sufferings. Only selfless service has kept the names of famous leaders like Lord Krishna, Lord Rama, Rishis-Munis, Bhagats and Gurus, living in the memory of human race.

Bhagwan Sri Chandra never tried to shun such a selfless service. Those who had a chance to study the biography of this great master are well versed that this unaltered mendicant, who had renounced all the facilities of easy going life, was busy moving from one place to another, humble and inferior people who were unable to look after themselves. What-else it was, if not selfless service to mankind. It is a matter of great concern that historical writers were biased while writing about this great man. They took no notice of his selfless and remarkable services towards this nation and the mankind as a whole. He was no doubt a preceptor of worldwide religion, yet a staunch supporter of Indian civilization and Vedic culture. He was indeed a great man who served with a smile. His saying "Nikarma Jeen, Tatva Ka Jora" (Matra Sastra) is the real essence of Geeta's theory of selfless deeds.

Topi Harichit Santosh Vichaarm

Once seeing Bhagwan Sri Chandra sitting by the side of his fire (dhuna), some of the aged Nath worshippers thought of planting a joke on him. They gathered around him. One of the mendicants enquired about his age? Bhagwan replied with a smile, it might be two or four years more than yours. The sadhu, who had enquired, was in his eightees. They were not satisfied and disbelieved him. But it was true, he was eighty four years of age at that time. He was a true Yogi and throughout his life looked like a child.

One Sadhu sitting by his side exclaimed. "You are looking so young, why were you telling that you were much older than your looks". It is not good to tell untruthful details. You seem to be unaware of the etiquettes and protocols of sadhus. What type of saint you are? You do not have the real symbols of saints such as Godri, Khintha, seli, topi etc."

Bhagwan Sri Chandra, who was listening to their taunting remarks, was amused at their ignorance. He pitted their lot because these gentlemen were still entangled in the outer details/symbols for a sadhu-saint.

These outer symbols are just like a uniform for a saint so that people could easily recognise him.

This outer uniform does not and can do no good/welfare to us and this is no media to gain the nearness of the God himself. To achieve God, we have to follow the path of knowledge, devotion and desireless deeds. They are unaware of these facts.

Then Bhagwan told these Naths that the symbols they have asked for, were already with him but they were unable to see those with their worldly eyes. To locate spiritual symbols, one has to acquire spiritual eyes too. You can never see these with your ordinary eyes because these symbols have somewhat different shapes. I always wear the khintha of truth, good conduct and forgiveness, seli (सैली) of truthfulness, and Godri (गुदड़ी) of knowledge.

On this mystical reply, those saints laughed at and remarked.

"He is really a child and does not know the attire of a saint. It looks that he has joined the saints fraternity lately. He will understand all the things in due course of time. He is saying that you can not see my symbols with your eyes. He is befooling us. Are we blind, who are unable to see the outer symbols like topi (cap) etc.?"

Knowing well that those were making a mockery of whatsoever he had said, politely he told them that they were not able to see and understand the things clearly due to their old age. Theirs development of intellect had also been obstructed due to ageing and so they are unable to get such simple facts.

Hearing this, all those aged Naths got irritated and furious. They remarked "If you are really wearing those symbols, then show us all. Bhagwan replied calmly that he had already explained that those topi, godri etc. were not made up of cotton or woollen thread and therefore you could not see all those by your human eyes.

Bhagwan was trying to tell them the reality of these symbols, but they got furious taking to be their derision. They remarked "either you will have to demonstrate those holy symbols or face the consequences."

Bhagwan in his mind, was laughing at their ignorance, senility and pitiable condition. They were taking him for an immatured and unacquainted person whereas they were themselves so. They have neither tried to understand the realm of spiritualism nor learned the method to realize the

God. They had left the world in a huff and wearing of large size rings in their ears had done no good to them. They had wasted their lives for triffles and dropped their gold like body into the gutter. They were now just like the washerman's donkey. Neither they enjoyed and discharged their duties nor did they serve the cause of their motherland. Now only the God himself could save them.

Bhagwan had to spare some time for debates with such ascetics belonging to the Nath Cult and residing in nearby jungles. Taking him to be just a child, they generally used to ask him questions about the outer attire of an ascetic. Not wasting valuable time, that he had to utilize in his meditation, he used to brief them through some pithy and pointed statement in a formulated form, having deep mystic disposition. In today's discussion also, they had enquired about the outer signs for a mendicant. On their constant insistance, he merely remarked.

TOPI HARI CHIT SANTOSH VICHARAM
DHARE SEES SO UTRE PAARAM

टोपी हरि चित्त संतोष विचारं।
धरे सीस सो उतरे पारं।।

Hearing the anecdote, the Naths started laughing and exclaimed you have not yet understood what we had asked you. O child it is none of your mistake, you are immature as yet, you are telling us the facts those learnt by rote, you have no experience of your own. You will learn all these details with the passage of time.

On the other side, there was a person in the form of Sri Sri Chandra, incarnation of the Shiva himself, a disciple of Sri Avinasi Muni, knowing each and every detail of Nigam and Aagam scriptures. He told those Naths that the outer cap (Topi) which you are wearing is only to save you from heat and cold, and can be seen with outer eyes, the cap and other articles which I wear are not a subject of these outer eyes. They are the spiritual symbols, and are out of your reach.

TOPI HARI CHIT SANTOSH VICHARAM
DHARE SEES SO UTRE PAARAM.
NAMASKAR TAKO BAHUBAAR.
DHARI SEES SIDH MUNI AVTAAR (1)

BRAHAMDIK, SANKADIK JOHAM
TAA KE SEES MAHIN YEH SOHAM
CHAAR VARAN MEN KOYU DHARE
BHAV BHRAM SINDHU TE PAR UTRE. (2)

Explanation

The cap that I am wearing, is made of contentment and thought by wearing it all the desires and lustfulness are destroyed for ever. The mind is well set to feel the holy presence of the God's kingdom. Any body who will wear this cap will certainly swim across the ocean of worldly enchantments.

I salute all those greatmen, sidhas, sadhus, munis who had worn this cap in the past on their heads.

CHAR VARAN MEN KOYU DHARE
BHAV BHRAM SINDHU TE PAAR UTRE

From any of the four varans (Kshatriya, Brahman,Vaishya and Sudra and the four races of the world, Black (Africans) Sufaid, white (Europians) Zard, yellow (People of Asiatic origin) and Red coloured race of Red Indians of American Continent, if any body wears this cap, woven from the threads of contentment and enlightenment on its head, all its misconceptions about the worldly affairs are removed.

Bhagwan said further that:

Yogi Yukti Rikhishwer Rakhi
Chaar Nigam mil deven Sakhi
Prathme Brahma Dhari Sudhaey
Hoye Ateet Baney Sidhaey

Bhagwan exclaimed all the four Vedas are a testimony to my saying that this cap was worn by all the Yogis and Rishis. What to say of others. The Brahama himself who has created whole of this universe, wore this cap and was called a Sidha. After wearing this cap Shiva earned the epithet of Yogeshwara or the Lord of Yogis as is said.

Aage Yogi Bhola Ishwar
Beng Paher Bhaye Yogeshwar

The cap worn by me is in destructible, nobody can ever steal or destroy it. It cannot be seen by human eyes. It is (अजर, अमर) undecaying and immortal.

Bhagwan Vishnu adored it and named it as his (Mukut). In the present times (that is Kaliyuga) Sri Chandra the son of Guru Nanak and disciple of Sri Avinashi Muni of Udasin Cult has worn it on his head.

Pehri Adi Shri Kartaaram
Mukut Naam dhar Kiyo Uchaaram
Kaliyug Pehri Nanak Poota
Pehirat Aaye Rishi Avdhoota

The cap which I am wearing is worn by all the great men of religion. So I appeal you all not to discard this uniform and outer signs of Sadhuism but you should try to wear the inner garments also.

Bhagwan Sri Chandra tried to bring to their notice that they must inculcate the inner qualities of truthful living, good moral conduct, forgiveness, kindness, meditation, concentration. Yogic exercises and the worship of the omni-present and omni-potent God. This real uniform of the human body is the only way to salvation.

It may not be an exaggeration if we say that the Matra is the essence of all the holy scriptures because all the important aspects of human relevation have been incorporated and formulated in it.

Some people think that this Matra is useful for the Udasin cult only; others can have no benefit out of it but they are mistaken over here. It was not revealed to the Nath Sidhas for their enlightenment exclusively. It has a message for the whole of mankind.

He wanted to serve this whole of mankind as the formulations are useful to all the sects and cults who are after knowledge, devotion, worship, love and affection, selfless service contentment, enlightenment, righteousness and desire free service to humanity. So it cannot be reserved for the Udasin sect only.

It is recited with full devotion and faith it can be beneficial for all those devoted to spiritual accomplishment. Daily recital of the Matra given by Bhagwan Sri Chandra bestows upon the reciter all the affluence and grants deliverance from the clutches of ignorance and liberties the human soul from the bonds of Maya.

If a faithful devotee recites this Matra one and a quarter lakh times with all the faith devotion, oblation, worship through offerings of a lamp and incense etc. to be a deity for aboration, certainly gains/acquires desired results. Its daily devoted recital also gives rise to all facilities, pleasures and peace.

Truthfulness

We should take a vow to be truthful because it is an attribute of the God himself.

He is the eternal truth and delightful. So the path of truth is worshipping the God, His adoration, obeisance, his devotion.

If we go by the side of untruthfulness knowingly than He, who is just within us, watching all our deeds-misdeeds, will be displeased with us certainly. This human body, called rightly the door to salvation is rare and difficult to attain, who knows after how many unbearable sufferings it has come to our hands. So falsehood has no place at this door of salvation. All the holy books support the above statement. Bhagwan Sri Chandra also opines in favour of the above statement in his Matra Sastra.

1. Satya Vichar Pauri Hai Jap Ki "7"

सत्य विचार पौडी है जप की ।। ।७ ।।

2. Sat Vichar Godri (Gyan) Bhai "9"

    सत विचार गोदड़ी (ज्ञान) भई।।६।।

3. Dharam Ka Chola Satya Ki Seli, etc.

    धर्म का चोला सत्य की सेली।।

All the above extracts engulf the higher spiritual sentiments alongwith the secular and practical truth. These should be practiced in this world with all our might in daily life.

Shri Maatraa of Bhagwan Sri Chandra (Roman Version)

Kahu re Baala:

Kis ne moondaa Kis ne moondaayaa
Kis ka bhejaa nagri aayaa.....1

    Sadguru moondaa lekh moondaayaa
    Guru kaa bhejaa nagri aayaa.....2

Chetahu nagri taarahu gaam
Alakh purush kaa sumirahu naam 3

    Guru avinaashi khel rachaayaa
    Agam Nigam kaa panth bataayaa.....4

Gyaan ki godri khimaa ki topi
Yat kaa aadband sheel langoti.....5

    Akaal khinthaa nirash jholi
    Yukat ka top Gurumukhi Boli.....6

Dharam kaa cholaa Satya ki seli
Maryaad mekhlaa lai galey meli.....7

    Dhyaan kaa batuyaa nrit kaa suyidaan
    Brahma anchalaa lai pahirey sujaan.....8

Bahurangi morchhad nirlep vishti
Nirbhav jangdora naa ko dwishti.....9

    Jaap jangotaa sift udaani
    Singi shabda Anaahad Guruvaani.....10

Shyam ki mudraa Shiva vibhotaa
Hari Bhagati mrigani ley pahirey Guru pootaa.....11

Santosh soot vivek dhaagey
Anek talli tahaan laagey.....12

Surat ki suyi ley Sadguru seevey
Jo raakhey so nirbhau theevey.....13

Sayaah safaid Zarad surkhaayee
Jo ley pahirey so Guru Bhaayee.....14

Treygun chakmak agni mathi paayee
Dukh sukh dhuni dehi jalaayee.....15

Samyam kripaalee shobhaa dhaaree
Charan kamal men surati hamaaree.....16

Bhaav bhojan Amrit kar paayaa
Bhalaa buraa man nahin basaayaa.....17

Paatra vichaar faruaa bahuguaa
Karmandal toombaa kisteee ghanaa.....18

Amrit pyaalaa udak man diyaa
Jo peevey so sheetal bhayaa.....19

Idaa men aavey pinglaa men dhaavey
Sushuman ke ghar sahaj samaavey.....20

Nirasah math nirantar dhyaan
Nirbhav nagari Guru deepak Gyaan.....21

Sthir ridhi amar pad dandaa
Dheeraj tahudee tapkar khandaa.....22

Vash kar aasaa samdrishtee chaugaan
Harash shok nahin man men aan.....23

Sahaj veraagee karey viraag
Maayaa mohanee sakal tyaag.....24

Naam ki paakhar pawan kaa ghoraa
Nikarma jeen tatwa kaa joraa.....25

Nirgun dhaai Guru shabda kamaan
Akal sanjoh preeti ka baan.....26

Akai ki barchhee gunon ki kataaree
Man ko maar karr aswaaree.....27

Visham garh tor nirbhau ghar aayaa
Naubat shankh nagaaraa baayaa.....28

Guru Avinaashee Susham Ved
Nirvaan vidyas apaar bhed.....29

Akhand janeyu Nirmal dhotee
Sohag jap sach maal pirotee.....30

Sikshaa Guru mantra Gaayatree Harinaam
Nischal aasan kar vishraam.....31

Tilak sampooran tarpan Yash
Poojan prem bhog mahaaras.....32

Nirvair Sandhya darshan chhaapaa
Vaad vivaad mitavey aapaa.....33

Preeti pitaambar man mrigshalaa
Cheet chitambar Runjhun maalaa.....34

Budhi bighambar kulah posteen
Khauns Khadawaan Eh mati leen.....35

Todaa chooda aur janzeer
Ley pahirey udaasi fakeer.....36

Jataa joot Mukut sir hoyee
Muktaa firey bandh nahin koyee.....37

Naanakpootaa Srichand boley
Jugat pachhaaney tatva viroley.....38

Aisee Matraa ley pahirey koyee
Aavaagaman mitavey soyee.....39

Sri Maatraa (Commentary)

Sidhas asked Bhagwan Sri Chandra, who has initiated

you in the Sanyas System and by whose order have you come to this world?

Bhagwan replies that my preceptor is Avinashi Munu and he has taught me the ways of Nigam and Aagam (Vedas and Shruties etc.)

He has ordered me to spread his message to the Urban and Rural people so that they may recite the name of that omnipotent God.

In the following stanzas, Bhagwan details the outer symbols and inner qualities of a real Sadhu of Udasin Sect.

Knowledge is my Godri.

Forgiveness is my cap.

Subjection of passion is my Aadband cover.

Sheel; Good conduct is my Kopin i.e. the piece of cloth worn over the privities.

My Kanthaa. The patchworl garment keeps me free from all bondages.

I wear the Jholl of desirelessness.

Tacties is my cap.

Guru's word is my language.

Religion is my cloak and truth is my sacred thread, Sell.

decorum and self-restriction is my girdle.

I keep the purpose of meditation always with me.

Brahm, God is my Anchal; outer covering cloth.

Under is my whisk made of peacock feather.

Goodwilling, fearlessness is my jangdora.

Worship is my underwear and merit is my flight.

Horn is the mystical sound or Anaahad Naad.

Knowledge is my Ear rings.

God Shiva is my Sacred ash, Vibhuti.

Devotion to God is my deer skin.

Contentment is the cotton and enlightenment is the thread for patching up the torn clothes.

Sadhus wearing Black, White, Yellow and Red clothes are our brothers by virtue of preceptoral affinity.

We lit the fire of pleasures and pains within our body with the help of fire stones of the three basic qualities of rajo, sato and tamo gunas.

Contentment is my begging boul and I always think of the lotus feet of my lord.

Conception is my divine food.

Judicious assessment of good and bad aspects is our wooden spade.

Kamandalu, a pot made out of scooped gourd; Tumbi and Kishti are our utencils.

He, who drinks the nectar, Amrit attains the real peace of mind.

That real power, the vital breath moves in Ida and Pingala and resides in Sukhmana.

We should desirelessly contemplate in the pessimistic monastery of his Name.

We try to light the lamp of guru's knowledge in the city of fearlessness, according to the instructions of our guru.

Stability of mind is our prosperity.

Eternity, immortality is our staff made up of wood.

Courage is our pick axe and penance is our sword.

To hold the staff, Aassa is to control the ten organs.

Equanimity is our support. We are not disturbed by jubiliation and bereavement.

A spontaneous renunciator should undo the web of Maya, web of worldly illusion and confusion; practising complete detachment from mundane attachments and bonds.

The name of God works like a Kavach, an amulet, for such renouncer.

We should control the horse of breathing with the bridle of detachment from deeds.

Truth is our family. The unattributed Nirguna God is our shield; Guru's word being our bow; Intellect acts as anulet, Love as arrow, deftness is like a dagger. Quality is like a Kataari a stiletto; a small dagger for self-defence.

Such a devotee breaks the fortress of wordly illusion and returns to his home fearlessly. He is greeted there with pomp and show and eulogical narrations are sung in his praise.

Only the immortal preceptor, Avinashi Guru knows all the intricacies of this Knowledge of Salvation; the Nirvana Vidya.

Our sacred thread is unbreakable. Our Dhoti; lower cloth is spotless.

We worship Soham on the beeds of truth.

We will return to our permanent abode by wearing the Shikha; topknot of hair of the formula given by our preceptor and reciting the Gayatri of God's name.

Concentration of mind in God's name is the ornamental religious vermillion mark on our forehead. Fame and glory is offering of water to our deceased ancestors as a mark of gratification.

Love is our worship. The eternal bliss is our food.

Humanity is our prayer; Sandhya.

Realization of God is our holy imprint; Chhaapaa.

Wearing of all these holy signs enables to undo the concepts and alternatives of mind.

Love of God is Pitambar or yellow cloth. Mind is deer skin.

Meditation in the void of ones mind on the tunes of Runjhun; the unhurt sound that yogis try to hear in their samadhi.

Such a devotee by breaking all the bonds of outer sectarian symbols, takes over the real robe of an Udasin Sadhu. By locking his matted hair over his head like a head-gear, undoes all the bondages of rebirth and attains salvation.

(Bhagwan) Sri Chandra, son of Guru Nanak has given this Maatraa for the salvation of mankind. Whosover worships it with true devotion should surely attain Nirvana, the extinction.

AARTEE

SRI GURU SRI CHANDRA BHAGWAN JEE KI

OM JAYA SRI CHANDRA DEVA SWAMI JAYA SRI CHANDRA DEVA

SUR NAR MUNIJAN DHAYAAVAT..2, SANTAN KE SAHIBAA HARI OM...

KALIYUG CHOR ANDHAKAR DEKH KAR DHARIYO AVTAARR SWAMI...

SHANKAR ROOP SADAASHIV..2, HAR APARAMPAARAA HARI OM...

YOGENDRA AVDHOOT SADAA TUM BAALAK BHAHMCHAAREE, SWAMI BAALAK...

BHEKH UDAASEEN PAALAK-2, MAHIMAA ATRI BHAAREE... HARI OM...

RAMDASS GURU ARJUN SODHI KUL BHOOSHAN...

SWAMI SODHI....

SEWAT CHARAN TUMHAREY-2, MIT GAYE SAB DOOSHAN. HARI OM...

RIDHI SIDHI KE DAATAA, BHAGTAN KE TRAATA,
SWAMI BHAGTAN ....

ROG SOG SAB KAATO 2, SHARNI JO AATAA... HARI
OM ....

BHAGAT GIRI SANYASSE, CHARNAAN VICH GIRIYO..
SWAMI CHARNAAN

KAAT DIYO BHAV BANDHAN-2, SISHYA APNAA
KARIYO... HARI OM......

UDASEENON KE MAALAK PAALAK, DUKH
GHAALAK, SWAMI PAALAK....

AACHAARYA SHIR DHARYA -2, JAG KE
SANCHAALAK, HARI OM.....

BEDI BANSH RAKHIYO JAG BHEETAR, KRIPA KAR
BHAAREE, SWAMI KRIPA

DHARAAM CHAND UPDESHIYO -2, JAVAAN
BALIHAAREE.... HARI OM......

GAUR VARNA TAN BHASMI KAAN MEN SAJEY
MUDRA.... SWAMI KAAN......

BAWARIYAAN SIR SHOBHIT -2, PIKH KAR JAG
UDHRAA.... HARI OM......

PADMAASAN KO BAANDH, YOG KO LIYO DHARO..
SWAMI YOG......

ALSO ROOP TUMHAARO-2, MAN MEN NIT
DHAARO...... HARI OM......

JO JAN AARTEE NISHDIN BAABEY KI GAVEY......
SWAMI BAABEY.......

BASEY JEE BAIKUNTH NAR NAAREE-2, SUKH
YASHFAL PAAVEY......HARI OM......

RAM NARAAYAN AARTEE BAABEY KI SAAJEE....
SWAMI BAABEY......

BAAL YATI SRI CHAND JEE-2, JAN PAR RAHO
RAAJEE..... HARI OM......

(Courtsy and with kind permission of Renerad Mahant
Ananatanand Ji Maharaj of Sangalwala Akhara, Amritsar)

MATRA SASTRA

KAHU RE BAALA

KIS NE MOONDA KIS NE MOONDAAYAA

KISKAA BEHJAA NAGARI AAYAA......1

SADGURU MOONDA LEKH MOONDAAYAA

GURU KAA BHEJAA NAGRI AAYAA......2

CHETAHU NAGARI TAARAHU GAAM

ALAKH PURUSH KAA SUMIRAHU NAAM......3

GURU AVINAASHI KHEL RACHAAYAA

AGAM NIGAM KAA PANTH BATAAYAA......4

GYAAN KI GODRI KHIMAA KI TOPI

YAT KAA AADBAND SHEEL LANGOTI......5

AKAAL KHINTHAA NIRAAS JHOLI

YUKATI KAA TOP GURUMUKHI BOLI......6

DHARAM KAA CHOLAA SATYA KI SELI

MARYAAD MEKHLAA LAI GALE MELI......7

DHYAAN KAA BATUYAA NRIT KAA SUYIDAAN

BRAHMA ANCHALAA LAI PAHIREY SUJAAN......8

BAHURANGI MORCHHAD NIRLEP VISHTI

NIRBHAV JANGDORA NAA KO DWISHTI......9

JAAP JANGOTAA SIFT UDAANI

SINGI SHABAD ANAAHAD GURUVAANI......10

SHARAM KI MUDRAA SHIVA VIBHUTAA

HARI BHAGATI MRIGANI LEY PAHIREY GURU POOTA......11

SANTOSH SOOT VIVEK DHAAGEY

ANEK TALLI TAHAAN LAAGEY......12

SURAT KI SUYI LEY SADGURU SEEVEY

JO RAAKHEY SO NIRBHAU THEEVEY......13

SAYAAH SAFAID ZARAD SURKHAAYEE

JO LEY PAHIREY SO GURU BHAAYEE......14

TREY GUN CHAKMAK AGNI MATHI PAAYEE

DUKH SUKH DHUNI DEHI JALAAYEE......15

SAYAM KRIPAALEE SHOBHAA DHAAREE

CHARAN KAMAL MEN SURATI HAMAAREE......16

BHAAV BHOJAN AMRIT KAR PAAYAA

BHALAA BURAA MAN NAHIN BASAAYAA......17

PAATAR VICHAAR FARUAA BAHUGUNAA

KARMANDALU TOOMBA KISTEE GHANAA......18

AMRIT PAYAALA UDAK MAN DIYAA

JO PEEVEY SO SHEETAL BHAYAA......19

IDA MEN AAVEY PINGLAA MEN DHAAVEY

SUSHUMAN KE GHAR SAHAJ SAMAAVEY......20

NIRAASH MATH NIRANTAR DHYAAN

NIRBHAV NAGARI GURU DEEPAK GYAAN......21

STHIR RIDHI AMAR PAD DANDAA

DHEERAJ FAHUDEE TAP KAR KHANDAA......22

VAS KAR AASAA SAMDRISHTI CHAUGAAN

HARASH SHOK NAHIN MAN MEN AAN......23

SAHAJ VERAAGEE KAREY VIRAAG

MAAYAA MOHINI SAKAL TYAAG......24

NAAM KI PAAKHAR PAWAN KAA GHORAA

NIKARMA JEEN TATWA KAA JORAA......25

NIRGUN DHAAL GURU SHABAD KAMAAN

AKAL SANJOH PREETI KE BAAN......26

AKAL KI BARCHEE GUNON KI KATAAREE

MAN KO MAAR KARO ASWAAREE......27

VISHAM GARH TOD NIRBHAV GHAR AAYAA

NAUBAT SHANKH NAGAARAA BAAYAA......28

GURU AVINAASHEE SUSHAM VED

NIRVAAN VIDYAA APAAR BHED......29

AKHAND JANEYU NIRMAL DHOTEE

SOHANG JAP SACH MAAL PIROTEE......30

SIKKHAA GURU MANTRA GAAYATREE HARI NAAM

NISCHAL AASAN KAR VISHRAAM......31

TILAK SAMPOORAN TARPAN YASH

POOJA PREM BHOG MAHAA RAS......32

NIRVAIR SANDHYAA DARSHAN CHHAAPA

VAAD VIVAAD MITAVEY AAPAA......33

PREETI PITAAMBAR MAN MRIGHAALAA

CHEET CHITAMBAR RUNJHUN MAALAA......34

BUDHI BAGHAMBAR KULAH POSTEEN

KHAUNS KHADAAWAAN EH MATI LEEN......35

TODAA CHOODA AUR JANZEER

LEY PAHIREY SADHU UDASSI DHEER......36

JATAA JOOT MUKUT SIR HOYE

MUKTAA FIREY BANDH NAHIN KOYE......37

NAANAK POOTAA SRI CHAND BOLEY

JUGAT PACHHAANEY TATVA VIROLEY......38

AISEE MAATRAA LEY PAHIREY KOYEE

AAVAAGAMAN MITAAVEY SOYEE......39

Bhagwan Sri Chandra deputed his four trusted pupils (called dhunas in udasin literature and said Mandalpatis by the Author of this book) to carry on his remaining task.

He stayed for some days at Barath and marched towards Chamba alongwith (Baba) Gurditta. On his way he stopped for a while at Mamoon village, (Teh, Pathankot, Distt. Gurdaspur).

Books Published by Priyatam Prakashan

Akhara Sangal Wala Amritsar

1.	Sankshipt Jeevani	Hindi	1962	Shravan Dass Shastri
2.	Shri Chandra Pushpanjali	Hindi	1967	Sh. Ananta Nand
3.	Avinashi Chandra	Hindi	1968	Jeevan Prakash Jeevan
4.	Shiv Vivah	Hindi	1970	Sh. Ananta Nand
5.	Panch Pushp	Hindi	1971	Kishor Chand Rajiv
6.	Sri Chandra Jyoti	Hindi	1972	Sh. Ananta Nand
7.	Aarti	Hindi	1972	Sh. Ananta Nand
8.	Durga Fulwari I, II, III	Hindi	1972	Sh. Ananta Nand
9.	Udasi De Tarle	Hindi	1974	Sh. Ananta Nand
10.	Bhav Bhey Mochan	Hindi	1974	Sh. Ananta Nand
11.	Udasi Di Fariyad	Hindi	1975	Sh. Ananta Nand

12.	Udasi Ki Pukar	Hindi	1975	Sh. Ananta Nand
13.	Dhur Di Vani	PBI	1978	J.P. Jeevan
14.	Matra Makrand	HDI	1978	J.P. Jeevan
15.	Avinashi Chandar	PBI	1978	J.P. Jeevan
16.	Jeewan Mukti	HDI	1979	J.P. Jeevan
17.	Sri Chandra Chalisa	HDI	1979	J.P. Jeevan
18.	Sri Chandra Viney Vandna	HDI	1980	J.P. Jeevan
19.	Aarti	HDI	1983	Mahant Ananta Nand
20.	Sri Chandra Chandrika	HDI	1984	J.P. Jeevan
21.	Nirvan Priyatam Charit	HDI	1991	Mahant Anantanand
22.	Bhagwan Sri Chandra Kuchh Shikshayan	HDI	1992	Mahant Ananta Nand
23.	Nitya Niyam	HDI	1992	Mahant Ananta Nand
24.	Sikhiawan Matra Satra Ate Arti	PBI	1992	Mahand Ananta Nand
25.	Sri Chandra Sidhant Manjri	HDI	1993	Mahant Anantanand
26.	Sankhshipt Parichaya Mandir Longan Wali	HDI	1993	Mahant Ananta Nand
27.	Matra Mahima	HDI	1993	Mahant Ananta Nand
28.	Priyatama Prabha	HDI	1993	J.P. Jeevan
29.	Sadguru Mahima	HDI	1993	Gyan Inder Singh
30.	Satsang Mahima	PBI	1993	Gyan Inder Singh
31.	A Brief History of Akhara Sangal Wala	ENG.	1994	Gyan Inder Singh
32.	Bhagwan Sri Chandra: Kahi Sikhsha	Marathi	1994	Mahant Ananta Nand
33.	Bhagwan Sri Chandra Some Teachings	ENG.	1994	Mahant Ananta Nand
34.	Nirwan Pritam Charit	PBI	1994	Mahant Ananta Nand
35.	Sri Chandra Sidhant Sagar	HDI	1994	Mahant Ananta Nand
36.	Sri Chandra Sidhant Manjri	PBI	1994	Mahant Ananta Nand
37.	Avinashi Chandra II Ed.	HDI	1995	J.P. Jeevan

38.	Amritanjli	HDI	1994	Mahant Ananta Nand
39.	Manavta Ke Pratik	HDI	1995	Mahant Ananta Nand
40.	Sri Chandra Dohavali	HDI	1995	Shravan Dass Shastri
41.	Amritanjali	PBI	1975	Mahant Ananta Nand
42.	Manavta Ke Parteek	HDI	1975	Mahant Ananta Nand
43.	Sri Chandra Prakash	PBI	1975	Mahant Ananta Nand
44.	Man To Sarva Dev Vasi Hoye	HDI	1996	Mahant Ananta Nand
45.	Kahu Re Bal	PBI	1996	Haman Das Sahraye
46.	Manavta De Pratik	PBI	1996	Mahant Ananta Nand
47.	Amratanjali Sateek	HDI	1996	Gyan Inder Singh
48.	Sri Chandra Bhajan Mala	HDI	1997	Mahant Ananta Nand
49.	Matra Bani Tatha Arti	HDI	1997	Mahant Ananta Nand
50.	Matra Banik Ate Arti	PBI	1997	Mahant Ananta Nand
51.	Matra Makrand	ENG.	1997	J.P. Jeevan
52.	Avinashi Chandra	ENG	1997	J.P. Jeevan

Works of Bhagwan Sri Chandra

1. Matra Makrand (मात्रा मकरदं)— This book with hindi commentary by Jeevan Prakash 'Jeevan' has been published in the year 1997. English version of this book is also available.

2. Shri Chandra Siddhant Manjari (श्रीचन्द्र सिद्धांत मंजरी)— This book Udasinacharya Bhagwan Sri Chandra has been published by Mh. Ananta Nand Ji Maharaj in the year 1993. It contains 'Guru Mahima Chalisa' in hindi language and two sets of Slokas containing 108 each.

3. Shri Shri Chandra Siddhant Manjari (श्री श्रीचन्द्र सिद्धांत मंजरी)— This book has been translated in Punjabi by Doctor Gyandra Singh of Amritsar.

4. Shri Chandra Dohavali (श्रीचन्द्र दोहावली)—108 Slokas of this book has been translated in hindi with commentary

has been done by well known Udasin intellectual Shravan Das Ji Udasin, Shastri M.A. in the year 1995 and published in the same year.

5. Shri Chandra Siddhant Sagar (श्रीचन्द्र सिद्धांत सागर) Vikrami Samvat 2051 (1997 A.D.)— This book which contains 674 pages has been published by Mahant Ananta Nand Ji Maharaj on the 500 anniversary of Bhagwan Sri Chandra. This was released in a special function organised in Delhi. The hindi version of this book contains 31 poems of Sri Chandra Acharya Maharaj. The prominent among them are Matra Shastra, Dohavali, Amritanjali, Barhamasa, (In Ramkali Rag), Shatrittu Vernan, दिनरात, Sapatvar, Shukla and Krishan Parkash, Varanmala, Barahmasa in Rag Vilaval, Tithiyan Tatha Tin Varon, Sankar Ki Var, Vilaval Ki Var and Anand Ki Var can be said.

6. Amritanjali Gutka (अमृतांजली गुटका)— This book is a version of a book entitled 'Om Jap Amrit Anjali (ओम जाप अमृतांजली) by Shri Chandra Charya Maharaj in ordinary Hindi and Punjabi for the daily use of common man.

7. Amritanjali Steak (अमृतांजली सटीक)— On the persistent demands of various sects of Sadhus Shri Mahant Ananta Nand Ji Maharaj with the collaboration of Doctor Gyandra Singh with a hindi commentary was published in the year 1996.

8. Shri Chandra Prakash (श्रीचन्द्र प्रकाश)— 108 Punjabi Pads of Sri Chandra Ji Maharaj with a commentary and compilation by Mahant Ananta Nand Ji Maharaj and Doctor Gyandra Singh was published by Akhara Sangalwala, Amritsar in the year 1996.

9. Baraha Maha (बारह माहा)— written by Shri Chandra Charya has been published which has been approved and appreciated by Sadhu Samaj.

During his stay in Kashmir Sri Chandra Ji Maharaj made commentary on Brahm Sutra and Vedas. It is available in parts. The full texts of these books has not been traced. Various scholars have discussed about his 'Teera Matrain (तेरह मात्राओं) in which the present system of Matra Shastra is the first and foremost. Except this Shri Chandra Sudha Siddhant Panchkam, Rattan Panchkam and these are known as Mukti Manjari writings (मुक्ति मंजरी रचनाए).

In the book entitled Acharya Shri Chandra, Sadhna Siddhant and Sahitya under the sub title Shri Chandra Shabad Sudha—Ganpati Vandana, Parvati Vandana, Shiv Vandana, Surya Vandana, Vishnu Vandana, Ram Vandana, Ganga Vandana, Yamuna Vandana, and alongwith Hanuman Vandana, 56 Padas have been included.

In the name of Sanskrit writings Shri Chandra Siddhant Panchkam, Rattan Panchkam, and Mukti Manjari like small writings has been published. This book was edited by Dr. Vishnu Dutt and was published by Panchayati Akhara, Udasin Nirvan, Rajghat, Kankhal in the year 1986.

(Translated in English from Professor Gurendra Kaur, Rajkiya Mahavidyalaya, Sector 42, Chandigarh. Hindi translation done by Dr. Gyandira Singh—Shri Chandra Jyotsna 1997).

12

Baba Sri Chand Ji
(A Chronological Study)
(1494 A.D-1643 A.D.)
(Vikrami Samvat 1551-1700)

1469 A.D.	April 15—(Vikrami Samvat 1526—Baisakh Sudi) (20 Baisakh: Full Moon) Birth of Guru Nanak Dev at Rae Bhoi di Talwandi known as Nankana Sahib, in Pakistan.
1469 A.D.	Oct.-Nov.—(Vikrami Samvat 1526—Kartik Sudi (Full Moon) Birth of Guru Nanak Dev.
	Note: Guru Nanak's birthday in the Sikh world is, invariably, celebrated on full moon night, in the month of Kartik (Kattak).
1485 A.D.	Engagement of Guru Nanak with Mata Sulakhani.
1487 A.D.	Marriage of Guru Nanak with Mata Sulakhni daughter of Mool Chand, Patwari of Batala.
1489 A.D.-1517 A.D.	Sikander Lodi ruled India.
1494 A.D.	September 8 (Samvat 1551—Bhadon Sudi 9) —Birth of Baba Sri Chand at Sultanpur.

1496 A.D.	(Vikrami Samvat 1553, Phagun)—Birth of Baba Lakhmi Chand at Sultanpur.
1502 A.D.	(Vikrami Samvat 1559)—Baba Sri Chand went to his maternal home.
1505 A.D.	(Vikrami Samvat 1562) At the age of 11 years Baba Sri Chand went to Srinagar (Kashmir) for his studies.
1507 A.D.	August 23rd—Visit to Heaven.
1507 A.D.	August 26th—Guru Nanak's Return from Heaven
1507-1515	First and Second journey of Guru Nanak— East and South India and Sri Lanka— approximate distance—6400 miles.
1508 A.D.	(Vikrami Samvat 1565)—Baba Sri Chand's discourses with well known Kashi Pandit Somnath Tripathi.
1509 A.D.	(Vikrami Samvat 1565)—Guru Nanak reached Sultanpur after completing his first Udasi (tour).
1510 A.D.	(1515 A.D.)—Second Udasi (tour) of Guru Nanak.
1515-1517	Third Journey of Guru Nanak—Himalayas and Tibet—1000 miles.
1517-1521	Fourth journey of Guru Nanak—West Asia, Bagdad, Mecca, Medina—6000 miles.
1517 A.D.	1526 A.D.—Ibrahim Lodi ruled India.
1518 A.D.	(Vikrami Samvat 1575)—Guru Nanak came back to Sultanpur after completing his second tour.
1518 A.D.	(Vikrami Samvat 1575)—Death of Jai Ram, husband of Bibi Nanki.

1518 A.D.	(Vikrami Samvat 1575)—After few months the death of her husband Bibi Nanki also expired.
1518 A.D.	(Vikrami Samvat 1575)—After the cremation of Bibi Nanki Sri Chand went to Pakkhoke.
1518 A.D.	(Vikrami Samvat 1575)—Meeting with Abinashi Muni at Srinagar.
1519 A.D.	(Vikrami Samvat 1576)—Daulat Khan Lodi, the Governor of Punjab invited Babur to invade India.
1520 A.D.	(Vikrami Samvat 1577)—After staying at Srinagar about years came back to Barth.
1521 A.D.	(Vikrami Samvat 1578)—First marriage of Baba Lakhmi Chand.
1522 A.D.	(Vikrami Samvat 1579)—After completing his third tour of seven years Guru Nanak reached Talwandi and set up a permanent home at Kartarpur. Sri Chand also reached there to stay with his parents.
	(Source: Sikh Itihas Ki Jhalkiyan—Teja Singh).
1522 A.D.	(Vikrami Samvat 1579)—Guru Nanak met his wife after a period of about 21 years.
1523 A.D.	(Vikrami Samvat 1580)—After the death of his first wife Baba Lakhmi Chand's second marriage took place.
1523 A.D.	(Vikrami Samvat 1580, Phagun 15, Sunday)—Marriage of Baba Buddha with Bibi Maroa at Kathuanangal. Guru Nanak Dev alongwith Mata Sulakhani and other members of the family. He was the father of four sons; namely Sudhari, Bhikhari, Mehmu and Bhana, Mahant Raghubir Singh

the author of biography of Baba Buddha has written that when the marriage of Sudhari son of Baba Buddha took place on that occasion Guru Angad Dev, Baba Sri Chand Ji, Baba Lakhmi Chand Ji alongwith his wife and his son Dharam Chand attended the function. Baba Buddha touched the feet of all the three great men; Guru Angad, Baba Sri Chand and Baba Lakhmi Chand. Guru Angad's wife Mata Khivi and Lakhmi Chand's wife Mata Dhanwanti met each other at this place.

In the marriage of Bhai Mehmu, Guru Angad alongwith his both sons Datu and Dasu and Baba Sri Chand, Lakhmi Chand alongwith Dharam Chand also participated. (Bakhshi Singh Adil p. 87-88).

1524 A.D.	(Vikrami Samvat 1581)—Baba Sri Chand set out for his First Udasi alongwith his colleagues of student life, residents of Firozabad distt. He ·visited Haridwar, Kankhal, Rishi Kesh, Lachman Jhoola, Hemkund and reached Tapat (Uttar Pradesh) village.
1524 A.D.	(Vikrami Samvat 1581)—Stayed in the Tapat village Krishan Temple and met Bhagat Dhanna.
1524 A.D.	(Vikrami Samvat 1581)—After staying in the village Tapats Krishna Temple Baba Sri Chand proceeded towards Mathura, Agra, Kanpur, Lucknow, Faizabad, Ayodhya, Prayag (Allahabad).
1525 A.D.	(Vikrami Samvat 1582)—From Kashi alongwith Pandit Somnath Tripathi via Gaya visited Patna, Mokamah across the river Gaya reached Hari Hari Chhattar Fair.

After staying there for few days he went to visit Kamrup Kamakhya Temple, Assam and from there reached Bengal's 24 Pargana Murshidabad, Midnapur and Orissa's Balasore district reached Cuttack.

1525 A.D.   (Vikrami Samvat 1582)—Baba Ji reached Kashi and visited Vishwanath and other temples there. (This was the same temple which was demolished by Emperor Aurangzeb (1658-1707 A.D.) and a mosque was constructed at that place.

1526 A.D.   (Vikrami Samvat 1583)—After staying for few days in Cuttack, reached Jagannathpuri.

1526 A.D.   (Vikrami Samvat 1583)—Uday Sen, Raja of Jagannathpuri called on Baba Sri Chand alongwith his wife for his blessing for a son. Due to the kind blessing of Babaji Raja and Rani were blessed with a beautiful son after a year.

On his return journey from Jagannathpuri via Orissa Babaji reached 'Amarkantak' Pilgrimage of Satyuga' times in the dense jungles and horrible mountains of Madhya Pradesh. It is situated at about 7 miles west to Pindra Road station at the top of a mountain. It is a historical temple. From this pilgrimage there is a source of Four rivers:

Sone river towards Bihar.

Maha Nadi river towards Orissa.

Godawari river towards Andhra Pradesh and

Narbada river towards Gujarat and Maharashtra.

It is said that in the olden times great sages of India came for meditation to this pilgrimage (Amarkanta). There is ancient Shiva Temple at this place.

1526 A.D.	(Vikrami Samvat 1583)—After staying for few days in Cuttack (Sanglabad Udasin Math) Baba Ji reached Jagannath Puri. In the memory of Babaji's visit a Math namely Mangu Math of Balu Hasan has been established. The Raja of Puri has donated 3000 bighas of land to this Math.
1526 A.D.	Babar in collision with the forces of Rana Sanga—defeated the armies of Ibrahim Lodhi, a descendent of Sikander Lodhi.
1526 A.D.	Ibrahim Lodhi was killed by Babar in the battle of Panipat.
1526 A.D.	(Vikrami Samvat 1583)—Baba Sri Chand had attained the age of 32 years when he met his father Guru Nanak Dev. When Guru Nanak left for his first Udasi (tour) Baba Sri Chand was only 3 years old.
1526-1527 A.D.	(Vikrami Samvat 1583-84)—Baba Sri Chand was about 32-33 years old when he travelled about 400 miles on foot and visited various places.
1527 A.D.	(Vikrami Samvat 1584)—After staying for some time with His (Bua) father's sister Bibi Nanki at Sultanpur Lodi, came back to Kartarpur and stayed with His parents. (Guru Nanak established Kartarpur in the year 1506 A.D. and settled their permanently after the year 1523 A.D.).
1527 A.D.-1538 A.D.	Baba Sri Chand Ji visited Kashmir Bohd Wadala, Galdi, Barath, Memoon and Achal

Batala (Bakshi Singh Adil).

1527 A.D.	(Vikrami Samvat 1584)—Nawab of Sultanpur Lodi called on Baba Sri Chand when he visited that place.
1528 A.D.	Rana Sanga was poisoned to death by one of his relatives.

(Avinashi Chandra - Jeevan Prakash Jeevan)

1528 A.D.   Baba Sri Chand countered the Vam margis propaganda of Matsya (fish), Madira (wine) Maithun (Sexual intercourse), Mansa (meat) and Mudra (Women).

(Avinashi Chandra Jeevan Prakash Jeevan)

1529 A.D.   Mughals succeeded in taking over entire India under their rule.

1531 A.D.   (Vikrami Samvat 1588)—After completing his fourth tour Guru Nanak reached Kartarpur.

(Source: Rattan Singh Jaggi—Jeevan Charit Baba Shrichandra ji).

1538 A.D.   (Vikrami Samvat 1595)—Baba Sri Chand came back to Kartarpur and stayed with his parents. During his tours between 1527-1538. He travelled for about 1200 miles journey.

1539 A.D.   (Vikrami Samvat 1596)—Alongwith Guru Nanak Dev Baba Sri Chand participated Shivratri Fair near Achal Batala (Bakhshi Singh Adil, p. 94).

1539 A.D.   Guru Nanak Dev came to Achal Batala for discussion with the Sidhs. He was accompanied by Baba Sri Chand and Baba Lakhmi Chand also.

1539 A.D.   (Vikrami Samvat 1596)—Death of Guru Nanak at Kartarpur. Both the sons, Baba Sri

Chand and Baba Lakhmi Chand performed the last rites of their father according to family traditions.

1540 A.D.　(Vikrami Samvat 1597)—During his Kandhar visit one day Baba Sri Chand in a dense jungle was in deep medittion. Kamran the king of Kandhar alongwith his colleagues while hunting killed a deer. When the servant of the king taking away the body of the dead animal Babaji came out of the Smadhi and he was shocked to learn when he saw the servants taking out the eyes of the deer. After a few moments the King Kamran happened to pass near Baba Sri Chand. Seeing Babaji the king paid his obeisance. Then Babaji pointing towards Kamran said, "Kamran! to kill innocent animal is not a justified act. He further said, look! if some one may take out your eyes from your body how will you feel? Babaji further said, have mercy on the poor and innocent and be God fearing. Kamran could not utter a single word from his mouth. He silently regretted his acts and promised not to repeat them in future and after a　long time when Kamran was defeated by Humayun, and put him in a prison cell and in the same manner took out Kamran's eyes and put lemon juice in it.

(Bakhshi Singh Adil page 99).

1540 A.D.　(Vikrami Samvat 1597)—Baba Sri Chand again reached Kashmir. He stayed there for few months and came back to Kartarpur. After few days stay there he proceeded towards Pakhoke and proceeded towards Amritsar, Sultanwind, and reached Lahore. After few days stay reached Multan and then to Peshawar.

1540 A.D.	(Vikrami Samvat 1597)—Visited Haridwar and other religious places.
1543 A.D.	(Vikrami Samvat 1600)—Started Haridwar visit - During that visit he generally stayed at Kankhal, as it was a historical place of Udasi sect. The ancient Udasin sage Acharya Sanat Kumar also used to stay at Kankhal.
1543 A.D.	(Vikrami Samvat 1600)—At Haridwar Baba Sri Chand had decided to go to Rishikesh. But on a urgent call from Sindh through a devotee named Ramchandra, Babaji proceeded towards Sindh.
	From Haridwar he reached Bathinda, then Multan and ultimately reached Thadda. This place had been a centre of fanatic Muslims and meeting with Bhagat Giri.
	From Thadda via Kachh visited Dwarkapuri and Sudamapuri in Gujarat.
1545 A.D.	(Vikrami Samvat 1602)—Humayun had been defeated by Sher Shah Suri and fleded from India. In the meantime Humayun was sitting score with his brother in Kandhar.
	From Kandhar Baba Sri Chand reached Baghdad, had religious discourses with the Maulvis and via Baluchistan and Peshawar reached Kartarpur.
1545 A.D.	(Vikrami Samvat 1602)—After attending the marriage of Bhai Mehmu Baba Sri Chand stayed at Pakhoke and used to go to deliver His sermons in the nearby villages - Jaityan, Abdal, Dhuan, Dalam Nangal, Bohad Wadala, Kalanaur, Panwann, and Barath etc. (Bakhshi Singh Adil).

1545 A.D.	(Vikrami Samvat 1602)—Marriage of Bhai Mehmu - the third son of Baba Buddha took place when he was 17 years old. Baba Dharam Chand aged 23 alongwith his father (Lakhmi Chand) and uncle (Baba Sri Chand) also attended the marriage (Bakshi Singh Adil) p. 85.
1548 A.D.	(Vikrami Samvat 1604, 2 Har)—Baba Manak Chand Son of Baba Lakhmi Chand was born (Origin and growth of Udasis by Swami Harnam Das Udasin).
1553 A.D.	(Vikrami Samvat 1610, Kartika)—Baba Mehar Chand, the second son of Baba Lakhmi Chand was born (Origin and growth of Udasis by Swami Harnam Das).
1553 A.D.	(Vikrami Samvat 1610)—Humayun defeated Sher Shah Suri and took over his empire from him after 13 years exile. (Bakhshi Singh Adil, p. 103).
1554 A.D.	(Vikrami Samvat 1611)—Baba Sri Chand asked his Kamalia to bring Baba Buddha immediately to Kartarpur as He had foresighted that very shortly Kartarpur will flow in the river Ravi before that a new Township would be constructed. The Smadhi of Guru Nanak had already drowned in the river.
	Baba Buddha accompanied Kamalia and reached Baba Sri Chand without moments delay they removed the mortal remain of Guru Nanak Dev and installed in a safer place in the new Kartarpur. (Bakhshi Singh Adil).
1555 A.D.	(Vikrami Samvat 1612, Baisakh 16)—Death of Baba Lakhmi Chand at the age of 59 years at Kartarpur.

1555 A.D.	(Vikrami Samvat 1612, Baisakh 13)—Lakhmi Das died at Kartarpur (A History of Sikh People by Gopal Singh).
1557 A.D. •	(Vikrami Samvat 1614)—Ultimately old Kartarpur smashed by river Beas (Bakhshi Singh Adil.)
1558 A.D.	When Sri Chand was 7 years old Guru Nanak Dev left for his first Udasi (tour).
	(Baba Sri Chand's life and Teachings, by Bhai Kirpal Singh).
1560 A.D.	(Vikrami Samvat 1617)—Guru Amar Das Ji on this very place i.e. Barath, presented his son Mohan to Baba Sri Chand and it is assumed this is the place where Guru Amar Das wiped Baba Sri Chand's feet with his long black beard, (Bakhshi Singh Adil p. 1011)
	Note: It seems that Shri Bakhsi Singh Adil is confused this incident. Because it was done by Guru Ram Das and not by Guru Amar Das).
1560 A.D.	(Vikrami Samvat 1617)—Guru Amar Das alongwith his both the sons namely 'Mohari Ji' and 'Mohan Ji' and Bhai Jethaji came to meet Baba Sri Chand from Dera Baba Nanak to Barath. A sum of Rupees Five Hundred and a horse was presented by Guru Amar Das to Babaji. After staying with Babaji Guru Amar Das returned to Amritsar (Bakshi Singh Adil) p. 101.
1564 A.D.	(Vikrami Samvat 1621)—Baba Sri Chand proceeded on the tour of Western side of the country. From Barath he reached Dera Baba Nanak, from there to Lahore and

reached Multan. After staying there for few days he reached Sindh. In this tour Somdev, Virdas and Kamalia also accompanied Him. He stayed at Hinglaj Devi Temple.

Note: Hinglaj is the place where Plate (Talu) had fallen of Mother Parvati. Hinglaj temple is situated on the Hinglaj mountain in district Hyderabad Sind—Bakshi Singh Adil p. 102.

1564 A.D.

(Vikrami Samvat 1621)—From the Thatta Via Dwarka, Gujarat and Abu Baba Ji reached Barath. (Bakhshi Singh Adil p. 103).

1564 A.D.

(Vikrami Samvat 1621)—From **Thatta** to reach Devi Hinglaj's Temple take about 9 days (on foot). From this place where **Babaji** had camped reached Dwarka, Sudamapuri, Gujarat and Kathiawad. Thatta in Sindh district was the capital of Nawab Isa **Khan;** who was fanatic muslim.

Thatta was the place where Sher Shah Suri defeated Humayun and he fled away and approached Baba Sri Chand for blessing. (Bakhshi Singh Adil p. 103).

1564 A.D.

(Vikrami Samvat 1621)—When Baba Ji reached Dwarka and he stayed at sea shore and demanded for drinking water (Bakshi Singh Adil) .

1564 A.D.

(Vikrami Samvat 1621)—Due to the scarcity of drinking water at sea shore Babaji failed to get even a drop of drinking water. The women who were fetching water from a far off place in Pitchers on their heads said sarcastically that if your Guru is so powerful why cant he provide sweet drinking water by a miracles? The sentiments of the women were conveyed by his disciples to Babaji. He put his Sankh in the earth and mericulously a powerful shower of water came rushing from the earth. This place is known as 'Shankeshwar Dham'. (Bakhshi Singh Adil).

1568 A.D.	(Vikrami Samvat 1625)—Battle of Chittaur took place between Maharana Pratap and Akbar. (Bakshi Singh Adil).
1568 A.D.	(Vikrami Samvat 1625)—Mughal captured Chittor after defeating Maharana Pratap's father Maharaja Uday Singh.
1572 A.D.	(Vikrami Samvat 1629)—After the death of Maharaja Uday Singh, Maharana Pratap acceded the throne of Udaypur.
1574 A.D.	(Vikrami Samvat 1631)—In Kashmir Kamalson son of Pandit Brahamdatta become Babaji's disciple.
	(उदासीन आचार्य का Sanchhipat Jeevan Charita by Jankidasji - Itawah (U.P.)
	(Vikrami Samvat 1575)—Arrival of Avinashi Muni, the great sage on pilgrimage of Amarnath in Srinagar. (Avinashi Chandra Jeevan Praskash Jeevan).
1576 A.D.	(Vikrami Samvat 1633)—Battle of Haldi Ghati took place between Maharana Pratap and Akbar, Maharana Pratap was defeated. (Bakhshi Singh Adil).
1576 A.D.	(Vikrami Samvat 1633)—Maharana Pratap was defeated in the Halidighati battle and faced numerous difficulties for about 20 years.

1576 A.D.   (Vikrami Samvat 1633)—After the defeat of Haldighati when Maharana Pratap was recollecting his forces he met Baba Sri Chand at Abu Parbat. After having his blessing Rana recaptured entire Mewar from the Mughals except, Chittor Mandalgarh and Forts of Ajmer.

1577 A.D.   (Vikrami Samvat 1634)—Guru Ram Dass from Amritsar reached Barth to meet Baba Sri Chand.

1579 A.D.   (Vikrami Samvat 1636)—On the request of Guru Ram Das Baba Sri Chand visited Amritsar.

1585 A.D.   (Vikrami Samvat 1642)—To reform Yakub Khan of Kashmir Babaji reached Srinagar, (Bakhshi Singh Adil).

1587 A.D.   (Vikrami Samvat 1644)—Taking advantage of the atrocities of Mir Yakub of Kashmir on the people and discontentment among them Akbar invaded Kashmir. Yakub was defeated and Kashmir became part and parcel of Mughal Empire. (Bakhshi Singh Adil.)

1588 A.D.   (Vikrami Samvat 1645)—During the battle of Haldighati Maharana Pratap was seriously injured. It was due to his horse Chetak that miraculously escaped. He alongwith his Finance Minister Bhama Shah was passing their troubled days in the hideouts of various jungles.

Once they were going for the pilgrimage of the Shivlingam situated at Abu Parbat. Haldighati is situated in between Udaipur and Nathdwara. This Shivlingam is about 12 miles from Udaipur. There is a Ashram of Udasin Acharaya Harit Muni. On this very place a meeting took place between Bhama Shah, Maharana Pratap and Baba Sri Chand Ji (Bakhshi Singh Adil).

1597 A.D.	(Vikrami Samvat 1654)—Maharana Pratap expired.
1604 Aug. 21	(Vikrami Samvat 1661, Bhadon Shudi 1st)—Guru Arjan Dev (5th Guru) completed Guru Granth Sahib and displayed in Harminder Sahib, Amritsar.
1606 A.D.	(Vikrami Samvat 1663)—The Fifth Guru Arjan Dev was assasinated by Mughal Emperor Jahangir at Lahore (now in Pakistan) (Bakhshi Singh Adil).
1608 A.D.	(Vikrami Samvat 1665)—Did deep meditation alongwith his disciple Kamalia in the dense jungle of Nanak Chak, Gurdaspur.
1608 A.D. ·	(Vikrami Samvat 1665)—Baba Sri Chand stayed at Barath and Dera Baba Nanak for a long time. (Bakhshi Singh Adil).
1608 A.D.	(Vikrami Samvat 1665)—For a short while Baba Sri Chand went to Nanak Chak near Aliwal and Kadrabad which is about six-seven miles from Batala. Nanak Chak was a lonely place and it was a ideal place for meditation. (Bakhshi Singh Adil).
1608 A.D.	(Vikrami Samvat 1665)—While Babaji was at Nanak Chak the Sidhs who had been defeated thrice by Guru Nanak in discourses at Sumer Parbat, Nanak Matta and Achal) came for discussion with Baba Sri Chand (Bakhshi Singh Adil).
1609 - 1623 A.D.	(Vikrami Samvat 1666-1680)—Baba Ji visited

Southern India and made Somrath Ram Das His disciple.

1610 A.D.
(Vikrami Samvat 1665)—Nagar Dhuan, Tehsil Batala near village Mirza Jan - if one goes from Batala to Dera Baba Nanak from left hand side about 9 miles from Batala. There is a eight corners well in the memory of Baba Sri Chand's visit. It has been inscribed on a marble slab that perhaps when Baba Sri Chand from Nanak Chak went to Dera Baba Nanak He stayed in village Dhuan. It is said that on the occasion of every Amavas the taste of the water of the well changes mericulously and proved very useful to cure skin diseases. A fair is held on that occasion. (Bakhshi Singh Ail. p. 100).

1612 A.D.
(Vikrami Samvat 1669, Asij 15)—Death of Sri Chand at the age of 118. (A History of the Sikh People Gopal Singh).

1612 A.D.
Lastly seen while crossing river Ravi. (Sikh Itihas Ki Jhalkiyan - Teja Singh).

1613 A.D.
(Vikrami Samvat 1670 Kartik Sudi 15)— Baba Gurditta was born. His father's name was Guru Hargobind and mother's name was Damodari (Bakhshi Singh Adil).

1613 A.D.
(Vikrami Samvat 1670)—On the recommendation of Mian Mir, Jahangir handed over Chandu alongwith his colleagues who were responsible for the assasination of Guru Arjun Dev to the Sikh leaders and was killed in Labore (Bakhshi Singh Adil).

1618 A.D.
(Vikrami Samvat 1675, Kartik)—Death of Baba Manak Chand son of Baba Lakhmi

Chand. (Source-Origin and growth of Udasis by Swami Harnam Das Udasin. Sadhbela-Sindh).

1624 A.D.   (Vikrami Samvat 1681)—Marriage of Baba Gurditta.

1624 A.D.   (Vikrami Samvat 1681)—Guru Hargobind dhanded over Baba Gurditta to Baba Sri Chand.

1624 A.D.   (Vikrami Samvat 1681)—Guru Hargobind alongwith his entire family called on Baba Sri Chand at Barth.

1626 A.D.   (Vikrami Samvat 1683)—Guru Hargobind dagain called on Baba Sri Chand at Barth and with his due permission took Baba Gurditta alongwith him to Amritsar.

1626 A.D.   (Vikrami Samvat 1683)—After four battles with the Mughal Army Guru Hargobind decided to shift his Headquarter from Amritsar to a hill area. After acquiring land from Raja of Kahlur started building Kiritpur.

(Source: Rattan Singh Jaggi - Jeevan Charitar Baba Sri Chandra Ji).

1628 A.D.   (Vikrami Samvat 1685, Sawan Shudi 10)— Baba Atal Rai Ji expired.

1628 A.D.   (Vikrami Samvat 1685. Chet)—Death of Baba Mehar Chand, the second son of Baba Lakhmi Chand (Origin and growth of Udasis by Swami Harnam Das Udasin).

1628 A.D.   (Vikrami Samvat 1685)—When Baba Sri Chand from Dera Baba Nanak Chak, Kadrabad, Guldi Sahib and Barath was going to Kashmir. He stayed at Charan Paduka for few days.

(Nirvan Priyatam Charit by Mahant Anantanand).

1629 A.D.

January 13 (Vikrami Samvat 1685 Magh Sudi 1)—Baba Sri Chand died at Kiratpur.

1629 Laid the foundation stone of Kiratpur.

(Encyclopaedia of Sikhism—Harbans Singh).

1634 A.D. Guru Ram Das Ji visited Barath and waited for two days for opening of Babaji's samadhi, where he was sitting in deep meditation.

1634 A.D. On Baba Srichand's suggestions, Guru Ram Das Ji changed the name of the town which he was building from "Ramdaspur" to "Amritsar" (Baba Sri Chand's Life and Teachings - by Bhai Kirpal Singh (Living by the Example of Baba Sri Chand - New Delhi Gobind Sadan Publication).

1635 A.D. When Guru Arjun Dev Ji came to visit Babaji he had to wait because, he was in deep samadhi from which he did not emerge for a long time. Guruji discussed many subjects such as his brother Pirthia's mischievous behaviour, the collecting of writings for the Guru Granth Sahib, and the instability of the water supply in Taran Taran Tank.

1635 A.D. Out of his compassion for the suffering people, Babaji gave a vessel of water from his own baoli to be poured into the Taran Taran Tank, Guru Arjun Dev Ji carried the water on his own head from Barath to Taran Taran and since then the Taran Taran Tank has never become dry.

(Baba Sri Chand's Life and Teachings" - Bhai Kirpal Singh).

1636 A.D.	Baba Sri Chand's visit to Amritsar was welcomed with great enthusiasm and ceremony.

1643 A.D. (Vikrami Samvat 1700) - Babaji arrived in Chamba when he was 149 years old and declared his end. He gave Sahansarnama and Shri Arta to Baba Mehar Chand Ji, son of Baba Dharm Chand Ji, and advised the sangat to read them as part of their continuing worship of Guru Nanak. He bade farewell to Bhai Kamalia, his lifelong companion and gave his last message to his followers. Those who wished to remain brahmachari and keep the Udasi symbols must maintain very high character and renunciation and direct the sadhu samaj on correct lines. Those who wished to adopt Udasi symbols while remaining with families must follow Udasi teaching sincerely.

Thus saying, he crossed the river standing on a slab of stone which moved like a boat and in the twinkling of an eye disappeared. Babaji's body could not be found.

(Baba Sri Chand's Life and Teachings - Bhai Kirpal Singh).

1682 A.D. (Vikrami Samvat 1738)—Sadhu Hanuman Das went to Talwandi (most probably from Dera Baba Nanak; as stated by Bakhsi Singh Adil in his book Jeevani Baba Sri Chand (Punjabi) has mentioned that after Baba Lakhmi Chand's demise. Four generations of Guru Nanak stayed at Talwandi and afterwards a few of them shifted to Dera Baba Nanak. When Sadhu Hanuman has visited Talwandi he was much pained to see the deserted look of the birth place of Baba Sri Chand and Baba Lakhmi Chand. He constructed a beautiful building there as a memorial. It is also stated that Mahant Sadhu Ram; who was the 8th generation of this family served this place with great devotion.

1921- Feb. 20   In his book 'Avinashi' Chandra, Jeevan Prakash Jeevan has quoted that the descendents of Hanumanji's progressed well (at Talwandi) and in the time of his 8th descendent Mahant Sadhu Ram this placed progressed all round. Its 10th Mahant Narayan Das faced stiff opposition, and tried to save this place of Udasin worship with all his might, but failed to save it. It is most ironical that author like Jeevan Prakash has twisted the historical facts and misled the readers. For the guidance of the readers, I have added few pages on Nankana Tragedy in this book.

13

Udasi Sampardai

Definition of word 'Udas' by Guru Nanak

During his journey a Sanyasi asked him (Guru Nanak) to define the word Udas. The Guru replied: To make use of all things in this world and not deem them one's own, but only God's property, and even to possess a desire to meet Him is Udas. (Vol. I Page 106) (The Sikh Regligion by M.A. Macauliffe, Vol. 1, p. 106).

Udasi, an ascetical sect of the Sikh founded by Sri Chand (1494-1629), the elder son of Guru Nanak. Udasi is derived from the Sanskrit word udasin, i.e. one who is indifferent to or disregardful of worldly attachments, a stoic, or a mendicant. In Sikh tradition, the term udasi has also been used for each of the four preaching tours of Guru Nanak: in this sense, udasi meant a prolonged absence from home. Some scholars, including many Udasis, trace the origin of the sect back to the Puranic age, but, historically speaking, Sri Chand was the founder. The Matra, the sacred incantation or composition, attributed to the Udasi saint, Balu Hasna, records that Sri Chand, received enlightenment from Guru Nanak, the perfect Guru, and that, after the passing away of the latter, he started his own sect.

Sri Chand was a devoted Sikh and a saintly person. His object in establishing the order of the Udasis was to propagate the mission of his father. Sri Chand kept on amicable terms with the successors of Guru Nanak. According to Kesar Singh

Chhibbar, he sent two turbans at the death of Guru Ram Das in AD 1581, one for Prithi Chand, the eldest son of the deceased Guru and another for Guru Arjan in recognition of his succession to the Guruship. In A.D. 1629 Sri Chand asked Guru Hargobind to spare one of his sons to join him in his religious preaching. The Guru gave him Baba Gurditta, his eldest son. Baba Gurditta, although married, was disposed to saintly living. Before his death, Baba Sri Chand admitted Baba Gurditta to the Udasi order and appointed him his successor.

Baba Gurditta appointned four head preachers—Almast, Phul, Goind (or Gonda) and Balu Husna. He gave them his own dress which became the peculiar Udasi garb and smouldering embers from Baba Sri Chand's dhuni (sadhu's hearth) to be taken to their new monastic seats. These Udasi sadhus set up from those embers a new dhuan each at his seat and thus came into existence the four dhuans or hearths which became active centres of Udasi preaching. Each dhuan came to be known after the name of its principal preacher. The Udasis proved zealous preachers of Sikhism and carried its message to the far corners of the country and beyond. They especially rediscovered places which had been visited by the Gurus and which had fallen into obscurity with the passage of time. They established on such spots their deras and sangats and preached Gurbani. Thus the Udasi dhuans popularized the teaching of Guru Nanak not only in the Punjab but also in far-off places.

Besides the four dhuans, there emerged another set of Udasi seats called bakhshishan, which flourished during the time of Guru Har Rai, Guru Tegh Bahadur and Guru Gobind Singh. A bakhshish (lit. bounty) was a missionary assignment conferred upon an individual by the Guru. There were six prominent bakhshishan, viz. Bhagat Bhagvanie (followers of Bhagat Bhagvan); *Suthrashahie* (followers of Suthrashah); Sangat Sahibie (followers of Sangat Sahib); Mihan Shahitaie or Mihan Dasie, so called after Mihan, the title conferred by Guru Tegh Bahadur on Ramdev; Bakht Mallie (followers of Bakht Mall) ; and Jit Mallie (followers of Jit Mall). The saints of *bakhshishes* travelled widely and established their deras, sangats, maths and akharas in distant places throughout India.

The Udasis preached the message of Guru Nanak and reverred and recited the *bani* of the Gurus, but they retained their separate identity. Baba Sri Chand did occasionally visit the Guru's who treated him with respect for being a saintly personage as well as for being a son of Guru Nanak. But they extended no patronage to his sect. However, after Baba Sri Chand had from Guru Hargobind his eldest son, Baba Gurditta, to admit to his sect, the Udasis began to receive support and guidance from the Gurus. Guru Hargobind's successors conferred bakhshishes upon Udasi sadhus. Several of the Udasi saints are remembered with esteem in the Sikh tradition. For instance, the famous Bhagat Bhagvan, Bhai Pheru of the Sangat Sahiba order, who had served in the langar or community kitchen in the time of Guru Har Rai, and Ramdev (later known as Mihan Sahib), who was originally a mashki or water carrier in the service of Guru Tegh Bahadur and who had received from him for his devoted service the title of Mihan (bestower of rain) as well as the dress and marks of an Udasi consisting of seehi (woollen cord), topi (cap), *chola* (hermit's gown) and a *nagara* (drum). Ramdev established his own order of the Udasis which came to be known as Mihan Dasie or Mihan Shahie. Another notable Udasi sadhu was Mahant Kirpal who took part in the battle of Bhangani (1689) under Guru Gobind Singh.

After the abolition of the order of the *masands* by Guru Gobind Singh, the preaching of Guru Nanak's word fell to the Udasis who also gradually took control of the Sikh places of worship. When Guru Gobind Singh evacuated the Fort of Anandpur alongwith his Sikhs, an Udasi monk, Gurbakhsh Das, underlook to look after the local shrines such as Sis Ganj and Kesgarh Sahib. When after the death of Guru Gobind Singh, one Gulab Rai, an impostor, proclaimed himself guru at Anandpur and tried to take possession of the shrines, Gurbakhsh Das thwarted his scheme. Gurbakhsh Das's successors continued to look after the Anandpur shrines till their management was taken over in recent times by the Shiromani Gurdwara Parbandhak Committee. At Nanded where Guru Gobind Singh passed away, Mahant Ishar Das Udasi performed the services at Darbar Guru Gobind Singh (Hazur Sahib) and managed the shrine from 1765 BK/AD 1708 to 1782 BK/AD 1725. He was succeeded by his disciple, Gopal Das Udasi, who remained in charge of Darbar Hazur Sahib up to 1803 BK/AD 1746. Gopal Das was succeeded by his disciple Saran Das Udasi, who served the shrine for a long period of 30 years. After Saran Das the control of the Darbar passed into the hands of the Sikhs who had, by that time, come from the Punjab in considerable numbers and settled at Nanded. In 1768 BK/AD 1711 an Udasi sadhu, Sant Gopal Das, popularly known as Goddar Faquir, was appointed *granthi* at the Harimandar at Amritsar by Bhai Mani Singh, sent to Amritsar as custodian of the shrine by Mata Sundari. Gopal Das was later replaced by another Udasi, Bhai Chanchal Singh, a pious and devoted Sikh.

Udasis recruit their followers from all castes and professions. In their religious practices they differ from the Sikhs, though they revere Guru Nanak and Guru Granth Sahib like all other Sikhs. In their monasteries, Guru Granth Sahib is the scripture that is read. They do not subscribe to the Sikh rites. Their ardas also varies. Ringing of bells (*ghanti* or *gharial*), blowing instruments (*narsingha* or *singhi*) form part of their religious service. They worship icons of Guru Nanak and Baba Sri Chand. Their salutations are Vahguru (Glory of the God). *Gajo ji Vahguru* (Hail alud the glorious Lord) of Alakh (Hail the Unknowable). The Udasis believe that after gaining *matra* one can attain *param tattva* (the highest truth) and achieve *mukti* (release). The term *matra,* lit a measure or quantity, stands in prosody and grammar for the length of time required to pronounce a short vowel. But the term has acquired an extended meaning in the Udasi tradition, signifying an incantation or sacred text. An Udasi *matra* is the sacred formula addressed to the disciples as counsel and advice. There are a considerable number of these *matras* attributed to Guru Nanak, Baba Sri Chand, Baba Gurditta, Almast and Balu Hasna. But the *matras* attributed to Sri Chand have special significance for the Udasis and are highly cherished by them.

Some of the Udasis wear white while others prefer *gerua* (ochre) or red-coloured garments. Those belonging to the Nanga sect remain naked, wearing nothing except a brass chain around their waist. Some wear matted hair and apply ashes over their body. Some wear cord worn around the head, neck and waist. They abstain from alcohol, but not infrequently use bhang (hemp), charas and opium. They practise celibacy.

Besides disseminating the word of Guru Nanak, Udasi centres serve as seminaries of Sikh learning. *Chelas*, i.e. disciples, gather around the head of the monastery who instructs them in Sikh and old classical texts. The heads of these centres travelled with their pupils to places of pilgrimage and participated in debate and discourse.

The Udasi *bungas* or rest houses around the Harimandar were among the prominent centres of learning. Udasi cloister at Amritsar, Brahm Buta Akhara, ran a Gurmukhi school which attracted a considerable number of pupils. Some Udasi centres also imparted training in Indian system of medicine and physiology. One such seat was the *bunga* of Pandit Sarup Das Udasi who was a great scholar as well as an authority on 'Charaka Samhita, the famous treatise on *Ayurveda*.

In the troubled years of the eighteenth century when Sikhs suffered severe persecution, the Udasi sadhus took charge of their places of worship. Their control of the holy shrines lasted until the opening decades of the twentieth century when Sikhs through an enactment of the Punjab Legislative Council had the management centralized in the hands of a democratically elected board. The Udasis, however, have their own *deras* and monasteries spread all over the country. The most important of their centres in the North are Brahm Buta Akhara and Sangalanvala Akhara at Amritsar, Niranjania Akhara at Patiala and the Panchaiti Akhara at Haridvar.

Udasis—The genuine disciples of Guru Nanak

Trumpp a noted Orientalist, and the first government sponsored translator of the scriptures of the Sikhs was the most prejudiced and biased of all the Western writers of Sikhism. He disregarded the findings of Forster, Malcolm Cunnigham and followed Wilson's, the most inadequate and false estimation of the nature of Sikhism, Wilson seems to hold Sikhs and the Sikh faith responsible for his own ignorance of the subject. In one of his articles he writes, "This exposition of the Sikh faith, if anything so vague deserves the appellation of a faith, is known as the Adi Granth, the `First Book' to distinguish it from another scriptured authority of the Sikhs of a later date. It is a large volume but contains no systematic exposition of doctrines—no condensed creed—no rules for ritual observances. It is an unconnected compilation of the verses of a mystical or a moral purport, ascribed mostly to Nanak, except a general accordance in a sort of spiritual quietism and the acknowledgement of one divine cause and essence of things.[1] At another place, crediting the Udasis as the genuine disciples of Guru Nanak, he says "Many of the Udasis are well read in Sanskrit, and are expounders of the Vedanta philosophy on which the tenets of Nanak are mainly founded.[2]

Udasi Sect and Dharam Chand

The successor of Angad, Amar Das, became possessed of some temporal power, and built the fort of Kajarwal. It would appear, however, that secular aggrandisement was not regarded as altogether orthodox and the Sikh, who restricted their views to purely religious objects, separated from Amar Das and attached themselves to Dharam Chand the grandson of Nanak, as their Guru or spiritual head. They then became known as Udasis, or persons entranged from worldly hopes or fears, or as 'Nirmalas', individuals free from soil or sin. It is chiefly from these classes of Sikhs, the Udasis, and Nirmalas, that teachers of the theism of Nanak are to be found in almost every considerable city of Hindustan, sometimes singly or sometimes assembled in *sangats* or convents. They have nothing of a political or military character, but devote their time to daily prayers and observances addressed chiefly to the memory of Nanak and the perusal and adoration of the sacred volume which contains illustrations of his doctrines by various hands, in different dialects of Punjabi and Hindi (Civil and Religious Institutions of the Sikhs by H.H. Wilson from the book entitled—Western Image of the Sikh Religion— A source Book ed. by Darshan Singh, National Book Organisation, New Delhi, 1999 pp. 89.)

Udasis/and Dharam Chand

These may be regarded as the genuine disciples of Nanak, professing, as the name denotes, in difference to worldly *vicissitudes.* They are purely religious characters devoting themselves to prayer and meditation, and usually collected in *Sangats,* colleges or convents; they also travel about to places of pilgrimage, generally in parties of some strength. Individuals of them are to be met with in most of the chief cities of Hindustan, living under the patronage of some man of rank or property but in all situations they profess poverty, although they never solicit alms; and although ascetics, they place no merit in wearing mean garments or dispensing altogether with clothes. On the contrary, they are, in general, well dressed, and allowing the whiskers and beard to grow, are not infrequently of a venerable and imposing appearance. Though usually practising celibacy, it does not appear to be a necessary condition amongst the Sikhs to be found in the Gangetic provinces: they are usually the ministrant priests; but their office consists chiefly in reading and expounding the writings of Nanak and Govind Singh, as collected in the Adi Granth and Das Padshah Ka Granth. The perusal is enlivened by the chanting, occasionally, of Hindu Padas and Rekhtas, the compositions of Kabir, Mira Bai, Sur Das and others. With that fondness for sensible objects of reverence which characterises the natives of India, the Book is also worshipped, and rupees, flowers, and fruits are presented by the votaries, which becomes, of course, the property of the officiating Udasi. In return, the Udasi not uncommonly adopts the presentation of the Prasad, and at the close of the ceremony sweetmeats are distributed amongst the congregation. In some of the establishments at Banaras the service is held in the evening after sunset, and the singing and feasting continue through a great part of the night. Many of the Udasis are well read in Sanskrit, and are expounders of the Vedanta Philosophy on which the tenets of Nanak are mainly founded.

The Udasi sect was established by Dharam Chand, the grand son of Nanak, through whom the line of the sage was continued, and his descendants, known by the name of Nanak Putras, are still found in the Punjab, where they are treated by the Sikhs with special veneration.

(Source: Nanak Shahis by H.H. Wilson from the book— Western Image of The Sikh Religion—A source Book ed by Darshan Singh—National Book Organisation, H-39, Green Park Extension, New Delhi 110016, 1999, pp. 107-108).

Guru Amar Das eliminated Udasis from the Sikh Community

The Udasis—This body was founded by Sri Chánd, the eldest son of Nanak. There are four subdivisions amongst them, who only differ from each other by some outward signs. They no more marry, after they have given up their household and turned Udasis (i.e. indifferent to the world); they are therefore a society of monks, though they do not live together in monasteries. Some of them do not cut their hair, like the regular Sikhs, some have short cut hair, some wear long tufted hair, and some shave head and face. They practise the Hindu rites concerning birth, death, marriage and Shradh, as all the old Sikhs did. They wear clothes dyed with red ochre and apply to their forehead a high Tilak. Their sacred book is the Adi Granth, whereas they reject the Granth of Govind Singh. Formerly they were very strict in their religious duties and lead an ascetic life, subsisting on coarse bread, baked on live coals, which they begged. As they obstinately advocated a mode of life, which was irreconcilable with secular occupations, and as they refused to submit to the authority of the established Guru, Guru Amar Das eliminated them from the

Sikh community and they were thence no longer acknowledged as Sikhs, though they themselves never gave up this claim. The Udasis have set up a Guruship of their own and after the death of a Guru some disciples whom the Guru has elected, assumes the spiritual authority, they address each other by the title of (brother). Their devotional service is very simple; in the morning and evening they play a violin or a rebek and sing a song of praise to the Supreme Lord, which is mostly taken from the Granth, imitating in this way the simple worship of Baba Nanak.

The Udasis were always a small body, as their Principles found no favour with the population. Now-a-days they have much deviated from their former ascetic habits and have for the greater part taken to secular occupations, differing only by some outward tokens from other people. Some of them bore a hole through their privities and insert a large ring of iron or brass to prevent them from fornication.

(Source: Sketch of the Religion of the Sikhs by Ernest Trumpp from the book ' Western Image of the Sikh Religion— A Source Book ed. by Darshan Singh, New Delhi, National Book Organisation, 1999, pp. 145-146).

Udasi Headquarters

When a group of pilgrims was going through the lanes and by-lanes of Amritsar and they stood a while on a bridge, a student of the local Khalsa College joined them. This student left them by the tower and went on home, after having told them some details of their surroundings. He had pointed out, among other things, the headquarters of the Udasi Sikhs, across the street from the tower, mostly hidden from view amidst the thick cluster of buildings and accessible by a narrow alleyway.

One of the "easy going" pilgrims excused himself immediately, asking leave to act on the students information and to visit the Udasi guru. The others of the party prepared to go at once to the Darbar Sahib—not that they would have been unwelcome among Udasis. There were public kitchen to serve them food at the temple, and quarters where they might spend the night in a lesser degree the Udasi head-quarters made the same sort of provision for their own visitors. Perhaps the "easygoer" who spent the first night with the old Udasi guru knew more the next day about the temple itself then the others whose first acquaintance was merely with the present normal facilities and routine; for the guru had had long acquaintance with events.

(Source: The Sikhs in relation to Hindus, Muslims, Christians and Ahmadiyyas. A study in Comparative Religion by John Clark Archer New York, Russell and Russel, 1971, pp. 22-24).

Udasi Graves

Satnamis: Their very name is derived from the Sikhs own name for God, Sat Nam, but their connection with the Sikhs is by no means altogether clear. These Satnamis are, in general, a low caste stock and are to be found mainly in central parts of India, but their scriptures and their simple worship are those of Sikhism. The Satnamis are especially numerous in the villages north and east of Jabalpur, Central Provinces. They may have been first organized from among Hindu outcaste. Hindus at any rate, have considered them not only ceremonially unclean, but otherwise filthy and immoral. Moslems, also have sometimes despised them, and they have been at times oppressed and persecuted by Moslem rulers. The Satnami movement originally took hold among chamars, in leather workers in particular and actually offered them some hope and demonstration of improvement. When, for example, they adopted the worship of Sat Nam, the formless and eternal God, they ceased using flesh of animals and certain "bloody" vegetables for food, and they gave up their idols. While Sikhs on the other hand, in the stricter meaning of the word, have kept themselves separate from their Satnami Co-religionists, these letters have not been excluded from the Sikh Gurdwaras and they are welcomed at Darbar Sahib, although very few of them, we may suppose have ever visited this shrine.

One of the pilgrim band, whose movements now engage us, came from Jabalpur where he was a member of the Sabha or association whose gurdwara stands beside a small lake known as Mera Tal. The site was once occupied by Udasi Sikhs—a special type with whom we shall get better acquainted in Amritsar who had taken it over about 1880 from a Hindu sect. The regular Sikh association, the Guru Singh Sabha took possession of it about 1907. In the small compound near the gate of entrance are still some Udasi graves on whose flat cover stones are inscribed the "feet" (foot prints) of the Hindu deity Vishnu. While these marking are unorthodox, the regular Sikhs have not disturbed these graves—any graves are commonly respected by all Indians nor is there any other burial ground connected with this gurdwara.

(Source: The sikhs—in relation to Hindus, Moslems, Christians and Ahmadiyaas. A study in comparative Religion, by John Clark Archer New York, Russell and Russell, 1971 pp. 16-18).

The gurdwaras had sprung up locally and had often been together with their endowments, in the control of local patrons, if not under the management of their immediate custodians, the mahants, for example. Although orderly and uniform control was not established until after World War I, the Government made a move in 1863 by which all gurdwaras were placed directly under Sikh Control, many of them having passed meanwhile, curiously enough, into non-Sikh hands. Some gurdwaras in fact, had passed virtually into Moslem hands ! or so it was thought by Sikhs that is, the custodians were converts from Islam, whom original Sikhs called majhbis to distinguish them from themselves, the pakka, or "true" Sikhs. And some gurdwaras of the Udasis, for example, who were celibates, were subject to uncertain and questionable succession, which prompted Udasis now and then to abandon Celibacy and to marry for the sake of a retention of property control within their own families. By the action of the government, even though it was somewhat inconclusive, the gurdwaras became on the whole more appropriately Sikh in character and in management and the question of stratification within the ranks of Sikhs remained merely social.

Sikhism must reappraise itself in the light of its own history, with due regards for the fruitful vagaries of speculation among its members and with a just appreciation of their sincere devotion. It has known how to be communal inspite of inner variations and should know from this experience and by the sheer weight of its present numbers how to act in inter-faith relations, mindful of the very gospel which the founder Nanak advocated. Within the Sikh constituency for instance, are the quietistic, innocous Udasis, and the activistic, militant and even fanatical Akalis. The little pilgrim band, we may recall, whom we met by way of introduction to our study included such extremes as these. The Udasi hostel stands in Amritsar inclose proximity to the Akal Takht, and they both are neighbours of the Darbar Sahib itself! These extremes may meet, have often met, inspite of intermittent controversies, and many a Sikh has found some satisfaction in what they represent reference has been made already to comfort which a militant Singh had found at the ascetic Udasi hostel.

Nirbanji Phalhari (whom the present writer came to know in 1937) was until his recent death beyond three score and ten guru of the Udasis—a blind seer, kindly simple celibate. They say he knew the Adi Granth by heart, and the whole ritual of his order. He practiced various arts, including native Ayurvedic medicine and took no fees for his advice. The Ayurveda is Hindu, is an appendix to the classical Atharva Veda, and is India's oldest authority on medicine. Its lore has been to Hindus divine revelation instructive in the use of herbs and magic, with spells for the cure of fever, dropsy, baldness, snake bite, mania and many other human ailments. It holds also charms for love and vengeance, for prosperity in trade, for keeping cattle safe, for thwarting demons and all enemies and for the expiation of "offences, failures, stains transgressions", and whatever else is "sin" as Hinduism sees it. The guru cured colic in his practice, and one day a layman came to him for a charm against an evil spirit that was troubling his nephew-cures in absentia are possible. His niece had previously been cured of a similar delusion. The Sikhguru need not hesitate to use these Hindu assets. Nirbanji had use for them and for methods of his own, also with many types of Sikhs including some Keshdhari Singhs, and he was a thorough going Sikh in his own ascetic atmosphere with an ochre robe as garb and several sadhus in attendance. His shrine was a gurdwara but it contained, in addition to the normal furnishings, an image of Sri Chand, Nanak's son and the founder of the Udasi order a peaceful contrast with Gobind's sword that rests in the sanctuary of the nearby Akal Takhat. But has not Christianity had its Quakers and also its crusaders, and Islam its conquering Ghazis and its peaceful sufi's and spiritual Ahmadiyyas ! And Hinduism has its fighting Rajputs and its pacifistic satyagrahis.

(Source: The Sikhs in relation to Hindus, Moslems, Christians, and Ahmadiyyas. A study is comparative Religion, by John Clark Archer New York, Russell & Russell, 1946, 1971, pp. 321-322).

There was a Sanyasi called Bhagwan Gir, who in order to obtain spiritual consolation went to visit the Guru in Kiratpur. The Guru advised him to proceed to Dehra Baba Nanak and join the Udasis there. This was tantamount to ordering Bhagwan Gir to relinquish his sect for the Sanyasis worship Dattara, while the Udasis have as their Guru Sri Chand, the eldest son of Guru Nanak.

(p. 280 Life of Guru Har Rai (The Sikh Religion Macauliff p. 288).

Guru Gobind Singh and Udasis

The Guru's (Gobind Singh) scouts who had been sent to Bhangani, reported that the enemy were marching to the attacks. He must therefore proceed at once to intercept them, otherwise they would enter Paunta on the morrow. The Guru sent orders to a body of Udasis to put on their turbans take their arms and prepare for defence. The Udasis too did not wish to loose their lives. They said that there were other countries where they might beg for their living and that the Guru's kitchen from which they used to eat, was not the only one in the world which remained to them. It was not for the purpose of fighting they had left their homes and become pilgrims. They accordingly resolved to abscond during the night one by one, so that their departure might be unobserved.

Next morning the Guru was informed that the Udasis had all fled except their mahant Kirpal, who remained in a state of abstraction. The Guru smiled and said, "The root at any rate is left and since there is the root the tree shade bear blossom and fruit. If the mahant had gone the Udasis would have been totally extirpated, and excommunicated from Sikhism. The Guru then ordered the mahant to be sent for, and thus addressed him: "O mahant, wither have thy Udasis fled? Hearken to me. The disciples eat our sacred food, but when they see a green field elsewhere, they go to graze on it like cattle. They have all absconded in the present hour of need. The mahant calmy replied, All disciples of the Gurus are made by thee and then thyself canst pardon them."

While the Guru was conversing with the mahant two Sikhs arrived to report that the army of the hillmen had arrived near Bhangani. The Guru gave orders to his five cousins to take troops and stop the entrance of the enemy into the town. Then making all arrangements for the defence of Paunta during his absence, he sent for his arms and armour and offered the prayer:

(page 35 - Life of Guru Gobind Singh Vol. V page 35 - The Sikh Religion by Macauliff).

Once a company of Udasis brought the Guru a copy of the Granth Sahib, written with great elegance, for his attestation and signature. At that time no Granth was accepted as correct unless countersigned by the Guru. But petitioners had first to approach his minister, Diwan Nand Chand and submit the work to him for approval. The latter observing the beautiful penmanship of the volume formed the dishonest intention of appropriating it. He told the Udasis to come in a month's time and he would meanwhile find some means of obtaining the Guru's signature. When they returned after the expiration of that period, he told them he had not yet had an opportunity of speaking to the Guru on the subject, and suggested their waiting for another ten days. By similar subterfuges he kept the Udasis going backwards and forwards in suspense for six months. At the end of that time he asked them to take the price of the Granth Sahib from him, and prepare another for the Guru's approval. The Udasis refused whereupon he had them forcibly expelled from Anandpur.

One day, when the Guru went hunting, the Udasis found an opportunity of complaining to him of Nand Chand's conduct. The Guru at once ordered that their Granth should be restored to them. Nand Chand sent a message to the Guru that he was ready to return the book, but at the same time told the Udasis to leave the place at once if they valued their safety. If they made any further complaint to the Guru, they should be imprisoned and put to death. The Udasis were, however, not so easily deterred. They bided their time to approach the Guru on another occasion. They complained that Nand Chand had disobeyed his order forcibly expelled them from the city, and threatened them with death in the event of their return and making a further complaint against him. The Guru sent a severe message to Nand Chand, `Evil days have come for thee. If thou, desire thine own welfare, restore their Granth Sahib to the Udasis.' When the Guru's message was communicated to Nand Chand, he said, Go away; I will not, return the Granth Sahib... See, my friends, how the Guru Seeketh to frighten me. Were I to shake the dust off the skirt of my coats, I could make many Gurus like him.' The Sikhs replied, 'Very well; let the Guru come to thee, and thou shall see. He will draw no distinction between thee and thy brother masands.'

Nand Chand, shrinking from the consequences of the temerity, fled with the Granth Sahib to Kartarpur. When the Guru heard that he had fled through fear of death, he replied, 'Death will reach him there too. When Nand Chand reached Kartarpur, he sent a message to Dhir Mal. Hundreds of thousands of Sikhs adhore to thy cause; they will all worship thee, and make thee the Guru of the world. It is in my power to-day to raise thee to that eminence. Nand Chand was, however, seriously distrusted at Kartarpur. It was suspected that he had come from the Guru to practise some treachery - either to kill Dhir Mal or take possession of the town. Dhir Mal consulted his masands as to what was best to be done. They advised that Nand Chand should be put to death according to the following stratagem. As he came to pay a visit, a musketeer should be hidden within the house to fire at him. This was agreed on. When Nand Chand entered Dhir Mal's one room, he received a bullet, in the thigh. As he staggered the doors were closed to prevent his escape, and he then received several fatal bullets from the roof which had been opened for the purpose.

(Page 87-89 - The Life of Guru Gobind Singh -) (The Sikh Religion by Macauliff Vol. 5 - p. 87-89).

Divisions of Sikhs

There are two great divisions of Sikhs Sahijdharis and Singhs. The latter are they who accepted the baptism inaugurated by Guru Gobind Singh. All other Sikhs are called Sahijdharis. The Singhs after the time of Guru Gobind Singh, were all warriors, the Sahijdharis those who lived at ease, as the word denotes, and practised trade or agriculture. (Some say that the Sahijdharis received their name from the promises of certain Sikhs in the time of Guru Gobind Singh, that they would not accept his baptism at the time, but that they would gradually do so). In the Singhs are included the Nirmalas, and Nihangs; The Sahijdharis include the Udasis founded by Sri Chand son of Guru Nanak; the Sewapan this founded by a water carrier of Guru Gobind Singh; Ramraiyas followers of Rai Rai, son of Guru Har Rai; the Handalis to be subsequently described, and other sects of minor importance.

(Source: The Sikh Religion by Macauliffe Introduction page lii).

The first schism of the Sikhs began immediately after the

demise of Guru Nanak. Some of his followers adopted Sri Chand, his elder son as his successor and repudiated the nomination of Guru Angad. The followers of Sri Chand were termed Udasis or the solitary; and they now constitute a large body of devout and earnest men. Anand Ghan one of their number has in recent times written the Life of Guru Nanak. It contains an apotheosis of Sri Chand, and states that he was an incarnation of God and the only true successor of Guru Nanak.

(Ixxx- introduction - The Sikh Religion by Macauliff)

Vol. I Page 106... The Guru Nanak next proceeded to Dipalpur. During his journey a Sanyasi asked him to define the word Udas. The Guru replied: To make use of all things in this world and not deem them one's own but only God's property, and ever to possess a desire to make Him is Uddas. (The Sikh Religion by Maculiff - vol. I, p. 106).

Sri Chand formally abolished the Sect of Udasis

The martial exercises and hunting did not interfere with the missionary work of Guru Hargobind. Baba Sri Chand—son of Guru Nanak met the Guru during one of his tours at the village of Ramdas. Sri Chand formally abolished the sect of Udasis of which he was the Founder and requested the Guru to take the charge of four of his preachers—Almast, Gonda, Phool Shah and Balu Hasna. The Guru agreed to this arrangement and sent these missionaries to different regions for the propagation of Sikhism. The Guru went on preaching tours to Srinagar (Kashmir), Gurdaspur, Kartarpur, Goindwal and neighbouring villages. He inspired people with courage and fearlessness. He exhorted them to remain in a state of preparedness for the rulers did not want Sikhism to flourish. The death of Jahangir in 1627 was a signal for hostile forces to challenge the Guru.

(Source: A Hand Book of Sikh studies by Dr. Gobind Singh Mansukhani - National Book Shop. Pleasure Garden Market, Chandni Chowk, Delhi) Page 75.

Khushwant Singh on Udasi Sect

No rules had been made for the management of the gurdwaras nor were qualifications prescribed for their caretakers. In the days of Mughal persecution, the job of granthi (scripture reader) was a hazardous, one, and many important shrines were entrusted to members of the Udasi order, who did not fully subscribe to the Khalsa creed and being usually cleanshaven, could disclaim their association with Sikhism when their lives were in danger. Even after Mughal rule, these shrines continued to be looked after by Udasis, and the post of granthi-cum-manager passed from father to son. The less important gurdwaras were looked after by men who wished to dedicate their lives to prayer and the service of the Community.

With the establishment of British rule, new settlement records had to be made. In many of these, the lands and properties attached to the gurdwaras were entered against the names of the mahants.

Where the congergation was vigilant, the entry remained a nominal one, where the priests were able to have it their own way, they were recorded as owners and began to utilise and alienate the property as they wished. The Udasis who were as much Hindu as they were Sikh, anxious to attract Hindu worshippers, installed images of Hindu gods and goddesses in gurdwara premises. There were also some cases of misuse of the sacred precints. (p. 195).

The Lieutenant Governor, Sir Edward Maclagan tried to push through legislation to transfer gurdwaras to their rightful owners, the Sikh congregation. In March 1921 the Education Minister, Mian Fazl-in-Husain introduced a bill to set up a Board of Commissioners which would take over the management of Sikh shrines. The bill was opposed by the Sikh legislators, who objected to having non Sikh on a board whose sole function was to manage Sikh places of worship. Nor could the members agree on what constituted a gurdwara; a large number of Udasis declared their shrines to be Hindu temples and so gained the backing of Hindu and anti-Akali

Sikh members.[3] Mia Fazl-in-Husain had the bill passed into law as the Sikh Gurdwaras and Shrine Act VI of 1922. The Sikhs ignored the legislation.

The most significant outcome of the four years of intense agitation (Gurdwara Reform movement) in which the Hindus supported the Udasis Mahants against the Akalis, was to widen further the gulf between the two Communities (p. 213).

(Source: A History of the Sikhs Vol. 2, 1839-1988, by Khushwant Singh, pp. 194, 195, 202, 212 and 213)

Nanak's successors effected a separation between the Sikhs and the Udasis, or the followers of Sri Chand and Sikhism became essentially a religion of house holders. (p. 11)

The Udasis as the followers of Sri Chand were called, also prima facie possessed the same credentials and claimed the same amount of sanctity as Sikhism proper. Besides celibacy and asceticism the other tenets of the sect were the same as those of Sikhism and it regarded Nanak with the same veneration as the Sikhs did. (p. 162).

Evolution of the Khalsa. The Foundation of the Sikh Panth Vol. I by Indu Bhushan Banerjee p. 11, 162.

We do not know of any definite measure taken by Guru Angad to avert this danger, unless his active preaching and exposition of the hymns of Guru Nanak be so construed. It is said, however, that his successors Guru Amar Das, authoritatively declared that the active and domestic Sikhs were wholly separate from the passive and recluse Udasis and thus preserved the infant faith from disappearing as one of the many sects that have arisen and vanished within the fold of Hinduism.[4]

Guru Nanak and Udasi Sect

There is a story of Guru Nanak cooking a deer at Kurukshetra. Behind this important Kurukshetra story there may be a further point of interest. A pandit called Nanu figures in the account. Evidently he had been passing himself off as Guru Nanak, which implies that the Guru was already famous. However, when the deer is cooked it is Nanu who leads the critics in denouncing Nanak. Perhaps there is here some reference to the Udasi movement centred upon Guru Nanak's son, Sri Chand, which persisted well into the seventeenth century when the janam sakhis were being written. The movement as well as Hinduism, is implicity denounced in this incident[5] for being guilty of falsely claiming to be the true Nanak Panthis.

Here we see Guru Nanak's dispute with Hinduism extending beyond ritualism and dietary regulations to the whole way of life. What may have been implicit at Kurukshetra becomes explict in his meeting with a sanyasi at Dipalpur.[6] The Guru asked what purpose the ascetic was serving to which came a formal reply. A sanyasi should renounce his home and family, renounce all desires and perform penances. To this the Guru responded by suggesting that he had replaced one set of attachments by others, with desire for occult powers. The sanyasi then asked Guru Nanak what the creed of an ascetic, an Udasi was, for the Guru was dressed like one. In reply the Guru said:-

An Udasi is a missionary who does not renounce the world. He lives in it but remains completely detached from it. He considers nothing to be his own. Everything he has is a gift from God to be used for God's creatures without any thought of 'I and mine'. He is individual in his search for truth but he lives in society and for society. Meeting with other enlightened people he gains more knowledge and enlightenment and in sadhu sangat where there are three, four or five seekers after truth, there is the spirit of God. Life's purpose is to serve others. The Sanyasis weekness is his dependence on others for food and shelter while professing individualism. The sanyasi became a disciple.

According to McLeod, Nanakmata consists of little more than a temple in the jungle.[7] He states that it was Udasi sadhus led by a mahant named Almast who drove out the Nath yogis during the guruship of Hargobind (1604-1644) and probably renamed the place. Sikhs describe him as a follower of the Guru. The Udasi Sikh distinction which certainly exists is recorded in the janam sakhis particularly with regard to Guru Nanak's passing over his son Sri Chand in favour of Lehna.

According to Guru Amar Das

Family life is superior to ascetic life, in a sectarian garb because it is from householders that ascetics meet their needs (by begging) (AG. 586).

This strong affirmation of the grihastha life may be accounted for first as a response to the need to give the steadily growing. Panth more precise guidance upon the way of life appropriate for a Sikh and second, the need to rebut the ascetic teachings of Sri Chand, Guru Nanak's surviving son. Though he never disputed the leadership of Guru Amar Das, he persistently argued that his way of life, that of an ascetic was the proper one for a Sikh to follow. For the first time too there is mention of apostasy in a Guru's hymns. However, this time the reference is not to Sri Chand but Datu, the son of Guru Angad, who had not accepted his father's choice of Guru and made concerted efforts to unseat the man he regarded as a usurper. It would appear that a faction among the Sikhs regarded Datu as Guru throughout his lifetime, to the embarrasment of Amar Das.

(Source: Sikhism and its Indian Context 1469-1708 by W. Owen Cole. p. 229.)

As the Panth was growing in size and was threatened by internal dissension, Guru Amar Das felt it necessary to require his followers to assemble in his presence at Goindwal at the festivals of Baisakhi and Diwali. At least twice a year Guru and disciples would meet and Sikhs would have to decide to whom they owed allegiance, to Sri Chand, Datu or Amar Das. Coincidentally, they would have to observe the festivals in the Hindu way or by assembling before the Guru; they could not do both.

(Source: Sikhism and its Indian Context 1469-1708 by W. Omen Cole.)

Contribution of Udasin Sampardai to Society

Mahamandleshwar Acharya Swami Raghvanand Ji Maharaj in his article entitled, 'Udasin Sampardai Ki Samaj Ko Dein" appeared in Shri Chandra Jyotsna 1997 has mentioned that:-

Udasin Sampardai is an ancient Vedic Sampardai of India. Probably from the earliest period the proofs of its existence are sufficiently available. According to its history the reformer Acharya Sri Chandra, the son of Shri Guru Nanak Dev Ji was an incarnation of Lord Shiva.

Acharya Sri Chandra Bhagwan had four disciples namely:

1. Shri Balu Hasan

2. Phool Sahib

3. Govind Dev and

4. Almast

These four disciples added numberless saints as their followers and strengthen the Udasin Sect. It appears that in the beginning that this Sect had great impact in the provinces of Punjab and Sindh. Gradually this Sect spread throughout India. Nearly fifty or sixty years ago those who believed in service to suffering mankind and spirit of dedication used to join this organisation. Due to the drastic changes in the Society's set up, it had a great impact on the Sadhu Samaj also.

Consequently the number of Sadhus had immensely decreased. Inspite of all these changes the Sadhu Samaj of Udasin Sampardai had set up near about 3000 Ashrams, Deras, Temples and Akharas. In the foreign countries the centres of this sects are being set up.

According to the teachings of Acharya Sri Chandra

Bhagwan, the saints of Udasin Sampardai alongwith their spiritual growth they devote their valuable time in social service and have undertaken numerous schemes to reform the society.

Through Shri Guru Ramroy Darbar Dehradun Institution in the field of education an examplary works has been done. The Institution had set up more than one hundred schools, Public Schools and Colleges. In these educational institutions by more than 2000 teachers near about fifty thousand students are studying. Out of these schools and colleges a few of them are being run free of any charge and in others by charging nominal feeses the best education is given. During the regime of Mahant Indresh Chandra's marvellous progress have been made in the education and social field.

Sadhu Bela Udasin Ashram Sindh Sakhar is an ancient Institution; where hundred of Sadhus used to take shelter. These Sadhus with their selfless service had brighten the name of this area. After the partition of India this famous Institution have migrated to Bombay. In the dynamic leadership of Mahant Ganeshdas this Institution is progressing in leaps and bounds. Due to great skills of planning and keeping in view of the protection of ancient Indian Culture always provided with modern technique to safeguard the interest of the society. Due to his historical contribution in the building up this organisation he called and known as Rajrishi Ganeshdas.

Guru Ganeshwar Spiritual Mission whatsoever progress have made in the past should be strictly followed by Sadhu Samaj in India. This Mission has been set up by Sadgurudev Swami Ganeshwranand Ji Maharaj and Sadgurudev Swami Sarvanand Ji Maharaj. Its 13-14 branches are busy serving the people in various villages, towns and cities. It includes Schools, Colleges, Hospitals and Sant Sewa and Social Welfare centres.

Shri Karsahini Udasin Ashram, Ramanreti Mahavan is such an organiation with a difference in which even in this modern period is functioning within the framework of ancient Indian Culture. One must appreciate the spirit of service to saints, cows and guests. Under the kind control of Present Mahamandleshwar Mahant Swami Guru Sharnanand; spiritual, social, and educational awakening alongwith to look after the purity of temples; importance of temples has done a commendable job. From the beginning this institution has taken a laborious attitude. For sightedness of the present Mahant is highly appreciated in the Samaj.

Sangalwala Panchayati Akhara was established by Bawa Priyatam Das. The traditions set up by Bawa Priyatam Das are quite safe in the hands of present Mahant Shri Anantanand Ji Maharaj. He has introduced lot of development schemes in the Akhara including free of charge Gurukul, a dispensary, library. This akhara under the able guidance of Mahant Shri Ananta Nand Ji Maharaj has played a prominent and historical role in publishing authentic books on Udasin Movement in India. Not only that to propagate the ideals of Udasin Sect. Audio and Video cassetts are being distributed among the people.

Shri Harihar Udasin Ashram, Delhi, Shad-darshan is a vast sarovar of Sadhu Samaj. The motive of this Institution is service to Sadhu Samaj. Impressed by Sadhu Samaj numerous persons have joined this Institution. Hundreds of saints have set up their Ashrams in Gujarat, Rajasthan and many other places and spread the ideals of this prestigious organisation as torch bearers.

Kalyan Seva Ashram has been set up by Baba Kalyan Das in Amar Kantak. Baba Kalyan Das have set up Schools in the backward areas of Madhya Pradesh, Orissa and Uttar Pradesh. After selecting meritorious students out of the whole lot sent them for higher studies to Banaras. In this manner he is preparing a team of well educated students. He has also set up a 100 beded hospital in the area. In the field of Art and Culture he has also established Research Centre. This is a unique institution working for the development of Social, educational and religious field.

Dera Baba Charan Shah Udasin Ashram, Bahadurpur,

near Hoshiarpur, Punjab is being looked after by Mahant Shri Ramendra Das. This Ashram is contributing its share in the educational field and other social welfare activities.

All these Udasin Ashrams are being run and looked after by highly qualified and intellectuls all over India.

1. Haridwar Udasin Ashram is being looked after by Mahamandleshwar Swami Ram Sawrup Ji Maharaj.

2. Munimandal Ashram is being looked after by Mahant Swami Ananad Raghavji Maharaj.

3. Ramshankar Udasin Ashram, Haridwar is being looked after Mahant Swami Prakash Muni Ji Maharaj.

4. Hare Ram Udasin Ashram is being looked after by Mahamandleshwar Swami Kapil Muni Ji Maharaj.

5. Bhagvaddham Udasin Ashram, Haridwar is being looked after by Swami Vivekanand Ji.

6. Jagadguru Udasin Ashram, Haridwar is being looked after by Swami Sahdev Muni Ji and Swami Sanatan Muni Ji etc. All these saints in their respective fields contributing their mite to look after the interests of the people by running Sanskrit Schools, Gurukuls, Hospitals, Libraries and by publishing religious books are serving the people continuously.

Chetan Dev Udasin Avdhoot Ashram known as Chetan Dev Kutiya but in reality it is a big fort where hundreds of Sadhus take shelter. Keeping inview its big halls and beautiful buildings structure one can imagine the greatness of this institution. The senior most intellectuals and after ex-Mahamandleshwar Swami Braham Hari, the present Mahant Mohan Das Ji is trying his level best to materialise the scheme which can change the lot of millions. To implement schemes for the welfare of people is very costly and time consuming factor. This is being done within the frame work of the Udasin Sampardai's traditions.

Similarly an institution run by Mahant Ishwar Das is a

historical city Thatha's organisation—is busy in Social, Religious and educational activities. `Bapu Ki Jhonpari' being run by reputed Mahant Thakur Das is busy in propagating the ideals of Udasin Sampardai and doing social service among the needy people. Govind Dham which is situated in Khar (Bombay) and run by Mahant Mohan Das it has also become an active centre for social, educational and religious activities.

Guru Ramroy Udasin Ashram in Delhi is more than 200 years ancient institution. Discources on Bhagvat Gita are conducted thrice a week by Mahant Mahamandelshwar Acharya Swami Raghvanand Ji Maharaj and arranged Bhajan Kirtan everyday. This is a unique institution run by Vedantacharya Swami Raghvanand Ji. There is an excellent Library with a rich collection of books on religion, children books and other social science subjects. Homeopathic Dispensary is serving the needy persons free of charge. The credit of smooth functioning of this Udasin Ashram goes to Mahant Raghvanand Ji Maharaj and Doctor Sant Devi संविदानन्द 'Udasin'.

Mahamandaleshwar Mahant Ishwar Das Ji Mahraj who is incharge of a new Akhara of Udasin Sampardai has set up many new Akharas in Jalandhar (Punjab) area and doing utmost social service. Being an intellectual and specialist in Ayurved thousands of patients take advantage by taking medicines from this Ashram. This Ashrfam also specialise in music and modern educational system. Thousands of students have been benefitted by the schools and colleges being run by this Institution.

Similarly Mahant Shri Swarupanand Ji Maharaj of Dera Tap (Bathinda), Sant Narayan Muni Ji of Dera Karipur Dumbh and his disciple Swami Muni Ji Shivanand Ji of Dera Kewal and Avdhoot Jagat Ram Udasin Ashram's Mahant Surindra Muni Ji Maharaj and so many other sanyasis have devoted their lives for the upliftment of the masses.

All these Ashrams have their Gaoshalas (cow sheds), Dispensaries, Guest Houses and students hostels.

Though there exists number of Udasin Ashrams in Patiala City (Punjab) but Chhatta Magni Ram's Ashram being run by Mahant Atma Ram is a unique one. It has many branches all over the states and other provinces. All these centres are managed by a powerful Trust which has decided to run educational institutions under the patronage of this Trust. Being social by nature Mahant Atma Ram has a vide circle of colleagues and friends. Not only Sadhu Samaj but also people from all walks of life approach him for the removal of thier grievances. Sadhu Samaj have great expectation from this young and energetic Mahatma.

Acharya Shri Chandra College of Medical Sciences and Hospital—Jammu

On the auspicious occasion of the 500th birth anniversary of Udasin Acharya Sri Shrichandra Maharaj, Shri Chandra Bada Akhara Udasin Trust and Society, Sri Nagar (Kashmir) has decided to set up a biggest Medical College in the Sidhra area, which will be a biggest Medical College in Northern India.

There will be a hospital consisting of 700 beds. It has been named as 'Acharya Sri Chandra College of Medical Sciences and Hospital'. The Jammu and Kashmir Government has agreed to allot a 60 Acre of land for this prestigious project. An amount of Rupees 70 crore will be spent on the construction on the buildings. A vast temple of Bhagwan Sri Chandra will be constructed in the compound of the College and Hospital. The foundation stone of this Medical College and Hospital was laid down by Mahamandleshwar Swami Govindanand by performing all vedic rituals including "Bhoomi Poojan", and preservation of "Tamar Pattar" on 18th April 1994. The foundation stone was laid down by Shri V. Krishna Rao, the Honourable Governor of Jammu and Kashmir. In this ceremony Shri Farooq Abdullah the Chief Minister of Jammu and Kashmir also participated. Shri Shrichandra Medical College and Hospital will be a one of the best and exemplary college in Northern India.

As it has been mentioned earlier that Udasin Sect has more than 3000, Maths, Temples, Akharas, Dharamsalas etc. in India. It will not be possible give complete details of all these temples in this article. A Directory (in Hindi) comprising more than 1500 entries about these Udasin Centres in India. Shri Chandra Panchshati Janam Samaroh Samiti has decided to prepare a comprehensive Directory of all such Udasin Centres in India.

We will be failing in our duty if we fail to mention the contribution of 'Panchayati Akhara Bada Udasin and Panchayati Akhara Naya Udasin in the Udasin Movement. Both these organisations are functioning under democratic norms. By the continuous efforts made by both institutions in the spiritual and social fields a lot of awakening is seen among the masses. Both these organisations have numberless centres in the various parts of the country. In these centres stay the representatives of the Sect and propagate the ideals of Udasin Sampardai and solve the day to day problems being faced by these Akharas, Maths, and temples. Both these organisations in their perspective areas look after the interests of Sadhu Samaj and the property of the sects.

Though this Sampardai (Sect) is like a big and ancient banyan tree and have countless numbers of Sadhus. They are contributing their share in every sphere of life to reform the Hindu samaj. Keeping in view their selfless service to the suffering mankind is worth appreciable. I vow my head and pay my heartfelt obeisance to all sanyasis of Udasin Sampardai.

Those great reformers and Udasin Asharms which I fail to mention in this article, is due to my lack of knowledge and I am sure the great saints and reforms of the udasin Sampardai will excuse me.

(Translation from Hindi article entitled "उदासीन सम्प्रदाय की समाज को देन द्वारा महामण्डलेश्वर आचार्य स्वामी राधावानन्द जी महाराज, महन्त, गुरूराम राय उदासीन आश्रम, पंचकुई रोड़, नई दिल्ली, appeared in Shri Chandra Jyotsna, 11 September 1997, pp. 35-39).

David N. Lorenzen on Udasis

The recent discovery of a document dating back to 1783 is a good indicator of how the categories Sahajdhari, Nanak-Panthis and Udasi overlapped in middle period Sikh tradition. This Gurmukhi document was compiled by a Nanak-Panthi Sikh and was primarily addressed to the head of an Udasis establishment in Bihar, but it also sought to instruct Sahajdhari Sikhs. Given the major importance of this document—for it not only exemplifies the close correspondence in the religious identities of Sahajdharis, Nanak-Panthis and Udasis, but it also illuminates the normative order they all were asked to subscribe to—it is reproduced almost in its entirety below:

A guidance and direction in the road to salvation, of Bawa Mansha Ram Faqir, given to Ramgarela Ram in 1783. It behooves the mahant of the Udasi establishment in Rajgir to remain celibate; be truthful and contented; spread the panth; share his means with others; recite the Name of the True one with every breath; not to forget the true teachings of the Sikh Gurus, daily recite gurbani (the Guru's words); uphold the pages of the granth; not to deviate from the service of the Sadhus and the members of the Congregation; take the bath early in the morning; repeat the Name; refrain from vices; tell the people of the magnitude of the name of the Guru; go to the houses of the Sikhs and instruct them to recite the Name; practice charity; perform ablutions; be benevolent and compassionate; observe religious duties; practice contentment and observe the laws of good conduct and morality; root out differences between the high and low; serve the saints and priests of every tradition; observe no discrimination; not to defame any deity; not to obliterate the propriety of conduct towards the Guru Sikh and the Chela Sikh; to preserve the dignity of the two *gurpurabs* ; continue the distribution of *Karah Parshad*; not to stop rendering service to the saints and sadhus on the occasion of the *lound* (intercalary month) fair; to continue the preaching of the Sikh tenets. The first duty of the Sahajdhari Sikh is to repeat the True Name and recite the *gurmantara*. The pure Sikh is he who regards the Guru's words of supreme importance and does not harbour hostility to anyone. No one should remain idle. It is obligatory to learn the gurmukhi script. Be not proud and arrogant. Remove the sufferings of the distressed ones. Do not practice deceit and hypocrisy. Give up greed and avarice. The mahant of the Udasi establishment in Rajgir will have to observe these rules. The mahant, who will abide by these rules, will not invite the punishment of the God of death on him, and he will have an easy access to heaven.

Note: This document was first located at an Udasi establishment in/Rajgir, Bihar, by historian Ved Prakash. He provides a translation of it in his book, The Sikhs in Bihar (Patna 1981) pp. 167-168.

If there had been fundamental differences among Sahajdhari, Nanak-Panthi and Udasi Sikhs, it is highly unlikely that the above quoted text could have ever been written. Both in the sequence of its production and contents, it supports our contention that non-Khalsa Sikhs may be meaningfully considered under the category Sahajdhari, and where possible we further explore and specify its plural constituency.

The differences between Khalsa and Sahajdhari categories of thought and concepts of the Sikh persons can be better understood by looking in some detail at the Udasis, perhaps the most conspicious and widely patronized segment among the Sahajdhari Sikhs. Although historians continue to dispute whether the Udasis originated with Sri Chand, the eldest son of Guru Nanak, or Baba Gurditta, the eldest son of sixth Guru Hargobind, of greater significance here are some of the doctrines, religious practices, and functions of the Udasis. The word *Udasi* is derived from the Sanskrit *Udas*, meaning detachment, and can signify renunciation or indifference to worldly concerns. The Udasis first seem to have come into prominence during the seventeenth century. Early Sikh tradition records ten major Udasi orders:-

The ten orders were: 1. Almast 2. Balu Hasna 3. Phul,

4. Goinde, 5. Suthre Sahi 6. Bhagat Bhagwane 7. Sangat Sahiba 8. Mihan Sahie 9. Bakht Mahe 10. and Jit Male.

Members of these orders gradually began to manage key Sikh shrines across northern India including the Harimandir for a short period of time, and also set up their own establishments in pilgrimage centres like Amritsar, Haridwar and Banaras.

From these rapidly expanding shrines and establishments Udasis enunciated a model of Sikhism that was at considerable divergence from that of the Khalsa Sikhs. The differences between the two can be briefly conceptualized by contrasting their attitude at three levels:

1. depletion of hair

2. dress code and

3. mode of salvation

The Udasis did not consider the Khalsa rahit-namas to be binding on them and accordingly, unlike the Khalsa Sikhs, felt free to cut their hair. Even when the Udasis maintained long hair, they would mat it rather than knot it under a turban like the Khalsa Sikhs. Whereas the Khalsa Sikhs laid great emphasis on wearing a Kachh and sporting arms, the items respected by the Udasis were quite different. An inventory of their dress code would include items like a cap, a rosary of flowers, a cotton bag, a gourd vessel, ash for smearing on the body, a chain to tie around the waist and a deer skin to perform hathayog on. In appearance perhaps no two persons would have looked more different than a Khalsa Sikh and a Udasi in the eighteenth century. Difference in physical appearance invariably reflect much deeper distinctions in thought and modes of being. This certainly holds true for the Khalsa and Udasi Sikhs. In the worldview of the former, salvation could be attained by living in the world and pursuing secular objectives like political power or accumulation of resources like agrarian land. These secular objecives, however, had to be attained within a particular framework of beliefs and religious practices. Paramount among these beliefs was the Khalsa normative order discussed at length in an earlier section of this essay. Salvation was assured to all those who subscribed to Khalsa identity.

Udasis interpreted the issue of salvation differently. For them secular pursuits were not compatible with the goal of human liberation, and to achieve this objective one had to renounce the world. Starting with this postulate the Udasis ended up by rejecting a whole series of doctrines and practices which were very dear to the Khalsa Sikhs. In the eyes of the Udasis, any individual could become an equal of the Sikh Gurus by following certain mystical practices. Such heterodox thinking ran contrary to the popular Khalsa belief that no individual could match the divine status of the Sikh Gurus. Ordinary Sikh could only emulate the Gurus, but never themselves turn into Gurus, for the Gurus were indistinguishable from God. The Udasis, by veering towards a grostic position, made suspect the orthodox line of succession from Guru Nanak to Gobind Singh and encouraged figures both within their own tradition and outside it to be viewed as Guru. But perhaps the most radical attitudinal difference between the two was on the issue of liberation. For Khalsa Sikhs considered Khanda Ki Pahul and the resulting corporate identity to be a major prerequisite for liberation from the transmigratory cycle. Udasis did not endorse this view and encouraged their own esoteric methods to overcome the constant cycle of birth and death.

(Source: Bhakti Religion in North India—Community Identity and Political Action) ed. by David N. Lorenzen pp. 55-59).

Jeevan Prakash Jeevan on Udasi Samparda

Meaning of the Word Udasin

Udasin word in general means a person who has renounced the world, who is imbiassed and unattached an ascetic who is averse to mundane affairs of the world, a fully detached person; who neglecting its perishable body relations, keeps on moving sted fastly on the path of mental progress, Merging all its faculties into the Brahma, detaching the mind away from the worldly attachments, having nothing to do with the give and take activities of this world, regardless of the pleasures and anger. He, who living in this world, remains aloof of the strings of mayajal of this world. He perfumes the atmosphere like a lotus flower grown amid a clean water tank. He toils for the uplift of his fellowbeings in the society, who are suffering from five major ills like Kama, Krodha etc. and works for his own spiritual upliftment.

Udasin is such a great soul who has realised the worthlessness of all the worldly activities, names and forms alongwith their false pretentions and as such has touch of real Brahma, the ultimate reality of this universe, in secular terms also an udasin person is he, who remaining aloof of the mundan activities tries to have a glance of the real truth. He who has no worldly attachment with any worldly being is a real udasin. In real terms, he is paraphysical being though having his individual body as he does not care for the pleasures and pains of his body. He is always busy in spiritual realm.

Udasin is that state of mind in which one does not have any malice towards any human being. He takes every body equal to his ownself and feels himself in everybody. This is a special faculty. Only is the higher stages of supreme oneness with the God himself that state of human mind emerges when one feels for the well being of the society at large and absorbs itself in the service of humanity. He feels whole heartedly in the oneness of all human beings. Udasin in real words is the person as per the quote of Mahakavi Tulsidass, the famous poet of Ramcharit Manas.

> "Siya Ram Maya Sab Jag Jani
> Karon Parnam Jori Jug Pani"

as a follower of Shri Rama feels the existance of Rama in every particle of this world, similarly a real udasin observes Brahma in every nook and corner of the universe.

Udasin is a word made up of two parts such as Ud + Asain; Ud—meaning elevated and Aasin meaning seated i.e. a person seated on a raised platform or an elevated personality is termed as Udasin in Sanskrit Grammar.

He who is elevated from the bonds of this visible (subtle) world and resides in the finer stage of the world just like a lotus in the marshy land, who always remains in the thoughts of God and is busy in the impriftment of general public, keeping himself above the social regimentation of class and creed, take everybody as equal is an udasin in the real sense of the word.

Historical Evolution of Udasin Sect and Gurudom

Puranic studies reveal that Bhagwan Vishnu was resting in the ocean of Milk, when one fine morning a strange lotus emerged out of his naval: from this lotus flower Brahma Ji appeared. He meditated for a long period, had the holy communion and was ordered to create conditions favourable for the emergence of life in this biosphear.

The very idea of handling the responsibility of planning and construction of this universe diffused the SATO & RAJOGUN capability of creation and the TAMO GUN faculty got infused resulting in the emergence of this creation full of five great mental hurdels such as Kama (Desire) Krodha (Anger), Lobha (greed) Moha (Attachment) and Ahankar (proud/ego) Brahmaji turned sad upon the scene of this undesired development. He started pondering over this anti-clockwise movement of the wheel of fate. He had to meditate for a long time till the emergence of Satvik Budhi (Pure Wisdom). From his Satvik (pure) conception four psycoprogenic children emerged who were named as SANAK, SANANDAN, SANATAN and SANAT KUMAR. Sanak & Sanandan are synonimus with Anand (BLISS) and Anand (Bliss) could only be attained in the devotion and dedication of God. Everyone of these four sons of Brahma was deeply absorbed in the thoughts of God and had nothing to do with the mundane desires. Even cupid was unable to divert them from their path.

Similarly Sanatan as per his name was just akin to Brahma and Vishnu, so he abohered the ties of this world. So he also followed the way his brothers had gone. Sanat Kumar also choose to tred the right path. Everyone of these four brothers, the sons of Brahma, devoted his precious time in meditating upon the 'Soham' Mantra. They considered world as perishable and had adopted udasin, attitude of non-alignment and aloofness from the strings of this world.

Brahma Ji ordered them to work for the development of this world but they refused bluntly. He gave them many alurements but they refused to budge and remained stuck to their original stand.

As they were themselves, a product of Sudha Satvik guna Pure intellect, so the desire too propagate did not propel in their mind. They were detachment from this world from the very beginning and absorbed in the thoughts of attaining knowledge and eternal bliss i.e. God himself. So they beg a pardon and requested Brahma Ji to bless them with the love and affection of God throughout their life time. They lived together. It came to their mind that when a person grows older, he falls a pray to the five sensual abuses such as kama, krodha, lobha, moha and goes astray of the real path of Bliss, thus leaving aside the path of God's grace, wastes its precious life time. Understanding this, with the grace of God they remained just like a child, through out their life, devoid of these five sins; meditating the name of God the great. It is told that the renowned sage Narada had given them discourses on the Shrimadbhagwata and Jai-Vijay; two brothers had to go through the Rakhshasha yoni for three consecutive births due to their curse. They lived in this world just like the lotus flower in the muddy land. Sanat Kumar was considered more experienced and adapt so he is considered as the originator of this udasin order.

Another story tells us that these four brothers came to Brahma Ji, to have some clarifications about the renunciational path and asked so many complex questions baffeling him. As he was himself busy in the recreational work of this world following the Pravriti Marg (प्रवृत्ति मार्ग) so he could not satisfy their quest about Nivriti Marg (निवृत्ति मार्ग). It was the initial stage of the world formation so it was practically impossible to find some suitable guide who could quentch the thirst of these four seekers of the ultimate truth. Hence they requested Shri Vishnu Bhagwan to show them the real path; Bhagwan Vishnu heeding to their request incarnated himself in the form of a swan; called Hansa Avtar and gave complete discourse on Nivriti Marg along with the real knowledge to these four sons of Shri Brahma.

This story tells us about the lineage of Guru-Chela i.e. preceptor and the disciple system. Sanat Kumar received his knowledge from the Hansa avtar so it becomes clear from the Puranic and other historical/mythological scriptures that in recent times also all the famous Rishis, munis and other learned people had one or the other person as their Guru or preceptor, through whom they attained their enlightenment without the guidance of some guru one can not attain the knowledge of one's self. Even in day-to-day life we have to take the help of some teacher then how can one persue the complicated path of knowledge about one's self without the guidance of some kind of a preceptor.

We have a strange of die-hard followers of some sects who insist on saying that the founder of their sect had no worldly guru or preceptor. They might be trying to prove that their sect guru was sent by the almighty fully trained and prepared for the job he was commissioned.

The follower of Budha, Muhamad and Guru Nanak believe that they were directed by the God himself and thus they required no worldly Guru or preceptor to teach them the ways of this world. Whereas in reality it is a simple case of little knowledge. Our religious books tell us that even the god men sent by God and his incarnates also need and had to follow in the footsteps of some guru.

Bhagwan Shri Ram Chandra had to go to Guru Vashistha and Yogiraj Shri Krishna had to go to the school of Rishi

Sandipan to learn the religious teachings. We would like to question such blind foliowers that if their religious preachers had no religious teacher then why did they themselves had started the Gurudom system in their sect. So it is an established fact that without a Guru one can not attain eternal bliss or have a communication with the God.

Well, we come to the original point that according to the puranic tales Guru-shishya Prampara i.e. Preceptor-disciple lineage emerged from the Hansavtar and Sanat Kumar etc. This Sanat Kumar is regarded as the founder preceptor of Udasin sect., and this lineage is still in vouge. Balyogi Bhagwan Srichandra became the disciple of Shri Avinashi Muni and hence inturn maintained the line of udasin sadhus.

Now we give this line of udasin sadhus as given in the old scriptures.

Udasin Line of Sadhus

1. Shri Sanat Kumar

2. Shri Narad Muni Ji

3. Shri Wabhravya Muni Ji

4. Shri Dalabhya Muni Ji

5. Shri Jai Muni Ji

6. Shri Sanjiwan Muni Ji

7. Shri Dev Muni Ji

8. Shri Arvind Muni Ji

9. Shri Govind Muni Ji

10. Shri Sahasrabhanu Muni Ji

11. Shri Shat Bhanu Muni Ji

12. Shri Shachitra Bhanu Muni Ji

13. Shri Varad Muni Ji

14. Shri Divya Muni Ji

15. Shri Sudharma Muni Ji

16. Shri Suvarma Muni Ji

17. Shri Aditya Muni Ji

18. Shri Ram Muni Ji

19. Shri Bhuri Sain Muni Ji

20 Shri Maha Sain Muni Ji

21. Shri Himanshu Muni Ji

22. Shri Gopal Muni Ji

23. Shri Narayana Muni Ji

24. Shri Padma Muni Ji

25. Shri Krishna Muni Ji

26. Shri Shiva Muni Ji

27. Shri Ritudev Muni Ji

28. Shri Vamdev Muni Ji

29. Shri Tilak Muni Ji

30. Shri Gagan Muni Ji

31. Shri Vibudh Muni Ji

32. Shri Sudev Muni Ji

33. Shri Bhudev Muni Ji

34. Shri Shanta Muni Ji

35. Shri Satya Muni Ji

36. Shri Vidhi Dev Muni Ji

37. Shri Nidhi Muni Ji

38. Shri Vijay Muni Ji

39. Shri Sujan Muni Ji
40. Shri Sharuti Sidh Muni Ji
41. Shri Madhav Muni Ji
42. Shri Manohar Muni Ji
43. Shri Dharma Dhwaja Muni Ji
44. Shri Jai Dhwaja Muni Ji
45. Shri Giridhar Muni Ji
46. Shri Satya Sandho Muni Ji
47. Shri Brahma Dev Muni Ji
48. Shri Vishal Muni Ji
49. Shri Yogendra Muni Ji
50. Shri Ravindra Muni Ji
51. Shri Pragya Muni Ji
52. Shri Sharish Muni Ji
53. Shri Devesh Muni Ji
54. Shri Chidananda Muni Ji
55. Shri Sugyan Muni Ji
56. Shri Vigyan Muni Ji
57. Shri Shudha Muni Ji
58. Shri Vishudha Muni Ji
59. Shri Lokesha Muni Ji
60. Shri Aacharana Muni Ji
61. Shri Subhushan Muni Ji
62. Shri Sidha Muni Ji
63. Shri Nrideva Muni Ji

64. Shri Narendra Muni Ji
65. Shri Dev(van) Muni Ji
66. Shri Pratap Muni Ji
67. Shri Sudhakar Muni Ji
68. Shri Ratnakar Muni Ji
69. Shri Himkar Muni Ji
70. Shri Devrat Muni Ji
71. Shri Surat Muni Ji
72. Shri Vishnu Muni Ji
73. Shri Shankar Muni Ji
74. Shri Hiranya Muni Ji
75. Shri Suvesha Muni Ji
76. Shri Ripuji Muni Ji
77. Shri Madanji Muni Ji
78. Shri Hayalok Muni Ji
79. Shri Sulok Muni Ji
80. Shri Sukirti Muni Ji
81. Shri Punyakirti Muni Ji
82. Shri Lok Pal Muni Ji
83. Shri Suyatra Muni Ji
84. Shri Sunaya Muni Ji
85. Shri Abhaya Muni Ji
86. Shri Rochishnu Muni Ji
87. Shri Deepan Muni Ji
88. Shri Sutej Muni Ji

89. Shri Sutapa Vudh Muni Ji
90. Shri Shachindra Muni Ji
91. Shri Sri Nayan Muni Ji
92. Shri Hari Narayan Muni Ji
93. Shri Sulochan Muni Ji
94. Shri Shriplochan Muni Ji
95. Shri Braham Bodh Muni Ji
96. Shri Virja Muni Ji
97. Shri Sujanma Muni Ji
98. Shri Susharma Muni Ji
99. Shri Sudham Muni Ji
100. Shri Trilok Muni Ji
101. Shri Bhisham Muni Ji
102. Shri Sukhada Muni Ji
103. Shri Mangal Muni Ji
104. Shri Pundreek Muni Ji
105. Shri Jitanand Muni Ji
106. Shri Mahesh Muni Ji
107. Shri Shakti Muni Ji
108. Shri Shanti Muni Ji
109. Shri Hansa Muni Ji
110. Shri Susang Muni Ji
111. Shri Asang Muni Ji
112. Shri Vigya Muni Ji
113. Shri Kritartha Muni Ji

114. Shri Subodh Muni Ji
115. Shri Kundal Muni Ji
116. Shri Vrihadra Muni Ji
117. Shri Suratha Muni Ji
118. Shri Suvarcha Muni Ji
119. Shri Shobhan Muni Ji
120. Shri Harit Muni Ji
121. Shri Suman Muni Ji
122. Shri Brahma Datta Munni Ji
123. Shri Tapodhan Muni Ji
124. Shri Shuchi Muni Ji
125. Shri Puran Muni Ji
126. Shri Harshna Muni Ji
127. Shri Toshana Muni Ji
128. Shri Diwakar Muni Ji
129. Shri Suchit Muni Ji
130. Shri Suvrat Muni Ji
131. Shri Shamvit Muni Ji
132. Shri Sudhan Muni Ji
133. Shri Priyamvad Muni Ji
134. Shri Shawet Ketu Muni Ji
135. Shri Vidhuta Muni Ji
136. Shri Sudhanva Muni Ji
137. Shri Prastava Muni Ji
138. Shri Vithavya Muni Ji
139. Shri Rudh Java Muni Ji

140. Shri Pijvana Muni Ji

141. Shri Udaya Muni Ji

142. Shri Swa Prakash Muni Ji

143. Shri Swata Sidha Muni Ji

144. Shri Prabhakar Muni Ji

145. Shri Chayava Muni Ji

146. Shri Sham Priya Muni Ji

147. Shri Lok Priya Muni Ji

148. Shri Prabhu Prasada Muni Ji

149. Shri Hari Nirupan Muni Ji

150. Shri Nahush Muni Ji

151. Shri Vishwasharva Muni Ji

152. Shri Suyasha Muni Ji

153. Shri Dharam Setu Muni Ji

154. Shri Chitra Ketu Muni Ji

155. Shri Lakshameer Muni Ji

156. Shri Sumeru Muni Ji

157. Shri Hari Gambhir Muni Ji

158. Shri Rishi Ram Muni Ji

159. Shri Chatur Bhuj Muni Ji

160. Shri Bhaskar Muni Ji

161. Shri Ramrati Muni Ji

162. Shri Atit Muni Ji

163. Shri Ved Muni Ji

164. Shri Avinashi Muni Ji

165. Shri Sri Chandra Muni Ji

Sri Sri Chandra Ji Maharaj was the last preceptor of the udasin sect. He appointed (4) four of his early disciples as four sacred fires or dhunas of Udasin order who in turn started Bakshish system to propagate their religion.

Approved Granths of Udasin Sect

1. Rigveda

2. Samveda

3. Yajurveda

4. Atharved

5. Upanishad

6. Gita

7. Ramayan

8. Purans

9. Other Sanatan Vedic Granths

(Source: Udasin Kalptaru (Hindi) p. 12)

References

1.   Wilson, Civil and Religious Institutions of the Sikhs—The Sikh Religion: A symposium, pp. 55-56.
2.   Wilson, Religious Sects of the Hindus (edited by Ernst R. Rost), pp. 149-50.
     Source: Western Perspective of the Sikh Religion—Darshan Singh Sehgal Publishers Service, 1991 - Page 91.

3.   Mehtab Singh retaliated by a vitriolic attack on the mahants: The mahants are a class of parasites. They have become infected with the poison which in accordance with a saying of our guru, is contained inthe income derived from the alms of the worshippers, and this poison has made devil of a man. If the government is honestly prepared to help us in this matter we have no objection to receiving this aid; but we are not prepared to admit that sadhus belonging to the Nirmala or Udasi sects possess the right of interferring in our religious affairs and of wondering our religious susceptibilities. P.L.C.D. April 5, 1921 pp. 544-545. (Page 202).

The Sikh Gurdwaras Act of 1925 had two schedules; the first listed 252 shrines. Another 28 were added to the list which were recognised as Sikh gurdwaras without further enquiry. The second schedule listed 224 akharas of Udasis or Nirmalas which were not to be declared gurdwaras unless they fulfilled certain conditions. Any Sikh could put in a petition within one year to have any institution (except those listed in the second schedule) declared a gurdwara.

4.   Cunningham op. cit. p. 50 Narang op. cit. p. 22, Glossary of Punjab Tribes and Castes, vol. I p. 681. It should be pointed out, however, that there is no clear evidence for attributing this measure particularly to Guru Amar Das, Mohsin Fani merely says that the Sikhs established that an udasi or one that has abandoned the world, is not to be esteemed higher than any other man (Vol. II, p. 271). Only Malcolm states distinctly that Amar Das made this separation (Sketch of the Sikhs p. 27). Evolution of the Khalsa. Indu Bhushan Banerjee.

5.   The whole story is linked with a prince, Raja Jagat Rai, who came to Guru Nanak to be blessed, so that his lost kingdom might be restored. The blessing the Guru gave was a lesson in serving not a conferring of powers. No mention of political help is found or implied in the sakhi. It is difficult to avoid linking this story with Prince Khusrau's visit to Guru Arjan. This resulted in the Guru's imprisonment by Jahangir, and his eventual death. Sikhs have always denied that Guru Arjan gave Khusrun's any support in his campaign to defeat Jahangir in a bid for the Mughal throne. The purpose of the sakhi may have been to demonstrate that the Gurus did not meddle in Political affairs.

6.   Kirpal Singh's, Mani Singh appendix, p. 363.

7.   Mc Leod 1968, p. 83.

(Source: Sikhism and its Indian Context 1469-1708 by W. Owen Cole Page 190).

Bibliography

1.   Randhir Singh, Bhai, *Udasi Sikhan di Vithiya*, Amritsar, 1959.

2.   Nara, Ishar Singh, *Itihas Baba Sri Chand Ji Sahib ate Udasin Sampardai*, Amritsar, 1975.

3.   Macauliffe, Max Arthur. *The Sikh Religion: Its Gurus, Sacred Writings and Authors* Oxford, 1909.

(Source: Encyclopaedia of Sikh Religion by Harbans Singh)

14

All India Udasin Parishad

After the Punjab Sikh Gurdwaras Act 1925 coming in force litigation started between the S.G.P.C. on one hand and several Udasin Institutions on the other wherein the S.G.P.C. claimed these institutions to be Sikh Gurdwaras.

In one of such cases a direct Issue was framed "Whether Udasis are Sikhs for the purposes of the Sikh Gurdwaras Act".

The matter having been decided by the Tribunal went up in Appeal to the Lahore High Court and ultimately to the Privy Counsel and the decision is reported in AIR 1936 P.C. 93.

This decision has elaborately given the history of the two sects, their distinctive features concerning Religious beliefs, ceremonies and observances.

This decision has been made the basis of all decisions subsequent. Thereto wherever the questions arose regarding Udasin Institutions.

These Judgments from Supreme Court, Punjab & Haryana High Courts and The Sikh Gurdwaras Tribunal further throw considerable light in this respect.

Any attempt from any quarter to take away the control

and management of these Holy Shrines from the Udasis or convert these places into Sikh Gurdwaras would not only be against the Freedom of Religions as enshrined and guaranted under our constitution but would undo the whole law so far established over more than half a century.

These five recent Judgments have held:

1. Udasis were not Sikhs while the teachings of Sikhs were against asceticism and were apposed to Hindu rites, the Udasis though 'using the same sacred writings as the Sikh kept up much more of the old Hindu Practices followed asceticism, were given to the veneration of Samadhis or Tombs and continued the Hindu Rites concerning birth, marriage and Shradh.   "From Supreme Court Judgment"

2. The Udasis being a separate sect having their separate Institutions, an Institution established by an udasi containing Samadhi and claimed as Dera cannot be declared a Sikh Gurdwara. Reading of Granth Sahib cannot also be a factor for treating the Institution as Sikh Gurdwaras, because the Udasis use the same sacred writings as the Sikhs and recitation of Guru Granth Sahib in Udasi Dera is a Common feature.

    "From High Court Judgment"

3. Gurdwara Sahib Sri Guru Granth Sahib of Kot Fatta is a Dera of udasis. It is not possible to believe that the Parkash of Guru Granth Sahib would be in the room where their is the Smadh. Although Guru Granth Sahib is read there by the Udasi Mahant and Sikhs attend these readings. Mere fact that the Udasis also read Guru Granth Sahib, a book they do venerate, does not make the institution a Sikh Gurdwara, so as to entitle the Sikhs to claim to be associated in the management of the Institution.

From: AIR 1975 SUPREME COURT 1069

AIR 1975 SUPREME COURT 1069

(From: ILR (1968) 2 Punj 499 (FB)

A.N. RAY, C.J., P. JAGAMOHAN REDDY, H.R.
KHANNA AND P.K. GOSWAMI JI

Dharam Das etc. etc., Appellants v. The State of Punjab and
others, Respondents.

Civil Appeals Nos. 354, 1222 and 1251 of 1969, D/- 14.1.1975.

From Page 1073 Para 12

12. The main question in these appeals is whether the
appellants have the right to challenge the provisions of the Act
by and under which a Gurdwara or an Institution is declared
or assured or assumed to be a Sikh Gurdwara. The full Bench
of the Punjab and Haryana High Court in its detailed
judgment has considered several aspects in the light of the
contentions advanced before it which contentions have been
repeated before us. Before we examine the impugned
provisions it is necessary to state that in order to remedy a
situation arising out of certain historical landmarks of Sikh
struggle to retain their shrines which had come into the
possession subscribing to non-Sikh faiths the Act was passed.
The Sikhs believe in the ten Gurus the last of whom was Guru
Gobind Singh. They further believe that there is no other Guru
after Guru Gobind Singh who enjoined on his followers that
after him they should consider Guru Granth Sahib as the
Guru. They do not subscribe to idol worship and polytheism,
nor do they have any Samadhi in their shrines. The teaching
of Sikhs was against asceticism. They believe in Guru Granth
Sahib, which is a Rosary of sacred poems, exhortations, etc.
During the time of the Sikh Gurus,the Gurdwaras were under
their direct supervision and control or under their Masands
or missionary agents. After the death of Guru Gobind Singh
the Panth is recognised as the corporate representative of the
Guru on earth and thereafter they were managed by the Panth
through their Granthis and other sewadars who were under
direct supervision of local Sangat or congregation. During

Maharaja Ranjit Singh's time Sikhism became the religion of the State and large estates and Jagirs were granted to the Gurdwaras, apart from the Jagirs which had been earlier granted during the Mugal period. The position of the Gurdwaras changed during British regime. The Mahants who were in charge of the Sikh Gurdwara could either be a Sikh Mahant or Udasi Mahant. It may here be stated that the Udasis were not Sikhs while the teachings of Sikhs were against asceticism and were opposed to Hindu rites, the Udasis though using the same sacred writings as the Sikhs, kept up much more of the old Hindu practices, followed asceticism were given to veneration of Samadhis or Tombs and continued the Hindu rites concerning birth, marriage and Shradh."

Note: Law relating to Udasi institutions was made the basis for deciding the nature of a Nirmalas Dera.

From: A I R 1967 Supreme Court 1915 (V 54 C 298)

A I R 1967 Supreme Court 1415 (V 54 C 298)

(From: Punjab: 65 Pun L R 94)

K.N. WANCHOO, R.S. BACHAWAT AND V. BHARGAVA, JJ.

Mahant Harnam Singh, Appellant v. Gurdial Singh and another, Respondents Civil Appeal No. 1377 of 1966, D/ 24.2.1967.

Civil P.C. (1908), S. 92— Nature of Interest —Institutions running a free kitchen serving free food to visitors—Resident of the village where such food is served do not have any interest entitling them to file suit under S 92—Institution proved to be meant for Nirmala Sadhus—Plaintiffs as lambardars and followers of Sikh religion cannot be said to have interest entitling them to file the suit as Nirmala Sadhus are not Sikhs—Even in their capacity as lambardars they cannot be said to have such interest. 65 Pun L R 94, Reversed. A I R 1919 Mad 384 and A I R 1924 PC 2 1 (2), Rel. on., A I R 1930 Lah I and A I R 1936 PC 93 AND A I R 1939 Lah 239 Ref.

Cases Referred: Chronological Paras (1939) A I R 1939 Lah 239 (V 261) 41

Pun LR 777, Ishar Das v. Dr. Mohan Singh

(1936) AIR 1936 pc 93 (v 23) 63 IND App 180: Hem Singh v Basant Das

(1930) AIR 1930 Lah 1 (V 17): ILR 11 Lah 142, Kirpa Singh v. Ajaipat Singh

(1924) AIR 1924 PC 221 (2) (V 11): 51 IId App. 282, Vaidyanath Ayarr v. Swaminatha Ayarr.

(1919) AIR 1919 Mad 384 (V6); ILR 42 Mad 360, Ramachandra Aiyar v. Parameswaran Unni

Mr. Naunit Lal for Appellant, M/s. I.M. Oberoi, S.K. Mehta and K.L. Mehta Advocates, for Respondent No. 1.

The following judgement of the Court was delivered by

BHARGAVA J.: This appeal, under certificate granted by the Punjab High Court at Chandigarh has been filed by Harnam Singh appellant against a decree passed by the High Court, decreeing a suit under section 92 of the Code of Civil Procedure, after setting aside the dismissal of the suit by the district Judge, and resolving the appellant from the office of the Mahant of an institution described in the plaint as "Gurdwara Jhandawala". The suit was brought by two plaintiffs after obtaining permmission from the Advocate-General. One of the plaintiff-respondents Ishar Singh, died and his legal representatives were not brought on the record. However, in view of the nature of the suit, no objection was raised before us about the maintainability of this appeal on this ground and consequently, we refrain from dilating on this aspect.

(2) The respondents claimed in the plaint that there is one Guru Granth Sahib at village Jhandawala in the name of Gurdwara Jhandawala which is managed by Mahant Harnam Singh appellant as a Mahatmim, and that he is in possession of the 'Dera' and agricultural land belonging to Guru Granth

Sahib, Gurdwara Jhandawala. The Gurdwara was alleged to be a public religious place which was established by the residents of the village, and it was pleaded that this religious institution was a public trust created by the residents of the village for the service of the public to provide food to the visitors from the Lungar (free kitchen) to allow the people to fulfil religious beliefs and for worship, etc. The plaintiff respondents stated that in the capacity of representatives of owners of lands situated at village Jhandawala and of residents of village Jhandawala, they submitted an application for permission to institute this suit on the ground that the appellant was indulging in various undesirable activities and was misusing the funds of the trust which justified his removal from the office of the Mahant. The respondents claimed that, in their capacity of representatives of the owners of the land situated at village Jhandawala and of residents of village Jhandawala, they were entitled to institute this suit under S. 92, C.P.C.

(3) The suit was contested by the appellant on various grounds, amongst which the principal one, with which we are concerned, is that the plaintiffs respondents had no such interest in this public trust as would entitle them to institute the suit. At the initial stage, the appellant did not admit that there was a public trust in existence at all, but the trial Court held that the institution was a public trust of a religious character, and that finding was not challenged on behalf of the appellant grounds, before the High Court. The two principal grounds, on which the dismissal of the suit by the District Judge was sought to be justified before the High Court, were that plaintiffs-respondents had no right to institute the suit under S. 92, C.P.C., for want of interest in the trust, and that the respondents had failed to prove that the appellant had indulged in any such activities as would justify his removal from the office of the Mahant.

(4) In this appeal, we heard learned counsel for the parties on the first question as to whether the plaintiffs respondents had any such interest in this trust which could

entitled them to institute the suit under S. 92, C.P.C.As has been mentioned above in the plaint the claim was that the plaintiffs were interested in the capacity of representatives of the owners of the land situated at village Jhandawala and of residents of village Jhandawala. On behalf of the plaintiff-respondents, the pleading was that this Gurdwara was established as a public trust on behalf of the residents of the village, but during the course of evidence, even the plaintiffs themselves admitted that, before the residents of the village donated any property at all to this institution the institution was already in existence. According to the plaintiffs, the institution, was then known as Guru Granth Sahib Dera Bhai Saida Ram, and Bhai Saida Ram was the Mahant of the institution. On February 19, 1904 Shamilat land belonging to the inferior proprietors of the village measuring 92 bighas and 12 biswas was donated to Guru Granth Sahib known as Dera Bhai Saida Ram by way of charity. That gift was subsequently confirmed in a mutation order of the revenue authorities on 1st July, 1905. Some time later, it appears that Mahant Mehtab Singh Sadhu Nirmala became the Mahant of this institution and he was succeeded by his Chela, Mahant Narain Singh. On 20th July, 1926 Mahant Narain Singh, describing himself as the Chela of Mahant Mehtab Singh, executed a will bequeathing his rights in the Dera to his Chela. Harnam Singh appellant. It also appears that a construction, described as Gurdwara, was built over an area of 8 kanals and 17 marlas out of the land donated to the Dera by the inferior owners of the village. This suit under Section 92, C.P.C. was instituted on 21st September, 1953 on the allegation that the appellant had stated indulging in activities which unfitted him for the position of the Mahant, as he had been responsible for abduction of women harbouring of dacoits, malversation of the trust income, closure of the Langar, stoppage of religious activities and perpetration of immoral acts.

(5) During the trial of the case it appears that the plaintiffs, attempted to show their interest in the trust property on one other alternative ground. The plaintiffs were admittedly Sikh by religion and the claim put forward was

that this Gurdwara was a religious institution   meant for Sikhs, and in fact, evidence was also sought to be led on behalf of the plaintiffs to show that the Mahant of this institution were not Sadhu Nirmalas, but were Sikhs. One of the plaintiffs-respondents specifically stated to that effect, but their is a concurrent finding by the District Judge and by the High Court that all the Mahants of this institution from Bhai Saida Ram to the present Mahant Harnam Singh appellant, have been Sadhu Nirmalas. The trail Court held that Sadhu Nirmalas are not Sikhs and that this institution was not a Sikh institution at all. The High Court disagreed and held that Sadhu Nirmalas are a section of the Sikhs and,consequently, that Sikhs had in this institution because of its being a Sikh Gurdwara. The High Court thus found in favour of the respondents that they had an interest as required by S. 92. C.P.C. because they were Sikhs and that the Institution was a religious institutions of Nirmala Sadhus who were a section of Sikhs. It was also mentioned by the High Court that the villagers having made the original donation of land which is the nucleus of the institution, the plaintiffs-respondents could not be said to be devoid of interest in the trust of whose property the appellant now asserts himself to be the sole owner. The correctness of this decision was the main point canvassed before us on behalf of the appellant.

(6) As we have indicated earlier, in the plaint the plaintiffs claimed interest in the trust property in their capacity of representatives of the owners of the land situated at village Jhandawala and of residents of village Jhandawala. The findings of fact recorded show that the land, which was donated to this institution was given by the inferior owners of this village out of their joint land. The plaintiffs respondents did show that they were Lambardars in the village but no attempt has been made at any stage to prove that any of the two plaintiffs was an inferior owner of any land situated in this village or that he was a descendant or a successor in interest of any of the inferior owners who donated the land to this institution in the year 1904. The mere capacity as Lambardars does not entitle the plaintiffs respondents to

claim that they are representatives of the inferior owners of the land who donated the land to this institution. The second ground of claim was that the plaintiffs/respondents were residents of village Jhandawala, but again, there is no pleading and no evidence tendered to show that the residents of village Jhandawala in general had any such interest in this trust which could entitle them to institute such a suit. The only allegation was that a Langar used to be run in this institution where free kitchen was provided to visitors. It was nowhere stated that any such free kitchen was being run for the general residents of village Jhandawala who could as of right, claim to be fed in the Langar. Mere residence in a village where free kitchen is being run for providing food to visitors does not create any interest in the residents of the village of such a nature as to claim that they can institute a suit for the removal of the Mahant. The nature of the interest that a person must have in order to entitle him to institute a suit under S. 92 C.P.C. was first examined in detail by the Madras High Court in T.R. Ramachandra Aiyar v. Parameswaran Unni, ILR 42 Mad 360: (AIR 1919 Mad 384). After the dismissal of the suit under S. 92; C.P.C. by the District Judge, the case came up in appeal before Wallis, C. J., and Kumaraswami Sastri, J., who delivered dissenting judgments. The appeal was dismissed and then came up before a Full Bench of three judges under the letters Patent. Three different judgments were delivered by the members of the Full Bench, Abdur Rahim, Oldfield and Coutt-Trotter, JJ. Wallis, C.J., when dealing with the appeal at the earlier stage, expressed his opinion that to entitle him to sue under S. 92, C.P.C. it is not enough that the plaintiff is a Hindu by religion, but he must have a clear interest in the particular trust over and above that which millions of his countrymen may be said to have by virtue of their religion: and this opinion was expressed even though the word "direct" in S. 92, C.P.C. had been omitted. It is not necessary to refer to other opinions expressed by the learned Judge in that case in view of the decision of their Lordships of the Privy Council in Vaidyanatha Ayyar v. Swaminatha Ayyar, 51 Ind App 282: (AIR 1924PC 2 1) (2), where they approved the opinion expressed by Sir John

Wallis, C.J. in the case cited above, and said: "They agree with Sir John Wallis that the bare possibility, however remote, that a Hindu might desire to resort to a particular temple gives him an interest in the trust appears to defeat the object with which the Legislature inserted these words in the section. That object was to prevent people interfering by virtue of this section in the administration of charitable trusts merely in the interest of others and without any real interest of their own." Agreeing with the view expressed by the Privy Council, we hold that in the present case the plaintiffs/respondents who were merely Lambardars and residents of village Jhandawala had, in those capacities, no such interest as could entitle them to institute this suit.

(7) The alternative ground on which the High Court accepted the claim of the plaintiffs/respondents that they had an interest in this institution entitling them to institute the suit because it is a Sikhs Gurdwara meant for all persons following the Sikh faith, was not specifically taken by the plaintiffs in the plaint. However, it appear that during the trial of the suit as well as in the appeal before the High Court, the claim of the plaintiffs that they had an interest entitling them to institute the suit was actually pressed and examined on this ground. The District Judge rejected this claim, but the High Court held in favour of the plaintiffs on its view that Nirmala Sadhus were Sikhs. It appears from the judgment of the High Court that, in arriving at this decision, the Court relied on only two items of evidence consisting of some observation made in Sir Edward Maclagan's Census Report and in Macauliffes Treatises on the Sikh Religion. The High Court made a reference to a judgment of Bhide, J. in Kirpa Singh v Ajaipal Singh, ILR II Lah 142 (AIR 1930 Lah 1) in which this question whether Nirmala Sadhus were Sikhs was examined in great detail, An error however appears to have been committed by the High Court in taking from that judgment a few extracts from Sir Edward Maclagan's Census Report and Macauliffe's Treatises on the Sikh Religion and relying on those extracts without examining the entire material that has discussed by Bhide J. in his elaborate and well considered judgment.

(8) Bhide, J. referred to various books which gave the history and description of Nirmalas and rightly held that, though the origin of Nirmalas was somewhat obscure, it appears to be clear that they were originally the followers of Guru Gobind Singh, but the important point for consideration was whether they had become distinct from the general body of the Sikhs and had ceased to be regarded as such.

(9) The quotation from Macauliffe's book "The Sikh Religion" relied upon by the High Court, is to the following effect:—

There are two great divisions of Sikhs, Sahijdharis and Singhs. The latter are they who accept the baptism inaugurated by Guru Gobind Singh which will be described in the fifth volume of this work. All other Sikhs are called Sahijdharis. The Singhs after the time of Guru Gobind Singh, were all warriors, the Sahijdharis those who lived at ease, as the word denotes, and practised trade or agriculture. In the Singhs are included the Nirmalas and Nihangs. The Sahijdharis include the Udasis founded by Sri Chand, son of Guru Nanak."

References was also made to an article written by Macauliffe on "Sikhism" in the Calcutta Review in 1881 where he described Nirmalas as only nominally Sikhs. The extract from Sir Edward Maclagin's Census Report, on which reliance was placed, runs as follows:—

"It is said that Guru Gobind Singh sent three followers named Karam Singh, Har Chand and Mihr Rai to Benares to acquire a knowledge of Sanskrit, when the pandits of that city refused to come themselves to Gobind Singh, and that, on their return the Guru blessed them as being the only learned men among the Sikhs and called them Nirmala. They were allowed to take the pahul and founded the order of Nirmala Sadhus. They are almost always celibate, and almost always in monasteries. Their principal Akhara is at Hardwar and it is said that their societies throughout the province are periodically visited by a controlling council. They have three considerable monasteries in the Hoshiarpur District at Munak, Adamwal and Alampur Kotla and by our returns they appear to be strong in Gurdaspur, where they are mainly returned as Hindus and Ambala, Ferozepore and in Amritsar where they are mainly returned as Sikhs. It is supposed that they to be found in some numbers in Patiala, but our tables would intimate that they are as strong in Faridkot. They are looked on as unorthodox by most true Sikhs, and it will be observed that more of them are returned in the census as Hindus and Sikhs."

We are unable to agree that these Passages agreed upon by the High Court are enough to lead to an inference that Nirmala Sadhus are Sikhs and that they still retain the essential characteristics of the Sikhs faith. It is true that in their origin Nirmala Sadhu started as a section of Sikhs who were followers of Guru Gobind Singh but subsequents in the period of about 300 years that has since elapsed, they have veered away from the Sikh religion. That is why, after given their historical origin, Macauliffe expressed the opinion that Nirmalas were only normally Sikhs. In Maclagan's Census Report also it was mentioned that Nirmala Sadhus are treated as Sikhs in some places, while in other places they are returned as Hindus. He has mentioned the Districts in Punjab where they are returned mainly as Hindus, and others where they were considered as Sikhs. Faridkot, the District within which the institution with which we are concerned is situated, is mentioned, as a place where they are regarded as Hindus and in the Census they have been returned as such. In these circumstances, we do not think that this material by itself which the High Court called out of the judgment of Bhide, J., could properly lead to the inference that Nirmalas are Sikhs.

(10) Bhide, J. quoted Sir Edward Maclagan's Census Report in greater detail and mentioned how in that Census Report there was a description that the Nirmala Sadhus were at first devoted to the regulations of Gobind Singh, but their taste for Sanskrit literature led them to imbibe the principles of the Vadanta and to re-adopt many of the customs of the Shastras. They gave up the use of meat and spirits and they adopted the dress of the Indian "faqir which was strictly prohibited to the true followers of Guru Gobind Singh. They

had so far deviated from the orthodox Sikhs that they were hardly distinguishable from the Udasi followers of Nanak. They were looked on as unorthodox by most true Sikhs and it was also observed that more of them were returned in the census as Hindus than as Sikhs. Then the "Glossary of the Tribes and Caste of the Punjab and N.W.F. Province by H.A. Rose contained a statement that the Nirmalas, having adhered to the study of the orthodox Hindu scriptures, had lost touch with Sikhism. In Oman's "Mystics, Ascetics, and Saints of India" Nirmalas were described as followers of Vedanta philosophy. From all these authorities an inference clearly follows that Nirmalas have a close affinity to Hindus and in the Census Report for the Punjab for the year 1891 a large number Nirmalas actually declared themselves as Hindus Bhide, J., on these materials, rightly came to the conclusion that Nirmalas Sadhus are not Sikhs.

(11) Further, in this case, there was material showing that this institution at Jhandawala was registered as one of the branches of the principal institution of Nirmala Sadhus known as the Panchayati Akhara situated at Kankhal near Hardwar. There was further evidence showing that in this institution the worship is primarily of a Samadh which is against all tenets of the Sikh religion. Nirmala Sadhus, it appears, as a class worship at Samadhs which goes to show that they can no longer be regarded as people following the Sikh religion. In their beliefs and practices, the Nirmala Sadhus are now quite akin to Udasis, and there is a series of cases which has laid down that members of the Udasi sect are not Sikhs. We need only mention the view expressed by the Privy Council in Hem Singh v. Basanta Das, 68 Ind. App. 180; (AIR 1936 PC 93) holding that "paralled with the growth of this movement, there seems from the time of Sri Chand, Nanak's son, to have been a sect of Udasis who while using the same sacred writings as the Sikhs kept up much more of the old Hindu practices, followed asceticism, were given to the veneration of samadhs and tombs, and continued the Hindu rites concerning birth, marriage, and Shradhs...the Udasis, so far as the matter can be decided by beliefs and

practices, are from the point of view of Sikhs, sehismatics who separated in the earliest days of the movement and never merged thereafter." Relying on these observations of the Privy Council, the Lahore High Court in Ishar Das v. Mohan Singh AIR 1939 Lah 239, held: "It is clearly established in the present case that this is an Udasi institution and that the Sikhs have nothing to do with it except that they may have gone there to listen to the reading of the Sikh scriptures which is also done by the Udasis." These decisions clearly indicate the principle that, though the Sikh Guru Granth Sahib is read in the shrines managed by the members of the Udasi sect, that was not enough to hold that those shrines were Sikh Gurdwaras. In the case before us, the mere fact that at some stage there was Guru Granth Sahib in this Dera cannot thus lead to any conclusion that this institution was aeant, for or belonged to, the followers of the Sikh religion. Clearly, the Dera was maintained for an entirely distinct sect known as the Nirmala Sadhus who cannot be regarded as Sikhs and consequently in their mere capacity of followers of Sikh religion residing in village Jhandawala, the plaintiffs/respondents could not be held to have such an interest as could entitle them to institute the suit under S. 92 of the Code of Civil Procedure. The judgment of the High Court has to be set aside on this ground.

(12) In view of the fact that we are holding that this suit was not instituted properly by persons interested as required by Sec. 92, C.P.C. we consider it unnecessary to express any opinion at all on the second main point decided against the appellant by the High Court, viz. that there were sufficient ground for the removal of the appellant from the office of the Mahant. In this case it is not at all necessary to record any finding on that aspect of the case and, consequently, we refrain from commenting on the finding recorded by the High Court on this question.

(13) The appeal is allowed with cost. The degree of the High Court is set aside and degree passed the by the District Judge is restored.

FF/VSD/G.G.M.   Appeal allowed

From AIR 1976 Punjab & Haryana Page 185
Bhopinder Singh Dhillon and
S.P. Goyal Ji

Joginder Singh and others, Appellants v. The Shiromani Gurdwara Parbandhak Committee, Amritsar, Respondent.

F.A.O. No. 72 of 19766, D/- 20.1-1976*

(A) Sikh Gurdwara Act (8 of 1925), Section 16(2) (iii)— Applicability—Essentials— Institution established by Udasi Faquir — Reading of Granth Sahib in institution—Institution claimed to be Dera and not Gurdwara — Institution is not a Sikh Gurdwara.

Before any institution can be declared as Sikh Gurdwara, two facts have to be established. That the institution was established for use by the Sikhs for the purpose of Public worship and that it was so used before and at the time of the presentation of the petition under Section 7(1) of the Act. The Udasis being a separate sect having their separate institutions, an institution established by an Udasi Faqir having his Samadh and claimed as Dera cannot be declared to be a Sikh Gurdwara. The fact that Granth Sahib is read in the institution, cannot also be a factor for treating the institution as Sikh Gurdwara, because the Udasis use the same sacred writings as the sikhs and the recitation of Guru Granth Sahib in Udasi Dera is a common feature. AIR 1936 PC 93, Ref. on AIR 1934 Lah 63 (2) and AIR 1934 Lah 319 and AIR 1936 Lah 825, Dist.

---

*From order of Sikh Gurdwara Tribunal, Punjab at Chandigarh, Dt. 6.9.1965.

(Paras 8, 12, 13 and 17)

Cases Referred Chronological Paras

AIR 1936 PC 93 = 63 Ind App 180 11, 13

AIR 1936 Lah 825   9, 16

AIR 1934 Lah 63 (2) = 148 Ind Cas 45

9,15

AIR 1934 Lah 319 = 147 Ind Cas 834

9.15

Achhra Singh,for Appellants Narinder Singh for Respondent.

S.P. GOYAL J.:— This is an appeal against the judgment of the Sikhs Gurdwara Tribunal (hereinafter referred to as the Tribunal) dated February 8, 1966 whereby three institutions, namely Gurdwara Deg Sahib, Gurdwara Akal Garh and Gurdwara Guru Granth Sahib, situated in the revenue estate of Gharuan, Tahsil Sirhind, District Patiala, were declared to be Sikh Gurdwaras and the petition of the appellant was dismissed.

On a petition having been presented under sub-section (1) of Section 7 of the Sikhs Gurdwaras act (hereinafter referred to as the Act) the State Government published a Notification No. 1999- C.I. dated November 6, 1962, under the provisions of sub-section (3) of section 7 of the Act describing the said institution as a Sikh Gurdwara. Two claims were filed under Section 8 of the Act one by Joginder Singh and 34 other residents of the said village and the other by Amar Singh and others, which were registered as claims Nos. 272 and 273. Both these claims were filed by more than 20 Sikh worshippers of the institution stating themselves to be more than 21 years of age. The Tribunal consolidated both the claims as they related to the same institution and recorded evidence is claim No. 272 alone. Though the notification and the claim related to the said three institutions, namely, Gurdwara Deg Sahib, Gurdwara Akal Garh and Gurdwara Guru Granth Sahib and the appeal was also filed respecting all the three institution but at the time of arguments the learned Counsel had not pressed the appeal qua the two institutions, Namely Gurdwara Deg Sahib, Gurdwara Akal Garh, and hence we are only concerned with the third institution, that is, Gurdwara Guru Granth Sahib.

3. In their claim petition, the appellants had stated that the institution in dispute was not a Sikh Gurdwara within the meaning of Sec. 16 of the Act, that the petitioner under Section 7 sub-section No. (1) had not been properly presented the persons alleged to have signed or thumb marked, actually did not sing or thumb mark the petition, that the petition under Section 7 had not been presented within limitation and that the Sikh Gurdwara Act was ultra vires of the Constitution: The claim petitions were opposed by the Shiromani Gurdwara Parbandhak Committee (hereinafter referred to as the Committee) who pleaded that the institution in dispute had been established in the memory of a Sikh Saini Bhai Jagga or in the alternative, had been established for worship by the Sikhs and was so used till now. It was, therefore, claimed that the institution in dispute may be declared to be a Sikh Gurdwara by application of the provisions of either Section 16 (2) (iv) or Section 16 (2) (iii) of the Act. The Committee also raised a preliminary objection that the petition, as framed, was not maintainable which gave rise to the following preliminary issue in petition No. 272:—

Whether the petition, as such, is not maintainable?

4. After hearing the parties this issue was decided against the Committee whereafter two more issues were framed in Petition No. 273 which read as under:

1. Whether the Act is ultra vires as noted in the preliminary objection of the petitioners?

2. Whether the institution in dispute is a Sikh Gurdwara or not?

5. Arguments were heard on the issue regarding the vires of the Act before the trial of the issue on merits and this issue was decided in favour of the respondent Committee.

6. Both the parties led oral and documentary evidence on the issue or merits and after hearing the parties and the perusal of the record the Tribunal by application of the provisions of Section 16 (2) (iii) of the Act held the institution

in dispute to be a Sikh Gurdwara. The claim of the respondent—Committee to declare the institution in dispute as a Sikh Gurdwara by application of 16(2) (iv) of the Act was rejected by the Tribunal and we are not concerned with the same in this appeal as the learned counsel for the respondent has not challenged this finding of the Tribunal.

7. The only question before us in this appeal is as to whether the Tribunal has rightly declared the institution in dispute to be a Sikh Gurdwara by applying the provision of Section 16(2) (iii) of the Act which reads as under:—

If the Tribunal finds that the Gurdwara was established for use by Sikhs for the purpose of public worship and was used for such worship by Sikhs before and at the time of presentation of petition under sub-section (1) of Section 7, the Tribunal shall decide that it should be declared to be a Sikh Gurdwara and record as order accordingly."

8. From a bare reading of the said provisions, it is clear that two facts have to be established before any institution can be declared a Sikh Gurdwara, namely, that the institution in dispute was established for use by the Sikhs for the purpose of public worship and that it was so used before and at the time of the presentation of the petition under sub-section (1) of Section 7 of the Act.

9. To substantiate their claim the Committee had examined 5 witnesses Gurdial Singh (R.W.1.) Maghar Singh (R.W. 2), Gurbachan Singh (R.W. 3) Jagan Nath (R.W. 4) and Rattan Singh (R.W. 5) and tendered in evidence certified copies of the revenue record Exhibits R. 1 to R. 15. The appellants in support of their claim examined 7 witnesses, namely Devinder Singh (P.W. 1), Harnarain (P..W. 2), Pritam Dass (P.W. 3) Mansa Dass (P.W. 4), Narat Singh (P.W. 5) Sawan Singh (P.W. 6) and Teja Singh (P.W. 7) and also tendered in evidence certified copies of the revenue record Exhibits P-1 to P-7. Out of the documentary evidence produced by the parties only Exhibits R-9 to 15 and Exhibits P-1 to P-7 relate to the institution in dispute. Exhibit R-10 is

a copy of jamabandi for the year 1960-61 B.K. (that is 1934-4 A.D.) and in the column of ownership Sukha Nand Chela Brahma Chetan Sadh is shown to be the owner of the land which is claimed to be the property of the institution in dispute, Exhibits R-11 and R-11A are copies of the Jamabandis for the year 1973-74 B.K. and 1985-86 BK respectively, whereas Exhibits R-9 and R-12 are copies of the Jamabandis for the year 1960-61 A.D. In the column of ownership in all the Jamabandis the Granth Sahib is entered as the owner of the land in dispute under the management of the then Mahant. Exhibit R-13 is a copy of R-14 a, the statement given by Brahma Nand Chela Chattar Dass and Exhibit certified copy of the joint statement of certain residents of the village forming a part of the Muafi file concerning the institution in dispute. The sum and substance of the statements is that Brahma Nand serves wayfares and the Faqirs who visit the Dera, provides all sorts of comforts to them and Parkash of the Adi Granth Sahib is regularly done in the institution. Exhibit R-15 is a copy of the relevant part of Naksha Muafiat. The recipient of the Muafi in this document is shown to be Dera Makan Granth Sahib under the management of Brahma Nand Chela Chattar Dass, Faqir Udasi. In Column No. 7 reference is made to an order of the Settlement Commissioner dated October 15, 1907 A.D. whereby the Muafi was entered in the name of Granth Sahib under the management of Sukha Nand Chela Brahma Chetan Faqir Udasi on the condition that he will look after the comforts of the wayfarers and Faqirs, recite Granth Sahib and be of good conduct. From these documents, the Tribunal arrived at the conclusion and rightly so that from the years 1960-61 Bk. till the time the said notification was made, the institution was described as Dera Granth Sahib. Further, on the basis of the oral evidence adduced by the parties, the Tribunal found that the village Gharuan where the institution in dispute is situated is a Sikh village and it was the village community who appointed or removed the Mahants of this institution. The Tribunal also found, though without any evidence on the record, that the land attached to this Dera was donated by the Sikh Sardars. On the basis of these findings and relying upon some decisions of the Lahore High Court, namely Bishan Das v. Gurbaksh Singh, AIR 1934 Lah 63 (2) Gurmukh Das v. Partap Singh, AIR 1934 Lah 319 and Harnam Dass v Kartar Singh, AIR 1936 Lah 825 the Tribunal held that the respondent had succeeded in substantiating both the ingredients of establishment and user as laid down in Section 16 (2) (iii) of the Act with respect to the institution in dispute and consequently decided the same by Gurdwara.

10. Mr. Achra Singh, the learned counsel for the appellant, has challenged the said finding of the Tribunal and has urged that neither the institution in dispute has been proved to have been established for use by the Sikhs for the purpose of public worship nor was it so used before and at the time of presentation of the petition under sub-section (1) of Section 7 of the Act. According to the learned counsel, the most material document on the record Exhibit P-3 a copy of Kafiyat Delhi, had not been taken into consideration by the Tribunal which conclusively shows that the institution in dispute was established in the memory of Bhai Jagga who an Udasi Faqir. The perusal of the said document shows that village Chandesar where part of the land claimed to be belonging to the institution in disputed is situate, was a Rajput village. Due to famines, the Rajputs were turned out, one by Gurta, a resident of village Gharuan. After the death of Guria, his descendants accepted the suzerainty of Maharaja Karam Singh. Guria, during his lifetime distributed the estate amongst his sons and gave some land by way of Muafi to Bhai Jagga. During the regime of Maharaja Sahib Singh a regular Patta Muafi was granted concerning the said Muafi. It is admitted between the parties that Maharaja Sahib Singh died in the year 1813 A.D. It is, therefore, evident that the land attached to the institution in dispute was granted to Bhai Jagga as Muafi sometime before the year 1813 A.D. At the time of the first settlement in the erstwhile State of Patiala which took place in the year 1960-61 Bk., (1903 A.D.) the ownership of the land was entered in the name of Sukha Nand Chela Brahm Chetan Sadh Udasi, but regarding the Muafi a note was made in the remarks column that the matter was under consideration.Ultimately the Muafi was entered in the name

of Granth Sahib by the order of the Settlement Commissioner as entered in Exhibit P. 15.

11. As regards the institution in dispute, it is a common case of the parties that the same was established in the memory of Bhai Jagga, who was an Udasi Faqir. It is also not disputed by the respondent that the smadh of Bhai Jagga exists at the premises of the said institution. The existence of the smadh naturally must have come into being on the death of Bhai Jagga and consequently the institution in dispute must have been in existence when Bhai Jagga died. The pedigree-table Exhibit P. 4 relating to Faquir Udasis shows that Bhai Jagga was succeeded by Pritam Dass. There were two more succession till Sukha Nand who was alive at the time of first settlement. There is neither any evidence produced nor any suggestion that these Udasi Faqirs had any other Dera, apart from the one in dispute. The presence of the Smadh of Bhai Jagga establishes beyond doubt that it was the institution dispute which was the Dera of Bhai Jagga and his descendants. There is no evidence worth the name on the record to show that Bhai Jagga was a Sikh or his descendants were Sikhs or had faith in Sikh religion. In Hem Singh v. Basant Dass, AIR 1983 PC 93, It was held:—

Parallel with the growth of this movement (Sikh religion) there seems from the time of Sri Chand, Nanak's son, to have been a sect of Udasis who while using the same sacred writings, as the Sikhs, kept up much more of the old Hindu practices followed asceticism, were given to the veneration of Smadhas or tombs, and continued the Hindu rites concerning birth, marriage and Shradh."

12. The Privy Council further approved in the said case a finding given by the Tribunal that:—

"xxxx both from the historical aspect of the case and from the observation of outward practices and inward beliefs of Udasis. I would have no hesitation in holding that Udasis are not Sikhs for the purpose of the Sikh Gurdwaras Act."

Since the said decision, it has never been disputed that

the Udasis are a separate sect and have their separate institutions. There can, therefore, be no manner of doubt that the institution in dispute was established by Bhai Jagga or his spiritual descendants who were all Sadh Udasis.

13. There is another very important circumstance which goes a long way to show that the institution in dispute was an Udasi Dera and not a Sikh Gurdwara. The documents Exhibits R—13 and R—14 are the statements of Brahma Nand and some of the residents of village Gharuan where the institution in dispute is situated. These statements were recorded in the year 1938 A.D. to decide if the Muafi was to be continued or not. Brahma Nand is described in Exhibit R—13 as Chela Chattar Dass Faqir Udasi Mohtmim Dera Baba Jagga. In his statement also Brahma Nand stated that he was looking after the comforts of the wayfarers and Faqirs coming to the Dera and that Parkash of Guru Granth Sahib had been done in the Dera by him. The other residents of the village also described the institution in dispute as a Dera and not a Gurdwara. It would be futile to say that as late as the year 1938 the residents of the village who were mostly Sikhs and gave their statements would not be knowing the distinction between an Udasi Dera and a Gurdwara. Had it been a Sikh Gurdwara it was highly improbable that they would term it as a Dera. All these facts and circumstances had been completely ignored by the Tribunal and instead the said documents were used by the Tribunal to record a finding in favour of the respondent on the ground that Granth Sahib was admittedly recited in the institution in dispute and no other object of worship had been mentioned in the said documents. The fact that in the statement of Brahma Nand it is mentioned that Granth Sahib was recited to the Dera and the fact that no other object of worship was mentioned in the said statement or in the statements of the other villagers can be easily explained. The proceedings in which those statements were made were instituted by the State to find out if the Muafi was to be continued or not. The institution was situated in the erstwhile Patiala State which was a Sikh State. In his anxiety to secure the continuance of the Muafi, Brahma Nand must

have thought it inadvisable to mention and other object of worship in the Dera and confined his statement to the fact that Parkash of Guru Granth Sahib was done in the Dera. So far as the recitation of Granth Sahib in the institution in dispute is concerned it is well known that the Udasi used the same sacred writings as the Sikhs and the recitation of Guru Granth Sahib in Udasi Dera is a very common feature. With respect to a similar statement, their Lordships of the Privy Council to Hem Singh's case AIR 1936 PC 93 (Supra) observed:—

Comment has been made that the only references to worship are to the reading of Granth, but these are directed to showing the diligence and worthiness of the applicant. Before inferences can be drawn from the absence of any reference to other forms of worship, one must remember that they might well have seemed both unnecessary and tactless when the backing of Sikh officials and persons of local influence was being sought."

14. The appellants had produced nine witnesses who had all stated that Smadh of Bhai Jagga was the object of worship in the institution in dispute. No cross-examination was adverted to, to discredit their statements in this respect. The respondents produced five witnesses who stated that the only festival celebrated in the institution was that of Maghi which was held in the memory of Bhai Jagga. They had all admitted the existence of the Smadh and none had the courage to depose that the Smadh of Bhai Jagga was not the object of worship on the said festival. All the witnesses of the respondents had depose that no Gur purb or other Sikh festival was ever celebrated in the institution in dispute. Moreover, the oral evidence adduced is not concerning the establishment of the institution. The institution was established many years before any of the witnesses was born. There being clear documentary evidence available as to the nature of the institution at the time of the establishment, the oral evidence is meaningless.

15. The other two factors relied upon by the Tribunal to record a finding in favour of the respondent were that the

grant of the Muafi was described in the revenue records since the year 1907 in the name of either Makan Granth Sahib or Granth Sahib and that the lands standing in the name of the institution were granted by the Sikh Sardars. There is absolutely no evidence on the record to support the observation that the land attached with the institution were donated by the Sikh Sardars. On the other hand, from the Kafiyat Delhi Exhibit P-8 it is proved beyond doubt that the land situated at village Chandesar was donated by one Guria to Bhai Jagga. It is no body's case that Guria was a follower of Sikh religion or of the Gurus. Regarding the rest of the land standing in the name of the institution, there is no evidence on the record as to who donated the same. The observation made by the Tribunal that the land standing in the name of the institution in dispute was donated by the Sikh Sardars is therefore, without any basis and is based on mere conjectures. The other fact, which weighed with the Tribunal that the Muafi was entered in the name of the Makan Granth Sahib or Granth Sahib since the year 1907, can hardly justify a finding that the institution in dispute was a Sikh Gurdwara. It is not disputed that prior to the year 1907 the Muafi stood in the personal names of the Mahants for more than 100 years. The fact that in the regime of a Sikh ruler the Muafi was entered in the name of Granth Sahib, would by no stretch of reasoning, be an indication of the situation as it prevailed in the 18th an earlier period of 19th century when the institution in dispute came in existence. The facts and circumstances in Hem Singh's case AIR 1936 PC 93 (supra), though similar to the facts and circumstances of the present case in many respects were much stronger and still their Lordships of the Privy Council held that the institution could not be held to have been established by the Sikhs for public worship. The decisions relied upon by the Tribunal have actually no bearings on the facts of the present case. In Bishan Das v. Gurbaksh Singh, AIR 1934 Lah 63(2), apart from the fact that the institution in dispute was the only place of worship in the village, it was found that the original institution which was an Udasi Dharmsala had fallen down and abandoned and the institution in dispute was a different foundation which had been built by the Sikh residents of the village at their own expense. It was under those circumstances that institution was declared to be a Sikh Gurdwara and the decision obviously has no relevancy to the facts of the present case. In Gurmukh Das v. Parap Singh, Air 1934 Lah 319, the other case relied upon by the Tribunal, what weighted with the Bench was that there was no Smadh on the premises of the institution and all the Smadhs of the office-holders were situated outside the village and that the Mahant, at the time when the question of Muafi was being investigated in the year 1052, stated that the lands were Muafi for the expenses of the Gurdwara. Moreover, in the said case there was no allegation much less any proof that the institution was established in the memory of an Udasi Faqir whose Smadh was in existence at the premises of the institution the object of worship. The ratio and the decision in this case is, therefore, of no help and guidance for the determination of the nature and was also on the present institution in dispute.

16. The third case of Harnam Das AIR 1936 Lah 825 (supra) relied upon by the Tribunal, if read as a whole, supports the conclusion that the Institution in dispute is an Udasi dera and not a Sikh Gurdwara. The facts found and the findings given in that case are contained in detail in head-note (b) which reads as under:—

"The Dharamshalas were managed by Mahants, the Udasi Fakirs. They had their chellas as Mahants of the institution. Muafi of land was granted on condition of Granth Sahib being regularly read. The Dharamshalas were not called Dharamshalas but were referred in documents as deras. There were smadhs on the land of Mahants and smadhs were commonly found in Udasi institution. Though there was langar or an alms-house, there was no place shown where Granth Sahib was read or recited.

Held: that the institution was not a Sikh Gurdwara and that the mere fact that the Granth Sahib was read was not sufficient to make it a Sikh Gurdwara."

17. Mr. Narinder Singh, the learned counsel for the

respondent, however, contends that the institution in dispute holding the Muafi has been continuously in the revenue record as Makan Granth Sahib or Granth Sahib since the first settlement which took place in the year 1907 A.D. and relying on certain decisions of the Lahore High Court has argued that from this use of the institution for a long period of more than 50 years, a presumption can be raised that the institution in dispute was established for use by the Sikhs for the purpose of public worship. There can be no dispute with this principal of law, but as discussed above, in the present case the facts proved on the record give a clear indication that the institution in dispute was established by Bhai Jagga who was an Udasi Faqir. Moreover, the institution in dispute was claimed to be a Dera by the then Mahant Brahma Nand as late as in the year 1238 A.D. and so was it described by the residents of the village. In view of these facts and circumstances it is not possible to raise a presumption from the latter use of the institution that it was established or used by the Sikhs for the purpose of public worship.

18. As a result, this appeal is allowed, the judgment of the Tribunal is set aside and a declaration is granted in favour of the appellant that the institution in dispute is not a Sikh Gurdwara. The parties are, however, left to bear their own costs.

B.S. DHILLON, J: I agree
Appeal allowed

Sikh Gurdwara Act (8 of 1925), S 16 (2)—Whether Gurdwara is Sikh Gurdwara—Onus—Discharge of.

The onus to prove that the Gurdwara in question, was a Sikh Gurdwara was on the Shiromani Gurdwara Prabandhak Committee. The committee was required to prove the following essential ingredients: (1) that the Gurdwara was established for use by Sikhs for public worship, (2) that it was being actually used for worship by Sikhs and, (3) that it was being used by Sikhs for public worship both before the presentation of the petition and at the time of presentation of the petition under S. 7. As there was no direct evidence to establish that the Gurdwara was established in the above mentioned circumstances was being used as such so as to satisfy the ingredients of the above provision, the Court was left to draw inference from the documentary and oral evidence on the record, Under (iii) of sub-sect. (.) of S. 16, two condition have to be satisfied. Even if one condition is not satisfied, the ouns is not discharged.

It was clear from the various documents that the Dera to begin with was founded by a Fakir Udasi, Mahant Garib Dass, and the land was onwed by him in his own name and the said Dera was more a charitable institution that a religious one. Only Muafi was granted by a Sikh ruler subsequently.

Held that the mere fact that the grant of the Muafi was subject to the condition of the existence of the Dera as well as Guru Granth Sahib would not convert the Dera into Sikh Gurdwara. There was no evidence on the record to warrant the conclusion that the Dera had been brought into existence by the Sikhs for the purpose of public worship. The committee had not been able to discharge its burden. AIR 1937 Lah 290; F. A. O. 64 of 1966, Dt. 12.5.1976 (Punj.) Dist, AIR 1937 Lah 280, Rel. on.

(Paras 12, 13, 15, 16)

Case Referred Chronological Paras

(1977) 79 Pun LR 298	11
AIR 1976 Punj & Har 130 (FB)	5
1976-78 Pun LR (Delhi) 238	9
ILR (1976) I Punj & Har 594 (FB)	9
(1976) F.A.O. No. 64 of the D 12.5.1976 (Punj & Har)	15
AIR 1972 SC 2526 : (1972) 2 SCC 461	11
(197) F.A.O. No. 111 of 1965, Dt. 23.8.1971 (Punj)	15
(1970) F.A.O. No. 177 of 1968, Dt. 8.1.1970 (Punj)	6, 7

P.K. Palli with Amarjit Markan, for Appellants Narinder Singh for Respondent.

From Para 15 Page 52

15. The learned counsel for the respondent has urged that from the evidence on the record, it is established that there was no other mode of worship except that Guru Granth Sahib in the Dera, that Guru Granth Sahib was installed in the Dera and that the Muafi was granted in favour of this Dera by a Sikh ruler and, therefore according to the learned counsel, the only conclusion which can be drawn is that the institution known as Dharamsala or the Dera was established by Sikhs for the purpose of worship and use by the Sikhs. It was also urged that Dharamsala, Dera or the Gurdwara are inter-changeable expression and in all cases, the institution is a Gurdwara: In support of this contention, reliance has been placed on F.A.O. No. 64 of 1966 (Jaswant Dass v. The Shiromani Gurdwara Parbandhak Committee) decided on May 12, 1976 (Punj & Har) and Ram Kishan Das v. Shiromani Gurdwara Parbandhak Committee, Amritsar, AIR 1937 Lah 290. In the former case, on the basis of evidence adduced by the Committee, the finding was reached that from the very inception of the institution known as Dera, land had been gifted by the Sikh rulers to the first ancestor and the founder of the Dera and the Muafi had been granted on the sole condition that the holy Guru Granth Sahib will be kept there and recited. It was under these circumstances the conclusion of the Tribunal that the Gurdwara, in question, was a Sikh Gurdwara, was upheld.

In the latter case, the Court came to the conclusion from the evidence on the record that there was no doubt that when the institution was endowed with the Muafi by the Sikh Sardar towards the end of 18th century, it was not only a Dharamsala to which the Samadh of a Sikh Sardar was attached but also a Makan Guru Granth Sahib. Further conclusion was also reached that the institution was not a Udasi Dera, but the ordinary Sikh village Dharamsala. As against this, reliance has been placed by the learned counsel for the appellants on F.A.O. No. 111 of 1965 (Shiromani Gurdwara Parbandhak Committee, Amritsar v. Prabhu Dayal) decided on August 23, 1971, wherein the institution was not held to be a Sikh Gurdwara though the finding was that the land had been donated by a Sikh Maharaja and the Muafi had been granted on the ground that expenses for Doop Deep etc. will be met from the same. It was also held that the mere fact that the holy book of Guru Granth Sahib is installed in the institution does not lead to the conclusion that it is a Sikh Gurdwara. In Arjan Singh v. Harbhajan Das, AIR 1937 Lah. 280, the originator of the shrine was generally known as udasi Fakir and the institution from its inception was more a charitable institution than the religious one. It was held that the mere reciting of the Guru Granth Sahib by Sikh under the circumstances would not convert an institution which was Udasi from its inception into a Sikh institution. The facts, in the present case, are almost similar. It is clear from the discussion of the various documents referred to above; Exhibit P-22, that the Dera to begin with was founded by a Fakir Udasi. Mahant Garib Dass, and the land was owned by him in his own name and the said Dera was more a charitable institution than a religious one. Only Muafi was granted by a Sikh ruler subsequently. The mere fact that the Muafi was subject to the condition of the existence of the Dera as well as Guru Granth Sahib will not convert the Dera in the present case into a Sikh Gurdwara.

16. There is no evidence on the record to warrant the conclusion that the institution, that is, the Dharamsala or the Dera had been brought into existence by the Sikhs for the

purpose of public worship, under Cl. (iii) of subsec. (2) of S 16 two conditions have to be satisfied. Even if one condition is not satisfied, the onus is not discharged. We are firmly of the opinion that in the present case, the respondent has not been able to discharge its burden. Consequently, we reverse the finding of the Tribunal on Issue No. 2 and hold that the institution notified under S. 7 of the Act has been proved to be a Sikh Gurdwara.

17. Besides, the documentary evidence both the parties also produced a number of witness who supported the respective case of the party on whose behalf they put in their appearance as witnesses. Their evidence is more or less of a partisan character and cannot be given much ordence especially when the case of the appellants is clearly established from the documentary evidence as mentioned above.

18. For the reasons mentioned above, we accept the appeal, allow the petition of the appellants under S. 8 of the Act and declare that the institution, in question, is not a Sikh Gurdwara. There will be no order as to costs.

Appeal allowed.

Before the Sikh Gurdwara Tribunal Punjab Chandigarh

Petition No. 478 of 1966   **Decided on 29.8.1978**

Mahant Man Dass Chela Mahant Hans Dass, Sadh Udasi of village Kot Fatta Tehsil and District Bhatinda

.......Petitioner

Versus

Shiromani Gurdwara Parbandhak Committee, Amritsar

........Respondent

Petition under Section B of the Sikh Gurdwara Act, 1925.

Quorum: **Sardar Pritam Singh Pattar, President and Sardar Bhan Singh, Member.**

Mr. P.K. Palli, Counsel for the Petitioner.

S. Charan Singh, Counsel for the respondent Committee

Judgment: (per President)

Bhakhtawar Singh and fifty-nine others, residents of village Kot Fatta, Tehsil and District Bhatinda, made a petition under sub-section (1) of section 7 of the Sikh Gurdwaras Act, 1925 (hereinafter called the Act) to declare the institution in dispute namely Gurdwara Sahib Sri Guru Granth Sahib, situated in the revenue estate of Kot Fatta, Tehsil and District Bhatinda to be a Sikh Gurdwara under the Act, and also to declare that the property whose list was attached to the said petition belonged to the above said Gurdwara. In pursuance of the provisions of sub-section (3) of section 7 of the Act, the Punjab Government published this petition vide Notification No. 721 G.P. dated the 17th April, 1964 in the Punjab Govt. Gazette dated the 17th April, 1964, alongwith the list of rights, titles and interests in properties claimed to belong to the said Gurdwara. Thereafter Mahant Man Dass Chela Mahant Hans Dass, Udasi Sadh resident of village Kot Fatta, filed this petition under section 8 of the Act, alleging that the institution in dispute is not a Sikh Gurdwara but is a Dera of Udasi Sadhus and that the property mentioned in the Notification No. 721-G.P. dated the 17th April, 1964 belongs to this Dera and that he is a office holder of this religious institution and the said notification may be quashed. It was claimed that the Dera of Udasi Sadhus and other buildings alongwith the well and the Smadh of Bassu Dass Khadesari are situated in Khasra No. 406 measuring about 40 Bighas-14. Biswas. This petition was forwarded by the Punjab State Government to this Tribunal for disposal in accordance with law. Notice of this petition was issued to the persons who originally moved the petition under section 7 (1) of the Act but none of them appeared in spite of service. Notice was also issued to the Shiromani Gurdwara Parbandhak Committee, Amritsar which was added as a respondent in this case. The respondent-committee contested this petition. It was alleged that the institution in dispute is a Sikh Gurdwara having been established for worship for Sikhs and that Gurdwara Granth Sahib is the only object of worship there and the land owned by the institution is entered in the name of Guru Granth Sahib. It was denied that the Gurdwara was an Udasi institution. It was alleged that the petitioner Mahant Man Dass was not a hereditary office-holder and had no locus-standi file the petition. It was claimed that the office holders in this institution have all to been Sikhs.

On these pleadings of the parties the following issues were framed by this Tribunal on 22.8.1966:

1. Whether the petitioner is a hereditary office-holder entitled to present petition ? O.P.P.

2. Whether the Institution is a Sikh Gurdwara? O.P.R.

It appears that later on the Tribunal was abolished in 1966 and was again constituted in the year 1970. The counsel for the parties stated on 27.10.1970 that issue No. 1 relating to the locus-standi of the petitioner to file that this petition may be treated as preliminary issue and it may be decided first. After recording the evidence of the parties the Tribunal held on 5.11.1971 that the petitioner Mahant Man Dass failed to prove that he is a hereditary office holder and thus had no locus-standi to file the petition and the same was dismissed with costs. Feeling aggrieved Mahant Man Dass petitioner filed F.A.O. No. 345 of 1971 against the decision in the Punjab and Haryana High Court which was accepted on 19.1.1978 and the decision of the Tribunal on issue No.1 was set aside and the case was remanded for being tried on merits.

Issue No. 2

The onus to prove this issue lies on the respondent-committee. In the written statement it was not mentioned that under which clause of Section 16 (2) of the Act the case of the respondent-committee, fall. However, during arguments the counsel for the respondent committee stated that the case of the respondent, committee falls under section 16 (2) (iii). The relevant portion of Section 16 of the Act reads as follows:

"16(1) Notwithstanding anything contained in any other law in force, if in any proceeding before a Tribunal it is disputed that a Gurdwara should or should not be declared to be a Sikh Gurdwara, the Tribunal shall before enquiring into any other matter in dispute relating to the said Gurdwara, whether it should or should not be declared a Sikh Gurdwara in accordance with the provisions of sub-Section (2).

(2) If the Tribunal finds that the Gurdwara-

(i) ....

(ii) ....

(iii) was established for use by Sikhs for the purpose of public worship and was used for such worship by Sikhs, before and at the time of the presentation of the petition under sub-section (1) of section 7, or

(iv) ....

(v) ....

the tribunal shall decide that it should be declared to be a Sikh Gurdwara and record an order accordingly.

To declare an institution to be a Sikh Gurdwara under section 16(2) (iii) of the Act, it is necessary to prove: (1) that the institution was established for use by Sikhs for the purpose of public worship and (2) that it was used for such worship by Sikhs, before and at the time of the presentation of the petition under Sub-Section (1) of section 7. Both these conditions must co-exists and if any of these conditions is not fulfilled, then the provisions of Section 16(2) (iii) would not be satisfied. The onus to prove that the institution in dispute is a Sikh Gurdwara is on the respondent-committee. Both the parties have produced oral and documentary evidence to prove their allegations. The respondent-committee produced six witness and thirteen documents, while the petitioner produced thirteen witnesses and seventeen documents.

All the six witnesses examined by the respondent-committee belong to village Kot Fatta, Tehsil and District Bhatinda where the institution in dispute is situated. It is undisputed that the institution in dispute is located at a distance of two miles from Abadi of village Kot Fatta, Dalip Singh R.W.-1 testified that the buildings of this Gurdwara in dispute was constructed before he attained, the age of discretion and that ancestors told him that one person whose name was Basau Dass meditated at that place while standing and therefore he was also known as Khadesari. He went on to state that the said Basau Dass used to recite Wah-Guru Wah Guru and that the residents of his village and also of villages Tungwala, Naiwala, Sabhir, Kartar Singh Wala and Bhara- which are stated to be situated at a distance of two miles from this institution constructed the building of this Gurdwara. He testified that one Gurdit Singh who was his ancester had donated land to this institution and this fact was told to him by his father and grand-father. The building of this Gurdwara, according to him, is a domed shape which is a pucca one, wherein Guru Granth Sahib is kept and it is the only object of worship there and that this building is in the original shape and there are about 8-9 rooms of this Gurdwara which are used for residence by the petitioner and also for the stay of the travellers and for running a Langar (free kitchen). According to him there is also a Nishan Sahib in the premises of this Gurdwara besides a tank. The first Granthi of this Gurdwara whom he saw, was Karam Singh, and the first person who was managing the affairs of this Gurdwara whom he saw, was Hans Dass. He deposed that the Sikh residents of his village and also of the above mentioned adjoining villages go to this Gurdwara for worship of Guru Granth Sahib and that during the time of Hans Dass 5-10 persons also used to reside in this Dera to assist him and they used to perform Kirtan in the morning and that in the evening the Path of Rehras Sahib was performed and thereafter the Sukhassi of Guru Granth Sahib was performed in the domed shape building and the Langar was distributed. Hans Dass according to him, was a Keshadhari Sikh. He started that the petitioner Mahant Man Dass is also a Keshadhari Sikh (However, when on 27.3.1978 the statement of this witness was recorded Man Dass petitioner was present in court and he removed his turban and the hair on his head were found cut and he had small trimed hair on his beard.) He deposed that Gurpurabs of Guru Nanak Dev and Guru Gobind Singh are celebrated in his Gurdwara. He admitted in cross-examination that the new 8-9 Pucca rooms in the premises of the institution were constructed by the petitioner only 4-5 years ago and prior to that there was on Deori and two big rooms (Kutcha built). In his cross-examination he denied that there was any Smadh of Basau Dass in the domed shape building. He did not know to which village the first Granthi Karam belonged. To the same effect are the statements of Joginder Singh, RW-2, Gurbux Singh RW-3, Kartar Singh RW-4, Parduman Singh RW-5 and Bakhtawar Singh RW-6. It was deposed by Joginder Singh RW-2 that inside the domed-shape building there in a Thara and on that Thara there is a Palki (i.e. Manji Sahib) and in that Palki there remains a Parkash of Guru Granth Sahib. He admitted that this Palki was donated by him about 3-7 years ago. Joginder Singh RW-2 admitted that in villages Tungwala, Kot Shamir, Kot Bhara, etc. which are situated at a distance of two miles from the institution in dispute there is one Gurdwara in each those villages. He deposed that Karam Singh Granthi was brought by the villagers to this Gurdwara about 17-18 years ago and he died about 2-3 years ago.

Both Joginder Singh RW-5 and Dalip Singh RW-1 deposed that Shaukin Dass is working as a Granthi in this Gurdwara for the last some years and he is residing in this Gurdwara since his childhood. This Shaukin Dass is a Gurbhai of the petitioner and he was examined as PW-12, and he contradicted the evidence of these two witnesses. He testified that he is a Mahant of the institution at Chindse, District Ferozpore and he resides there. He deposed that he is registered as an Ayurvedic practitioner and is the President of the Ayurved Association of Ferozepore District and that he was given Tamre-Patra in recognition of his sacrifices in the freedom movement. He deposed that he never worked as a Granthi in the institution in dispute nor is there any Parkash of Guru Granth Sahib in this Gurdwara that he had never seen any Granthi in this Gurdwara and that Man Dass petitioner is illiterate and so was his Guru Hans Dass. He admitted that about 40 years ago when he was still young, he was convicted and sentenced for committing theft of gun but he was acquitted on appeal. This witness, thus contradicts the statements of these two witnesses Joginder Singh RW-2 and Dalip Singh RW-1, that he is working as a Granthi in the Gurdwara in question for the last several years.

Dalip Singh RW-1 deposed that for the last 5-7 years Shaukin Dass was performing the work of Granthi in this institution. But as against the Joginder Singh RW-2 stated that Shaukin Dass is working as Granthi in the Dera for the last 10-12 years and he, thus, contradicts the statement of Dalip Singh RW-1.

Gurbux Singh RW-3 stated in his cross-examination that he was told by his ancestors that the land was donated in the name of Guru Granth Sahib kept in this Gurdwara and that the Sadhus residing in the institution in dispute are called Nirmala Sadhus. Parduman Singh RW-5 deposed that there is no Smadh in the domed type room in this Gurdwara and that there is Parkash of Guru Granth Sahib. According to him, Man Dass petitioner is illiterate and that Baba Basau Dass Khandesari belonged to their village and he did not originally construct the building of this Gurdwara. He went on to State that Sewa Dass performs the function of a Granthi in the ˈinstitution in dispute and prior to him Jaggar Dass used to work as Granthi and that Hans Dass nominated Man Dass as Mohtmim of this Gurdwara and also gave him the land attached to the Gurdwara. All these witnesses admitted that the petitioner is a Brahmin of their village and he is illiterate.

The oral evidence of these witnesses of the respondent-committee is vague and inconsistent and is contradicted by the documentary evidence which shall be discussed below. Name of them known when this institution was established and by whom and for what purpose. They simply stated that their ancestors told them that one Gurdit Singh donated land and that one person called Baba Khadesari, who meditate there, and the residents of their village Kot Fatta and of the adjoining villages constructed the building of this institution. None of them gave the name of the ancestors who told them these facts. Moreover, these statements are not admissible under any of the provisions of section 32 of the Indian Evidence Act. The institution in dispute is situated at a distance of 2 miles from the village Abadi. From the documentary evidence on the file it is clear that this institution was established more than 150 years ago and none of these witnesses was born at that time.

Mahant Hari Kishan Dass PW—a, aged 70 years, Mahant Dera Chhata Baba Magani Ram, Patiala, deposed that he is a Mahant in the Udasi Bhek and the General Secretary of the Udasin Mahamandal, Punjab and member of Akhil Bhartiya Udasin Parishad, Hardwar and he often visits the institution in dispute. He deposed that it is the Dera of Udasi Sadhus and is known by the name of Dera Baba Khadesari who used to meditate by standing and he founded this Dera. The succession is from Guru to Chela to the post of Mahant of this Dera and that the only object of worship in the Dera is Samadh of Baba Khadesari, which is located in the domed type room and there are Smadhs of the previous Mahants also there. There is no other object of worship in that room excepting the Smadh and Murti of Sri Chand. He deposed that about 2½ years ago, the petitioner built a new temple and shifted the Murti of Sri Chand in that temple and he was present at that time. He went on to state, that there is no Parkash of Guru Granth Sahib in the premises of this Dera; that no Sikh ceremony including Gurpurabs or Kirtan is performed in this Dera and that no free kitchen is run in this Dera. However, food is prepared for the residents who reside in the Dera and for the Sadhus who visit the Dera. He denied that there is any tank. According to him, there is a kutcha pond where water collect during the rainy season. The first Mahant of this Dera, whom he saw, was Mahant Hans Dass, who had long Jattas (matted hair) on his head. To the same effect are the statements of Banarsi Dass PW-1, Baldev Singh PW-2, Sivjant Singh PW-3, Mathra Ram PW-4, Jagir Singh PW-5 and Mukhtar Singh PW-6, who are all residents of village Kot Fatta Bhajan Singh PW-7, of village Tungwali, Shaukin Dass PW-12 and Man Dass petitioner PW-13.

Mahant Sewa Dass PW-II is the Mahant of Dera Baba Jamuna Dass situated in the Abadi of village Kot Fatta and he deposed that he never worked as a Granthi in this Dera and that there is no Parkash of Guru Granth Sahib in this Dera. He deposed that he cuts hair on the beard as well as on the head and smokes and is an Udasi Sadhus. Gurbanta Singh PW-10 is an Udasi Sadhu, who is the Mahant of Dera Tapa, District Bhatinda and is the President of the Zila Mandals of Districts Bhatinda and Hissar. He deposed that he often visits the Dera in dispute in his capacity as President of Zila Mandals of Bhatinda and Hissar and there is no Parkash of Guru Granth Sahib in any part of this Dera, that no Sikh festival is celebrated there nor any Kirtan is held. As stated in the earlier part of the judgment, Shaukin Dass PW-12 is a Mahant in the Dera situated in village Dhindsa, District Ferozepore and he, being the Gurbhai of the petitioner, helps him in the conduct of this case. Man Dass petitioner PW-13 deposed that he smokes and other Sadhus who reside in this Dera all smokes and that he had never kept long hair on the head and beard. He deposed that the only object of worship in this Dera are the Smadh of Baba Basua Dass, Gola Sahib and the Murti of Baba Sri Chand.

Mahant Shankar Dass PW-9, who is the Mahant of Panchayati Bara Akhara Udasin, Allahabad (U.P.), deposed that this institution is a Dera of Udasis, that Bassau Dass Khadesari was its founder and he had visited this institution about 5-10 times. He visited this Dera for the first time in 1954-55 and thereafter he had been visiting this Dera with the Jamat of the Akhara, which goes to various Udasi institution in the country. He deposed that this Dera is affiliated to their

Akhara and that the only object of worship in this Dera is the Smadh, Gola Sahib and the Murti of Sri Chand and there is no Parkash of Guru Granth Sahib in any part of this Dera. He deposed that the petitioner is illiterate and so was Mahant Hans Dass. The petitioner had matted hair with beard and he got the same cut off during his illness some years ago. He fully corroborates the evidence of the petitioner and his other witnesses.

The evidence of the witnesses of the petitioner is consistent and cogent and there is no discrepency. From the oral evidence of the petitioner, as discussed above, it is established that the institution in dispute was founded by Baba Basau Dass Khadesari, who was an Udasi Sadhu, that the succession to the office of Mahantship of this Dera devolves from Guru to Chela and all the successors of Baba Khadesari upto Man Dass petitioner have been Udasi Sadhus and that the objects of worship in this Dera are the Smadhs of Baba Basau Das Khandesari and his successors the photo of Siri Chand son of Sri Guru Nanak Dev Ji, and Gola Sahib. It is also clear from their evidence that Guru Granth Sahib was not the object of worship in this Dera and there is no Prakash of Guru Granth Sahib in any part of this Dera.

The plan Exhibit R-1/x of the building of the institution in dispute is at page 975 of the Punjab Government Gazette dated the 17th April, 1964 wherein Notification No. 721-GP. dated the 17th April, 1964 was published. In this plan the boundaries of this building are given as follows:—

North : Bir (Jungle)

South : Bir (Jungle)

East : Digi and Bir (Digi is a Katcha pond)

West : Agricultural land of the Gurdwaras

The building of this institution consist of Deori, room for Langar, Baithak and room for cattle, besides one room marked 'A' wherein it is written Smadh with Parkash Kita (i.e. There is Smadh and the Prakash). This room is domed type and is in the original shape. The Smadh of Baba Khadesari of this Dera is there which is stated to be the only object of worship. The Parkash of Guru Granth Sahib is alleged to be done in this room.

Before discussing the evidence of the parties I may point out that the respondent committee produced certain documents, which the petitioners had also produced. Besides some documents have been produced by the parties in duplicate. Reference to these duplicate copies of the docucments will be made while discussing the contents of the same. Exhibit R-6 is the copy of the Jamabandi for the year 1960-61 B.K. of the land belonging to this institution. In the ownership column the entry is "Sunder Dass Chela Charan Dass Quam Udasi Sakina Deh. Some land is recorded in self-cultivation and the remaining land is in possession of tenants. Similar are the entries in the Jamabandi for the year 1968-69 B.K. whose copy is Exhibit R-12/ Exhibit R-1 (same as Exhibit R-7 and P-11) is the copy of mutation order No. 1189 attested on Phalgun 10, 1974 B.K. pertaining to the succession of Mahant Sunder Dass Chela Charan Dass. As is clear from Exhibit R-6 and R-12 the land is dispute of the Dera was recorded as owned by Sunder Dass Chela Puran Dass. On the death of Sunder Dass a report was made by Hans Dass that Sunder Dass had died and that on the basis of writing executed by Sunder Dass he was to succeed to this land and that the other person whose name was mentioned in that writing was a gambler. This report is recorded in the remarks column of the mutation order. The order of the revenue officer on exhibits R-1, R-7 and P-11 shows that Hans Dass stated before the Revenue Officer that some Mahant may alienate this property by mortgage or sale and, therefore this land may be mutated in the name of the Guru Granth Sahib kept in the Dera Baba Khadesari. The revenue officer therefore, mutated this land in the name of Guru Granth Sahib, kept in dera Baba Khadesari Br-ihtman Hans Dass. After the attestation of this mutation order the entry in the Jamabandi of this land was entered in the name of Guru Granth Sahib. Exhibit R-2 is the copy of Jamabandi for the year 1976-77 BK. which was prepared after the attestation of this mutation order and in the ownership column the entry is "Sri Guru Granth Sahib Baihtmam, Mahant Baba Hans Chela Sunder Dass Sadh Udasi Deh".

To the same effect are the entries in the subsequent Jamabandi whose copies are Exhibits R-3 for the year 1984-85 B.K. R-4 and R-5 for the year 1951-52 A.D. R-8 for the year 1980-81 B.K. and R-10 for the year 2000-2001 B.K. Exhibit R-9 (same as Exhibit P-10 and P-12) is the copy of the mutation order No. 6,300 attested on 6.5.1959 A.D. pertaining to the success Hans Dass in favour of Man Dass petitioner.

Exhibit P-1 and Exhibit R-13 are the copies of Shajr Nasab of village Kot Fatta, relating to Udasi Sadhus. Exhibit R-13 was prepared much earlier. The following is the pedigreetable of the Udasi Sadhus of this Dera as is given in Exhibit P-1 and P-13.

Baba Basau Das

Chela

Charan Dass

Chela

Sundar Dass

Chela

Hans Dass

Chela

Man Dass

In exhibit P-1 Khewat and Khatauni numbers and the area of the land are also given. It is, thus clear from Exhibits P-1 and P-13 that the original owner of the Agricultural land in dispute of this Dera was Baba Basau Dass, an Udasi Sadhu, and it devolved from Guru to Chela. The land was rcorded in the revenue papers as owned by the Mahant of the Dera for the time being.

Exhibit P-2 is the copy of the statement of the Lambardars of the village recorded by the Nazim on Baisakh Badi 4, 1920 relating to the file of Muafi of land measuring 25 Bighas Biswas of the Dera in dispute. The statement is in the form of questions and answers. The Lambardars stated the Gurdit Singh who was their colleateral, made in a gift of 25 Ghumaons of land in favour of Basau Dass Khadesari and it was a Muafi in his favour, that this land has never been forfeited, that the produce of this land has been used by the Muafidar to feed Sadhus and the travellers, who visited the Dera. They stated that this land was being cultivated by the tenants and that the character of the Muafidar Sadhus was good. To the same effect was recorded by the Nazim of Sant Dass Chela Charan Das of this. In those days, Charan Dass was the Mahant of this Dera who used to it outside the Dera and the affairs of the Dera and its land were managed by his Chela Sant Dass, who made the statement which is exactly the same as made by the Lambardar in the copy Exhibit P-2. The Nazim by his order dated the 5th August 1873 A.D. whose copy is Exhibit P-4, recommended that the land should continue as muafi with the Muafidar and he sent the file for sanction to the Maharaja Patiala, and after the report was made by the Diwan who was then dealing with these matters, the orders were finally passed by the Maharaja Patiala on 18th August, 1874 and its copy in Exhibit P-5. This fact is also clear from Exhibit R-11 produced by the respondent-Committee regarding the Muafi of this land.

It is, thus, clear from the documents produced by the petitioner, discussed above, that this Dera was founded by Baba Khadesari, who was an Udasi Sadhu: that this Dera is situated in the jungle of village Kot Fatta and the land in dispute was donated by one Gurdit Singh, a proprietor of this village in favour of Baba Khadesari and that this land developed from Guru to Chela, who used to the Mahant of this Dera for the time being and that the income of the land used to be spent by the Mahant an Udasi Sadhus residing there and also to serve food to the travellers who visited the Dera.

Exhibit P-6 is the copy of Jamabandi for the year 1958-59 B.K. (equivalent to 1901-02 A.D.) wherein Sunder Dass Chela Charan Dass, Udasi Sadhu was recorded as the owner. To the same effect are the entries in the subsequent Jamabandi Exhibits p-7, p-8, p-14 and p-15 for the years 1962-63 B.K., 1971-72 B.K. 1973-74 B.K. and 1960-61 B.K., respectively. In all these Jamabandis Sunder Dass Chela Charan Dass was recorded as the owner of this Dera.

In Part No. 1 attached to the Punjab Government Gazette Notification No. 721-GP dated the 17th April, 1964, the boundaries of the building of the institution in dispute are given as follows:

East — Digi and Bir

West — Agricultural land of the Gurdwara

North — Bir (Jungle)

South — Bir (Jungle)

It is mentioned in this part that this Gurdwara is situated in Khasra No. 1586/406. To the same effect are the entries in the plan Exhibit R-I/X attached to the above said Notification.

The copy of the Jamabandi for the year 1951-52 of the land belonging to the institution in dispute and also of the land where the building of this institution is situated was attached to the Punjab Government Notification No. 721-G.F. dated the 17th April, 1964, published in the Punjab Government Gazette. The agricultural land of this institution which was gifted by Gurdit Singh proprietor of this village bore Khewat No. 222, Khatauri No. 640. As regards the land wherein the building of the institution in dispute is situated it bore Khewat No. 57/255. In the ownership column of this Khewat the entry is Teja Singh and others 1/2 share; Nand Singh and others 1/4 share; Pritam Singh and others 1/5 of 1/4 share; and other 4/5 of 1/4 share. In the cultivation column the entry is Hans Das Chela Sunder Dass Sadhu. There is no entry in the rent column of his Jamabandi for the year 1951-52. The total are of the Khasra No. 406 was more than 40 Bighas and out of it Gair Mumkin was 5 Bighas 10 Biswas; Banjar Kalan 33 Bighas 11 Biswas and Nehri 8 Bighas 13 Biswas; This Khasra No. 406 had two parts, namely, 1585/406 measuring 3 Bighas 13 Biswas and 1585/406 measuring 43 Bighas-I Biswas. The building of the institution in dispute is situated in Khasra No. 1585/406 as is clear from Part No. 1 and its pain Exhibit R-I/X is attached to the above mentioned Notification.

Exhibit P-16 is the copy of the order dated 28.9.1954 of the Assistant Consolidation Officer, Kot Fatta wherein he observed that the land belongs to Teja Singh and others, but it was in adverse possession of Mahant Hans Dass prior to the settlement of the year 1960-61 B.K. and he was in adverse possession for more than fifty years and, therefore, he rejected the objection of the proprietors of this land and held that this land will continue to be in possession of the person mentioned above. The Dera in dispute, admittedly, is situated in Khasra No. 1586/406 as is clear from Part I and the plan attached to the petition made under section 7(i) of the Act, which was published in the Punjab Government Gazette vide Notification No. 751-GP dated th 17th April, 1974. This land has been in adverse possession of the Udasi Sadhus, and the building of the institution in dispute is situated in this Khewat number.

The documentary evidence of the petitioner, discussed above, fully corroborates the oral evidence produced by them. It is established from the evidence of the petitioner that the institution in dispute was founded by Basau Dass Khadesari, who was an Udasi Sadhu; that all his successors Mahant Charan Dass, Mahant Sant Dass, Mahant Hans Dass and Mahant Man Dass petitioner have been Udasi Sadhus; that the succession of the office of Mahant of this Dera was from Guru to Chela; that this Dera is situated in Jungle at a distance of two miles from the village Abadi and even at present, it is surrounded by Jungle on three sides. From the documents Exhibits P-2, P-3, P-4, P-5 and P-17 it is clear that this Dera was foudned more than 150 years age; that the gift of the land in dispute measuring 25 Ghumaons was made by Gurdit

Singh of village Kot Fatta about 30-40 years prior to Samvat 1920 i.e. in or about 1890 B.K. to Baba Basau Dass Khadesari, who was an Udasi Sadhu, whose Dera in dispute was situated in jungle that and devoted from Basau Dass to his Chela Charan Dass and after his death is developed upon his Chela Sunder Dass. (This land continued to be recorded in the revenue record as owned by the Mahants of the institution is dispute till the death of Sunder Dass. After the death of Sunder Dass this land was mutated by the revenue authorities on the basis of the statement made by Hans Dass in the name of Guru Granth Sahib B-Intmam Hans Dass Chela Sunder Dass, Sadhu Udasi and this mutation, whose copies are Exhibits R-1, R-7 and P-11 was attested on Phagun 10, 1974 B.K. Till the attestation of this mutation in the year 1917 A.D. there is no evidence on the file to show that this institution was established for use by Sikhs for the purpose of public worship and was used for such worship by Sikhs, before and at the time of the presentation of the petition under Secton 7(1) of the Act. On the other hand, it is proved from the oral and documentary evidence of the petitioner that this Dera was founded by Basau Dass Khadesari and the object of worship in this Dera was the Gola Sahib and photo of Sri Chand and the Smadh of Baba Basau Dass Khadesari. This fact is corroborated by the entries in the plan Exhibit R-1/x, which is attached the Notification No. 721G.P. dated the 17th April, 1964, discussed above. It is clear from this plan that inside the domed-type from shown as 'A' in the plan, there is the Smadh and the Parkash of Guru Granth Sahib is also there in. It is not possible to believe that the Parkash of Guru Granth Sahib would be in this room where there is the Smadh. This fact controverts the statements of the witnesses of the respondent committee that there is no Smadh in this institution. The land which was originally donated by Gurdit Singh, in favour of Basau Dass Khadesari, and Udasi Sadhu of this Dera was mutated in the name of Guru Granth Sahib kept in this Dera vide mutation order, whose copies are Exhibits R-1,R-7 and P-11. These facts do not prove any of the ingredients laid down in Section 16(2) (iii) of the Act.

The counsel for the parties cited a number of decisions in support of their contentions. The counsel for the respondent-committee relied on Puran Dass Chela V. Kartar Singh and others, A.I.R. 1934 Lahore 398, wherein it was held as follows:

"Where an institution is founded by inhabitants of Sikh village for their own benefit for religious and charitable purpose, the religion being the worship of the Granth Sahib as a Sikh Gurdwara, the fact that the incumbents had always been Udasis immaterial, as in a large percentage of cases Udasis are found to be incumbents of Sikh Gurdwara."

In Sohan Das v. Bela Singh and others, A.I.R. 1934 Lahore 180 it was held:—

"Where in a petition under S.8, Sikh Gurdwaras Act , the petitioner asserts that he is the mahant of a dharamsala and claims that the dharamsala is not a Sikh Gurdwara and even it appears that from its foundation the mahants have been Udasis and that there are at the dharamsala samadhs of the petitioner's ancestors, the onus is on the objectors to establish the character of the institutions. When it is proved by documentary evidence that the dharamsala has been a place of public worship since 1858 and that such worship has been connected with the Granth Sahib and it also appears that the village is a Sikh village and the evidence of the objectors goes to show that the existence of a samadh dates only from recept times more than probably after the Sikh Gurdwara controversy had become acute and the importance of a samadh had been realized by the udasi mahants, it should be held that the institution falls within S 16(2) (iii)" In Ram Piari Vs. Sardar Singh and others, A.I.R. 1937 Lahore 786 it was held:-

"Gurdwara Baba Narain Singh was established by Narain Singh who was a Keshadhari Sikh and he read and reverted the Granth Sahib in the institution Gurpurabs were celebrated and several Granthis were in charge from time to time. The place had been used for congregational worship and prayers since the founder's time. Held: that the institution had been used for the purposes of the public worship of the Granth Sahib by the Sikhs ever since the time of the founder and the evidence was sufficient also to justify the inference under the circumstances that the institution was established for public worship."

In Gulab Das vs. Foja Singh and others, A.I.R. 1937 Lahore 826

It was held:—

"A dharamsala was founded by Udasis and many of its subsequent managers were also Udasis. Yet it was used as a resting place and a langar was maintained. It was endowed by Sikh Sardars and Granth Sahib was read every day and pictures of Sikh Sardars were hung round the wall. No Hindu Gods were worshipped or Hindu scriptures read:

Held: that the institution was a Sikh Gurdwara."

To the same effect is the law laid down in Ram Kishan Dass vs. Shiromani Gurdwara Parbandhak Committee, Amritsar and another, A.I.R. 1937 Lahore 290.

The Counsel for the respondent committee also relied on F.A.O. No. 106 of 1965 decided on 24.12.1970 by the Punjab and Haryana High Court. The fact of this were that the institution was founded by Bibi Rattan Kaur wife of Maharaja Fateh Singh of the erstwhile Kapurthala State before the year 1980-81 B.K. She also donated some land for the expenses of the Dharamsala which was constructed. In another document it was found that this Pucca Dharamsala is situated on the bank of stream bein and got constructed by Mata Rattan Kaur and that Narain Dass and Amar Dass lived in the Dharamsala and the travellers were served food and water and that Guru Granth Sahib was always read therein and that Mai Sahib granted land for the maintenance of the Dharamsala. On these facts it was held that the institution in dispute was established for use by Sikhs for the purpose of public worship and the institution declared to be a Sikh institution within the meaning of Section 16, subsection (2) Clause (iii) of the Act.

All these decisions are distinguishable and are not applicable to the facts of the present case. In all these decisions it was held that the institutions in dispute were established for use by Sikhs for the purpose of public worship and were used for such worship by Sikhs, before and at the time of the presentation of the petition under sub-section (1) of Section 7 and the conditions laid down in section 16(2)(iii) were satisfied. In the instant case, it is not proved that the institution in dispute was established for use by Sikhs for the purpose of public worship and was used for such worship by Sikhs, before and at the time of the presentation of the petition under Section 7(1) of the Act.

The first decision relied upon by the counsel for the petitioner is Joginder Singh and others v. The Shiromani Gurdwara Parbandhak Committee, Amritsar A.I.R. 1976 Punjab and Haryana 185, wherein it was held as follows:—

"Before any institution can be declared as a Sikh Gurdwara two facts have to be established. That the institution was established for use by the Sikhs for the purpose of public worship and that it was so used before and at the time of the presentation of the petition under section 7(1) of the Act. The Udasi is being a separate sect having their separate institutions, an institution established by an Udasi Faqir having his Samadh and claimed as Dera cannot be declared to be Sikh Gurdwara. The fact that Granth Sahib is read in the institution, cannot also be a factor for treating the institution as Sikh Gurdwara, because the Udasis use the same sacred writings as the Sikhs and the recitation of Guru Granth Sahib in Udasi Dera is a common features".

In Mahant Budh Dass and Mahant Purana Nand through his guardian Smt. Vidya Wanti Legal Rept. of Mahant Jiwan Mukta Nand v. The Shiromani Gurdwara Parbandhak Committee, Amritsar, A.I.R. 1978 Punjab and Haryana 39(F.B.) it was laid down as under:—

"The onus to prove that the Gurdwara in question

was a Sikh Gurdwara was, on the Shiromani Gurdwara Parbandhak Committee. The Committee was required to prove the following essential ingredients:

(1) That the Gurdwara was established for use by Sikhs for public worship, (2) that it was being actually used for worship by Sikhs and (3) that it was being used by Sikhs for public worship both before the presentation of the petition and at the time of the presentation of the petition under S.7. As there was no direct evidence to establish that the Gurdwara was established in the above mentioned circumstances and was being used as such so as to satisfy the ingredients of the above provision, the Court was left to draw inference from the documentary and oral evidence on the record. Under Cl. (iii) of sub-sec. (2) of S. 16 two conditions have to be satisfied. Even if one condition is not satisfied, the onus is not discharged.

It was clear from the various documents that the Dera to begin with, was founded by a Faqir Udasi, Mahant Garib Dass, and the land was owned by him in his own name and the said Dera was more a charitable institution that a religious one, only Muafi was granted by a Sikh ruler subsequently. Held that the mere fact that the grant of the Muafi was subject to the condition of the existence of the Dera as well as Guru Granth Sahib would not convert the Dera into a Sikh Gurdwara. There was no evidence on the record to warrant the conclusion that the Dera had been brought into existence by the Sikhs for the purpose of public worship. The Committee had not been able to discharge its burdon." In Harnam Das v. Kartar Singh and others A.I.R. 1936 Lahore 825, the facts were as follows :—

> "The dharamsala were managed by Mahants, the Udasi Faqirs. They had their chelas also a Mahant of the institution. Muafi of land was granted on condition of Granth Sahib being regularly read. The Dharamsalas were not called Dharamsala but were referred in documents as a dera. There were samadhs on the land of Mahants and samadhs were commonly found in

Udasi institution. Though there was langar or an alms house. There was no place shown where Granth Sahib was read or recited:

Held: That the institution was not a Sikh Gurdwara and that the mere fact that the Granth Sahib was read was not sufficient to make it a Sikh Gurdwara."

To the same effect was the law laid down in Mukand Singh v. Puran Das. A.I.R. 1936 Lahore 924. Hardit Dass v. Gurdit Singh and others A.I.R. 1936 Lahore 819 and Arjan Singh and another v. Harbhajan Das, petitioner and others, A.I.R. 1937 Lahore 280. Further it was held in Bawa Ishar Dass and others v. Dr. Mohan Singh and others, A.I.R. 1939 Lahore 239 as follows:—

"The Udasi order constitutes a separate sect, distinct from the orthodox sikhs. The Udasi occupy an intermediate position between strictly orthodox Sikhs and Hindus. They are in fact a monastic order in their origin and are followers of Bawa Sri Chand, son of the first Guru. Though they worship samadhis, etc. they do reverence to the Granth Sahib without completely renouncing Hinduism. They are often in charge of a village Dharamsala or Gurdwara which is a Sikh institution but in other cases the Sadhu and his chelas constitute a monastery or college. Owing to their intermediate position, it is possible for Udasis to be in charge of a Sikh Gurdwara property so called but it does not follow that the institution is Sikh Gurdwara and not a true institution merely because the Granth Sahib is read in it.

Where therefore, it is established by evidence that the mahants of an institution have all along been Udasis, that the institution is an Udasi monastery that although the Guru Granth Sahib is read there by the Udasi Mahant and Sikhs attend these reading still, the other ceremonies observed by the Udasis and Hindus, are performed at the institution is a genuine Udasi institution and the mere fact that the Udasis also read the Guru Granths Sahib, a book which they do venorate, does not make the institution a Sikh Gurdwara so as to entitle the Sikhs to claim to be associated in the management of the Institution."

To the same effect was also the law laid down Arjan Singh and another V. Inder Dev and others, A.I.R. 1934 Lahore 13, and Naginder Singh and another V. Pal Das A.I.R. 1934 Lahore 60.

The counsel for the petitioner also relied upon certain unreported judgments of Punjab & Haryana High Court, Chandigarh and these are:F.A.O. 59 of 1964 Mahant Kirpa Ram V.S. C.P.C.) decided on 14.11.1969, F.A.O. No. 11 of 1865 (S.G.P.C. Zora Singh and others).

Decided on 19.8.1971, F.A.O. No. 111 of 1965 (S.G.P.C., v. Prabhu Dayal and others decided on 23.8.1971, F.A.O. No. 4 of 1964 (Shambhu Nath v. S.G.P.C. decided on 8.4.1970 F.A.O. No. 47 of 1964 (Mahant Pargat Singh v. S.G.P.C. and others) decided on 4.5.1970 and F.A.O. No. 166 of 1964 (S.G.P.C. v. Lal Singh) decided on 11.3.1970. The facts of these cases were similar to the facts of the present case and in all these cases was held by the High Court that the Institution in dispute was not a sikh Gurdwara the ingredients laid down in section 16(2)(iii) of the Act were not proved.

For the reasons given above, it is held the respondent-committee failed to proved that the institution in dispute was established for use by Sikhs for the purpose of public worship and it was used for such worship by Sikhs, before and at the time of the presentation of the petition under sub-section (1) of Section 7 of the Act. one of the ingredients laid down in Section 16(2)(iii) of the Act is established. It is, therefore held that the respondent-committee has failed to prove that the institution in dispute is a Sikh Gurdwara within the meaning of Section 16(2) (iii) of the Act and this issue is decided against it.

As a result, this petition No. 478 of 1966 is allowed and it is hold that the Institution in dispute known as Gurdwara

Sahib Sri Guru Granth Sahib, situated in the reven estate of Kot Fatta, Tehsil and District Bhatinda, is not proved to be a Sikh Gurdwara and the Punjab Government Notification No. 721 G.P. dated the 17th April, 1964 under Section 7(3) of the Act is quashed. Under the circumstances of the case there will be no order as to costs.

Counsel's fees Rs. 250/-   Pritam Singh Pattar
Dated Chandigarh   President
the 28th August, 1978

I agree
sd/-

Bhagwan Singh
29.8.78

Order:

Pronounced, this 29th day of August, 1978 in open court in the presence of S. Charan Singh, Counsel for the respondent-Committee. The counsel for the petitioner may be informed.

Balwant Singh   Pritam Singh Pattar
Member   President

15

An Appeal to the followers and disciples of Bhagwan Shri Sri Chandra Ji Maharaj

In our country every house holder worship their gods of clay and stone in the firm faith that the Divine spirit dwells therein. In every street there is a temple. In every locality there is a Gurdwara, in every chowk there is a Masjid and in every city there is a Girja Ghar. There are countless number of living Gods in our country with sufficient following. The religious places are found always flooded with devotees, and pilgrim places have no place to accommodate pilgrims. Katha Kirtan, Jagratas observed daily. In nutshell we can say our is a God fearing nation. Lakhs of Sadhus, Mahatama, Rishis, Munis, Yogis and Saints are there to guide and to deliver sermon to common man. Religious books like Ramayan, Gita, Gurugranth Sahib, Quran, Bible, Ved Shastra and Purans are recited with full devotion. Mother India has been blessed by the God Almighty by sending its messengers to guide and help misguided human beings. The land of Bhagwan Ram and Bhagwan Krishna, Lord Buddha and Shankrachary, Guru Nanak Dev Ji and Bhagwan Shri Sri Chandra Ji Maharaj, Bhagwan Mahavir, Goswami Tulsi Das, Kabir Sahib and Surdas, and so many other great personalities also blessed this country.

There was a time when our greatest Dharam Acharyas

were there to guide the Nation in the religious affairs and they had full control and authority in the religious fields because they were the person with a highest range of character. In their presence no body could dare to do any mischief in personal or Public life because they were treated as Dharam Gurus and their motive of life was to give sincere advice to the ruling class in particular and masses in general. They commanded full respect and regards every where. They were well read persons having complete knowledge of their subject and full control on the public.

The administration also had full control on the state affairs and fear in the mind of general public.

But, what is happening in free India? The population has crossed 100 crores figures. Is there any Dharamacharya or any political leader who has full control on the masses? or is there any body in any field? (Religious, Political and Social) who could be followed blindly? Is there anybody who represent the common man? Ironically every sphere of Indian life is full of corruption. Majority of them in every circle are characterless and opportunists. Kursi has become 'Dharam' of every leader. No body bother about for that India which stands for certain customs and traditions. The dreams of Mahatma Gandhi, Pandit Jawaharlal Nehru, Netaji Subhash Chandra Bose, Bhagat Singh, Chandra Shekhar Azad, Jaya Prakash Narayan and Dr. Rammanohar Lohia and other stalwarts of freedom movement that country will be managed by the intellectuals and every citizen without any distinction will get its share according to his/her capability. There would be no role of money and muscle power in the day to day Indian life. Unfortunately all the dreams of our beloved leaders and numerous martyrs who laid down their lives for the country have been shattered. The dream of socialistic pattern of society seems no where. Entire set up viz Political, Social, cultural religious and Economic and Commerce is arranged, managed and ruled by the capitalist class, oppressed, depressed, poor and down trodden, scheduled castes, Tribals and middle class have no role and place in any sphere of life.

Whatsoever is seen in day to day life is only eyewash and vote catching fraud of the leadership. Can any God fearing country is ruled in such a fashion.

I quite agree and of the firm opinion that no body can reform everybody on earth. But? what our socio-cultural, National, Secular, religious, Reformist and Voluntary organisations based on the concept of The Unity of India, with the motive to help and work for the suffering Mankind-are doing? India was the country where elderly parents were worshipped and no junior could dare to defy their wishes. In the same country the parents who sacrifices their every thing for the well being of their children-the same children-after 53 years independence throwing them on road side from their own houses-even then we are religious people. God fearing people? It is most unfortunate that people who are posing themselves as religious in Public life and they are most Pakhandis in personal life. Dual character of Indian people is most condemable. Materialistic approach in Indian culture and traditions have no place. India was great only when was following selfless service to suffering mankind.

Through this book most humbly and respectfully I wish to draw the attention of all the mahants of more than 3000 Akharas ! Ashram ! Maths ! Dharamsalas of Udasin Sampardai (sect) set up by Baba Sri Chand Ji Maharaj and his followers through the length and breadth of this vast country to propagate the ideals of Baba Sri Chand Ji, Bhagwan Ram and Bhagwan Shri Krishan Ji Maharaj and to safe guard the Sanatan Dharam in India.

I regret to say that majority of these institutions have been converted into personal properties. The occupants in the name of Baba Sri Chand leading a luxurious life, their attitude towards common men is most shameful and objectionable. They are treating themselves as Feudal Lords of donated lands/jagirs to such religious organisation. They are not only misusing the funds of these institutions but also creating a bad prescedent to the coming generation. There functioning is worse than Mahant Narayan Das of Nankana Tragedy fame

(1921). They have completely forgotten the norms laid down by Nirvan Shri Pritam Dass Ji in the constitution for Udasin Sect. If these mahants have to marry, wish to have 'keeps' taking of wine and other intoxicants have become a part and parcel of their lives—they have no moral right to stay in these dharamshalas to defame the pious name of great saint Baba Sri Chand Ji Maharaj. Such Pakhandi mahants are black spot on the forehead of Udasin Sampardai. They should be kicked out of these places and real sanyasis may be appointed as mahants. If the present regime of Udasin Sect is so hopeless and helpless-an Udasin Foundation or Udasin Trust on All India level may be constituted with immediate effect to look after and to manage the affairs of the Sampardai.

Failing which coming generations will not forgive the present management for this lacuna.

With due regards and apology I want to say that I do not agree with revered Mahamandelshwar Mahant Ragvanand Ji Maharaj's of Guru Ram Rai Udasin Ashram, Panchkuan Road, New Delhi about the comments made by Swami Ji due to his ignorance or he has purposely exaggerated the facts about certain Udasin Deras. I do not want to discuss the entire report but I will be failing in my duty and feel guilty if I could not disclose the facts of our village Udasin Dharamsalas (Village and Post Office-Jandoli, via Basi Kalan, Police Station Mahilpur, Tehsil Garhshanker, District Hoshiarpur Punjab) which is under the control of Bhadurgarh Dharamsala management.

I am very sorry to say that in the above quoted Dharamsala, no religious function is held for the last about one hundred years. The building of the Dharamsala had collapsed long long ago. The Samadhis of Baba Mehar Das and other saints have been converted into Burmese (Snake holes). The Dharam Granths had been eaten by white ants.

The present gang of so called mahants are posing themselves as 'Samants' of olden times. They themselves living as Lords enjoying luxurious lives—increasing number of children. What to talk of any Sadhu Samagam or shelter and fooding and lodging to anyone, they even don't permit poor farmers to come across their fields whosoever raised any voice about their anti-social and anti-national activities is put in false cases. Not only that their kiths and kins are threatened to face dire consequences.

What to talk of their long list of atrocities and their most bulgar and revengeful attitude towards respectable persons of the village and that area are insulted by them. They have no regards for anybody.

This Dharamsala having more than 500 Bighas of land, a big chunk of jungle lot of mango groves and garden of oranges, Beries etc. It is learnt that with the connivance of their masters they have sold all the jungles and mango groves and even sold out the earth to the contractor of Brick Klin. Not only that they have started selling Dharamsala's agricultural land which they got transferred in their names.

The poor petty farmers, the members of Scheduled Castes and Scheduled Tribes have told me that Dharamsalas so called Mahants have got allotted entire land of the village which was (Shamlat Deh) for centuries together with the connivance of village Patwari and other Revenue officers. There is no land left for poor Harijans and small farmers for grazing their animals.

I demand through the colums of this book which is a part of Baba Sri Chand's biography that if the management of Udasin Sampardai is so week and helps to check and stop the functioning of such mahants the said Dharamsala should be handed over to a duly constituted and legaly approved Trust or Foundation without any further delay as misuse of Public funds should not be tolerated any longer. If this is not possible, the entire land may be distributed among the Harijans and poor people of the village for residential and agricultural purpose and a piece of land for Baba Sri Chand Hospital and Baba Mehar Das Vocational College for Boys and Girls may be allotted; which is the need of the area residents.

Dear countrymen and most respected Sadhu Samaj and revered mahants of Udasin Sampardai to highlight the mismanagement and misuse of Public land by so called Pakhandi mahants is no more tolerable. And inspite of the wishes and humble requests of their well wishers have fell on deaf ears. These so called mahants have miserably failed to mend their ways; their lavish life styles, their Samant Shahis language, their vulgarily in conversation and what not....?

Dear Sirs, on the popular demand of the residents of nearby villages namely (Nasran, Badhna, Tajewal, Narunangal, Bachholi,Sarangwal, Soona, Chhoti Jandoli, Chak, Chanthu, Kalewal Bhagtann, Bilaspur, Singhpur, Chhoti and Badi Lahli, Parsowal and Ghukarwal and Jandoli—I request the Director, Central Bureau of Investigation, The Hon'ble Home Minister of Punjab Government to immediately appoint a high power inquiry committee—that how and why and with who's permission—the Jundoli Dharamsala management have got transferred the Dharamsala land in their personal names and occupied hundred and thousands of Acre Shamlat Deh Zameen, and under who's instructions and connivance they are harassing poor farmers and involving them in false and cooked up cases. I also request the Udasi Sampardais all Mahants of All the Akharas to please intervene in the matter without any fail most urgently as these Mahapurush of Jandoli Dharamsala are assasinating the roots of Udasi Sampardai.

Whatsoever I have recorded in this appeal the facts of life without any prejudice and any ill will against anybody. This has been brought to your kind notice on the popular demand of the residents of the local people.

I am quite hopeful that voice of the aggrieved persons of the villages will be heard and immediate necessary action may be taken in this regards. Thanking you.

Appendices

Appendix 1
The Nankana Tragedy (1921)

Nankana Sahib, being the birth place of Guru Nanak occupies the most important position among the Sikh places of religious worship. Nankana Sahib and other Gurdwaras related to Janam Asthan were controlled by Mahant Sadhu Ram. These Mahants belonged to the Udasi sect of the Sikhs and had gradually grown into wealthy feudal landlords. They deprived the poor peasantry of their rights. The Mahants misappropriated the Community's income from the Gurdwaras and their land and flouted the traditions and customs of the Sikhs.

To bring these temples under the control of the Community, the Sikhs convened a conference at Amritsar in July 1920. A small Committee to administer the temples affairs was constituted in this conference. A mandate was issued from the Akal Takhat to summon an assembly of the Sikhs to meet on 15 November 1920 to elect a representative body of the panth to govern and control the Golden Temple and other shrines.

Mahant Sadhu Ram, who was leading a luxrious life and had nothing to do about his religious duties. Mahant Narain Das, who succeeded Mahant Sadhu Ram followed the foot prints of his predecessor.

The local Sikhs tried too curb the evil practices adopted

by the Mahants, but of no avail, as the Mahants had the backing of the local British officials. The Mahant used to spent lakhs of rupees out of the Gurdwara funds in offering rich presents to the local officials on whose goodwill and support depended their appointment and continuance in office. Soon after his appointment as the Mahant, Narain Das had kept a Muhammadan drummer's wife, invited dancing girls to Nankana Sahib and permitted profane singing even in the sacred precincts of Janam Asthan.

It will not be out of place to mention here that during 1918 one Sindhi retired I.A.S. officer happened to visit Gurdwara Nankana Sahib alongwith his daughter. He stayed in one of the rooms of the Gurdwara. When the programme of evening prayer was in progress his 13 years old daughter was being raped by one of the Mahant's colleague in the Gurdwara Complex. Mahant was requested to expel the concerned person from the Gurdwara premises but he did not paid any head towards this heinous crime.

In the same year a group of six women visited Gurdwara on a 'Pooranmasi Day.' They also stayed in the Gurdwara. At night the Mahant's colleagues forcefully assaulted all these six ladies. This was the same place where Guru Nanak Devji had born to reform the suffering mankind.

This state of affairs in Nankana Sahib attracted the attention of the Sikh reformers. A resolution in a Dewan which was held at Dharowal during the month of October 1920. In this gathering a resolution was passed calling upon Mahant Narain Das to improve his habits and purify the administration of the temple. On the contrary Mahant Narain Das began to recruit a strong force to resist the Akali Movement. Not only that with the blessing of Mr. C.M. King, the Commissioner of Lahore Division in consultation with Baba Kartar Singh Bedi and other Mahants, Narain Das arranged a meeting at Nankana which was attended by over sixty such types of Mahants.It was decided at the meeting not to recognise the authority of the newly formed S.G.P.C. and a parallel Committee was formed with Mahant Narain Das as its President and Mahant Basant Das as the Secretary. A newspaper entitled, 'Sant Sewak' was also started from Lahore to carry on propaganda against the Akali Movement.

On the pretext of self-defence and fortification of the shrine, Mahant Narain Das collected about 400 mercenaries, including notorious outlaws like Ranjha and Rehana, and armed them with swords, lathis, chhavies, takwas and other lethal weapons. Arms and ammunition and kerosene were kept in ready stock. A large number of pistol cartridges were also brought by him from a dealer in Lahore. A further reinforcement of 100 Pathans under the leadership of Ismail Bhatti was also kept ready to strike at a movement's notice.

The local authorities had full knowledge of the said preparation by the Mahant and they had alerted their high ups. Inspite of these instances of the Mahants' preparation and the local officials and residents informing the Deputy Commissioner about his designs, the authorities failed to make any police arrangements or to dissuade the Mahant from coming into armed conflict with the Akali reformers.

In the meantime, the Shiromani Gurdwara Prabhandhak Committee was also considering ways and means to bring this important Gurdwara, like the Golden Temple, Akal Takhat and other Gurdwaras under Panthic Control. In a meeting held on 24 January 1921, a resolution was passed by the SGPC calling upon the whole panth to assemble in a Dewan at Nankana from 4 to 6 Marach 1921, and to impress upon the Mahant the need for reform. On 6 February 1921 another meeting of the SGPC was called in which a five member Committee was appointed to make longer arrangements for the proposed Dewan.

The reported decision of the SGPC frightened the Mahant. Meanwhile he might also have heard the rumours about Jathedar Kartar Singh Jhabbar's plans of a forcible seizure of the Gurdwara in case the Mahant failed to mend his ways. As such he showed some signs of compromise in a meeting with Kartar Singh Jhabbar agreed to the appointment of a Committee of management of certain conditions. However, before the meeting could take place the Mahant seems to have changed his mind. Instead of meeting with the Akali leaders he started making further preparations, including murder of topmost Akali leaders.

Keeping in view the murderous plans of the Mahant in view, the senior leaders of the Akali Dal deputed persons to persuade Jathedar Kartar Singh Jhabbar to abandon his plan for the forcible occupation of Nankana and to request Jathas not to proceed to Gurdwara Janam Asthan. After having informed Jathedar Jhabbar, Dalip Singh proceeded to Sunderkot to inform Bhai Lachman Singh not to start for Nankana as planned. On finding that Bhai Lachman Singh and his Jatha had already left the place, Dalip Singh then proceeded to the factory of Bhai Uttam Singh which was located about a mile away from Nankana.

Bhai Lachman Singh had started for Nankana late in the evening of 19 February 1921 with a few Companions. On the morning of 20 February 1921, the party reached a place half a mile away from Gurdwara Janam Asthan. Here they met a messenger of Bhai Dalip Singh and received a message containing the S.G.P.C.'s instructions not to proceed to Janam Asthan. Bhai Lachman Singh agreed, but the other members of his Jatha persuaded him that there would be no harm if they visited the Gurdwara and, after paying their homage, returned peacefully. Having been thus persuaded by his colleagues, Bhai Lachman Singh proceeded to the Janam Asthan and arrived there at the head of his Jatha at about six in the morning. The member of the Jatha, who were unaware of these designs, sat down after bowing before the holy Granth and started singing hymns. Immediately 25 of the Mahant's men went atop the roof of the Verandah and started firing at the Akalis sitting below. The rest of the Mahant's men and Sadhus began throwing bricks at the Sikhs, some of whom ran to take shelter in the side-rooms. Others who ran to the side of the sanctuary were shot dead there. About 25 members of the Jatha who remained inside the Gurdwara calmly suffered martydom. About 60 of the Akalis shut themselves is another sanctuary called Chaukhandi but the Mahant's men broke open the doors and killed them there. Then the siderooms were searched and 25 Akalis found there, were put to death.

After wounding and killing all the members of Bhai Lachman Singh's party and other Jathas along with their sympathisers, the Mahant and his men collected and burnt most of the dead and wounded by pouring kerosene which had already been stored for the purpose.

On coming to know of the tragedy, Bhai Uttam Singh, a local factory owner, and Sardar Karam Singh, the Station Master, tried to inform the higher authorities in the Punjab as well as the Akali and the national leaders. Urgent telegrams were sent to the lieutenant Govenor of the Punjab, the Deputy Commissioner of Sheikhupura, the Superintendent of Police, the Shromani Gurdwara Prabhandhak Committee and to Mahatma Gandhi. The lone Sub-Inspector at the nearby police station of Warburton was on leave on the day of the tragedy. He and another Sub-Inspector from Mangatwala arrived at the scene of the tragedy only after the arrivial of the Deputy Commissioner. According to the Press reports, even after the arrival of the Deputy Commissioner the burning of the dead and the wounded continued for about an hour and a half.

Mahant Narain Das, with two of his henchmen and 26 Pathans was arrested and sent to Lahore, but a large number of hooligans succeeded in escaping. The Gurdwara Janam Asthan was placed under military guard.

Jathedar Kartar Singh Jhabbar along with his Akali Jatha was stationed at Khara Sauda when he heard of the tragedy. Marching at the head of his Jatha, Jhabbar was stopped on the way near village Khipwala on 21 February 1921 and surved with an order from the Deputy Commissioner forbidding the Akalis to proceed towards Janam Asthan. According to the biography of the Jathedar, he tore this order into pieces in front of the very eyes of the messenger and told him to inform the Deputy Commissioner, 'I am coming with my Jatha; you may do whatever you please. Jhabbar and his Jathas continued their march towards Janam Asthan when they were next stopped by the Deputy Commissioner himself, who according to the biographical account, warned the members of the Jathan that if they proceed further, they will face bullets. Ignoring the warning, the Jathedar ordered his followers to march on till they reached Janam Asthan and took control of the Gurdwara. At this development the Deputy Commissioner seems to have yielded and, after consulting the Commissioner, he agreed to handover the keys of the Janam Asthan to Jhabbar provided the Akalis agreed to the formation of a Committee of management for the Gurdwara. After some discussion, the charge of the Gurdwara was handed over to a Committee consisting of seven members under the Presidentship of Sardar Harbans Singh Atteri, a moderate Chief Khalsa Dewan leader.

The native Press was unanimous in its attack on the Mahant. Even papers opposed to the Akali leadership condemned the cruel and savaged deed of the Nankana Mahant and sympathised with the families of the Nankana martyrs. National leaders like Mahatma Gandhi, Maulana Shaukat Ali, Dr. Saifuddin Kitchlew, Lala Duni Chand and Lala Lajpat Rai, visited the scene of the tragedy and expressed sympathy for the Akalis. Prominent Sikh leaders, Members of the Punjab Legislative Council, the Sikh League the Chief Khalsa Diwan and other Sikh organisations reached the spot. In a big Shahidi Diwan held at Nankana on 3 March 1921, Jathedar Kartar Singh Jhabbar, who had played a prominent role in taking over the keys of the Janam Asthan from the Deputy Commissioner, narrated the incident in brief and pointed out that the happening had awakened the Sikhs from their slumber and the march towards Swaraj had been quickened.

The tragedy greatly perturbed the Sikhs in different parts of the country who vehemently condemned the action of the Mahant and sent messages of sympathy for the Akali Martyrs. Resolutions were passed everywhere demanding the death penalty for the Mahant and his associates.

Appendix 2
Nankana Sahib Tragedy and Mahatma Gandhi

In February 1921 when an open clash occurred at the Nankana Sahib Gurdwara between the armed men of the local Mahant and the Sikh volunteers who made an attempt to seize the Gurdwara Mahatma Gandhi was already touring the Punjab with a view to guiding the non-co-operation movement and inspiring the people of Punjab to join the movement in large numbers. Actually the Mahant of the Nankana Sahib Gurdwara as well as the Akali leaders had already been in touch with him. The Mahant had asked Gandhiji to condemn the violent methods by which the Akalis were seizing the various Gurdwaras. The following series of lectures and letters of Mahatmaji are very useful to understand the nature of the Congress-Akali relations with regard to the Gurdwara Reform Movement.

The following is the substance of Mahatma Gandhi's Hindustani speech delivered at Nankana Sahib Gurdwara when he visited it together with Maulana Shaukat Ali on 3 March 1921.

I have come as a pilgrim to tender you my sympathy. I have received a wire about the Tragedy on February 20, 1921 when I was at Rawalpindi. I showed it to Lala Lajpat Rai and other friends. The news was so staggering that they would not believe without confirmation. We hastened back to Lahore to find that the news was all terribly true. I cancelled my visit to Multan and awaited further information. The next day I proceeded to Lyallpur and attended a Sikh Diwan on February 1921. I heard there that the cremation was taking place that day. It was too late to attend when the news was received. I could not make this pilgrimage earlier as I was bound to keep important appointments at Amritsar and Lucknow. In the meantime I have heard much about the immolation.

I need hardly give you many assurance that your grief is mine. I am so constituted that the sufferings of others make me miserable. When I heard of the tragedy of Nankana I felt like wanting to be among the victims. I must confess that I have not yet been able to come to any final conclusion to what actually happened. It seems almost unbelievable that not a single man died at the hands of the Akali Party. Did not the brave men who were armed with kirpans and battle-axes retaliate even in self-defence? If they did not, it is an event that must electrify the whole world. Condemning the cruel deed of the Mahant and commending the Akalis for their passive sufferings, he described the martyrdom of the Akali reformers as an act of national bravery. He also denounced for foreign Government whose rule, he said, `was based on devlish tricks.' Later, in the message to the Sikhs in Lahore, while comparing the tragedy of Nankana to a similar one in April 1919 at the Jallianwala Bagh, Amritsar, Mahatmaji said, 'Everything I saw and heard points to a second edition of Dyerism, more barbarous, more calculated and more flendish than the Dyerism of Jallianwala. Mahatmaji also advised the Akalis to offer non-co-operation in the matter of official enquiry in the Nankana Tragedy and consented to serve as Chairman of non-official Commission of Enquiry set up by Sikh League provided the Sikhs adopted a formal resolution affirming non-co-operation and agreed not to take recourse to the British law courts for getting the murderers punished.

Official support to the Mahants and their indirect involvement in the Nankana tragedy convinced the Akali leadership that it was not possible for them to liberate their Gurdwaras till they accepted Mahatma Gandhi's advice to liberate the bigger Gurdwaras, i.e. India, by throwing off the foreign Yoke. After ensuring active co-operation and support from the national Press, the Indian National Congress and other nationalist forces in the country, the Akalis formally joined the nationalist movement and launched a two-pronged struggle directed against the Mahants, priests and other vested interests in the Sikh shrines on the one hand and against their supporter, the British Government in the Punjab, on the other. Under the new programme of non-violent non-co-operation, which received the blessings of Mahatma Gandhi and other nationalist leaders. Akali struggle against the foreign Government became a synonym for struggle far reform in the Sikh shrines.

While delivering his judgement in the Akali versus C.M. King defamation case, the judge clearly fixed the responsiblity on Mr. King when he observed. The plea that the police was not available is ridiculous. No Government could be worthy of the trust which could not help keep an eye on the doings of its people. It appears that the British Officials in the Punjab were playing a double game. On the one hand they did not wish to lose the goodwill of the Sikh Community and therefore, followed a policy of non-interference in the religious affairs of the Sikh's and on the other, they did not want to withdraw themselves from the direct or indirect control of the Gurdwaras. Under the circumstances, the policy of local officials, i.e. secretly encouraging the Mahants, to offer tough resistance to the Akalis and outwardly professing 'sympathy' with the movement of reform, promised best results. It appears from the facts about the tragedy that the officials wanted the growing movement of the Akalis to be crushed through the Mahants and thus to save themselves from incurring the displeasure of the Sikh Community. Hence, the lower-level officials not only allowed the Mahant to prepare himself to meet the growing movement but secretly encouraged and patronised him wishing him success in his mission.

But this policy of the Government and the failure of the

local officials to take precautionary measures to avert the tragedy became a subject to severe criticism both in the Executive Council of the Viceroy of India and in the office of the Secretary of State for India in London. In a letter addressed to Lord Reading, the then Viceroy, Mr. E.S. Montague, Her Majesty's Secretary of State for India, criticised the official action with regard to the Sikh situation and observed that the Government action comes after the trouble and not in anticipation of it.

The most interesting part of the whole story is that inspite of the strong criticism of the action of the local officials and their responsibility for the tragedy of Nankana having been established, neither did the Viceroy of India nor any other member of his Executive Council ask the Government of the Punjab to take any action against the concerned officials.

After the Nankana tragedy all the routes to Nankana were ceased and halting of all trains passing through Nankana Sahib Railway Station was stopped. At night at about 9 p.m. Lahore Police Commissiooner King and D.I.G. Police reached Nankana by a special train alongwith 100 British Officers and one hundred Indian Sepoys. After their arrival Mahant Narain Das alongwith his two henchman and 26 Pathans were arrested and sent back by the same train to Lahore. Many other miscrents managed to escape.

(*Source*: Gurdwara Reform Movement and the Sikh Awakening—Teja Singh, The Akali Movement,—Mohinder Singh, India's struggle for Freedom. Role of Associate Movements—P.N. Chopra, India as I knew it—Sir Michael O Dwyer, Akali Morche TeJ habbar—Narain Singh, Select Documents Gurdwara Reform Movement 1919-1925—An Era of Congress—Akali Collaboration Ed.by M.L. Ahluwalia. Young India 16 March 1921, Collected Works of Mahatma Gandhi Vol. 19).

Appendix 3
Martyrs of Nankana Sahib Tragedy
February 21, 1921

Name	Father's Name	Village	District	Province
		A		
Arur Singh	Nihal Singh	Jhothian Khurd (Now in Pakistan)	Sheikhupura	Punjab
Atma Singh	Hira Singh	Mustafabad	Gurdaspur	"
		B		
Bachint Singh	Sunder Singh	Farala	Jalandhar	"
Bachitra Singh	Sunder Singh	Dagala	Jalandhar	"
Bagga Singh	Ranga Singh	Nazampura	Chak No. 38	"
		Dewan Singh wala (Now in Pakistan)	Sheikhupura	
Bagh Singh	Pala Singh	Bundala	Amritsar	"
Banta Singh	Bhola Singh	Bihala	Hoshiarpur	"
Banta Singh	Bhola Singh	Tahihara	Hoshiarpur	"
Bela Singh	Maya Singh	Kartarpur	Jalandhar	"
Bara Singh	Pala Singh	Bandala	Amritsar	"
Bhag Singh	Amir Singh	Nizampura	Chak No. 38	Punjab
		Dewan Singh Wala (Now in Pakistan)	Sheikhupura	"

Contd...

Name	Father's Name	Village	District	Province
Bhagat Singh	Amar Singh	Shahbazpur	Amritsar	Punjab
Bhagat Singh	Bur Singh	-	-	"
Bhagwan Singh	Lehna Singh	Nizampura (Now in Pakistan)	Sheikhupura	
Bora Singh alias Rachpal Singh	Sat Singh	Jalal Usman	Amritsar	"
Budh Singh	Surjan Singh	Kartarpur (Now in Pakistan)	Sialkot	"
Budh Singh	Surjan Singh	Kotha Pardhan Singh (Now in Pakistan)	Sialkot	"
Budh Singh	Surjan Singh	Kartarpur (Now in Pakistan)	Sialkot	"
Budh Singh	Surjan Singh	Sahowal (Now in Pakistan)	Sialkot	"
Bur Singh	Mul Singh	-	-	"
		C		
Chanda Singh	Hukm Singh	Nizampura (Now in Pakistan)	Sheikhupura	"
Charan Singh	Gurdit Singh	Kotla Sant Singh (Now in Pakistan)	Chak No. 43 Lyallpura	"
Charan Singh	Gokal Singh	Dinga (Now in Pakistan)	Gujarat	"
Chet Singh	Jawala Singh	Bundala	Amritsar	"
		D		
Dal Singh	Masuda Singh	Nizampura (Now in Pakistan)	Chak No.38 R.D. Devan Singh wala Sheikhupura	"
Dalip Singh	Karam Singh	Sahuwal (Now in Pakistan)	Sialkot	"
Darbara Singh	Jeewan Singh	Jaraga	Patiala	"
Darbara Singh	Kehar Singh Shahid Shasind	Jang	Patiala	"

Contd...

Name	Father's Name	Village	District	Province
Dasoudha Singh	Hira Singh	Haripur	Janandhar	Punjab
Dayal Singh	Devan Singh	Ghasitapur	Amritsar	"
Dewan Singh	Hari Singh	-	-	"
Dewan Singh	Hira Singh	-	Jalandhar	"
Dharam Singh	Santa Singh	Nazampura (Now in Pakistan)	Sheikhupura	"
Dharam Singh	Sant Singh	Bandala	Amritsar	"
Dhera Singh	Jaimal Singh	Pandori Nirjanu	Jalandhar	"
Dhera Singh	Hira Singh	Pandori	Jalandhar	"
		G		
Ganda Singh	Hukam Singh	Nizampura (Now in Pakistan)	Sheikhupura	"
Ganda Singh	Karan Singh	Bhasin (Now in Pakistan)	Lyallpur	"
Ganga Singh	Hukam Singh	Nazampura Chilawala (Now in Pakistan)	Sheikhupura	"
Hukam Singh	Sunder Singh	Pharala	Jalandhar	"
Gopal Singh	Hukam Singh	Bahedu (Now in Pakistan)	Lyallpur	"
Gopal Singh	Hukam Singh	Buhuru (Now in Pakistan)	Chak No. 18 Sheikhupura	"
Gujjar Singh	Jhanda Singh	Nizampura Chilawala (Now in Pakistan)	Sheikhupura	"
Gulab Singh	Hira Singh	Sonabad	Jalandhar	Punjab
Gulab Singh	Hira Singh	- (Now in Pakistan)	Sheikhupura	"
Gurbakhash Singh	Chanda Singh	Sonabad	Jalandhar	"
Gurbanhash Singh	Chanda Singh	- (Now in Pakistan)	Sheikhupura	"
Gurbux Singh	Ganda Singh	Sonabad	Jalandhar	"

Contd...

Name	Father's Name	Village	District	Province
		H		
Hukam Singh	Ghania Singh	Dingrian	Jalandhar	Punjab
Hari Singh	-	Dhadeka	Feroozepur	"
Hari Singh	Ghania Singh	Bibian (Now in Pakistan)	Sheikupura	"
Hari Singh	Kanahya Singh	Jhothian Khurd (Now in Pakistan)	Chak No. 10 Sheikhupura	"
Hari Singh	Kanahya Singh	Thothian	Amritsar	"
Hira Singh	Sewa Singh	Pandori Nirjan	Jalandhar	"
Harnam Singh	Dhanna Singh	- (Now in Pakistan)	Sheikhupura	"
Harnam Singh	Ishar Singh	Nizampura (Now in Pakistan)	Sheikhupura	"
Harnam Singh	Sunder Singh	Dhaisian Kahna	Jalandhar	"
Hazara Singh	Lal Singh	Bundala	Amritsar	"
Hira Singh	Buta Singh	Tongawali (Now in Pakistan)	Gujranwala	"
Hukam Singh	Kanahya Singh	Hazara	Jalandhar	"
		I		
Inder Singh	Mehtab Singh	Daroli	Jalandhar	"
Inder Singh	Mehtab Singh	- (Now in Pakistan)	Sheikhupura	"
Inder Singh	Sarmukh Singh	Pandori Nijjran	Jalandhar	"
Isher Singh	Attar Singh	Bohrn	Amritsar	"
Isher Singh	Attar Singh	Baheru (Now in Pakistan)	Chak No. 18 Sheikhupura	"
Isher Singh	Attar Singh	Baheru (Now in Pakistan)	Lyallpur	"
Isher Singh	Gurdit Singh	Dharowal	Gurdaspur	"
Isher Singh	Gurdit Singh	Dharowali (Now in Pakistan)	Sheikhupura	"

Contd...

Name	Father's Name	Village	District	Province
Isher Singh	Hardit Singh	Parowali	Gurdaspur	Punjab
Isher Singh	Sant Singh	Bandala	Amritsar	"
Isher Singh	Santa Singh	Nizampura	Amritsar	"
Isher Singh	Wadhwa Singh	Rupowali	Gurdaspur	"
Isher Singh	Wasawa Singh	Rupowali (Now in Pakistan)	Sheikhupur	"
		J		
Jagat Singh	Maghar Singh	-	-	"
Jahal Singh	Chanda Singh	Nizampura	Amritsar	"
Jawala Singh	Keser Singh	Nizampura Deva Singh wala (Now in Pakistan)	Sheikhapur	"
Jawand Singh	Ala Singh	Nizampura Deva Singh wala (Now in Pakistan)	Sheikhupura	"
Jeewan Singh	Pohu Mal	Landewali (Now in Pakistan)	Gujranwala	"
Jetha Singh	Kaku Singh	Gudu	Ludhiana	"
Jhera Singh	Jaimal Singh	Pandori Nijran	Jalandhar	"
Jur Singh	Mal Singh	Mula Singh Wala (Now in Pakistan)	Sheikhupura	"
Joginder Singh	Devi Ditta	-	-	"
Kanahaya Singh	Sunder Singh	Farala	Jalandhar	Punjab
Kanahya Singh	Sunder Singh	Dayala	Jalandhar	"
Karam Singh	Hakam Singh	Lahake	Lyallpur	"
Kaham Singh	Jiwan Singh	Jarg	Patiala	"
Kesar Singh	Milan Singh	Walto hianwala (Now in Pakistan)	Gujranwala	"
Kesar Singh	Milan Singh	Bharki (Now in Pakistan)	Guranwala	"
Kesar Singh	Pal Singh	Nizampura (Devi Singh wala) (Now in Pakistan)	Sheikhupura	"

Contd...

Name	Father's Name	Village	District	Province
Khushal Singh	Budh Singh	Nizampura (Devi Singh wala) (Now in Pakistan)	Sheikhupura	Punjab
Kishan Singh	Sunder Singh	Rattoka	Amritsar	"
		L		
Lachhman Singh Granthi	—	Dalla (Now in Pakistan)	Sheikhupura	"
Lachhman Singh	Meher Singh	Dharowali (Now in Pakistan)	Sheikhupura	"
Lachhman Singh	Meher Singh	Dharowal	Gurdaspur	"
Lachman Singh	Nankg Singh	Bura Dala	Gurdaspur	"
		M		
Mangal Singh	Kirpan Bahadur Ratta	Udoke (Now in Pakistan)	Sheikhupura	"
Mangal Singh	Lachhman Singh	Ratta	Gurdaspur	"
Mangal Singh Kirpan Bahadar	Ratta	Udoke	Gurdaspur	"
Mangal Singh	Ratan Singh	-	-	"
Mansu Singh	Pala Singh	Bundala	Amritsar	"
Mehanga Singh	Jhanda Singh	Lahuke	Lyallpur	"
Mota Singh	Hari Singh	Bassi	Hoshiarpur	"
Mota Singh	Hari Singh	Baheru (Now in Pakistan)	Sheikhupura	"
Mota Singh	Nand Singh	Shahkot (Now in Pakistan)	Sheikhupura	"
Mula Singh	Jeewan Singh	Wāla Sahib	Amritsar	"
		N		
Nand Singh	Bhagwan Singh	Jhothian Khurd (Now in Pakistan)	Sheikhupura	"
Nand Singh	Bhagwan Singh	Bibian (Now in Pakistan)	Sheikhupura	Punjab

Contd...

Name	Father's Name	Village	District	Province
Narain Singh	-	Warah (Now in Pakistan)	Sheikhupura	Punjab
Narain Singh	Warhan	-	Amritsar	"
Narain Singh	-	Nawan Vavihar	Amritsar	"
Narain Singh	Jawahar Singh	Lahuke (Now in Pakistan)	Lyallpura	"
Narain Singh	Pahu Singh	Nizampura Devi Singh wala (Now in Pakistan)	Sheikhupura	"
Narain Singh	Phala Singh	Nizampura Devi Singh wala (Now in Pakistan)	Sheikhupura	"
		P		
Pal Singh	Hukam Singh	Boheru (Now in Pakistan)	Sheikhupura	"
Punjab Singh	Mian Singh	Nizampura (Now in Pakistan)	"	"
Punjab Singh	Pahu Singh	Nizampura (Devi Singh wala) (Now in Pakistan)	"	"
Punjab Singh	Phul Singh	-	-	"
		R		
Ram Singh	Jhanda Singh	Nizampura (Now in Pakistan)	"	"
Rur Singh	Nihal Singh	Bibian (Now in Pakistan)	"	"
		S		
Santa Singh Suhre	-	Shakar Chak	Amritsar	"
Santa Singh	-	Daroli	Jalandhar	"
Santa Singh	Mohar Singh	Fatehgarh Churian	Amritsar	"
Santa Singh	Nand Singh	Daruli	Jalandhar	"

Contd...

Name	Father's Name	Village	District	Province
Santa Singh	Isher Singh	Nizampura Mala Singh wala (Now in Pakistan)	Sheikhupura	Punjab
Shama Singh	Pala Singh	Bandala	Amritsar	"
Sohan Singh	Kesar Singh	Kala Kakkar (Now in Pakistan)	Gujranwala	"
Sohan Singh	Sher Singh	Dingrian	Jalandhar	"
Sudershan Singh	Mit Singh	Nizampura (Now in Pakistan)	Sheikhupura	"
Sunder Singh	Bishan Singh	Dudial	Jalandhar	Punjab
Sunder Singh	Bishan Singh	(Now in Pakistan)	Gujranwala	"
Sunder Singh	Chanda Singh	Nizampura (Now in Pakistan)	Sheikhupura	"
Sunder Singh	Jagta Singh	Bham (Now in Pakistan)	Sheikhupura	"
Sunder Singh	Jagat Singh	Bham	Gurdaspur	"
Surain Singh	Meet Singh	Nizampura Deva Singh wala (Now in Pakistan)	Sheikhupura	"
Surain Singh	Ram Singh	Nizampura Mula Singh wala (Now in Pakistan)	Sheikhupura	"
		T		
Tehl Singh	Chanda Singh	Nizampura (Devi Singh Wala) (Now in Pakistan)	Sheikhupura	"
Teja Singh	Mehann Singh	Bibian (Now in Pakistan)	Seikhupura	"
Teja Singh	Mihan Singh	Thothian	Amritsar	"
Teja Singh	Mihan Singh	Thothian Khurd	Sheikhupura	"
Thakar Singh	Inder Singh	Manak Ghuman	Jalandhar	"

Contd...

Name	Father's Name	Village	District	Province
		U		
Ujagar Singh	Jagat Singh	Sambhwal	Amritsar	Punjab
Ujagar Singh	Jagat Singh	Bundala (Now in Pakistan)	Lyallpur	"
		W		
Wadhawa	Sara Singh	-	-	"
Waryam Singh	Bhag Singh	Nizampura (Now in Pakistan)	Sheikhupura	"
Waryam Singh	Bhagwan Singh	Tibbi Jai Singh (Now in Pakistan)	Mintgomery	"
Waryam Singh	Bulaka Singh	Mandhiala Chathian (Now in Pakistan)	Gujranwala	"
Waryam Singh	Buta Singh	Haripur	Jalandhar	"
Waryam Singh	Dula Singh	Sambhwal	Amritsar	"
Waryam Singh	Dula Singh	Sambhwal (Now in Pakistan)	Sheikhupura	"

Source: Indian National Movement—Punjabi Martyrs of Freedom (Specially written on Diamond Jubilee Year of Jallianwala Bagh Tragedy) Vol. I. by O.P. Ralhan.

Index